HEGEL AND AFTER

SCHACHT, Richard. Hegel and after; studies in Continental philosophy between Kant and Sartre. Pittsburgh, 1975. 297p bibl 74-4526. 15.95. ISBN 0-8229-3287-3. C.I.P.

CHOICE   JAN. '76

Philosophy

The well-known and respected author of *Alienation* (CHOICE, May 1971), a student of Tillich and Kaufmann, has pulled together some of his previously published articles and added new chapters to create a work that successfully covers the mainstream of Western European philosophy since Kant. The work is organized thematically rather than historically, and does not compare with standard histories, yet ends up covering the essential development of Continental philosophy quite adequately. Thus it is useful either for a general historical overview, or as a more specific resource for separate research into Hegel, the early Marx, Kierkegaard, Nietzsche, Husserl, Heidegger, existentialism, Existenz-philosophy, or philosophical anthropology. The result is a clear, readable, absorbing work covering some of philosophy's most difficult material in a minimally technical way that makes it eminently suitable for every upper-division library. It is appropriate for juniors and seniors with some philosophy background, or for graduate students. Schacht writes specifically for Anglo-American philosophers largely unfamiliar with the Continental tradition since Kant.

HEGEL AND AFTER

Studies in Continental Philosophy
Between Kant and Sartre

RICHARD SCHACHT

University of Pittsburgh Press

Copyright © 1975, University of Pittsburgh Press
Feffer and Simons, Inc., London
Manufactured in the United States of America

Library of Congress Cataloging in Publication Data

Schacht, Richard, birth date
    Hegel and after; studies in continental philosophy
between Kant and Sartre.

    Bibliography: p. 271
    1. Hegel, Georg Wilhelm Friedrich, 1770-1831—
Influence.   2. Philosophy, Modern—19th century.
3. Philosophy, Modern—20th century. I. Title.
B803.S328   190   74-4526
ISBN 0-8229-3287-3

to the memory of
PAUL TILLICH,
who showed me where to look
and to
WALTER KAUFMANN,
who showed me how to see

So ist unsere Stellung ebenso, die Wissenschaft,
die vorhanden ist, zuerst zu *fassen* und sie uns
zu eigen zu machen, und dann sie zu *bilden.*

Hegel, *Vorlesungen über die Geschichte der Philosophie*

So likewise is it our place first to *grasp*
the knowledge which is at hand and make it our
own, and then to *develop* it.

Contents

Acknowledgments

I wish to thank those whose permission was required in order for me to include in this volume the following studies, which were published elsewhere previously:

"A Commentary on the Preface to Hegel's *Phenomenology of Spirit*" (chapter 3). Copyright © 1972 by D. Reidel Publishing Company. Reprinted from *Philosophical Studies*, 23, nos. 1/2 (February 1972), pp. 1–31, by permission of D. Reidel Publishing Company.

"Hegel on Freedom" (chapter 4). Copyright © 1972 by Alasdair MacIntyre. Reprinted from *Hegel: A Collection of Critical Essays* (Garden City: Doubleday & Company, Inc., 1972), pp. 288–328, by permission of A. MacIntyre.

"Kierkegaard on 'Truth Is Subjectivity' and 'The Leap of Faith' " (chapter 6). Copyright © 1973 by the Canadian Association for Publishing in Philosophy. Reprinted from the *Canadian Journal of Philosophy*, III, no. 3 (March 1973), pp. 297–313, by permission of the Canadian Association for Publishing in Philosophy.

"Nietzsche and Nihilism" (chapter 8). Copyright © 1973 by the *Journal of the History of Philosophy*, Inc. Reprinted from the *Journal of the History of Philosophy*, IX, no. 1 (January 1973), pp. 65–90, by permission of the Editor.

"Husserlian and Heideggerian Phenomenology" (chapter 9). Copyright © 1972 by D. Reidel Publishing Company. Reprinted from *Philosophical Studies*, 23, no. 5 (October 1972), pp. 293–314, by permission of D. Reidel Publishing Company.

"Existentialism, *Existenz*-Philosophy, and Philosophical Anthropology" (chapter 10). Reprinted from the *American Philosophical Quarterly*, 11, No. 4 (October 1974), by permission of the Editor.

All of the above studies are reprinted here in substantially the same form as that in which they first appeared, except for certain editorial changes and some minor alterations made by the author.

Grateful acknowledgment is also made to those whose permission was required to make numerous citations from translations of certain of the works discussed extensively in the course of one or more of the studies in this volume:

Excerpts from Søren Kierkegaard, *Concluding Unscientific Postscript,* translated by David F. Swenson and Walter Lowrie (copyright © 1941, 1969 by Princeton University Press; Princeton Paperback 1968), for the American Scandinavian Foundation; reprinted by permission of Princeton University Press.

Excerpts from *Hegel: Texts and Commentary,* edited and translated by Walter Kaufmann (copyright © 1965 by Walter Kaufmann); reprinted by permission of Doubleday & Company, Inc., and of George Weidenfeld and Nicolson Ltd.

Excerpts from *Hegel's Philosophy of Right,* translated by T. M. Knox (1942); reprinted by permission of The Clarendon Press, Oxford.

Excerpts from *Karl Marx: Early Writings,* edited and translated by T. B. Bottomore (copyright © 1963 by T. B. Bottomore); reprinted by permission of McGraw-Hill Book Company and of C. A. Watts and Company, Ltd., London.

Excerpts from Friedrich Nietzsche, *The Will to Power,* edited by Walter Kaufmann and translated by Walter Kaufmann and R. J. Hollingdale (copyright © 1967 by Walter Kaufmann); reprinted by permission of Random House, Inc., and of George Weidenfeld and Nicolson Ltd.

Introduction

Most Anglo-American philosophers and students of philosophy are reasonably well acquainted with the more important Continental (European) philosophers from Descartes to and including Kant, and many also have at least some idea of what is involved philosophically in the existentialism of Sartre and Camus and the "humanistic dialectical naturalism" of many recent neo-Marxists. Between Kant and Sartre, however, there is a period in the history of philosophy in Europe of nearly a century and a half that is largely terra incognita (aside from the work of the Vienna Circle and the thought of men like Frege and Tarski) for the great majority of English-speaking readers generally. To be sure, the more important names are familiar enough: Hegel, Marx, Kierkegaard, Nietzsche, Husserl, and Heidegger, in particular. For many philosophers and laymen alike, however, it is as though they were standing before a huge dark cavern, detecting motion and hearing sounds, but unable to make any sense of them. It is frequently the case that one knows—or at any rate *thinks* one knows—a thing or two about the thought of some of the writers mentioned; but what is thus "known" about them is all too often a mere label or slogan or perhaps a brief thumbnail sketch.

What is worse, few of those interested in philosophy who find themselves in this situation are at all disturbed by it. One reason is that they are preoccupied with their own, rather different concerns; but another is that most of Continental philosophy between Kant and Sartre has been treated so inadequately, and even shabbily, by many influential commentators that those who have tended to rely upon the latter for their information about the former are inclined to feel confident that they are not missing anything. This neglect is reflected in the fact that survey courses dealing with the history of modern philosophy prior to the emergence of analytic philosophy in the twentieth century generally end with Kant, and in the fact that, in most colleges and universities, neither undergraduate nor graduate students in philosophy are expected to know anything about these philosophers by the time they receive their degrees.

No doubt the neglect of Continental philosophers between Kant and Sartre is partly due to their association in many people's minds with extremist political movements of both the Right and the Left, and with an insidious undermining of many fundamental Western values and institutions. Indeed, this association has unquestionably accounted for much of the bad press which these philosophers have received in the English-speaking world, especially since the First World War. But the idea of such a link is as lamentable as it is unjust. In most of those cases in which it has any foundation in fact at all, this association is greatly exaggerated; and it is simply wrong to blame Hegel for what the Kaiser did, or Marx for what Stalin did, or Nietzsche and Heidegger for the actions of Hitler and Eichmann. Nationalism, totalitarianism, racism, and nihilism may indeed have posed enormously serious threats to Western civilization in the first half of this century, and may continue to do so. It is only by radically distorting the views of these philosophers, however, that one can rank them among those responsible for the existence of these dangers. This should become clear—if it is not already—in the following studies.

There are, however, at least two other factors of major importance in connection with the neglect of these philosophers, which are more pertinent than that just mentioned. One is that what the Germans call the *Fragestellungen* of many post-Kantian Continental philosophers—the kinds of questions with which they concern themselves—are rather different from those of most Anglo-American philosophers in the present century; and it is obvious that if one does not take the trouble to try to understand the questions another is asking and his reasons for asking them, one is unlikely to be able to make much sense of the answers the other proposes.

This is not to say that the two groups of philosophers have no common interests. On the contrary, they are active in many of the same areas of philosophical endeavor. Within these areas, however, each has discerned important issues where the other generally sees nothing problematical; and (as often happens in the courtroom) different lines of questioning, while starting from a common point (namely, Kant), have led those who pursue them to very different conclusions. The situation is further complicated by the fact that these differing conclusions derive much of their meaning and support from the often long and complex lines of questioning from which they issue. Consequently, they cannot easily be evaluated in relation to each other with respect to their relative validity and justification, or even be compared and juxtaposed, since these undertakings are possible only if meaning is either constant or different in a way that is clearly understood.

One who comes upon post-Kantian Continental philosophy from a recent philosophical tradition that has developed independently thus cannot hope to understand what philosophers from Hegel to Heidegger are saying, and to arrive at a proper determination of the meaning and validity of what they say, simply by seizing upon propositions here and there in their writings and examining them in isolation. In Part I of *Human, All-Too-Human*, Nietzsche nicely describes what must be done if one is ever to be in a position to do so:

Whoever really wishes to *become acquainted* with something new (whether it be a person, an event, or a book), does well to take up the matter with all possible love, and to avert his eye quickly from all that seems hostile, objectionable, and false therein,—in fact to forget such things; so that, for instance, he gives the author of a book the best start possible, and straightway, just as in a race, longs with beating heart that he may reach the goal. In this manner one penetrates to the heart of the new thing, to its moving point, and this is called becoming acquainted with it. This stage having been arrived at, the understanding afterwards makes its restrictions; the over-estimation and the temporary suspension of the critical pendulum were only artifices to lure forth the soul of the matter.[1]

This undertaking is admittedly a laborious and time-consuming one. Many English-speaking philosophers have shied away from it in the case of these writers, because they are doubtful whether there is enough to be gained from the expenditure of time and effort required to warrant making it. I am convinced that there very definitely is, but whether or not this is in fact the case is something that cannot be established in any easier way. If it is true, as Hegel observes, that there is no royal road to knowledge, it is also true that there is no royal road to the establishment of the verdict that there is little if anything of philosophical significance in a body of philosophical literature one has not explored. The rather alien *Fragestellungen* of philosophers from Hegel to Heidegger may help to account for their neglect in the Anglo-American philosophical community in this century, but this explanation is no justification. Rather, it only underscores the need for interpretations of their writings rendering them intelligible and so accessible for purposes of discussion and evaluation. The studies in this volume are intended as contributions along these lines.

A second factor, related to this one, constitutes an additional obstacle for English-speaking readers, even if they are sufficiently well disposed toward the philosophers under consideration to be willing to give them a hearing. It concerns the alien styles of writing of these philosophers. One who is accustomed to the relative clarity and simplicity of language and the straight-forwardness and orderliness of exposition of English-speaking philosophers from Locke and Hume to Russell and Quine, is easily put off by the turgidity, terminological artificiality, and longwindedness of many Continental philoso-phers; by the indirect and semiliterary style of some; and by the aphoristic and disjointed character of the writings of others.

Great patience and effort are required to interpret what these men are saying, to reconstruct their views and arguments in a recognizable form, and to render coherent the philosophical positions which underlie their frequently abstruse and sometimes seemingly "unphilosophical" discussions and pro-nouncements. The neglect of these writers is to no inconsiderable extent a consequence of the fact that many English-speaking readers lack the patience and the motivation required to put forth the necessary effort. The rationaliza-tion sometimes offered by philosophers disinclined to trouble themselves with these men, that one who does not clearly display his wares must have no wares worth displaying, is hardly conclusive; for this simply is not true.

There are a variety of reasons why post-Kantian Continental philosophers adopted their various strange (to us) styles of writing, but I shall not go into them here. My present concern is only to acknowledge the problem their styles present and at the same time to suggest that this obstacle need be no insurmountable barrier to the comprehension and appreciation of what they are saying. English-language studies of these philosophers often leave this obstacle in place, because their authors tend to adhere too closely to the styles of those with whom they deal. This is understandable but, given that style is a problem, it is no less unfortunate for that. And it is not inevitable. In the studies to follow I have attempted to avoid succumbing to this tendency and to employ a more familiar philosophical idiom, in the hope of alleviating this problem and of demonstrating by example that the task of interpreting these writers in this way is neither impossible nor unrewarding. To be sure, there are others who have done this, at times with considerable success (and here Walter Kaufmann in particular must be mentioned). But the lesson has not yet been sufficiently learned, and the enterprise of putting it into practice has barely gotten off the ground.

That this enterprise is worthwhile philosophically is of course something that can be established only by actually undertaking studies along these lines, and not merely by making assertions to this effect or by referring to the fact that many more recent Continental philosophers have been greatly influenced by one or more of the writers discussed in this volume. The proof of the pudding, as the saying goes, is in the eating (and not in either the recipe or the advertisements for it). And there is much more in the writings of the philosophers to be dealt with than is explicitly discussed or even hinted at in the following studies—much too much to be considered in any single volume.

Putting the matter very briefly, Continental philosophy since Kant may be viewed as a series of attempts to come up with viable alternatives to the traditional (unsatisfactory) categories in terms of which almost everything of concern to philosophers—for example, our nature as human beings, our relation to the world and to one another, our cognitive and practical activities, and our institutions and values, as well as the things we experience and reality generally—has been analyzed and characterized, both in philosophy and in ordinary and scientific discourse. At the same time it consists in a search for viable methodological alternatives to traditional (unsatisfactory) ways of carrying on the enterprise of philosophy. More precisely, if minds and things are not to be thought of as two types of substances; if indeed the subject-object distinction cannot be supposed to correspond to any irreducible ontological subject-object dichotomy; if a "faculty" analysis of human experience is unacceptable; if all talk of Kantian "things in themselves" is meaningless; if Descartes' epistemological program cannot be carried out; if the correspondence theory of truth—and the general conception of knowledge based upon it—must be abandoned; if the existence of a transcendent deity is no longer considered demonstrable, or beyond dispute, or even a rationally coherent hypothesis; if there are no divinely ordained values and divinely sanctioned moral principles; if man has no fixed essential nature by reference to which values and moral principles may be determined; and if, moreover, the philosophical methodologies of empiricism, rationalism, and Kantian "criticism" are found wanting, and neither science nor formal logic nor ordinary language is sufficiently unproblematical to serve as a reliable guide in dealing with most philosophical questions—how then may one best proceed to deal with the issues thus raised, and what is to be said of a substantive nature concerning them?

There are a number of ways in which one might approach the many and varied responses of Continental philosophers in the nineteenth and twentieth centuries to these problems, which remain among the main objects of contemporary philosophical concern. In this book I have combined two such ways. Three of the chapters to follow (chapters 1, 2, and 10) provide a general orientation to the period under study, indicating some of the philosophical background of it and some recent developments whose origins are to be found in it, as well as giving an overview of certain of the most important developments in this period itself. This overview, while general in one respect, is in another no less selective than is the series of more intensive studies (chapters 3–9) which make up the main part of the volume; for in both I deal only with a few of the many philosophers mentioned in any history of philosophy covering this period.

My reasons for concentrating on a relatively few figures are, first, that some such selection is necessary if the discussion is to remain manageable and reasonably detailed and if any degree of internal coherence is to be preserved; second, that those selected stand in at least some loose direct or indirect relation to one another; and third, that they are in my view the most important representatives of the main developments in Continental philosophy in this period. And I would be less than candid if I did not acknowledge a fourth reason: the philosophers with whom I deal are quite simply those on the Continent in this period of time in whom I am most interested, less only one or two.

A number of the chapters of this book have been published previously as separate studies, principally in various philosophical journals, and appear here in only slightly modified form. Several were written before I conceived of the book, but most were written either with the thought of such a volume in mind or especially for it.

One last word. This book is dedicated to two of my former teachers, Paul Tillich and Walter Kaufmann, for the reason that, in different ways, each has done much to draw the attention of English-speaking readers to the importance of Continental philosophers from Hegel onward and to render their thought accessible and intelligible to us; and for the further reason that, without Tillich's stimulation and Kaufmann's education of my interest in them, the studies contained in this volume would and could never have been written.

PART I

Perspective:
Two Approaches to Philosophy
in the Nineteenth Century

1:

From Hegel to Nietzsche:
A Selective Overview

The history of philosophy in Europe in the nineteenth century is a very complex and tangled affair; but among those whose efforts have earned them places in it, there are five whose thought is of particular importance. They are Hegel, Marx, Kierkegaard, Schopenhauer, and Nietzsche. The importance of their thought may be explained in part in historical terms but only in part. Much more than any others since Kant, they are the ones whose orientations, procedures, and convictions set the stage for the developments in Continental philosophy in the present century. Moreover, directly or indirectly, they have had an enormous influence in shaping the ways in which many people today view themselves, their societies, and their world. Beyond this, however, their thought is of special and continuing significance both for the conduct of ongoing philosophical inquiry and for the understanding of many matters of philosophical interest. They are no less deserving of attention by philosophers today concerned with a whole range of live philosophical issues than are most of those other pre-twentieth-century figures upon whom current interest in the English-speaking world largely centers—even though an appreciation of them presupposes a readiness to entertain certain sorts of deep and troublesome questions differing markedly from most of those with which contemporary Anglo-American philosophers tend to be preoccupied.

For those to whom the concerns and views of a group of philosophers are relatively unfamiliar, a general characterization and comparison of some of the basic contentions they advance often proves helpful. Indeed, to be able to determine what to make of their writings and of contemporary studies of various aspects of their thought, it is almost a necessity first to achieve a broad thematic perspective upon these writings. Otherwise one is very likely to be unable to see the forest for the trees. This chapter is intended to provide a general overview of some of the larger positions taken and specific conclusions reached by these five philosophers, and so to perform this function of basic orientation. My immediate aim is simply to indicate something of the nature of their concerns and differences; but my broader purpose is also to stimulate interest in their arguments and views, some of which are dealt with in more detail in later chapters.

Together with the following one, this chapter constitutes an introduction to the next two parts of this book. These first three parts together will supply the reader with an understanding of the historical background of the developments discussed in Part IV at least as adequately as chapter 1 does for Parts II and III. And if a twentieth-century sequel to the present chapter and its nineteenth-century overview is desired, one may simply turn to the final chapter of the book, and read it as such (although it too is admittedly selective).

The five philosophers to be considered, like many Continental philosophers before and after them, were concerned with a broad range of the most fundamental questions it is possible to raise: questions concerning the ultimate nature of reality and of life; man's nature, significance, and place in the general scheme of things; the basic character of social institutions and historical developments; and the highest or ideal form of human existence which men can and perhaps also ought to strive to realize or approximate (to mention only some). Questions of this sort are so large and difficult that many philosophers today are reluctant even to attempt to deal with them. Whether this hesitancy is the course of wisdom or merely of timidity is not easily determined, though which course it is must obviously be a matter of great consequence.

The very meaningfulness of such questions and the possibility of dealing with them coherently of course cannot be held to stand or fall with the efforts made along these lines to be found in the writings of any particular group of philosophers, any more than the views of any such group can be taken to exhaust the range of possible responses to them. However, the philosophers dealt with in this chapter, and again in others to follow, afford one a better opportunity to come to terms with this problem than one is likely to find elsewhere in the history of philosophy. If a serious encounter with their thought does not lead one to the conclusion that these questions are legitimate and important ones which may profitably be made objects of philosophical deliberation, it is doubtful whether anything can.

I

I shall begin this overview with Kierkegaard because his view of the world and of man's place in it is closer than that of any of the others to what might be termed the "traditional" Western understanding of these things: namely, the world interpretation (and self-interpretation) which took shape under the influence of Judeo-Christian religious belief, according to which the world is fundamentally a stage, created by a transcendent God, on which man is placed and where the drama of the individual's development and salvation (or damnation) is played out. For Kierkegaard the world in which man lives has little more significance than this. It does also serve to provide men with objects of aesthetic enjoyment, but these can be temptations which distract them from what is truly important. The world of social institutions too is merely part of the stage and is not of any intrinsic significance; and it too can have a negative value, insofar as it distracts men from what is most important in life by ensnaring them in the toils of role-playing and conformism.

What is truly important, according to Kierkegaard, is the individual's attainment of the proper relationship to God, and through it genuine self-hood and an enduring happiness. In attributing supreme importance to this goal, Kierkegaard clearly ties in with the traditional Judeo-Christian interpretation of man's significance and ideal condition. The proper God relationship, in his view, can be established only through a "leap of faith," which presupposes passion, inwardness, and subjectivity; but Kierkegaard maintains that becoming subjective and attaining true individuality are neither possible nor desirable on a plane of pure self-sufficiency. Human fulfillment and the enduring happiness which Kierkegaard so persistently pursues are held to be found only in the God relationship and thus to be achieved only through faith, rather than reason, revolution, or creativity.

The natural world itself does not, for Kierkegaard, develop in any significant manner; but men's lives are not lived merely on the plane of natural processes. Human life is also historical, and meaningful human existence is conceived by him in terms of an orientation to two historical events—or rather two events which transform human life into history. One is the pivotal moment in which the infinite and eternal God of Christianity paradoxically incarnated himself in the finite and temporal form of a man. The other is the moment which will bring history to an end and, therefore, gives it a direction: the last judgment. The world of nature and natural processes thus acquires its significance through the intrusion into it of a supernatural power, radically different in character from anything to be found in the natural world itself.

The highest form of human existence which Kierkegaard envisages has no distinctive outward features which would serve to set it apart objectively from any other form of it, as Kierkegaard suggests in his description of the "knight of faith" in *Fear and Trembling:*

The moment I set eyes on him I . . . leap backwards . . . : Why, he looks like a tax-collector! However, it is the man after all. . . . He is solid through and through. . . . He belongs entirely to the world, no Philistine more so. . . . He takes delight in everything. . . . He is absorbed in his work. . . . He takes a holiday on Sunday. . . . In the afternoon he walks to the forest. He takes delight in everything he sees. . . . Toward evening he walks home, his gait as indefatigable as that of the postman. On the way he reflects that his wife has surely a special little warm dish prepared for him. . . . His wife hasn't it—strangely enough, it is quite the same to him. . . . He lives as carefree as a ne'er-do-well.[1]

What makes the "knight of faith" a knight of faith, for Kierkegaard, is not the form of life he leads at all, but rather precisely *his faith,* which is something purely subjective or inward.

Subjectively, what it is to become a Christian is defined thus: . . . The thing of being a Christian is not determined by the *what* of Christianity but by the *how* of the Christian. This *how* can only correspond with one thing, the absolute paradox. . . . To *believe* is specifically different from all other appropriation and inwardness. *Faith is the objective uncertainty along with the repulsion of the absurd held fast in the passion of inwardness.* . . . This formula fits only the believer, no one else . . . , simply and solely the believer who is related to the absolute paradox.[2]

It is his faith which enables the believer to turn back to the world and involve himself in it, like the man described above. "He does not do the least thing except by virtue of the absurd . . . . He resigned everything infinitely, and then he grasped everything again by virtue of the absurd."[3]

II

Curiously, the kind of human being Hegel takes to embody the highest form of human existence has the same look of solid bourgeois respectability—of the good citizen, family member, society member—as the man just described by Kierkegaard. And he too is sustained in his involvement in this kind of life by the grasp of something which transcends and justifies it—at least in the ideal case. Only here the similarity ends, for in the case of Kierkegaard this "grasp of something" takes the form of faith in the truth of the paradoxical claim of Christianity and in the existence of a personal God. In the case of Hegel, on the other hand, it takes the form of "absolute knowledge" of the *Begriff,* or "system of pure reason," and its manifestation in nature and history; and this self-realizing "system" is the essential nature both of the whole of reality and of the only God that Hegel recognizes.

Related to this point is the fact that for Hegel, as for Kierkegaard, the individual's highest significance is to be found only in a condition which transcends both the life of the senses and mere particularity (Hegelian "subjective spirit") and social institutional life (Hegelian "objective spirit"). As for Kierkegaard, this condition for Hegel is one in which the individual relates himself to something which transcends him—in fact, something compared to which the individual is virtually nothing. For Kierkegaard, however, this condition is faith, and the transcendent reality to which he relates himself is a personal God; while for Hegel this condition is "absolute knowledge," and the transcendent reality is the *Begriff* and its phenomenal manifestations.

Further, for Hegel, what we ordinarily think of as the natural world and the social world do not merely constitute an indifferent stage on which everything of true significance occurs. Rather, they themselves constitute part of the unfolding development of the "Idea"—that is, the *Begriff* regarded not merely in itself but as requiring concrete embodiment for its completion— which is the truly significant event in the world of existence. Hegel agrees with Kierkegaard that the significance of human life can only be understood by reference to the historical as opposed to the merely natural, but he regards the historical as part of the actualization of the Idea. He sees the whole of reality (natural and social as well as personal and intellectual) as having a definite developmental direction and as having a meaning and significance in virtue of that which emerges through this development. For Hegel, as for Kierkegaard, this history is to be viewed in light of the fact that it is moving toward an *end*. According to Hegel, however, this end is not a last judgment of individual souls, but rather the completion of the process through which the *Begriff* comes to be concretely and fully existent. When this point is reached, it not merely will be true that "the actual is rational" (which is how "actual" is to be conceived), but moreover will be the case that reality generally is rational. What we ordinarily think of as nature, individuals, society, and knowledge will then form one perfect harmonious whole, conforming completely to the "system of pure reason."

This actualized rational whole is what has ultimate significance for Hegel. This means that before this development is completed, there is no concretely existing independent reality which as such gives significance to developments as they occur, as God is (and does) for Kierkegaard, even though the essential content of the Idea—the pure *Begriff*—is eternal. Significance is measured in terms of contribution to the actualization of this ideal, which is lifeless until it is realized in us—most emphatically *un*like Kierkegaard's God.

Since what is of value is the actualization in concrete form of the *Begriff*, the individual's ultimate or objective and absolute significance is a function of the extent to which the *Begriff* acquires actuality through and in him. This "system of pure reason" does not—as Kierkegaard's personal God does—care for each person's particular individuality; what counts is the extent to which he embodies it. It is in these terms that Hegel conceives the individual's place and significance in the world: not in terms of becoming subjective and making the "leap of faith" through which the proper God relationship is achieved, but rather in terms of becoming objective and ultimately of attaining absolute knowledge, thereby both achieving objective and absolute spiritual existence and fully actualizing the Idea.

It is illuminating to contrast Kierkegaard's world view, according to which everything revolves around the individual, his life in the world, his subjectivity, his faith, and his relation to God, with Hegel's view of reality summarized in the last paragraphs of his *Phenomenology of Spirit:*

[The world represents] the self-externalization through which spirit actualizes itself . . . , manifesting its pure nature outside of itself as time, and its structure as space. The latter of its manifestations, nature, is its living and immediate actualization. . . . The other aspect of its actualization—history—is its conscious, self-mediating actualization: spirit externalized in time. . . . This aspect takes the form of a slow procession or sequence of spiritual forms . . . ; it moves slowly because the self must submerge itself in the whole wealth of this its substance and appropriate it. Since the ultimate end of the self consists in knowing that which it is—its substance—completely, this knowing is a delving into itself in which it leaves behind its mere particular existence and gives itself over to recollection [i.e., the contemplation of its substance, these spiritual forms] . . . . Its transcended particular existence, however, is still retained; and this transformed existence—which is the same existence as before, only reborn through knowledge—is a new existence, a new world and mode of spirit. . . .

The realm of spiritual forms, which in this way attains concrete existence, constitutes a succession, in which one form gives rise to another. . . . The goal of this process is the revelation of the depths of the spirit, and this is the absolute *Begriff*. This revelation is [the process through which] these depths are brought to the surface and laid out in space and time. . . .

The goal, which is absolute knowledge, or spirit knowing itself as spirit, is reached through the recollection of these spiritual forms, both as they are in themselves [in philosophical logic] and as they bring about the organization of their existing spiritual domain [in a phenomenology of spirit]. Their preservation, as free existence appearing in the form of the contingent, is history; organized systematically in concepts, however, it is the science of the structure of appearances. Both together, history comprehended in concepts, form the recollection and the totality of absolute spirit.[4]

III

Marx combines Hegel's rejection of an other-worldly ground of the existence and significance of this world and Hegel's notion of a historical development of the human world generally (with its companion notion of an approaching culmination of this development in the form of an ideal, enduring, and harmonious state of affairs) with Kierkegaard's depreciation of objective spiritual life, his abandonment of any aspiration to absolute knowledge, and his relocation of ultimate significance in the life of the individual. For Marx the world develops *as if* it were gradually actualizing some essential rational structure, only it is the operation of purely "material" (natural and economic) laws that leads to this result. This is no mere happy coincidence, however; for Marx contends that history is shaped by men, as they struggle— however blindly—to achieve a form of life that is adequate to their human as well as merely animal needs. In this pursuit they cast off one form of social organization after another, as they will continue to do until they finally achieve one which will allow for the full flowering of human life as genuine social individuality.

Marx differs from Hegel in that, first of all, he regards nature as ontologically independent of consciousness and, secondly, he does not regard the emergence of the world of nature as itself constituting a part of the actualization of the ultimate end he envisages. For him the world of nature has significance primarily as material to be used in the realization of that end and, secondarily, as an object of aesthetic experience. But Marx also differs from Kierkegaard in that in his view this world is not merely a stage on which the drama of human self-realization is played out, but rather is essential to this self-realization; for the creative transformation of the world constitutes a crucial part of this process.

Marx also differs from both Kierkegaard and Hegel in that, for him, the ultimate significance of the individual is *not* to be found in a condition which radically transcends the realm of sensuous and practical life—neither in faith nor in absolute knowledge (nor, for that matter, in institutional social existence). And it is not to be conceived in terms of the attainment of a relation to something which transcends the individual himself—neither a God nor a "system of pure reason" (nor sociocultural institutions). Rather, it is held to be a matter of the individual's cultivation of the life of the senses, and of his productive and creative shaping and molding of the natural world. Marx adds to this that man is an essentially social being, but social existence obviously does not involve a relation of the individual to any kind of transcendent reality.

Marx's ultimate ideal is that of a world in which exploitation, suffering, degradation, physical need, and interpersonal conflict will be eliminated, and of a kind of human existence that will be characterized in terms of self-realizing creativity, aesthetic sensibility, and interpersonal unity and harmony. It is its instrumentality in actualizing this ideal which for him gives significance to what has happened in the past and what is happening now, and it is in terms of this ideal that he conceives the significance of human life. He characterizes the ideal state of affairs he envisages in terms of "communism" and his ideal of human existence in terms of humanization and the overcoming of all forms of alienation and self-alienation.

Communism is the positive supersession of private property, of human self-alienation, and thus the real appropriation of human nature through and for man. It is, therefore, the return of man himself as a social, i.e. really human, being. . . . Communism as a fully developed naturalism is humanism and as a fully developed humanism is naturalism. It is the definitive resolution of the antagonism between man and nature, and between man and man. It is the true solution of the conflict between existence and essence, between ojectification and self-affirmation . . . , between individual and species. It is the solution of the riddle of history, and knows itself to be the solution. . . .

The supersession of private property is . . . the complete emancipation of all the human qualities and senses. It is such an emancipation because these qualities and senses have become *human*. . . . Need and enjoyment have thus lost their egoistic character. . . . [This means] not only the five senses, but also the so-called spiritual senses, the practical senses (desiring, loving, etc.). . . . The cultivation of [these] senses is the work of all previous history.[5]

In communist society, as Marx conceives of it, an individual's labor will be "voluntary" and will be "his own spontaneous activity"; and through it he will "fulfill himself" and "freely develop his spiritual and physical qualities," and thereby his personality.[6] Marx has no doubt that men will find their lives both enjoyable and meaningful under these conditions, and that they will find the consolations of religious and metaphysical illusions quite dispensable. And he further is confident that it is well within men's power to bring these conditions about, supposing moreover that the time is not far off when they will actually succeed in doing so.

IV

It is of some interest, before turning to Schopenhauer, to consider a passage in Kierkegaard's *Fear and Trembling* that both intimates that Marx's optimistic humanism is naive and untenable, and also enables one to better understand Schopenhauer in relation to these two men. Kierkegaard writes:

If there were no eternal consciousness in man, if at the foundation of all there lay only a wildly seething power which writhing with obscure passions produced everything that is great and everything that is insignificant, if a bottomless void never satiated lay hidden beneath all—what then would life be but despair? If such were the case . . . , if one generation arose after another like the leafage in the forest . . . , if the human race passed through the world as the ship goes through the sea, like the wind through the desert, a thoughtless and fruitless activity, if an eternal oblivion were always lurking hungrily for its prey and there were no power strong enough to wrest it from its maw—how empty then and comfortless life would be![7]

Kierkegaard goes on to say, "But . . . it is not thus"; for he believes in the existence of a God, in relation to whom our lives acquire a significance that they would utterly lack under the circumstances just described. For Schopenhauer, however, no such God exists; and so life appears to him actually and inevitably to be the desperate and meaningless affair that Kierkegaard suggests it would be if there were no God.

Schopenhauer rejects a basic idea shared by all of the first three writers—namely, that history is meaningful in terms of the actualization of an ultimate ideal of some sort. In his view there is process in the world but no meaningful historical development. Instead, there is only blind striving—a manifestation of the "will to live" that is the essential tendency of all existing things—which does not and cannot produce perfection, salvation, or self-realization but, rather, only meaningless suffering. As for Marx, there is for Schopenhauer no transcendent reality or ideality to which the individual can relate himself, thereby acquiring significance for himself and rendering his life meaningful. But contrary to Marx, there is also no hope of realizing some socio-politico-economic state of affairs in which the individual's life can acquire a positive meaning through his own creative efforts. The life of the individual can attain no positive significance either through social participation or through productive activity. In fact, individuality itself for Schopenhauer is scarcely more than an illusion, being a matter of essentially insignificant differences which thinly veil the same blind striving everywhere.

The world, for Schopenhauer, is nothing more than "will" and "idea" (or "representation"). It is *will*—by which Schopenhauer means something like the "wildly seething power" of which Kierkegaard speaks—in a whole scale of manifestations of differing complexity, each enduring for a time at the expense of others and then itself succumbing to others, the higher emerging only through the exploitation and suppression of the lower, the lower struggling against the higher to survive. There are higher and lower forms; but these are not value terms, for they only serve to designate varying degrees of complexity. Science, social institutions, and other such expressions of the human spirit are only means through which certain of these particular manifestations attempt to assert themselves in a hostile world.

The world is "will"—and "idea." This addition for Schopenhauer means only that with the attainment of a certain kind and degree of organizational complexity, one such type of manifestation of this "will"—man—developed a distinctive way of relating to the others, involving the ability to experience, reflect, and reason. But this development—which issues in knowledge—does not in any sense serve to make life more worthwhile, for Schopenhauer, or to lend meaning and significance to the developments which led up to it.

A being with the capacity for knowledge, however, is capable of stepping back out of involvement in reality and viewing it objectively; and thus he is capable of a certain kind of dignity—the only kind possible, according to Schopenhauer, and the closest thing to something meaningful to which man can aspire. This dignity is achieved through registering a protest against the absurdity and meaninglessness of this blind striving, and through refusing to play along with it. This attainment does not amount to much and does not suffice to endow existence with a positive significance after all. But a living protest against the stupidity and absurdity of life is a kind of victory over it; and this victory, Schopenhauer feels, is more meaningful than a quick exit through suicide.

In taking this position, Schopenhauer is closer than any of the other four (Kierkegaard and Nietzsche included) to the kind of attitude which characterizes the existentialism of Camus and Sartre. Schopenhauer could be considered more consistent than they are, however, in that he carries this position to its logical conclusion, by advocating a life of the severest asceticism. He too has an ultimate ideal of a sort: the elimination of blind striving not only in one's own case but generally, and thus the end of the world as "will." And this means the end of the world as "idea" too—in short, the end of the world altogether: nirvana, nothingness. In the last pages of his most important work *The World as Will and Idea*, Schopenhauer writes:

We have recognized the inmost nature of the world as will, and all its phenomena as only the objectivity of will; and we have followed this objectivity from the unconscious working of obscure forces of Nature up to the completely conscious action of man. Therefore we shall by no means evade the consequence, that with the free denial, the surrender of the will, all those phenomena are also abolished; that constant strain and effort without end and without rest . . . , in and through which the world consists; the multifarious forms succeeding each other in gradation; the whole manifestation of the will; and finally, also the universal forms of this manifestation, time and space, and also its last fundamental form, subject and object: all are abolished. No will: no idea: no world. . . . [When] the will has turned and denied itself, this our world, which is so real, with all its suns and milky-ways—is nothing.[8]

Toward this end Schopenhauer's human ideal—the ascetic—

disowns this nature which appears to him. . . . Essentially nothing else but a manifestation of will, he ceases to will anything, guards against attaching his will to anything, and seeks to confirm in himself the greatest indifference to everything. . . . Voluntary and complete chastity is the first step. . . . Asceticism [further] shows itself in voluntary and intentional poverty. . . . He compels himself to refrain from doing all that he would like to do. . . . He practices fasting, and even resorts to chastisement and self-inflicted torture, in order that, by constant privation and suffering, he may more and more break down and destroy the will. . . . If at last death comes, which puts an end to this manifestation of that will . . . , it is most welcome, and is gladly received as a longed-for deliverance.[9]

V

Nietzsche takes a stand against one or another of the central aspects of all these interpretations and ideals. With Schopenhauer he rejects the tendency to view the world historically, and with it both the idea that historical development will eventuate in the emergence of a world of enduring and complete harmony and perfection (as Hegel and Marx hold), and also the ideas that any historical event is of unique and ultimate importance and that the world has a beginning and will have an end (as Kierkegaard and other Christians believe). He holds, on the contrary, that the world has no begin-ning and no end, and that, far from following a course of continuous development, it presents the spectacle of a cyclical rise to heights and fall to depths, recurring eternally.

He also rejects the view that the world and man have any preestablished or essential end, direction, or purpose. He agrees for the most part with Schopen-hauer's characterization of the fundamental principle of reality, only, instead of referring to it simply as "will," he refers to it as "will to power." He departs from Schopenhauer, however, in finding value in a certain type of development of this basic force. He holds that any scheme of value which ignores or opposes the basic character of reality as "will to power" is bound to be a ludicrous failure, and perhaps dangerously nihilistic as well. The only positive and nonillusory valuation of existence actually possible, in his view, must take the form of positing as a goal a kind of life in which the "will to power" is present in its highest intensity and quality, and thus of affirming this basic principle as the fundamental standard of value.

To affirm this principle, however, is not to endorse human life in its present form; for Nietzsche feels that there is too much about men as they now are that is weak, limited, decadent, and nihilistic. To affirm this principle is to "will the overman"—to resolve that there shall emerge a form of life in which all that is "human-all-too-human" will be overcome. If life is to have value at all, its value must be conceived in terms of the realization of the Dionysian ideal of the "overman" (*Übermensch*). Under these circumstances it follows that one's life has meaning and significance only insofar as it serves to bring closer the realization of this ideal—and not in itself, as for Kierkegaard and Marx. For both of them the individual is an end in himself; for Nietzsche he is a bridge to higher men to come and a means to the end of the emergence of the "overman." As for Hegel and Kierkegaard, the present-day individual's highest significance is held by Nietzsche to be conceived in terms of his standing in the proper relation to something which transcends him. But for Nietzsche this "something" is nothing which transcends the natural order—neither the *Begriff* nor God—but rather is an ideal that is essentially naturalistic. It also follows that, like Hegel and Marx (and unlike Kierkegaard), Nietzsche determines the value of that which presently exists in terms of something which will find adequate concrete embodiment, if at all, only in the future; but it is something quite different for him than it is for either of them.

Like Marx, Nietzsche rejects the view that man's highest significance is to be conceived in terms of the attainment of anything like a condition of faith or absolute knowledge or conformity with sociocultural institutions. In fact, the terms in which Marx characterizes his own ideal come closer to describing Nietzsche's "overman" than those employed by any of the others; for creativity, cultivation, and even a certain form of fellowship are of paramount importance for Nietzsche as well as for Marx. Nietzsche, however, has a very different form of fellowship in mind than Marx does; for while Marx's (at least in principle) is to exclude no one, the form Nietzsche praises is highly selective, excluding all who are not one's true equals in ability. Nietzsche's ideal differs profoundly from Marx's in that he does not envisage all men attaining the same level of spiritual life (as Marx does), since he is convinced that men differ too greatly in their related natural capacities for equality to be achievable on any level other than that of mediocrity. For this reason he denounces both the myth of present equality and the goal of achieving equality, and affirms and stresses the differences between men.

He further differs from Marx—and from Hegel—in that he anticipates no end to exploitation, suffering, destruction, and tragedy; he accepts Schopenhauer's view that these are inseparable from life. But he differs from Schopenhauer in affirming this world of "will," and therefore these negative factors along with it. If life is to be affirmed at all, it must be affirmed on its own terms; and these are some of its terms. This means that one who would affirm it must affirm not only the exploitation of the lower men by the higher but also even the "overman's" own suffering and destruction. The coming of the "overman" will not mean an elimination of all conflict and the attainment of perfect harmony; the basic conditions of life will not change with the appearance of this ultimate ideal, which Nietzsche does not expect to have any permanence. In the last section of *The Will to Power*, he makes this point quite clear, and sums up the whole world view of which it is part:

And do you know what "the world" is to me? Shall I show it to you in my mirror? This world: a monster of energy, without beginning, without end; a firm, iron magnitude of force that does not grow bigger or smaller, that does not expend itself but only transforms itself . . . ; enclosed by nothingness as by a boundary . . . ; a sea of forces flowing and rushing together, eternally changing, eternally flooding back . . . , with an ebb and a flood of its forms; out of the simplest forms striving toward the complex, out of the stillest, most rigid, coldest forms toward the hottest, most turbulent, most self-contradictory, and then again returning home to the simple out of this abundance, out of the play of contradictions back to the joy of concord, still affirming itself in this uniformity of its courses and its years, blessing itself as that which must return eternally, as a becoming that knows no satiety, no disgust, no weariness: this, my *Dionysian* world of the eternally self-creating, the eternally self-destroying, this mystery world of the twofold voluptuous delight, my "beyond good and evil," without goal, unless the joy of the circle is itself a goal . . . ; do you want a *name* for this world? A solution for all its riddles? A light for you, too . . . ?—*This world is the will to power—and nothing besides!* And you yourselves are also this will to power—and nothing besides![10]

How different this is from Kierkegaard's religious drama, from Hegel's actualization of the "system of reason," from Marx's communist utopia, from Schopenhauer's nirvana—though how like Schopenhauer's "world as will and idea." And how different Nietzsche's ideal of human existence, which he characterizes as "Dionysian," is from Hegelian socio-politico-cultural "objectivity" and absolute knowledge, from Kierkegaardian "subjectivity" and God-relatedness, from Schopenhauerian asceticism and revulsion toward life, and from Marxian sociality and self-fulfilling productivity. The following passages, written near the end of his productive life, make this unmistakably clear:

The highest state a philosopher can attain: to stand in a Dionysian relationship to existence—my formula for this is *amor fati:* a Dionysian affirmation of the world as it is, without subtraction, exception, or selection. . . .

The word "Dionysian" means . . . : a reaching out beyond personality, the everyday, society, reality, across the abyss of transitoriness: a passionate-painful overflowing into the darker, fuller, more floating states; an ecstatic affirmation of the total character of life . . . ; the great pantheistic sharing of joy and sorrow that sanctifies and calls good even the most terrible and questionable qualities of life; the eternal will to procreation, to fruitfulness, to recurrence; the feeling of the necessary unity of creation and destruction.[11]

This is more or less Nietzsche's last word. Whether the last word really belongs to him, however, or to one of the others or to someone else is a question which obviously is still open after this brief overview, and which moreover will remain an open one even after these and other writers have been discussed in more detail in the chapters to follow. Indeed, it may well be a question to which there neither is nor can be any definitive answer. Yet the reflections of these men can be of great value to anyone who would concern himself with the kinds of issues and problems with which they deal, and no one who would do so should rest content until he has come to terms with them.

2:

The Philosophical Background of Hegel's Metaphysics

Any attempt to come to terms with developments in Continental philosophy since Kant, and in particular in the nineteenth century, must of necessity involve a consideration of Hegel—and not only of Hegel's social philosophy and philosophy of history but, even more importantly, of his metaphysics and the system in which the many implications of his metaphysics are worked out. Marx, Kierkegaard, and Nietzsche, for example, objected strongly to Hegel's thinking along these lines. Yet they all felt obligated to reckon with it in one way or another, in order to justify their treatment of various matters in ways differing from Hegel's manner of dealing with them in the context of his most formidable scheme. Better than most—and unlike many—of their admirers, these men recognized that Hegel's metaphysics might be superseded or rejected but could not properly be simply ignored.

Indeed, it is at least arguable that the emergence of Hegel's metaphysics is the single most important event in the history of European philosophy after Kant, not only because of its place in the all-embracing Hegelian system of philosophical idealism—which purports (with some justice) both to incorporate and to surpass the efforts of Hegel's predecessors—but also because it looms so large in the thinking of European philosophers after Hegel, up to the present day. The history of European philosophy since Hegel to a very considerable extent consists of a variety of responses to him—responses taking the form of attempts to ascertain fundamental defects in the broad and long tradition of philosophical thinking which culminates in his metaphysics and the system based upon it, and to recommence philosophical inquiry along lines that would correct these purported defects.

To understand what has happened in European philosophy in this period, therefore, one must first understand Hegel and, more specifically, at least something of his metaphysics. Achieving even a general understanding and appreciation of the latter, however, is no easy matter. The difficulty of doing so can in no way be completely eliminated; but it can be diminished to some extent by viewing his thought in the context of the philosophical tradition prior to him which he attempted to appropriate and carry to completion, and thus by approaching his metaphysics through a consideration of certain developments in the history of modern philosophy to which it is directly related. It is the purpose of the present chapter to provide this sort of historical perspective, and thus to render comprehensible both the views of Hegel discussed in the next two chapters and the countermoves made by certain of his successors to be dealt with subsequently.

The developments to be discussed pertain primarily to questions arising in connection with the interconnected issues of how reality in general and its various constituent elements are to be conceived, and what is involved in the kinds of experience and knowledge we do or can have; for it is above all with these matters that modern philosophers since Descartes have been concerned. Every serious student of philosophy will already be acquainted with at least the general nature of the views advanced with respect to these issues by the more important figures in the tradition from Descartes to Kant. For this reason they are dealt with relatively briefly here. The views of the two post-Kantian philosophers whose responses to Kant constitute the more immediate background of Hegel's thought, however, are much less familiar to most English-speaking readers, even if their names—Johann Gottlieb Fichte and Friedrich Wilhelm Joseph von Schelling—may not be completely unknown. Considerable attention is therefore given to them; for while the intrinsic philosophical interest of the positions they developed is not sufficient to render their general neglect a great misfortune, they played an important transitional role between Kant and Hegel, and must be examined in some detail if the circumstances surrounding certain of Hegel's most significant departures from Kant are to be comprehended.

Philosophers discussing some philosophical issue have often observed that if anyone who did not understand the relation between what they were saying and the issue with which they were concerned were to overhear them, he would think them to have taken leave of their senses. Unfortunately, these very same philosophers often fail to see that something similar holds true of the writings of a philosopher like Hegel. They are only too quick to conclude, on the basis of a glance at some of the things he says, that he is talking utter nonsense or that he is simply mad—forgetting to take into consideration the fact of their ignorance of the relation between various assertions he makes and the issues with which he is concerned, and failing to see that, as they would justly observe in their own case, the judgment of a person in such a state of ignorance is not really worth very much.

It is my feeling that at least a considerable part of Hegel's metaphysics, which taken by itself does seem bizarre to say the least, is in fact quite reasonable in relation to the philosophical background out of which it developed, and that this holds true of it in relation not only to the context set by Fichte and Schelling but also to the philosophical context in which *they* wrote, as it had been set by Kant and by the course of modern philosophy from Descartes to Hume before him. I would hesitate to go as far as to say that Hegel's metaphysics was the inevitable outcome of the sequence of philosophical development initiated by Descartes, or even of that begun by Kant. It does seem to me, however, that many of Hegel's metaphysical moves become plausible and even rather compelling if they are viewed in the light of the ways in which epistemological and metaphysical questions had been formulated and answered or treated by philosophers from Descartes to Kant.

Of course, it may be that the implausibility of Hegel's conclusions is sufficiently great to lead one to suspect that, if what I am suggesting is true, there must be something fundamentally wrong with the ways in which epistemological and metaphysical questions were formulated and dealt with before Hegel. And such a suspicion has been abroad for some time: Kierkegaard, Marx, and Nietzsche, for example, all suggest something of this sort. But even if this suspicion is well founded (and it is not my intention here to suggest that it is), the desirability of understanding what Hegel says and why he says it renders it important to consider those developments in the history of modern philosophy which affected the direction of his metaphysical thinking. I shall begin with some discussion of the situation before Kant and as Kant left it, and then shall turn to a consideration of Fichte and Schelling.

I

Prior to Kant philosophers had taken a variety of different positions on the metaphysical question of the nature and qualities of the world and of the entities which constitute it, and on the associated question of the relation between these entities and what we actually perceive. The view held by many Scholastics—today often called "naive realism"—is roughly that the world is *there,* created and existing independently of us and our perceptual experience, and that we exist *in* this world, endowed with the capacity to perceive it. We perceive it more or less as it is; it has (or the things which constitute it have) the kinds of qualities which we perceive, provided that our organs and faculty of perception are generally operating properly and that the conditions under which we perceive things are normal ones.

Philosophers such as Descartes and Locke felt there were certain difficulties in this position, and held that it must be modified to the extent of distinguishing between "primary" qualities and "secondary" qualities. On this view—which might be characterized as a qualified (or perhaps "sophisticated") realism—the world is still there, existing independently of us and our perceptual experience; but the things which constitute it, considered as they are in themselves, have only *some* of the kinds of qualities which we perceive: extension, size, shape, solidity, number, and motion or rest (the "primary" qualities). As for the others (the "secondary" qualities)—for example, color, heat, sound, taste—they cannot as such be attributed to things, but rather occur in our perceptual experience as the result of the action upon our senses of certain configurations of imperceptible "primary" qualities of things. Things exist independently of us and cause us to perceive secondary as well as primary qualities; but they themselves have only primary qualities, while the secondary qualities which they appear to have are as much the contribution of our senses as they are the contribution of the things we perceive.

After Descartes and Locke, philosophers like Berkeley and Hume took a further step away from the thesis of "naive realism," and indeed rejected any sort of realism as a defensible and coherent philosophical position. They argued that we have no better reason to attribute primary qualities to things existing independently of our perceptual experience than we have to attribute secondary qualities to them. Our experience of the so-called primary qualities is not significantly different from our experience of secondary ones; and since the latter cannot plausibly be said to exist independently of our perceptual experience, there is no good reason to suppose that the former can either.

This reasoning, however, raises doubts about the fundamental thesis of realism—the thesis, namely, that the world exists independently of us and our perceptual experience. For if none of the qualities of the things we perceive can be attributed to things existing independently of us, it follows that we do not encounter such things in experience at all. And if this is so, the question arises: What evidence do we have that *there are* things existing independently of our consciousness? There is, of course, a phenomenal world—that is, the "world" of our experience, consisting of the totality of those of our perceptions which can be integrated with one another in accordance with the laws or principles of association, consistency, and the like. But *this* "world" cannot be known to exist—indeed, it cannot even be conceived to exist—except in relation to our consciousness. It, therefore, cannot be that world existing independently of our perceptual experience of which the realists speak.

Nor is this all. Berkeley and Hume further maintain that we can say nothing at all about what lies *beyond* the realm of possible perceptual experience; for we can never know the nature or existence of something which we have never experienced, and we therefore cannot in principle know what lies beyond our perceptual experience—beyond the contents or objects of consciousness—or even if there is anything at all that does. Indeed, the very idea of something of which we can never even in principle have any experience is virtually meaningless, since we can form no idea whatever of what it would be like.

Further, this empiricist critique of realism has the consequence that all of the "knowledge" which we *can* have pertaining to the phenomena we *do* experience can only be inductive—that is, based on generalization from the experience of similar particular instances. And since induction from a limited set of particular instances can never render certain a general proposition ranging over all possible similar instances, we can never establish the truth of such propositions as "Every event has a cause." Such universal propositions can never be established by experience (a posteriori); they can only be formulated by reasoning independently of experience (a priori), or at least by going beyond what is given in experience. But as such, they cannot be supposed to yield or constitute knowledge of the world, even if the world is conceived in terms of our perceptual experience; for only perceptual experience itself can tell us anything about it.

Descartes, at the dawn of modern philosophy, had hoped that, starting with a systematic suspension of belief in everything which is in the least dubitable, he would be able to proceed to erect an ediface of knowledge which would be completely certain and would moreover—as luck would have it—accord with the basic ideas of the world, man, God, and morality adhered to by Scholastic philosophers and theologians, and by ordinary men of common sense as well. By the time of Hume, these hopes seemed to have been dashed from first to last. In Hume's hands Descartes' systematic doubt, applied more rigorously than it had been by Descartes himself, led to skepticism with regard to the nature and existence of everything except the actual contents of perceptual experience—and in particular, with regard to the nature and existence of the three objects of traditional metaphysics: the world, the soul, and God. It also led to the view that the concepts of traditional metaphysics are meaningless, to a denial of freedom of the will, and to a kind of conventionalism in ethics.

II

Confronted with this situation, Kant was profoundly disturbed. He was convinced, among other things, that (1) we have more knowledge (of the validity of such propositions as "Every event has a cause") than Hume was willing to allow; (2) belief in God, the soul, and immortality, more or less as they have been traditionally conceived, far from being mere groundless superstition, is in fact sound; (3) men have absolute moral duties and the freedom of will to respond to them; and (4) the central concepts of traditional metaphysics are not completely meaningless. His problem, therefore, was to show how these various propositions can in fact all be true—to show, indeed, that they actually *are* true—in spite of the fact that Hume's basic criticisms of realism (and rationalism) are sound.

Considering first our perceptual experience, Kant maintains that there are three elements of it which must be distinguished, rather than only one—sensible qualities or "impressions"—to which Hume had thought all experience ultimately may be reduced. They are, first, sensible qualities (Hume's "impressions"); secondly, the two basic *forms* under which all such qualities are experienced, namely, the forms of space and time; and thirdly, the *categories* under which these qualities are arranged and ordered in the course of our experience. The sensible qualities constitute the *content* of perceptual experience while the forms of space and time and the categories constitute its *formal* elements. Both, according to Kant, are indispensable in that, without the latter as well as the former, experience as we know it would be inconceivable.

Having reached this point, Kant is confronted by the question of how these various elements of experience are to be accounted for, and by the more specific question of what contribution the mind makes to the occurrence of each of them. His answers to these questions bring him close to the idealism of his successors; and, historically considered, they made its emergence almost inevitable. First, with regard to the sensible content or qualities of our experience, Kant agrees with earlier critics of realism who maintained that none of these qualities can be attributed to things in themselves, because of the various ways in which they can be shown to be conditioned by our faculties of sense. It does seem to him, however, that their *occurrence* is to be explained in terms of the action of some external agency upon our senses. We must suppose, therefore, that there are "things in themselves"; but we cannot attribute any of the sensible qualities of our perceptual experience to them.

This also holds, according to Kant, for the forms of space and time. For experience shows us only that these forms of perceptual experience have application *within* the realm of perceptual experience; and no reasoning a priori can establish that they have any application beyond it, that is, to things in themselves. Kant accepts the empiricist argument that we cannot legitimately extend beyond the limits of perceptual experience the employment of notions which we know to have application only within it. Indeed, Kant goes further, maintaining that the necessity and universality of certain kinds of mathematical and natural-scientific propositions (which he takes to be indisputably valid) presupposes that the forms of space and time are strictly phenomenal in character. He thus concludes that it must be *the mind itself* which supplies our sensibility with the forms of space and time. In short, the forms of space and time are a contribution of the mind, rather than of the nature of things in themselves, to our experience.

And this is also the case, Kant argues, with regard to the categories. They too cannot be regarded as features of things in themselves, which are simply mirrored in our experience. Rather, it must be the fact that the understanding has certain structures in accordance with which the sensible contents of our experience are arranged which accounts for the circumstance that they always *are* so arranged in our experience. Categories like unity, plurality, substantiality, cause and effect, and so forth, may legitimately be applied only to the phenomena we experience, and not to things in themselves; for there is neither any experiential ground nor any a priori reason to extend their application further.

Indeed, it is only if these categories are regarded as contributions of the mind to experience that the necessary and universal validity of a proposition like "Every event has a cause" can be understood. And Kant regards it as a virtually conclusive point in favor of his position that propositions of this sort clearly are necessarily and universally valid. His reasoning, reduced to its barest essentials, goes something like this: These propositions are necessarily and universally valid. For them to have this sort of strict validity, the categories would have to be understood as contributions of the understanding to experience. Therefore they are contributions of the understanding to experience. And thus the mind must be constituted in such a way that it structures experience along these lines. This is an instance of what has come to be known since Kant as a "transcendental argument." And if his premises are sound, his conclusion must be granted to have considerable force.

In short, we cannot, according to Kant, conceive of experience except in terms of the forms of space and time and the categories; but it is because the mind operates as it does, rather than because things in themselves are actually like that, that we experience things as ordered in space and time and as conforming to the categories. Consequently, while the existence of things in themselves must be supposed to account for the *occurrence* of our perceptual experience, Kant agrees with the critics of realism that we can have no knowledge of what things in themselves are like. He is thus a realist, but only in a very limited sense; for though he speaks of things in themselves, he holds that the entire phenomenal world—which is the whole world of our perceptual experience and which Kant quite appropriately identifies as "nature"—is ordered, organized, and colored (i.e., supplied with the particular sensible qualities it has for us) by various faculties of the mind. And all possible empirical and theoretical knowledge pertains only to the phenomenal world, and reflects not the natures of things in themselves but the nature of the mind.

So Kant says that the understanding "prescribes its laws to nature," rather than discovering laws of a nature which exists independently of it. Nature, as we experience and know it, has the forms and laws it does because the mind is responsible for the very forms and laws which structure it. This is Kant's "Copernican Revolution," and the parallel with the original Copernican Revolution should be obvious. Before Copernicus, it had been thought that the sun revolved around the earth. Copernicus reversed this picture. And before Kant (or rather, before his immediate predecessors), it had been thought that the mind took its cues from an independently existing nature. Kant's "revolution" consisted in his reversal of this picture: nature as we know it is now understood, not as existing independently of the mind, but rather as having no existence independent of it and as taking its cues (forms, structures, qualities) from the latter. The mind, therefore, far from being merely a sort of passive mirror of nature, is seen as playing a very active role indeed in the generation of experience.

Now, these activities of the mind obviously are not the sorts of mental acts of which we are or can be *self-conscious* (our various particular thoughts, decisions, choices, and the like) but rather the operations of what might be called the basic structures of the mind, which are essentially the same in all of us and which do their work prior to the emergence of our thoughts and perceptions into consciousness. The question then arises: Since "the mind" is not *identical* with the self-conscious, living, individual self which you are or I am, how do you and I and human beings generally fit into Kant's general scheme? "The mind" obviously is not part of the phenomenal world, since it orders and organizes the phenomenal world. For this reason, it may be referred to as the "transcendental ego." But what about individual human beings, who (ourselves included) occur in experience as *part of* the phenomenal world? Are they (or we) simply on a par with other phenomenal objects? If so, then it would follow that we would have no reason to regard ourselves as free moral agents; for, according to Kant, all events in the phenomenal world are connected with other events of a purely "natural" sort, in accordance with the principle of causality. If, therefore, we are purely natural entities, we must be determined causally in our actions as completely as any other natural entity.

Kant maintains, however, that, first, his reflections on the role of the mind in experience establish at least the logical *possibility* that we are not *merely* natural entities and to some extent transcend the natural or phenomenal world; and that, secondly, there are good—if not logically conclusive—reasons for supposing that we *do* transcend the natural world, and that we *have* a sort of freedom of the will which renders us responsible moral agents. On the first point, Kant is at pains to argue that there exist things in themselves which in some way are related to the occurrence of perceived objects in our experience, as their "ground." He further argues that categories such as that of causality have application only *within* the world of phenomena. It is possible, therefore, that, even if our phenomenal or empirical selves are part and parcel of the causally determined natural world, our transcendent or noumenal selves (our "selves in themselves") are *not* causally determined. Add to this the reflection that, after all, "the mind" which plays so active a role in the constitution of experience and which transcends the phenomenal world completely, is not entirely unconnected with *our* minds, and our transcendence of the phenomenal world with its network of causal laws seems like a very reasonable possibility.

Yet to show that our noumenal, rational selves are not subject to the principle of causality is not to *establish* that we are free, at least in any very significant sense. And no such conclusion can be demonstrated by any line of pure a priori reasoning based on considerations of the nature of the soul; for any such proof always presupposes some abstract definition—here, of the soul—which cannot be shown to be applicable to reality. What then is it which leads Kant to conclude that in point of fact we *are* free? Being unable to give a conclusive theoretical proof, he turns to practical experience and finds in our *consciousness of moral duty* a kind of "practical proof" or indication of our freedom. For duty presupposes the ability to act either in accordance with it or contrary to it. It presupposes, in short, freedom, at least with respect to the matters one's duty concerns. If I have a clear awareness of such obligation, therefore, I cannot but regard myself as free. And while this does not establish my freedom for theoretical purposes, it does establish this conclusion for practical purposes, since, once more, Kant has shown to his satisfaction that our freedom is theoretically *possible* and cannot be ruled out on theoretical grounds, even if it cannot be demonstrated on such grounds either.

Next, on the subject of metaphysical concepts, Hume had argued that all our genuine ideas derive ultimately from sense impressions and consist either of simple copies of them or of complex groupings of such simple copies. A term is meaningful, in his view, if and only if it is associated with an idea whose derivation from impressions of sense can be explained or demonstrated. It thus followed for Hume that if one can produce no such impressions in connection with the use of some term, the term represents no genuine idea at all, but rather is being used meaninglessly and in point of fact signifies nothing. And this, he had contended, is precisely the situation in the case of most metaphysical terms. They do not designate genuine ideas or concepts after all because they fail to pass his test of meaningfulness. Consequently, it had seemed to him that all metaphysical talk of such things as substance, the necessary connection of events, God, and the human soul must end—or at least must be acknowledged to be fundamentally meaningless according to strict (i.e., empiricist) philosophical standards.

Kant rejects this conclusion, even while granting to Hume that such terms as these do not refer to any simple sense impression or complex of impressions. He rejects the conclusion because he rejects Hume's empiricist criterion of meaningfulness. There are at least two basic types of concepts, he holds, which do not refer to simple or complex perceptual contents, but which nonetheless are meaningful and may legitimately be employed, at least subject to certain restrictions. These are the categories of the analytic faculty of understanding and the "ideas" of the synthesizing faculty of reason. The first two concepts mentioned at the end of the previous paragraph are examples of the former, while the next two are examples of the latter. These concepts, and others like them, may legitimately be employed, according to Kant, because they have a legitimate and even indispensable use in the analysis and systematic exploration of our experience. And they are meaningful, Kant contends, because they have legitimate and recognizable uses.

Kant does agree with Hume to this extent: he holds that we have no reason to suppose, on strictly theoretical grounds, that these concepts have any application to things in themselves—that there is a thing in itself corresponding to the term "God," for example, and that there are others corresponding to the term "souls." And he grants that, if the concepts which Hume had termed meaningless are thought to name or refer to metaphysical things in themselves, then they are indeed—from a theoretical standpoint—incoherent and meaningless. They derive, according to Kant, from the understanding on the one hand and from the reason on the other, and do not mirror things in themselves; and they may legitimately be used only in connection with our experience and only because the mind has shaped our experience in such a way that they apply to it or are helpful in the exploration of it.

Properly understood and employed, however, these concepts are both meaningful and useful. Where traditional metaphysics went wrong, Kant contends, was not in making use of terms which do not denote sensible particulars or complexes of them. Rather, it was in regarding the "ideas" of reason as terms denoting particulars of another sort—nonsensible, metaphysical entities—and in thinking that the "categories" of the understanding could legitimately be applied to them. Kant holds, instead, that the "categories" have application only to the phenomenal world of experience, and that the "ideas" of reason, such as those of "God" and "soul," serve as useful ("regulative") *guides* in our attempts to achieve a unified comprehension of the phenomena we experience, as opposed to naming entities which we do not experience, but whose existence and nature we somehow manage to discover through a priori reasoning.

In saying this, however, Kant does not mean to deny the existence of God and the existence and immortality of the soul. He might seem to be a skeptic like Hume, from what has been said above and from the fact that he subjects the traditional theoretical proofs of the existence of God and of the existence and immortality of the soul to devastating criticism. In point of fact, however, he is not. He is careful to point out that what he says about the theoretical status of the "ideas" of reason in no way implies anything about what does or does not exist beyond the realm of phenomena and in the realm of "noumena" or things in themselves. And he further maintains that there are compelling reasons for holding, on practical rather than purely theoretical grounds, both that there is a God and that the soul exists and is immortal. In brief, he holds that the moral law in part tells one to act so that one will be deserving of happiness. Happiness, therefore, ought to be proportionate to morality. But it plainly is not proportionate to morality in this life. A future life, in which things will be set right, thus must be postulated; and this presupposes both the immortality of the soul and the existence of a being sufficiently good and powerful to set them right.[1]

This may not seem to most readers to be a very compelling argument, but Kant deemed it sufficient to render the acceptance of certain basic theological propositions at least more reasonable than not. And, consequently, he felt that he had met the various challenges posed by Humean skepticism. Subsequent philosophers, such as Fichte, Schelling, and Hegel, were persuaded of the truth of some parts of his position—in particular, his new Copernican Revolution and his insistence and emphasis on man's freedom—but found others objectionable. And the development of their own positions may best be understood in the light of what they found acceptable and what they found objectionable in Kant.

III

Fichte, the first philosopher to gain widespread attention in central Europe after Kant, accepts Kant's argument for man's freedom; and he also is convinced by Kant's argument that it is the structures of the mind (i.e., the transcendental ego) which are responsible for experience having the basic features it does.[2] Thus he takes over the Kantian notion of mind transcending the realm of phenomena and elaborates upon the conception of the transcendental ego as a kind of spiritual thing in itself.

But Fichte cannot accept the Kantian idea of a counterpart "material" (or nonegological) thing in itself. Kant had argued that there must be something of this sort to account for the occurrence of sensation. But this indicates an apparent blindness to Hume's basic point and indeed to the implications of Kant's own argument that one cannot employ the categories of the understanding outside of the realm of experience. And that is what Fichte feels Kant was doing here—giving as his justification for introducing the notion of a nonegological thing in itself that the sensuous content of the phenomenal order must have a "ground" (which is really to say a cause) other than the mind itself. Since Kant himself had shown this type of reasoning to be illegitimate and since it is principally to serve as a cause that the nonegological thing in itself was introduced, Fichte considers it necessary simply to drop the idea. But he still feels compelled to ask: How are we to account for the *existence* of the phenomenal world—that is, for the occurrence of the phenomena we experience?

Fichte's answer to this question also shows the reasoning behind his postulation of an "absolute ego," which is ontologically prior to all particular existences. For Kant, once again, the mind performs an active function in experience; but its activity is confined to the ordering and categorizing of content which originates elsewhere—in the thing in itself. Fichte holds that the introduction of the notion of the thing in itself in this manner is illegitimate. He can see no way to account for the content of our experience other than to attribute its very occurrence, as well as its forms and the categories, to the mind—the existence of which cannot be called into question by the type of critical reasoning which shows the notion of the material thing in itself to be illegitimate. Thus the mind, for Fichte, is even more active than Kant had thought, though, once the mind had been shown to be that active, this idea was not too hard for Fichte and others like him to countenance.

Kant had rightly pointed out that his talk of the structuring of experience by "the mind" should not be taken to refer to anything which occurs at the level of explicit individual consciousness. He claimed to be speaking, instead, about operations which we do not experience directly, but infer as logical presuppositions of the possibility of the experiences we have. He therefore had called the "ego" in question here the "transcendental ego," as opposed to the "phenomenal" ego or self which each of us is conscious of in various ways and thinks of as being himself. Fichte likewise recognizes that one can no more attribute the production of the content of our experience to our phenomenal egos than one can its form or content. This too can only be conceived in terms of the activity of the transcendental ego.

But now a problem that did not exist for Kant arises. When the content as well as the form of experience is made dependent upon the transcendental ego, this ego can no longer be regarded simply as a basic structure common to autonomously existing individual minds. If it is to be regarded as capable of producing the content of our experience as well as its forms and organization, it must have an existence which both transcends our individual existences and subsumes them. For if one puts the source of the content of our experience in each individual mind, it would be inconceivable that the experience of one individual should have the degree of similarity of content to that of others that it unquestionably does have. To attribute to minds existing completely independently of one another a common structure that results in a common *ordering* of their experiences (proceeding from the same "ground" that is independent of each and all of them) is one thing; but to locate in each of them the *source* of their various experiences as well, which sources are coordinated in such a way that there can occur all of the actual subtle and substantial similarities in your and my and others' experience, is quite another. Leibniz may have believed that such a view is plausible, but Fichte does not.

Moreover, it would seem highly implausible to suppose that if all individuals were to disappear, then absolutely nothing would exist. This supposition would, among other things, make it difficult to account for the existence of individuals in the first place. Yet this would be the result if one (1) traces the phenomenal world to the activity of the transcendental ego, (2) rejects the notion of things in themselves, (3) rejects the notion of an omnipotent God existing independently of the mind and the world, and (4) considers the transcendental ego to have no reality in its own right, but rather to be a kind of common attribute of individual subjects. Kant did not have this problem because he assumed the existence of things in themselves and an independently existing God. Fichte, however, considers this assumption untenable. Rather than accept the above conclusions, therefore, he rejects (4), and attributes ontological ultimacy to the transcendental ego, to which individuals are related as concrete, ontologically dependent manifestations. And he then is led to attribute to it an impulse toward the achievement of concrete existence or embodiment and the capacity to give itself such embodiment, in order to explain the circumstance that it is in fact concretely existing—for *we* do in fact exist.

This marks the transition from Kantian "transcendental idealism"—which is actually still a kind of realism—to "absolute idealism"; the transcendental ego is transformed from the formal structure of the mind into the absolute ego, a (indeed, the) metaphysical entity. The argument for its existence, in brief, is that it is logically presupposed by experience, if one eliminates the notion of the Kantian nonegological thing in itself. And what has happened, again briefly, is that the transcendental ego (now "absolute") has had to take over the basic function—and therefore something of the character—of the discredited nonegological thing in itself: namely, that of independent existence and the capacity to give rise to experience.

Fichte had learned from Kant's criticism of traditional metaphysics, however (as Kant himself had not sufficiently learned, in his view), that this ego cannot be conceived of as a *thing*, and that, in particular, it is not to be conceived in terms of the categories of substance, spatiality, and concrete existence. One reason why he employs the term "ego" here is that, in the context of Kantian philosophy, it is clearly recognized *not* to designate a *thing*, such as might be found within the phenomenal world but, rather, to designate something transcending the phenomenal order. Fichte conceives of it as what can perhaps only (though inaccurately) be described as a dynamic *general principle* which has the tendency to seek concrete embodiment for itself and the capacity to give itself such embodiment. The term "ego" does have a certain aptness in this connection; for it can much more appropriately be used in conjunction with the ideas of a "complex of concepts" and of "activity" than the terms "substance," "object," "thing," and the like. This is a very difficult notion to comprehend. But it is difficult, according to Fichte, because our whole way of thinking is oriented primarily to relations obtaining *within* the phenomenal world. Here, however, we are trying to talk about the nature and foundation of the entire phenomenal world itself.

The question which must immediately be faced, of course, is that of Fichte's conception of the relation between the absolute ego and the phenomenal world; and it is perhaps best to approach this equally difficult matter from the standpoint of the *need* this ego has of the world. For Fichte, as for Kant, the notion of *freedom* is at the very heart of his conception of the character of the trans-phenomenal ego in terms of which our essential nature is to be conceived; and it is in *moral action* that freedom is most truly evinced and manifested. Freedom conceived in terms of the ability and opportunity to respond to the call of moral duty is an essential feature of

Kant's noumenal self, and Fichte incorporates it into his absolutized version of this self, the absolute ego. The full actualization of the absolute ego thus requires not merely concrete embodiment in the form of existing particulars, but moreover the provision of a context within which these existing particulars can engage in moral action. Such action requires the existence of a world like that of ordinary experience; for if the only objects with which we had to deal were purely intellectual (e.g., mathematical) ones, the opportunity for moral action would not exist, and thus freedom of the sort associated with the possibility of such action would not be a reality. For this reason the self-realizing impulse which Fichte contends must be attributed to the absolute ego is held to be an impulse to achieve that sort of concrete embodiment in which moral freedom can be manifested.

In short, this ego requires a world, as—in Fichte's words—"the material of duty." It therefore "posits" the realm of sensation—the sensible phenomenal world. "The subject posits the object," in his famous phrase; and thus the phenomenal world is "spun out of itself as the spider spins its web." You and I are not conscious of this process, just as we are not conscious of the Kantian shaping of experience by the structures of the mind; but it occurs nonetheless, in order that we may have the opportunity to be morally active and so render the absolute ego fully actual.

At this point one might be moved to attempt to undercut Fichte's extravagant speculations along these lines by accusing him of committing the same error that he himself attributes to Kant, of regarding the phenomenal world as having been caused by something outside of it. Fichte feels, however, that he is not; for he takes himself to be explaining the existence of the phenomenal world in terms of a radically different *kind* of causality than that which Kant had shown to be applicable only within the context of the phenomenal world. Kant's analysis applied only to the notion of *efficient* causality, whereas Fichte's explanation makes use of the notion of *final* causality. In Kant's analysis, to ask for the (efficient) cause of an event in the phenomenal world is to ask for a description of another event in the phenomenal world preceding it in the temporal sequence and related to it in accordance with a rule. Fichte grants that it is appropriate to speak of this sort of causality only within the context of the phenomenal world. If causality is understood in this way, he denies the appropriateness of speaking of the phenomenal world as having a cause. From this standpoint one can only say: It is a fact that there are these sequences of phenomena.

The applicability of the notion of *final* causality, on the other hand, is not restricted in this way. In fact, this notion has its most appropriate application in *practical* contexts, for it involves explaining an existing state of affairs in terms of a purpose, end, or goal. An explanation of the existence of the phenomenal world is not possible in terms of efficient causality; it is possible, for Fichte, only with reference to the goal set by the very nature of the absolute ego: namely, the emergence of a state of affairs in which both concrete existence and freedom are a reality. It is only in terms of this end, he holds, that one can give an answer to the question: Why is there the sort of phenomenal world which is given in experience? Fichte thus takes himself to be completing Kant's Copernican Revolution and to be incorporating the essential elements of Kant's moral philosophy into it in the bargain.

Fichte is left, therefore, with the absolute ego as that which alone is presupposed by our experience. And he holds that, since there is no Kantian nonegological thing in itself in contrast to which the phenomenal world of experience is *mere* appearance, the phenomenal world is restored to the status of the *real* world (because it is the *only* world)—as common sense is inclined to think anyhow. And thus it is the real world which reflects the structure of the mind. The phenomenal world is the real world, but it is the trans-phenomenal (or "transcendental") absolute ego which accounts both for the formal and material features of it and for its very existence.

Of course, this means that in a sense the phenomenal world has the character of "appearance" in relation to the absolute ego. But since this ego is no *thing* in itself and has no real existence independent of the phenomenal world in which it *achieves* realization, the use of the term "appearance" does not carry with it the kind of invidious distinction which it has for Kant. For the phenomenal world here is not regarded as *mere* "appearance," as opposed to something else which is "reality"; rather, it is the manifestation or realization of a principle which by itself lacks concrete reality. The phenomenal world for Fichte is thus "the appearance" of the absolute ego—that in which it "*makes* its appearance," so to speak, and thereby becomes something actual.

In conclusion, two more specific points warrant brief comment. First, the manner in which Fichte conceives of the individual may strike one as odd or objectionable, but it grows out of Kant's view and in turn is reflected in Hegel's. The individual is viewed by Fichte, not as something inherently unique, but rather as a particularized instantiation of the absolute ego. Each individual is essentially the same as other individuals, for all embody the same fundamental principle. It is helpful, in this connection, to think of Kant, who thought of each person essentially as a rational agent, with the same rational mental structure as all other persons. Empirical differences, on the other hand, were not regarded as essential. Thus, for Kant, individuals are fundamentally instances of a general type; and as instances of this general type, minds all have the same transcendental features. Fichte simply takes the additional step of suggesting that the absolute ego (a kind of hypostatization of the Kantian general type) must be in some sense ontologically *prior to* its particular instantiations, even though it lacks real, concrete existence until it finds embodiment in them. (Indeed, he at times equates it with God.)

Finally, Fichte's main originality is sometimes said to consist above all in his virtual invention of the notion of dialectical development; and there is much to be said for this observation. For him the story of the world is that of one principle (the absolute ego) giving rise to another which is its opposite (nature), and then achieving a synthesis with it, so that the apparent initial opposition (of "subject" and "object") is overcome. The synthesis is ultimately completed through the recognition on the part of concrete self-conscious mind that nature is not something foreign to it, but rather in a sense is its (because it is the absolute ego's) own creation, and through the subsequent appropriation of nature for the purpose of the realization of freedom through moral action. The result is a whole in which freedom no longer is merely implicit but rather has attained concrete, living reality. Both this general world view and the attendant notion of a dialectic in which something gives rise to its opposite whereupon this opposition is subsequently overcome greatly influenced Hegel and did not originate with him.

IV

Schelling's basic philosophical position does not differ greatly from Fichte's.[3] His contribution to the development of absolute idealism consists less in showing any great originality, as Fichte does, than in carrying certain ideas beyond the point to which Fichte carries them, in somewhat changing their relative emphasis, and in giving some of Fichte's ideas a rather different twist.

For example, he elevates Fichte's general notion of dialectical development to the status of what he calls "the law of triplicity"—the "law" that all action is followed by reaction, which in turn is followed by synthesis, which as a new action is followed by another, different reaction, synthesis, etc. For Fichte there is basically one such development, the absolute ego giving rise to nature and then appropriating it. Schelling sees this principle at work everywhere within reality as the general mechanism of change and development in it. Hegel is often associated with this "law of triplicity," but in fact Schelling is the one who proclaims it a "law"; and compared with him, Hegel makes relatively little use of it. Hegel makes a great deal of use of the notion of dialectical development; but for him it does not always need to take this three-step form. In fact, one of Hegel's departures from Schelling consists precisely in his liberation of the notion of dialectical development from the rigid confines of action-reaction-synthesis (or thesis-antithesis-synthesis).

Schelling's change of emphasis in relation to Fichte consists in part in his shift away from Fichte's strong emphasis on moral action. He is much more concerned with nature considered in itself than Fichte is, and does not view it (as Fichte does) principally as a setting in which moral action can occur and freedom can be realized. He still speaks of freedom, but for him freedom is to be conceived less in terms of human moral action than in terms of the realization of the absolute ego's essential nature. He holds that the essential structures of the absolute ego are reflected (as Kant argued of the transcendental ego) in the basic features of the phenomenal world, and it is in the form of the phenomena of perceptual experience that it finds its initial manifestation. But the highest form of mental activity is not mere perception. Reflective, rational self-consciousness (of the philosopher) is higher; and active, creative self-consciousness (of the artist) is higher still. And so Schelling concludes that the end toward which the realization of the absolute ego tends is the emergence of a form of concretely existing consciousness in which the full range of its essential structures is self-consciously exhibited.

Schelling takes a position similar to Fichte's on the question of our freedom in relation to nature. Both hold that nature appears to bind us only as long as we fail to recognize that its structure and laws reflect those of the mind—that is, of the absolute ego—rather than vice versa, and that, therefore, because we are concrete instantiations of it, and so are essentially identical with it, we are not subject to the tyranny of the laws of an alien nature, and hence enjoy at least the possibility of freedom. This means slightly different things for the two men, however. For Fichte, it means that we recognize that our phenomenal existence does not preclude the possibility of free, rational, moral action, but rather makes such action possible by supplying us with a context in which it can occur. And we actualize our potential freedom insofar as we conduct ourselves as rational beings in our actions in the world.

For Schelling, on the other hand, freedom means attaining a consciousness of the basic structures of mind and nature (which are ultimately one and the same), on the one hand, and engaging in creative activity, on the other. The difference is that for Fichte, with his moral concerns, freedom is essentially something practical and moral action is its principal manifestation, whereas for Schelling freedom is conceived without reference to this moral element. It is not the moral agent responding to the call of duty who is the paradigm embodiment of freedom, in Schelling's view, but rather the philosopher whose reason is subjected to no arbitrary restrictions and, above all, the artist who gives free reign to the creative impulse within him, which is essentially identical with the self-realizing impulse of the absolute ego itself. Both philosopher and artist are free because they are self-determined, in that each is one (albeit in different ways) with that which he essentially is (viz., the absolute ego). But the latter is more truly free, because the philosopher does not actually embody the creatively active element, as does the artist, but rather merely contemplates it.

For Schelling, as for Fichte, the individual is conceived essentially as an instantiation of the absolute ego. Or rather, each concretely existing individual is held to have certain essential characteristics which reflect those of the absolute ego. However, he may or may not achieve a form of consciousness according fully with them and a self-conscious identification with the absolute ego. For Kant and Fichte, this is primarily a moral issue, and is principally a matter of whether or not one *recognizes* that one is essentially a free rational being having the capacity to act as such and *acts* accordingly. Schelling puts the matter in somewhat different terms in order to avoid raising these moral issues—or, at least, to avoid making them so central. He takes the position that one is truly *actual* only insofar as one achieves a spiritual state which accords with the nature of the absolute ego. For if one fails to achieve an awareness of and identification with the basic elements of the absolute ego, then—since these are definitive of one's essential nature—one's essential nature remains merely implicit and unrealized. And if the actuality of a thing may be measured in terms of the degree to which it really *becomes* what it is *essentially*—what it "actually is"—then one who is essentially an individuation of the absolute ego but who (for example) exists and views himself on a merely sensuous or one-sidedly rational plane is not fully "actual." This is not to deny that he *exists,* but rather is to assert that one's existence does not really amount to much to the extent to which it does not reflect one's essential nature. (This is a view which it is well to keep in mind when reading Hegel.)

One other aspect of Schelling's early philosophy should be mentioned. Fichte introduced the idea of development into the static Kantian world view. He suggested the idea of a process through which the absolute ego, which is essentially free, brings forth a world in which it can manifest and actualize its freedom. Schelling seizes upon the idea of a developing actualization of the essential nature of the absolute ego, only he conceives this in terms of a development toward the end of the emergence of a form of spirituality in which the essential characteristics of the absolute ego become fully explicit. Obviously, he has in mind *man*, when man achieves an adequate comprehension of the absolute ego and its nature and becomes artistically creative.

Schelling holds, however, that before this end is attained, a long develop-ment is necessary. First, the emergence of the phenomenal world or nature does not in his view merely have the character of the provision of a framework within which, and material by means of which, moral action may be undertaken and freedom thus realized, as it did for Fichte. Rather, it is itself the first stage in this development—the first step in the process through which the absolute ego achieves a form of existence which adequately embodies its essential nature. This first stage is by itself inadequate, but it is presupposed by later ones. Subsequent stages which build upon it—higher stages of development—are, according to Schelling, those of creative imagina-tion, reflection, and the act of will, ultimately taking the form of artistic creation. In artistic creation man finally gives adequate expression to that freely creative force which characterizes the absolute ego most fundamen-tally, over and above the categories of the understanding that come to light at the stage of reflection; and thus the absolute ego achieves full actuality, in a concretely existing being which actually and self-consciously embodies its essential nature.

Now this admittedly seems rather wild. But Schelling takes the general position he does, and thus arrives at these conclusions, because he can think of no other way of conceiving the relation between what began as Kant's transcendental ego and the phenomenal world, in the light of Kant's strictures (which he takes very seriously—more seriously than Kant himself, and even Fichte, did) against applying the category of causality outside of the phenom-enal order. For while Fichte rejects the idea of nonegological things in themselves as the ground or cause of our perceptual experience, in Schelling's eyes he for all practical purposes proceeds then to treat the transcendental (now absolute) ego as the cause of it—in the sense of efficient, and not merely final, causality, Fichte's protestations to the contrary notwithstanding. To be sure, Fichte, unlike Kant, avoided using a term virtually synonymous with "cause" in this context, and spoke instead of "the subject *positing* the object" (namely, the phenomenal order). But it seems to Schelling that, as in the case of Kant, the basic idea here is still that of efficient causality.

Schelling holds that it is no more legitimate to regard the absolute ego and the phenomenal world as causally related (positor to positee) than it is to regard the phenomenal world as causally related to some nonegological thing in itself. But this position then leads him to try to conceive the relation between the two in some other way. He is able to think of only one other way of conceiving it: namely, as that of potentiality to actuality, of mere abstract essence lacking embodiment to the concretely existing realization of this essence. Thus he argues that nature is not to be regarded as the *product* of an action ("positing") on the part of an absolute ego which must therefore in some sense exist prior to it (in order to be able to do the positing). Rather, he holds that it must be conceived as the first stage in the actualization of an absolute ego which is utterly lacking in substantial existence prior to it. The idea that the ultimate essence of the universe has an inner impulse to achieve concrete realization had been around in philosophy for a long time (at least since Plotinus), so it does not seem to be utterly absurd to Schelling. And in view of the seeming lack of alternatives, he concludes that this account must be the correct one.

Schelling's developmental scheme of stages is virtually necessitated, if this view is taken. For while the phenomenal world of perceptual experience may be regarded as the initial embodiment of the otherwise merely abstract absolute ego, it certainly cannot be regarded as an *adequate* manifestation of its nature. It is, after all, a far cry from a philosophical grasp of the absolute ego's basic structures and from the creative activity of the artist. So it was only natural for Schelling to regard the emergence of the phenomenal world of sense as simply *one step* in the direction of an adequate manifestation of it, which is followed by others. The question, "Which other steps?" led Schelling to reflect upon the various forms of consciousness and ultimately to formulate the developmental sequence mentioned earlier.

This, in the space of a few short decades, is what reflection upon Kant's notion of the transcendental ego—and his argument that the forms of space and time and the categories of the understanding may not be applied beyond the realm of phenomena—led his most important and influential successors to maintain. And it was in a philosophical community dominated by the thought of Fichte and Schelling that Hegel's views took shape. Indeed, in the case of Schelling, the extent to which Hegel was exposed to his influence could scarcely have been greater; for they were students together—and close friends—at Tübingen, and remained in close association during the years which followed (though Schelling received widespread attention long before Hegel did), very nearly to the time of the appearance of Hegel's *Phenomenology of Spirit*. At that point they parted company over philosophical differences which emerged between them, but Hegel constantly had Schelling in mind in his formative years. Indeed, his first major publication consisted of an extensive analysis of the views of Schelling and Fichte.[4] More than anyone else's, therefore, it was Schelling's questions and answers which set the stage for Hegel's development of his own metaphysics. This will become clear in the following chapter.

PART II

Consciousness, Society, and Freedom:
From Absolute Idealism to Socio-Naturalism

3:

A Commentary on the Preface to Hegel's Phenomenology of Spirit

A preface to a book in philosophy is often a rather cursory affair, of little interest in its own right and of only marginal value with respect to the understanding of the views of its author. Over the past two centuries, however, something of a tradition among Continental philosophers has developed—that of using prefaces to reveal the aims, motivations, and commitments of the authors much more clearly, succinctly, and candidly than is generally done in the main body of the works to which the prefaces are affixed. Nietzsche's prefaces, for example, are masterpieces; Kant's are highly revealing; and Husserl's preface to the English translation of *Ideas,* Merleau-Ponty's to *The Phenomenology of Perception,* and Sartre's to his *Critique of Dialectical Reason* are invaluable as indicators of the nature of their concerns and positions.

Hegel's prefaces and introductions to his published works and series of lectures, however, are almost in a class by themselves; for of virtually no other philosopher can it be said that, if his introductory material alone remained available to us, we would still be in a position both to understand the essentials of his philosophy and to apprehend his greatness. And of this material the Preface to his *Phenomenology of Spirit* is of the greatest importance and value. It is a major work in its own right, and in it the main outlines of Hegel's thought are indicated and related to prior philosophical developments. Of all his writings and lectures, it constitutes the best point of entry into his philosophy as a whole and into his metaphysics in particular. In addition to facilitating the comprehension of what he goes on to do and say in the *Phenomenology* and elsewhere, the Preface is most helpful in enabling one to discern what it was that subsequent philosophers from Marx and Kierkegaard to Sartre both felt obliged to take seriously and reacted against. Making sense of the Preface, however, is a formidable task, for it is beyond question one of the most difficult as well as one of the most important prefaces any philosopher has ever written. For this reason the discussion of it in the present chapter is cast in the form of a commentary, meant to be read in conjunction with the Preface itself; but it is intended to be sufficiently informative and self-contained to serve as an introduction to Hegel's philosophy if read independently.

Hegel's metaphysics is commonly thought to be a relic of the past, swept into the dustbin of intellectual history by the series of philosophical reactions and revolutions occurring on both sides of the English Channel in the century following his death, and now commanding merely antiquarian or historical interest. In point of fact, however, a kind of neo-Hegelianism has begun to emerge in recent years in certain quarters of the English-speaking philosophical world; and in Europe, Hegelian tendencies have long been apparent in phenomenological (Husserl), existential (Jaspers, Sartre), and even Marxist (Lukács) circles. There may be few philosophers today who are strict Hegelians in the sense of adhering to each and all of the positions he takes in the form in which he sets them forth; but in this sense there are presently few if any Aristotelians, Cartesians, or Kantians either—and yet there clearly are numbers of philosophers whose orientations and views are such that they may quite properly be so styled. And in the sense in which Aristotelianism, Cartesianism, and Kantianism are thus still very much alive, Hegelianism is at least by no means dead and is showing signs of increasing vitality.

Hegel's metaphysics is no more self-evidently absurd than any of its more recent naturalistic rivals is self-evidently sound. One can dismiss it out of hand, as Dr. Johnson did Berkeley's idealism, but to do so is only to exhibit one's failure to comprehend what it involves. Hegel was anything but philosophically naive, and presents us with no mere result of an idiosyncratic flight of philosophical fantasy—as his more important opponents have clearly recognized. He felt there were compelling reasons for taking the positions he sets forth—and compelling they are. There may be even more compelling reasons for ultimately rejecting them, or at least modifying them, but that is an issue that can properly be resolved only after giving Hegel his day in court. The present chapter does not seek to settle the matter one way or the other, but it does indicate something of the nature of the issues which must be dealt with in any attempt to do so.

Hegel's *Phenomenology of Spirit* has come to be regarded by many Hegel scholars as his most important work—even though it was his first book and in many ways is more difficult to read than any of the others he wrote. And it is a matter of further widespread agreement that the Preface to the *Phenomenology* is the most important part of it. This may be illustrated by the remarks of some eminent Hegel scholars concerning it, cited by Walter Kaufmann in his introduction to his translation of it:[1] "It is not saying too much when I claim that anyone understands Hegel's philosophy if he completely masters the meaning of this preface" (Rudolf Haym, 1857). "[It is] the most important of all Hegel texts. . . . Whoever has understood the preface to the *Phenomenology* has understood Hegel" (Hermann Glockner, 1940). "The *Phenomenology* is preceded by a remarkable Preface, which is a literary as well as a philosophical masterpiece" (J. N. Findlay, 1958). And "The Preface of the *Phenomenology* is one of the greatest philosophical undertakings of all times" (Herbert Marcuse, 1941). Kaufmann himself also thinks it is of the greatest importance, as is shown by his publication of his own translation of it, together with a commentary on it.

Thus I will take the importance of the Preface, at least in the context of Hegel's philosophy, to be established on good authority. I myself think that, if one *can* understand it, one will have understood Hegel's basic conception of what philosophy is and how it ought to be done, and the essentials of his metaphysics as well. It *is* in my view the best summary of his philosophy that he ever wrote, even if it does not contain his arguments for his views. (And, after all, one should not expect to find arguments in a Preface.) In this commentary I shall attempt to expound and clarify some of the basic points Hegel is making in it, in order to facilitate the understanding of it. Such a commentary is needed because it *is* very difficult to understand. Ultimately, of course, the important thing is for one to come to some conclusion about the merit of what Hegel is saying, but one cannot do that until one achieves an understanding of him.

I

Near the beginning of the Preface, Hegel says, "The true form in which truth exists can only be the scientific system of it" (p. 12). First, the term "scientific" should not be understood in its usual sense, as referring to the empirical sciences. Rather, it should be understood in the sense of Hegelian philosophy and "logic." And secondly, Hegel's point here is that, since the "truth" or the essential nature of things consists in a network of logically related concepts, it can only be grasped accurately and completely through a philosophical mode of thought which is rigorously rational and logical, and systematic as well. So also, when he says a few pages later, "Truth finds the element of its existence only in the Concept [*Begriff*]" (p. 14), he means, first, that the truth or essential nature of reality is the *Begriff* (or "system of pure reason"), and secondly, that it can be grasped only through the mode of thought appropriate to it—namely, through conceptual, rational thought.

Those against whom Hegel is speaking here are not first and foremost previous philosophers like Hume and Kant, though he *would* want to criticize them too along these lines for not recognizing what the essential nature of reality consists in, and for failing to see both that the basic task of philosophy is to comprehend it in conceptual systematic thought and that it is possible for philosophy to do this. Those whom he has in mind are above all the romantics, or those associated with the view—widely prevailing at the time and to some extent once again today—that the ultimate and true nature of reality is to be apprehended (and can *only* be apprehended) through some sort of intuition or feeling. The romantics had seen—rightly, in Hegel's view—that mere analytical, empirical, or critical thought is not capable of revealing the true ultimate nature of reality; but from this they had proceeded to what Hegel regards as the erroneous conclusion that therefore something altogether different from rational thought is required to reveal it.

This way of thinking, Hegel says, characterizes "the stage the self-conscious spirit occupies at present" (p. 14)—in other words, the situation as *he* enters the picture. The human spirit which has reached the stage of romanticism has, in its intellectual development, passed beyond immediate, unreflective consciousness, beyond the stage of uncritical thinking and of naive faith in the ability of uncritical thinking to grasp the nature of reality, and also beyond the stage of skeptical thinking which despairs of being able to apprehend the fundamental nature of reality at all. But it now attempts to proceed, according to Hegel, "not by returning the chaotic consciousness to the order of thought and the simplicity of the Concept, but rather by . . . suppressing the discriminating concept, and by establishing the *feeling* of the essence" (p. 16).

Against the romantics who took this stance, Hegel contends that mere "enthusiasm" for "the beautiful, the holy, the eternal, religion, and love" is far from sufficient to yield an adequate apprehension of the nature of reality (p. 16). It took a long time for men to rise above mere mythical thinking about reality and to achieve a recognition of the importance of clarity of understanding and of careful attention to the actual contents of experience. This development of the ability to think analytically represented a step in the right direction, even if also a stage which itself must be surpassed if genuine knowledge of the nature of reality is to be attained. But instead of surpassing this stage of analytical thinking in the right direction, the romantics merely recognized its insufficiency, negated it, and in doing so reverted to an essentially more primitive sort of thinking—and thereby risked losing what had been gained in the development of the sort of thinking against which it was reacting. Their protest against the adequacy and ultimacy of analytical, critical thought was based upon the apprehension of something true about it; but romanticism did not itself represent a positive advance beyond this mode of thought. (Indeed, in Hegel's eyes Kant himself had contributed to the emergence of this deplorable state of affairs, with his suggestion that faith and faith alone could penetrate where the understanding could not go; recall Kant's assertion that "I have . . . found it necessary to deny *knowledge,* in order to make room for *faith.*"[2])

In the Preface, however, Hegel is concerned to criticize not only Hume, Kant, and the romantics, but also his immediate philosophical predecessors and contemporaries—and in particular, Schelling. Schelling, he feels, had moved in the right direction, beyond both Kant and the romantics, but his sort of speculative philosophy still leaves a good deal to be desired. Against Schelling, Hegel argues that speculative philosophy must certainly be able to come to terms with the various sciences and incorporate their findings; but one does not arrive at a satisfactory speculative philosophy simply by taking these findings and arranging them under a few abstract formulas (such as "thesis-antithesis-synthesis"), and subsuming them under a single general abstract principle (namely, that of identity, or "$A = A$"), which is then given the status of the "absolute" or fundamental principle of reality. This, in Hegel's view, is an empty formalism which—insofar as it goes beyond the various sciences at all—contents itself merely with vague and empty principles and vacuous formulas (pp. 24–26). He thus implies that in *his* version of speculative philosophy, the connections he proposes will be more significant than Schelling's, and his conception of the absolute more substantial.

II

With regard to the nature of the absolute or "the true" as *he* conceives it, Hegel says, "We comprehend . . . the true not [merely] as substance, but just as much as subject. . . . The living substance is . . . that being, which is in truth subject" (p. 28). As Kaufmann observes, there is an allusion to Spinoza (with his conception of the absolute as substance) and Fichte (with his conception of the absolute as ego or subject) here. The contrast in question—both sides of which Hegel wants to affirm—is between a conception of the absolute as something with an unchanging, determinate character and a conception of the absolute as pure activity or dynamic agency. In Hegel's view each conception, taken by itself, is inadequate to the true nature of the ultimate principle of reality (the "absolute"), although each conception does bring out an important aspect of the absolute. Retaining the traditional terminology, Hegel maintains that the absolute is to be conceived as *both* substance *and* subject—that is, both as having a determinate nature and as being active. Its substantial aspect, he holds, consists of the "system of pure reason," the system of thought forms which constitute the *Begriff* or "Concept." And its subject aspect consists of its dynamic, self-realizing impulse which accounts both for the unfolding of the *Begriff* in itself and also for the emergence of concretely existing consciousness, in which it is concretely embodied and ultimately actually thought.

A conception of the absolute which focuses solely on its substantial aspect, according to Hegel, fails to do justice to the interrelation of the very components of this substantial aspect itself, and also to the fact that this purely formal, abstract substantial aspect comes to attain the form of existing self-consciousness—and is something actual only insofar as it does so. On the other hand, Hegel holds that a conception of the absolute which focuses solely on its subject aspect does not do justice to the fact that determinateness is not merely something which it acquires in an accidental way in the course of its actualization, but rather is an essential feature of the absolute even when considered simply in itself as pure *Begriff*. And finally, as the case of Schelling shows, Hegel feels that it is also possible for a philosopher to grasp that the absolute is to be conceived both as substance and as subject, and yet to fail to conceive the nature of these elements of it and their relation to each other adequately. In his own conception of the absolute as the self-determining, self-realizing *Begriff*, Hegel feels that he makes good all these shortcomings.

Hegel's argument for his conception of the absolute, stated very briefly, would seem to be the following: (1) philosophical inquiry reveals that reality fundamentally has the essential character of a "system of pure reason," in terms of which everything that exists concretely can and must be understood, with no materialist or Kantian "things in themselves" left over as a meaningful remainder. And (2) the fact that there *are* natural and historical phenomena which manifest this "system of pure reason," and that there *is* thinking activity in which it is more or less accurately apprehended, cannot be explained except by attributing to the absolute an impulse toward the attainment of concrete, and ultimately self-conscious, existence. And from this it follows that the absolute must be conceived both as substance and as subject in the above senses.

Thus, to the description of the absolute as it is *in-itself*—which involves setting out the *Begriff* in all its determinateness and detail—it must be added that it is of "the nature of this life to be *for-itself*" (p. 30), that is, to achieve the form of existing self-consciousness. Only when it is *for-itself*—and so is *in-and-for-itself*—is it fully *actual*. Only then is it *actually* what it is *implicitly* or essentially. This is what Hegel has in mind when he says that "the form is no less essential to the essence than the essence itself," and that "the essence is to be comprehended . . . not merely as essence . . . , but just as much as form—and in the whole wealth of the developed form. Only as such is it comprehended . . . *in its actuality*" (p. 30). So, according to Hegel, the absolute is not presented "in its actuality" in philosophical logic; there only its essence—its skeleton—is indicated. It is presented "in its actuality" only in a phenomenology of spirit, in which "the whole wealth of the developed form"—that is, the various stages of consciousness through which the essence of the absolute comes to be explicitly manifested and adequately grasped in actual consciousness—is taken into consideration.

Hegel goes on to observe that "the result is the same as the beginning" and that "the actual is the same as its Concept" (p. 34)—at least in a sense. They are the same in the sense that, considered *formally,* the essential structure of "the actual" or "the result" of the whole developmental process will correspond exactly to the structure of the absolute considered merely in itself, as *Begriff.* But there is a profoundly important difference between "the actual" and "its Concept" at the *existential* level—very literally, all the difference in the world. For at "the beginning" nothing *exists;* "the Concept" merely by itself *is* nothing real at all. Whereas "the result" *does* exist; "the actual" *is* something real, something having the "form" of *existence.*

III

At this point something should be said about a notion which recurs frequently in Hegel's discussion in connection with the subject aspect of the absolute, the process of its actualization, and consciousness: namely, "negativity." How is "negativity" to be understood, in relation to these other notions? To begin with, "negativity" for Hegel—reasonably enough—is the opposite of "positivity"; and as Hegel uses the latter term, something has the character of "positivity," or is "positive," to the extent that it has a determinate content or form. Now, in the context of the substance-subject distinction, the aspect of the absolute with the character of "positivity" is its *substance* aspect.

Hegel wishes to distinguish between it and the *subject* aspect of the absolute, even though he also holds that they are simply different aspects of one and the same ultimate principle. So if the substance element may appropriately be characterized in terms of "positivity," what better way is there than in terms of "negativity" to characterize the subject element? For by so characterizing it, one brings out the difference between the latter as a dynamic impulse which impels development beyond all determinate forms that are incomplete—and which therefore is in a sense opposed to all (limited) determinateness—and the former, which is nothing if not determinate and which as such contains no impetus toward actualization. The absolute-qua-subject "negates" the abstract purity of the absolute-qua-substance, by impelling it in the direction of actualization, and it "negates" each merely transitional stage in the course of its actualization, by impelling the process in the direction of a mode of consciousness more adequate to the *Begriff.* And so it is quite understandable that Hegel characterizes this subject aspect in terms of "negativity."

He also characterizes "consciousness" in terms of "negativity" for equally good reasons. Consider the distinction between the contents of consciousness, whatever they may be, and consciousness itself. Consciousness itself is to be distinguished from each and every possible determinate (or "positive") content of consciousness, though of course it cannot exist without some such content. All consciousness is consciousness of something, but consciousness as an activity is not to be identified with its contents which are the objects of that activity. The contents of consciousness are always something more or less determinate, or "positive"; and so, in relation to its contents, consciousness itself is something *in*determinate, non-"positive," or "negative." In short, in relation to its contents, consciousness itself has the character of "negativity." It is something more than they are, something which transcends them in the direction of other possible contents; but even so it is not itself something determinate—not another determinate object, in the sense in which another possible content or object *of* consciousness *is* another determinate object. In this sense it is something "negative," like the subject aspect of the absolute, and for basically similar reasons. And this result should not be surprising, for according to Hegel consciousness and the subject aspect of the absolute are not unrelated. On the contrary he regards consciousness as the existing manifestation of the subject aspect of the absolute—the *form* it takes, in which its substance or essential *content* becomes something actual. (More will be said about "negativity" and "the negative" below.)

IV

Next, let us turn to Hegel's use of the term "spirit," in relation to the expressions "the true," "actuality," "science," "the absolute," "substance," and "subject." Hegel says, "That the true is actual only as [scientific] system, or that the substance is essentially subject, is expressed in the conception which speaks of the absolute as *spirit.*" And further: "The spirit that, so developed, knows itself as spirit is science. Science is the actuality of spirit and the realm that the spirit builds for itself in its own element" (p. 38).

Hegel has already characterized the absolute—the fundamental principle of reality or "the true"—as both substance and subject. Here he is suggesting that since the absolute has both of these characteristics, it might more informatively be referred to as "spirit." For this term more adequately expresses its subject character than does the merely formal term "the absolute." He also has already said that "the true"—or rather the *Begriff*—is "actual" only when it is actually *thought*, only, that is, when there exists an actual consciousness of its essential contents. Now "science," or "scientific system," as Hegel uses these expressions, is precisely a consciousness or explicit apprehension of the *Begriff*; the substance of it is "the true" grasped completely in actual consciousness. So it follows that "the true is actual only as [scientific] system"—only when it is comprehended in "scientific" or philosophical thinking. And "science" so conceived can also be characterized as "spirit knowing itself as spirit": that is, as spirit-as-subject knowing (or attaining the form of consciousness of) itself-as-substance.

"Science," Hegel says, "is the actuality of spirit." That is, it is a form of existing consciousness in which the substantial content of spirit or the absolute is actually thought. And "science . . . is the realm that the spirit builds for itself in its own element." For spirit's "own element" is thought or consciousness, since spirit is essentially subject as well as substance. And "science" or systematic thought is that form achieved by consciousness in which the substantial content of spirit may be grasped clearly and completely by spirit-qua-subject, that is, in which spirit becomes conscious of its essential substantive nature. This is what Hegel means when he says that spirit "must become an object for itself"; its substantial content must become an object of knowledge—something explicitly and adequately grasped in consciousness.

When this happens, spirit's "being-in-itself," or essential nature, is then also "for-itself," or something of which there exists an explicit consciousness. In short, it then is "in-and-for-itself." (And Hegel believes that, in him, this goal at last has been reached.) Before this happens, it is what it is only "in-itself," but not "for-itself." At the intermediary stage in which consciousness grasps the substantial nature of the absolute (what it is in-itself) more or less adequately, but does not yet see that it itself is really the subject aspect, there is for it a subject-object split. Here spirit-as-subject has its own content before itself in consciousness (for-itself), but it is not recognized as such. Consciousness does not realize that what it has before it (for-itself) is what *it itself* essentially *is* (in-itself). Only when consciousness recognizes this—only when it sees that "subject" and "object" are but two sides or aspects of the same fundamental reality (viz., spirit, which is both substance and subject)—is the appearance of a subject-object split overcome. Then genuine self-knowledge—which is also genuine knowledge of the nature of reality generally—is at last achieved. Only then is it appropriate to speak of the existence not merely of "spirit in-itself" and "spirit for-itself," but of "spirit in-and-for-itself." And with this the end of the process of spirit's self-realization is reached.

It is the second of these stages which Hegel has in mind when he speaks of "pure self-recognition in absolute otherness," which "is the ground and basis of science or universal knowledge" and which "the beginning of philosophy [proper] presupposes" (p. 40). That is, the philosophy which is going to usher in the third and final stage, according to Hegel (namely, his own), presupposes that the second stage has been reached. This is the same "presupposition of philosophy" (that is, of philosophy proper) which Hegel had spoken of in his earlier discussion, "The Need for Philosophy," in his essay on Fichte and Schelling:[3] namely, what he there called "the bifurcation of subject and object," which needs to be overcome.

V

Although Hegel feels that, in his philosophy, spirit has finally reached the third stage of "knowing itself as spirit" and of being both "in-and-for-itself," there still remains the practical problem of how *other individuals* may be brought up to this level or standpoint of "absolute knowledge" too. He says, "The individual has the right to demand that science should at least furnish him with the ladder [from his initial naive state] to this standpoint" (p. 40). And Hegel feels that he is furnishing us with such a ladder by writing the *Phenomenology*. Starting with ordinary sense experience—which is the simplest, lowest form of human experience—he proposes to lead the individual by the hand all the way up to the level of absolute knowledge, by retracing and leading him through the dialectical development by which the human spirit (or at least its advance units) has reached this goal.

Hegel's point in speaking of "self-certainty," or of consciousness becoming "certain of itself," is that if the individual is really to reach this goal, he must not simply be confronted with the results of this development, that is, with absolute knowledge in its final form. Rather, he must be brought to the point that he is completely certain that what Hegel's philosophical "science" says about reality and spirit both is an accurate, adequate account of them and applies to him. He must become just as certain of this as he is of himself in his initial, naive, commonsense understanding of himself. His initial "self-certainty" soon disappears, once his self-consciousness and his understanding become more sophisticated—and it *must* disappear if he is ever to reach the level of absolute knowledge; but so also must he dispel that *doubt*, which he surely would feel if he were suddenly confronted, completely unprepared, with Hegel's *Logic* or *Encyclopedia* or the final chapter of the *Phenom-*

enology on "Absolute Knowledge." It is only by being properly prepared for them that he will ever be able to be certain of their truth. And it is only when this new and ultimate form of "self-certainty" is achieved that he really will have ascended Hegel's "ladder" and attained absolute knowledge.

This is one way in which Hegel intends the *Phenomenology* to be viewed— as an educational device enabling the individual to attain absolute knowledge. But he further intends it to be viewed in another way; for it may also be conceived with reference simply to its *content.* So Hegel says, "This phenomenology of the spirit presents the becoming [or actual emergence] of science or universal knowledge" (p. 42). That is, it describes the development of consciousness from its most primitive form to its highest, final form, in which it achieves an adequate comprehension both of itself and of the true nature of the absolute (which is simply to say the same thing in different ways).

"Knowledge in its initial form," Hegel says, "is . . . the consciousness of the senses"—a form of consciousness, he adds, which "lacks spirit" (p. 42), that is, which does not in fact constitute genuine knowledge. "To become true knowledge," he continues, "it has to work its way through a long journey" (p. 42). This is what the human spirit has done in the course of its development; and this is what the individual also must do if his own consciousness is to reach that highest level of development which the human spirit has reached—which is that of "true" or "absolute" knowledge. There is no other way it can be reached, Hegel says—no "royal road to knowledge," which would spare the individual the necessity of following the long, hard path leading to it. He must work through the intervening stages of intellectual development himself, for there is no other way in which "self-certainty" at the level of absolute knowledge and a complete and adequate comprehension of its contents can be achieved.

Of the various stages in the development he describes, Hegel says, "Every moment is necessary" (p. 46). For each later one presupposes those which preceded it and could not have emerged without them.[4] And from this it follows that, for the individual, "the [whole] length of this way must be endured" (p. 46). Yet, fortunately for the individual, this is easier for him that it was at first; for those who have gone before him have done the work of initial discovery and have left a well-marked and relatively clear path for him to follow. So Hegel says, "The individual must also pass through the contents of the educational stages of the general spirit, but as forms that have long been outgrown by the spirit, as stages of a way that has been prepared and evened for him" (p. 44). And this makes it possible for an individual today to work through in a relatively short time a development which initially took the human spirit thousands of years.

This process or development can be viewed from two different perspectives. From one perspective—that of the individual—it is the process through which he "acquires what is given to him" and makes the hard-won knowledge of the content or "substance" of spirit his own. As such it is the process through which the individual consciousness becomes "universal"—an existing instantiation of spirit which is "in-and-for-itself." And from the other perspective, "from the point of view of the general spirit as substance, this means . . . that this [substance] acquires self-consciousness" (p. 46) and so becomes "actual"—or, if the individual is not the first to do it, renews and more firmly establishes its "actuality."

Or, as Hegel says on another occasion in the *Phenomenology*, the result is a "twofold actuality": an individual who is universal spirit and universal spirit which really exists. Unless and until this point is reached, neither the individual consciousness nor spirit generally is anything "*actual*": the individual consciousness, because it has not yet become in reality what it is essentially (namely, universal spirit), and spirit, because it has not yet attained a form of existence which fully corresponds to its formal essence. "Actuality" is achieved only with the emergence of a form of existing consciousness in which the essence of spirit is fully manifested.

VI

At this point, however, a number of questions still remain to be answered, such as: What is it that moves the human spirit from one stage of spiritual development to the next? How are the various successive stages related to one another? And, given that Hegel says that "every moment is a necessary one," and that the sequence he describes is that which spiritual development necessarily must follow, what accounts for the necessity?

In answer to the first question, Hegel says that it is "the power of the negative" which drives the development onward. His meaning becomes clearer when this statement is taken together with his view that each stage in the development short of the final one turns out to involve certain internal contradictions or inadequacies. As each particular level of consciousness emerges and achieves full explicitness, these contradictions and inadequacies become apparent. When they do so, those features of the particular type of consciousness in question which are responsible for the difficulties are identified and "negated"; and as a result of this "definite negation," a new level of consciousness is achieved. It is the "negation" of the previous level, but it is not *merely* that; for in "negating" the previous level in a "definite" or "determinate" manner, consciousness goes beyond it. It is a higher level or mode of consciousness than the previous one, because it is a positive one which is not characterized by the specific inadequancies of the previous one which led to the difficulties associated with it. But it itself then turns out to have other shortcomings, which result in other difficulties; and so *it* is eventually "negated," and yet another level of consciousness is achieved. And so it goes, until finally a level of consciousness is reached which has no such shortcomings. And this level, almost by definition, is that of absolute knowledge.

What *does* the negating, according to Hegel, is not something altogether different from consciousness. Rather, it is an element of the human spirit which is distinct from its particular features or determinate form at any given point. It is its pure subject aspect, which Hegel sometimes refers to as the "pure ego" to distinguish it from the various determinate modes of consciousness which emerge, are subjected to criticism, and are then left behind. But it is important to see that, for him, the "pure ego" is no *thing* which has any real existence separately and apart from various existing modes of consciousness. Both are simply different aspects of the spirit—the one being its determinate form at any particular point; the other, its ability to criticize and transcend any such forms that are limited and incomplete.

In short, each subsequent stage in the developmental sequence Hegel describes is viewed as the positive result of a specific, definite negation of the stage preceding it. The subsequent stage, as the result of the negation of the previous stage, presupposes the previous stage and cannot emerge until the previous stage has been reached. And, since for each stage there are certain specific difficulties which surface as it becomes fully explicit, the stage which succeeds it by negating those specific features of it that give rise to those difficulties will itself have a specific character and will be its *necessary* successor. In this way each stage is necessarily related to that which precedes it as its inevitable and indeed "logical" outcome, and it inevitably gives rise to that which follows it by virtue of its own particular shortcomings. It is for this reason that Hegel holds that "every moment is a necessary one," and that the sequence he describes is the one which spiritual development necessarily must follow. And it is in this sense that the term "dialectical" is to be understood, when Hegel refers to this development generally as one which proceeds "dialectically."

This all may sound quite reasonable, but one might well wonder why Hegel supposes that this in fact is the way in which the human spirit really has developed. In the Preface, he only *says* that it is. It is in the body of the *Phenomenology*, on the other hand, in which he actually sets out the various stages of spiritual development, that he tries to show how they *are* actually related to one another in the manner he describes. And so the only way of putting his theory to the test is to ask oneself while reading the *Phenom-*

enology: Has he accurately described the various stages through which the human spirit has passed in the course of its development? *Does* the history of human thought actually constitute the sort of development he describes? And, if so, *are* the various stages he distinguishes related to one another in the way he says they are? *Is* the transition from each to the next necessary, in the sense that they could not have occurred in any other order and that the human spirit could not have developed in any other way?

These are difficult questions, but they are the kinds of questions which must be answered before a final verdict on the validity and success of Hegel's enterprise in the *Phenomenology* can be given. And Hegel certainly would seem to be justified in saying that one has no right to pass judgment on him unless one meets him on his own ground, and that, if one dismisses what he is saying and trying to do simply out of hand, as absurd or ridiculous, one is no true philosopher, but rather the willing victim of mere prejudice, or at the very least a captive of unsubstantiated preconceived ideas.

VII

Having laid at least some of his cards on the table, Hegel at this point in the Preface turns to a further statement of what he is and is not going to be discussing: "What is no longer necessary at the point at which we are here taking up this movement [i.e., the development of spirit] is the *Aufhebung* [supersession] of [mere] existence. But what remains and still requires a higher transformation is the notion of the familiarity with the forms [which emerge in the course of this development]" (p. 48). He thus is not going to deal with the question of the initial emergence of consciousness. This is, to be sure, a very important metaphysical issue, which he does discuss elsewhere; but a discussion of it would obviously be out of place in a work entitled *The Phenomenology of Spirit*. Instead, he is going to begin with consciousness, in its basic forms, and trace its development or transformation from these basic forms into higher ones. And he also is going to be concerned with the explication or translation into appropriate terms or concepts of a variety of common notions (e.g., God, subject, object, nature, society, etc.), which emerge in the course of this development and are central to various stages of it, and which, while spoken of frequently, are seldom properly understood. For, he observes, "what is familiar is not known simply because it is familiar" (p. 48). And this holds true in the case of philosophers no less than in the case of ordinary men; for philosophers are often as guilty as anyone else of simply taking over expressions from ordinary usage and employing them in the discussion of philosophical issues, without first subjecting them to careful scrutiny.

Hegel maintains, however, that the requisite form of scrutiny does not consist merely in analyzing or breaking down such notions into simple components (in the manner of Hume), so that the familiar form of the notion is replaced by a form in which certain simple components are made explicit. This "activity of differentiating," as Hegel terms it, is all well and good; but it is not the end of the matter (p. 50). For analysis of this sort only leaves one with a set of *representations (Vorstellungen)*; and it is further necessary to proceed to supplant them with the appropriate *pure thoughts* (in the manner of Kant). But this is not the end of the matter either, for one must then introduce in *their* stead the appropriate philosophical or "logical" *Concepts (Begriffe)*. In this way, he says, "the pure thoughts become Concepts and [so] come to be what they are in truth" (p. 52). For then they no longer are regarded as fixed and opposed or unrelated to one another, but rather are grasped in their interconnection with one another. Thus Hegel speaks of "making fixed thoughts fluid," by "sublimating fixed, determinate thoughts" through relating them to the appropriate Concepts (p. 52). These Concepts, in turn, form "an organic whole" (p. 52). And it is only when the original notions have been replaced by Concepts of the appropriate sort, which in turn are grasped in their interrelation with the other elements of this "organic whole" (which is nothing other than the *Begriff* proper), that one's task of analyzing the notions which come to light at different stages in the development of the spirit is finished.

VIII

There is a seemingly curious passage about "death," occurring just before this discussion (on p. 50), which becomes comprehensible only if understood in relation to it. In this passage the term "death" is to be understood metaphorically; and the passage itself constitutes an oblique criticism of mere understanding or analytical thinking, mere "differentiating activity," in terms of what it can and cannot accomplish and what its results are. Hegel speaks of "the negative" in this passage as well, because he views the drawing of distinctions as something essentially negative—a matter of saying what things are not, and what is not the same as something else. And when he says, "Death . . . is what is most terrible, and to hold on to what is dead requires the greatest strength" (p. 50), he means that analytic differentiating by itself is negative and destructive in relation to that which is so analyzed, and that great mental powers are necessary in order for one to be able to go beyond it and see the underlying unity of the elements which are differentiated—which as such are lifeless or "dead," as opposed to the underlying unity, which is the living reality.

This theme is reminiscent of Hegel's discussion "The Need for Philosophy" in his essay on Fichte and Schelling. But here as in that essay, he goes on to affirm the necessity of such "differentiating activity" and "death." He says (revising Kaufmann's rendering): "But the life of spirit is not one which shrinks from death and keeps itself from being defiled by devastation, but rather one which endures death and preserves itself in devastation" (p. 50).

Hegel further says that the truly philosophical consciousness "looks the negative in the face and abides with it" (p. 50). In fact, it *must* do this in order ultimately to arrive at the full truth in all its structural complexity, as opposed to mere empty abstract formulas, like "A = A." That is, it must engage in this sort of "differentiating activity" and then go beyond it, and it cannot go beyond it unless and until it has engaged in it. So Hegel says, "Spirit gains its truth only by finding itself in absolute dismemberment" (p. 50)—and by then transcending this "dismemberment" through the synthesizing activity of reason. This is essentially what Hegel had said in his essay on Fichte and Schelling: "[Reason] is not against opposition and limitation in general; for bifurcation is a necessary feature of life, which forms itself through eternal opposing; and totality is possible in the highest liveliness only through restoration out of the highest separation."[5]

In the first three paragraphs of the next section of the Preface, which Kaufmann titles "The forms of consciousness and truth" (pp. 56–58), Hegel gives a capsule summary of the whole *Phenomenology*. For this reason these paragraphs are of the greatest importance, but just for that reason I shall pass over them at present and return to them at the conclusion of my commentary.

IX

The next issue Hegel takes up is that of "truth" and, more specifically, that of the difference between philosophical truth and knowledge and historical and mathematical truth and knowledge. His discussion of this issue is rather long, but his point may be stated relatively briefly. Historical knowledge and truth, he maintains, pertain to the merely particular. History (which is not to be confused with Hegelian *philosophy of* history) is concerned with particular facts, in all their detail and specificity, and as they happen to occur. Mathematics, on the other hand, does not deal with the merely particular and with the happenstance of its occurrence; but it is concerned with nothing more than magnitude, quantity, and arrangement. While history and mathematics in these respects differ radically from each other, both, according to Hegel, thus deal with the merely accidental or inessential—that is, with something other than *essence;* for both magnitude, quantity, and arrangement and the merely particular in its specific details are irrelevant to the question of the essential natures of things and of reality generally.

Philosophy, on the other hand, is held to be concerned precisely with essences—with the basic qualitative features of things, rather than with such accidental matters as their quantitative and merely particular features. "Philosophy," Hegel says, "considers not the inessential determination, but the determination insofar as it is essential" (p. 70). And this concern sets philosophy apart from history and mathematics—and also above them, in Hegel's mind, since in his view a discipline which deals with the essential is clearly to be ranked above disciplines which deal with matters which do not touch upon the essential. And it follows that philosophical truth and knowledge are more profound and more significant than the sorts of truths and knowledge which may be attained in history and mathematics.[6]

One may think it curious that Hegel does not mention natural science in this discussion. There is a reason for this, however; and this reason is that Hegel regards natural science as a kind of lower-order philosophy—or rather as a kind of naive investigation of reality which is not qualitatively different from philosophy, but which attains its true and proper form only when it becomes a *part of* philosophy as Hegel conceives it. Natural science for Hegel is a kind of thinking about reality which, as long as it remains merely empirical, is incapable of yielding genuine knowledge of reality, and of penetrating to the essential natures of things; but it makes a start in that direction and is ultimately transformed into a mode of consciousness which does at last yield absolute knowledge. Scientific knowledge which is based upon mere empirical investigation has its shortcomings; but they are not those of history and mathematics, which render the latter incapable ever of leading to the attainment of absolute knowledge. For science is concerned not merely with magnitude, nor with the mere description of particular facts as they occur. Rather, it is concerned with universals, as is philosophy—that is, with the natures of general types of things and the general laws which apply to them—even if it cannot attain true knowledge of them, until it is transformed into Hegelian "philosophy of nature."

X

It is important to observe that while Hegel holds the concern of philosophy to be with the essential, rather than with mere magnitude and particularity, he does not mean to say that *existence* is of no concern to philosophy. To be sure, it is of no concern to that part of Hegelian philosophy which deals with the *Begriff* as it is *in itself*—that is, to philosophical "logic." But existence *is* of great concern to those parts of Hegelian philosophy which deal with nature and the social and intellectual world, and it is of great concern to Hegel in the *Phenomenology*. For all of these parts of Hegelian philosophy are concerned with essences as they come to attain real existence.

Indeed, the whole of the *Phenomenology* is devoted to an examination of the different modes or levels of actually existing consciousness. And for Hegel, it would make no sense if someone were to say, Never mind about the various modes or levels of consciousness; let us talk about *what exists* more generally. For *what exists,* for Hegel, *is* precisely consciousness in its various forms, and nothing more. He regards it as meaningless to speak of anything else—such as Kantian "things in themselves"—as existing; for he regards it as meaningless to speak of them at all. Since the whole of the *Phenomenology* is devoted to an analysis of the various modes of the only thing which for Hegel may properly be said to *exist* at all, he would, therefore, regard it as very odd indeed—and certainly as wrong—if anyone were to accuse him of being concerned only with essences and of ignoring existence.

So while Hegel does regard existing particulars as "evanescent," he says, "The evanescent must . . . be considered essential" (p. 70). This is another way of saying that it is crucial, in his view, that essences should attain the form of real existence. Existence *in its particularity* is evanescent, transient, and ephemeral; but existence *as such* is indispensable and "essential" if spirit is to become something actual. So Hegel says, "The appearance is the coming to be and passing away of that which itself does not come to be or pass away; it . . . constitutes the actuality and the movement of the life of the truth" (p. 70). The particulars which achieve the status of appearance or explicit existence all are ephemeral and are of no essential importance *as particulars;* but *that there should be* such particulars—in the form of actual conscious events—is necessary in order for spirit to achieve actuality. So Hegel characterizes spirit at the conclusion of its development in terms of both its essential content and existence: "Its existence is knowledge of itself even as this knowledge is just as immediately existence" (p. 72).

There is a famous passage in this section of the Preface which at first glance seems both mysterious and—insofar as it is not completely mysterious—rather self-contradictory; but sense may be made of it if it is viewed in the light of what has just been said. The passage is: "The true is thus the bacchanalian whirl in which no member is not drunken; and because each, as soon as it detaches itself, dissolves immediately—the whirl is just as much transparent and simple repose" (p. 70). In this passage Hegel is suggesting that "the true" may be viewed both as a "bacchanalian whirl" of appearing and disappearing elements and as something in a state of "transparent and simple repose," just because "the true" as something actual has two elements: the element of substance, the *Begriff,* which is timeless and unchanging and is therefore in "transparent and simple repose," and the element of existence (the work of its self-realizing subject-aspect) taking the form of "appearance" or conscious events, which have the character collectively of a "bacchanalian whirl." The two elements are very different; but both are essential, according to Hegel, if "the true"—or the absolute or spirit—is to be something actual. So also he says, "The individual forms of the spirit endure no more than determinate thoughts do; yet they are just as much positive and necessary moments as they are negative and evanescent" (p. 70).

It may be observed in passing that this view of the status of particulars has important implications for us and our significance as existing individuals. For it follows that as *particular* individuals we have no essential significance, since we are merely transient and ephemeral, and—qua particular—merely accidental. But spirit is something that *exists* only in the form of particularity—only, that is to say, in the form of particular individual consciousnesses like ourselves, and so particular individuals like ourselves are essential to the actualization of spirit. In short, it is in virtue of the fact—and only in virtue of the fact—that we are explicit manifestations of various general modes of consciousness that we have essential or ultimate significance; and the higher the modes of consciousness we manifest, the greater our ultimate significance is. But as unique and individual personalities, we have no such ultimate significance. What is unique and particular about ourselves matters *to us;* but we are ephemeral, and when we are gone, what we have been as unique and particular individuals will have no enduring significance. The details of our lives may be of interest to the historian; but as has been seen, Hegel does not regard historical knowledge as knowledge of the essential. Our lives do really count for something—but only insofar as we are, in a manner of speaking, torchbearers of consciousness, and in particular insofar as we are torchbearers of the highest forms of consciousness.[7]

XI

But I digress; let us return to the Preface. Having characterized philosophical as opposed to historical and mathematical truth and knowledge, Hegel turns to the question of the nature of philosophical method, which is to yield such truth and knowledge. But it seems to him that little more really needs to be explained about it, since, in his words, "the concept of this method is implicit in what has been said, and its real exposition belongs to the Logic, or rather constitutes the Logic. For the method is nothing else than the edifice of the whole, constructed in its pure essence" (p. 72). Philosophical method, he contends, has neither the "looser gait of conversational arguments," nor the "stiffer gait" of mathematics, nor that of those so-called disciplines which merely record various particular facts and so are largely superficial. Rather, it consists in following out "the necessity of the Concept," as it unfolds both within itself (in philosophical "logic") and in the realm of appearance (in the *Phenomenology*) (p. 74).

But Hegel is very much concerned that it should not be confused with mere "schematizing formalism"; and so in the following section he returns to his criticism of Schelling—again, without mentioning him by name. His criticism is essentially the same as that which he levels against Schelling's version of speculative philosophy earlier in the Preface. The only difference is that here he goes on at greater length, ridiculing Schelling mercilessly. His main point once again is that Schelling simply imposed an empty, abstract, formal schematism on phenomena in a merely superficial way, instead of bringing to light the underlying, essential features and necessary relations of these phenomena, which consist of those aspects of the *Begriff* reflected in them. Schelling did not, in other words, "enter into the immanent content of the matter," as "scientific knowledge . . . demands." And it is only by doing this, Hegel argues, that we "confront and express its inner necessity" (p. 80) and thereby attain genuine philosophical knowledge and truth.

XII

Hegel then breaks off his criticism of Schelling and resumes the presentation of his own position. And here he reveals the very heart of it, committing himself explicitly to that form of idealism which he develops at much greater length in his *Logic* and *Encyclopedia*. He says: "By its quality an existence is different from another. . . . But through this it is essentially *thought.* —In this the fact is comprehended that being is thinking; and this includes the insight . . . of the identity of thinking and being" (p. 82). In other words, when we eliminate everything inessential (i.e., considerations of magnitude and quantity and of mere particularity), we are left with nothing but general qualities—and, of course, the activity of "thinking." But these general qualities are not *things*, which have any real existence independent of thinking activity or consciousness. Rather, they are only so many different thought forms. We thus find that at bottom reality consists solely of the system of these thought forms (or Concepts), insofar as they are actually thought in thinking activity or consciousness. "Being," therefore, is to be conceived in terms of these thought forms, on the one hand, and thinking activity or consciousness, on the other. And this is in effect simply to restate the claim that the absolute or ultimate principle of reality is both substance (the *Begriff*) and subject—and nothing more. To say that thinking and being are identical, as Hegel does here, is simply to say that at bottom, *what there is* is simply thought as content (the thought forms which constitute the *Begriff*) and thought as subject (thinking activity or consciousness).

Should it be objected that Hegel has left out existing things, he would reply that it is meaningless to speak of them except in terms of actual contents of consciousness, and that he has made reference to both consciousness and its possible contents in his statement of what there is. The form of *existence,* he holds, is supplied not by anything external to consciousness but rather by consciousness itself. Existence is inconceivable except in terms of events of consciousness. To associate existence with anything like Kantian things in themselves is to associate it with something the very notion of which is unnecessary, unwarranted, incoherent, and therefore inadmissible. There is no justification, either from experience or from a priori reasoning, for the extension of the notion of existence to something lying outside of consciousness altogether. Eliminate consciousness and one can only legitimately speak of the *Begriff* in itself, which as such lacks existence. In short, "Existence," Hegel says, "is . . . determinate thought" (p. 84). And he goes on to say that it is meaningful to speak of being only in terms of "its own inwardness" and in terms of "its becoming" (p. 84)—the former referring to the *Begriff,* and the latter to its actualization in the form of the various modes and states of existing consciousness.

Hegel is simply restating the point that the absolute or spirit is both substance and self-realizing subject when he goes on to say: "the *nous* . . . is the substance, [which] on account of its . . . self-identity . . . appears firm and enduring. But this self-identity is also negativity; therefore this firm existence passes over into its dissolution" (p. 84)—that is, into a process of becoming something actual. Hegel speaks of its "dissolution" here because it is only at the end of this process that it is self-identical once again. For at the beginning of this process and all the way through it until it is finally completed, its subject aspect—in the form of existing consciousness—is *not* identical with its substance aspect, but rather is only a partial and imperfect apprehension of it. And when Hegel says, "reasonableness is a becoming, and as such becoming it is rationality" (p. 84), his point is simply that rationality can come to exist explicitly only by that which exists—that is, consciousness—passing through a process of development; for the merely existent as such, in its simplest forms, exhibits little or no rationality. Since the development of existing consciousness is guided by the structure of the *Begriff* which is its implicit essential nature, however, the result of the process is existence that exhibits complete rationality.

So Hegel contends that this process is characterized by "logical necessity";

for it is in "the nature of beings," he says, "to be their Concept in their being" (p. 84)—that is, to move toward a state in which their existence will conform to their essence, as this is determined by the *Begriff*—which is something rational and which indeed is the measure of rationality. He is simply restating this point in another way when he goes on to say, "This alone is the rational and the rhythm of the organic whole." And it should be observed that Hegel is here giving a *definition* of the notion of "logical necessity" as it applies to the process through which spirit is actualized. The basic notion here is "the rational," which is to be understood in the sense of the *Begriff*; and Hegel is defining "logical necessity" in terms of it. The logical necessity of the developmental process is the necessity with which that which exists (i.e., consciousness) develops through a necessary sequence of stages in the direction of conformity to the rational (or the *Begriff*).

This process, Hegel says, "is in itself the transition into formalism" (p. 86)—that is, the transformation of existence into a form which corresponds to or reflects the formal structure of the *Begriff*. If the claim Hegel is making here is a questionable one, it is at least not the claim that "logical necessity" in the modern sense alone renders a transition in a process rational. Rather it is the claim that existence is impelled by an internal principle in the direction of conformity with essence, with the *Begriff*. This may be a questionable claim, but if it is, it is much less so than the other. And it should be observed that it is quite reasonable of Hegel to make it, given his view that existence and essence are ultimately simply different aspects of one and the same thing—namely, spirit or the absolute.

XIII

In the next part of the Preface, Hegel turns to what he considers the proper and improper ways of viewing philosophical assertions and to the consequences of viewing them improperly. He is particularly concerned with what he terms "the conflict between the form of a proposition and the unity of the Concept that destroys it" (p. 94). He suggests that the subject-predicate form of propositions has misled philosophers into taking a substratum-attribute view of things and thereby into regarding the grammatical-subject term as designating "a subject at rest that carries its attributes unmoved" (p. 92). He argues against this view and contends that it is necessary to emancipate philosophical thinking from subjection to grammar, for he holds that in fact there are no such enduring substrata to which various attributes merely adhere. Rather, as has already been seen, he contends that there *is* only consciousness—which is no material substratum—and the various thought forms which provide it with content.

Hegel is especially concerned with the proper interpretation of a certain class of propositions: namely, those of speculative philosophy—such as "Spirit is subject and substance." And his main point is that one should not be misled by the form of such a proposition into thinking that (to take the example under consideration) "spirit" is some *thing* which has the *attributes* of "subject" and "substance." Rather, the proposition is properly understood only if it is seen that the content of the expression "spirit" is exhausted through these specifications, and that the subject of such a philosophical proposition is essentially nothing over and above what the various specifications of it collectively convey, except their unity. This is part of what he has in mind when he speaks of "the identity of subject and predicate."

There is a sense of "subject" and of "predicate," however, in which he suggests that they are still to be distinguished, even while constituting a fundamental unity. This is the sense in which the "subject" is not conceived as a material substratum or thing in itself denoted by the grammatical subject, but rather as the "knowing [or conscious] ego," or explicitly existing spirit-as-subject. And it is the sense in which the "predicate" is conceived not as a particular attribute or set of attributes of a material thing in itself, but rather as the whole or some part of that complex of thought forms which supplies the knowing ego or spirit-as-subject with definite content—that is, spirit-as-substance.

It is in this way, Hegel contends, that "subject" and "predicate" are truly to be conceived. For, as he has already argued, the philosophical analysis of all possible proper predicates reduces them to one or another of the concepts which collectively make up the *Begriff*. And, as he also has already argued and argues here again, philosophical analysis also shows that the notion of the subject of predication as a material substratum or thing in itself is indefensible and incoherent, with the consequence that "this subject is replaced by the knowing ego which connects the predicates and becomes [itself] the subject that holds them" (p. 94)—that is, that supports and unites them. Any other way of viewing that which predicates denote is held to be naive and to indicate that philosophical analysis has not yet been carried far enough. And any "realist" interpretation of that which supports and unites various collections of qualities denoted by predicates is held to constitute a naive and erroneous view, resulting from one's having been misled by the subject-predicate form of linguistic propositions.

If "subject" and "predicate" are understood as "spirit-as-subject" and "spirit-as-substance"—then, to repeat, Hegel suggests that, while there is an "identity of subject and predicate," there is also a distinction to be drawn between them. He says, "The identity of subject and predicate is not meant to destroy the difference between them . . . ; rather, their unity is meant to emerge as a harmony" (p. 94). The point is simply one which should be quite familiar by now: namely, that spirit or the absolute is to be conceived both as subject and as substance, and that the failure to recognize that it has these two aspects has far-reaching and fatal philosophical consequences; but that while these two aspects must be distinguished and while, in the course of its development, the concretely existing spirit-as-subject can and does fail to conform adequately to the nature of spirit-as-substance, the two are still both merely different aspects of one and the same ultimate principle. They are both "spirit," only one consists of its essential structure, while the other consists of the form in which its essential structure comes to be actualized.

XIV

Of the remaining pages of the Preface, little needs to be said; for in them Hegel devotes himself primarily to the further development of points which have already been discussed (e.g., the need to subject expressions like "God" to philosophical analysis, the fact that the content of grammatical-subject terms in philosophical propositions is exhausted by the predicates applicable to them, the distinction between genuine philosophy and philosophizing and other modes of thinking, and the fact that there is "no royal road to knowledge").

One final point is worth mentioning, however, and that is contained in Hegel's warning against trying to understand and evaluate any proposition of speculative philosophy simply by itself in isolation from all others. Any such proposition, he says (p. 98), can be properly understood only in the context of the speculative system as a whole; for by itself it is bound to be either vacuous or one-sided. This follows from his general position, stated near the beginning of the Preface, that "the true form in which truth exists can only be the scientific system of it" (p. 12). This is a statement in part about the conditions under which the *Begriff* achieves full existence or actuality; but because philosophical knowledge is knowledge of "truth" so understood, this statement also has the sense that genuine philosophical knowledge must take the same form as its object—namely, the form of "scientific system."

More concretely stated, the point is that for Hegel philosophical knowledge must take the form of an all-embracing system and cannot be achieved through isolated bits and pieces of analysis. And, since philosophical truth is to be found only in such a system as an interconnected whole, in which the appropriateness of each part may be understood only in terms of its relations to all the others, it follows that any proposition which is anything less than a complete and exhaustive specification of the whole system—as all conceivable propositions of manageable length are—will suffer from one of two faults. Either they will characterize the whole, but in too general a way to indicate its specific content—for example, "The absolute end and aim of the world is freedom actualized," or "Science is the actuality of spirit," or "Spirit is substance and subject"—or they will characterize some part or aspect of the whole in a more determinate way but in a way which is one-sided or which otherwise leaves a great deal unsaid—for example, "The state is spirit objectified," or "Existence is determinate thought," or "The actual is the same as its Concept." Both sorts of speculative propositions leave a good deal to be desired, and that which they leave to be desired can be supplied only by viewing them in relation to the rest of the system of speculative philosophy of which they are a part. And, whatever the merit of this position may be as a general thesis about philosophical knowledge (which may be considerable), it is essential to keep it in mind when reading Hegel; for his system is meant to be viewed as a whole, and his various particular assertions can only be understood properly as parts of this whole.

Still, it by no means follows that everything Hegel has to say about the many issues he discusses either stands or falls with his system as a whole. Even if one ultimately rejects his metaphysics, one can still gain a great deal of insight into such matters as the nature of social institutions, the development of personality, the relation between human freedom and social institutions, and the dependence of self-consciousness upon interpersonal interaction, from considering what he has to say about them. It may run counter to the spirit of Hegelian philosophy to read Hegel with a view of discovering the various particular insights it contains, but he can be read in this way with much profit. And it is better to read him in this way than not to read him or take him seriously at all because one finds his metaphysics unacceptable.

XV

In conclusion, I shall turn to a brief consideration of the first paragraphs of the section of the Preface which Kaufmann entitles "The forms of consciousness and truth" (pp. 56–58), which, as I have suggested above, contain a capsule summary of the whole development presented in the body of the *Phenomenology*. What Hegel says here is this. Spirit *exists* in the form of *consciousness*. Consciousness contains two elements: an objective element and a subjective element. That is, consciousness is always consciousness *of something*—it always has some object before it—and this object is always the object *of* some sort of thought process or thinking *activity* (and exists only in relation to it). It is through the interaction of conscious activity and the objects of this activity that spirit develops and realizes itself, passing from simpler forms of consciousness and naive ways of conceiving the nature of its objects, to higher forms of consciousness and more sophisticated ways of conceiving its objects. Spirit therefore exists as a variety of *forms of consciousness,* some of which emerge out of others, and all of which may be related to each other in a developmental sequence. The study of actual, existing spirit is thus the study of these different forms of consciousness, in themselves and as they relate to one another. And in such a study the "substance" or structural content of spirit is dealt with, not as it is simply in itself but rather as it gradually comes to be revealed and known, in the form of the succession of types of experienced objects of the various forms of consciousness in the developmental sequence.

Consciousness can have knowledge only of that which is an object for it—only of "what lies in its experience"—for it surely could have no knowledge of something which was *not* an object for it. But (although it does not recognize this to be the case until it reaches the end of its development) its object is never anything other than the "substance" or structural content of spirit—which is nothing other than its own substantial content. Thus its object, in other words, is always only its *self;* but in its naive and simpler forms it fails to see this and regards its objects as something *other* than itself. Its objects *are* something other than itself-*qua-subject* or thinking activity, for they are itself-*qua-substance.* And until it achieves an adequate knowledge of its own nature, as "spirit" which is *both* substance *and* subject, it conceives itself only *as subject.*

This process, in which spirit assumes the double form of conscious subject and object of consciousness, and in which the object of consciousness is first regarded as something "other" than consciousness and then is recognized by consciousness as being merely its own substantial nature in objectified form, is the process through which spirit becomes actual and self-conscious. And this process is nothing other than *experience,* which is initially naive and then is gradually transformed into genuine knowledge. In the simplest forms of experience, there is no explicit distinction between consciousness and its objects; the former is completely absorbed in the latter. With the development of a degree of self-consciousness and greater sophistication, subject and object are distinguished, but are regarded as radically different and independent of each other. Finally, their underlying unity and interdependence are recognized. This development might be characterized as a process in which a stage of immediate unity gives way to a stage of "separated opposites," which in turn gives way to a stage of higher, "mediated" unity. It is in these terms that Hegel characterizes it in his early writings. Or it might be characterized—as he characterizes it here—as a process in which a stage of unity gives way to a stage of "estrangement" or "alienation," which then gives way to a final stage in which this separation is overcome.

In the middle stage there is what Hegel terms a "nonidentity" of subject and object, or of "ego" and "substance." As "nonidentical" they are both defective, for each is what it ought to be only when it is at one with the other. But this "nonidentity," which is something "negative" in itself, is also something of positive significance, since this very "negative" element is *experienced* as a defect or deficiency, and so provides the dynamic impetus which drives the development onward, until a form of consciousness is attained in which this "nonidentity" is seen to be not absolute, but rather merely a difference which is relative to an underlying identity or unity.

When this point is reached, the "ego" or consciousness ceases to regard its object as something external to it which impinges upon it from without. It recognizes its object as its own substance and so is conscious of itself both as subject and as substance. And, since it is something concretely existing and since it exists in the form of "spirit knowing itself as spirit"—that is, as both subject and substance—it *is* spirit "in-and-for-itself." In it spirit has become something fully *actual,* or completely and self-consciously realized. Thus "spirit has made its existence equal to its essence." The *Begriff* is no longer mere abstract essence; it has come to life and, more than that, to self-conscious life.

And, Hegel says, "With this the phenomenology of the spirit is concluded." For now spirit exists in the form of absolute knowledge—knowledge both of its own essential content and of the whole course of its development through the various forms of explicitly existing consciousness. The systematic exposition of the former is the proper task of philosophical logic while the sequential exposition of the latter is the proper task of a phenomenology of spirit. These, taken together, contain the whole of absolute knowledge. And even an omniscient deity could know nothing more.

In fact, Hegel implies in the last pages of the *Phenomenology* itself that God—insofar as it is legitimate philosophically to speak of "God" at all—*is* nothing other than "spirit knowing itself as spirit," as this notion has been developed in the preceding discussion. God's *nature* is nothing other than the *Begriff,* as this is set forth in philosophical logic. And God's *life* is nothing other than existing consciousness, which develops from the simplest forms of consciousness to its highest form, absolute knowledge. It is with this thought that Hegel concludes the *Phenomenology,* saying that philosophical logic and the phenomenology of spirit together "form the recollection and the Golgotha of absolute spirit; the actuality, truth, and certainty of its throne, without which it would be something lifeless and empty. Only 'from the cup of this realm of spiritual forms does its infinity foam forth for it.' "[8] With these words, which are the last lines of the work, I conclude my commentary on Hegel's Preface to it. And to repeat what I said at the beginning: to understand this remarkable and difficult Preface is to understand the heart of Hegel's philosophy—even if not the whole body of it, to which, after all, this is *only* a preface.

4:

Hegel on Freedom

Hegel's metaphysics is the heart of his philosophy, but the philosophical system he developed around it comprehends virtually every aspect of human life and experience. His system is a tightly integrated one, unified not only because his analyses of various particular matters all ultimately refer back to the same metaphysical scheme, but also because he employs a number of basic concepts across a wide range of areas of philosophical inquiry. The concept of freedom is one of the more important of these, figuring centrally in his analyses of morality and ethics, social and political life, human history and intellectual life, and even human nature and reality in general. For Hegel there is no great gap between metaphysical and practical philosophical questions; and there would seem to be no more illuminating way to exhibit the relationship he conceives to exist between them and at the same time to indicate the central features of his understanding of the nature and norms of human personal, social, and ethical life than to examine his uses and elaboration of the notion of freedom. The present chapter consists of such an examination.

Hegel's interest in freedom is by no means purely abstract and speculative. He is concerned to achieve an understanding of human life as people actually do and can live it, as particular persons, moral agents, ethical subjects, and members of social and political communities, as well as thinking and reasoning beings; and he is convinced that it is necessary to understand such dimensions of our existence in terms of freedom and at the same time to construe freedom in terms of these dimensions. Further, he attempts—as he considers it incumbent upon him as a systematic philosopher to do—to make room for both in his larger system and the metaphysical scheme on which it rests, while at the same time drawing upon this system and scheme to clarify their status and significance in relation to phenomena of other kinds.

Freedom may fairly be styled the watchword of the modern Western world; and Hegel joins such different philosophers as Kant, Marx, and Sartre in acclaiming it. He is hardly in complete agreement with them, however (nor are they with one another), with regard to the nature of the kinds of freedom human beings have and are capable of attaining, the relative importance of each of them, and the relations between them, human nature, thought, action, and the world of nature and society; and, as he recognizes, these are matters of great practical significance as well as of substantial theoretical importance. Nearly every war and revolution fought over the past two hundred years has been fought—by one or both of the parties involved—in the name of freedom; and freedom is commonly reckoned among our most priceless possessions, without which life would scarcely be worth living. People have risked and given their lives in the cause of freedom—either in the attempt to achieve it or in an effort to resist threats to it. And, on a somewhat different but related level, the issue of whether human choices, thoughts, decisions, and actions are or can be "truly free" or else are inevitably determined by impersonal biological, psychological, social, and/or economic forces is debated with a fervor suggesting that the very nature and value of human existence are felt to hang in the balance pending its resolution.

For Hegel, as for many subsequent Continental writers, these concerns are by no means misplaced; and the interconnection between what might be termed interpersonal and intrapersonal freedoms, far from being merely terminological, is a very intimate one. Yet, obviously, a great deal depends upon the meaning to be assigned to the notion of freedom as it is applied to actual human life. Freedom obviously has to do with self-determination, as contrasted with compulsion and constraint; but what is to count as the former, and what as the latter—and under what circumstances is the former impossible, possible, and actual? What is the relation between freedom and such things as desire, spontaneity, reason, self-consciousness, and social and political laws and institutions? If the answers to these and other such questions seem to be simple and obvious, one would be very much mistaken, even if one's intuitions should happen to be sound—and one should not be too sure that they are.

Hegel's answers to these questions are in certain respects consonant with conventional wisdom on these matters, while in others they cut rather strongly against it. Marx found highly unsatisfactory Hegel's contention that freedom in the fullest—highest and also broadest—sense is possible and actual only in the context of a socio-politico-economic system of the general sort exemplified by the more advanced states of the Western world in the early nineteenth century, for reasons which shall be explored in chapter 5. One would do well, however, not only to view Marx as a powerful critic of Hegel's position, but also to read Hegel as a powerful critic of that of Marx, and to take Hegel's analysis of freedom and what its realization involves no less seriously than one may presently take Marx's, or any other philosopher's—or, for that matter, one's own.

No concept is more central to Hegel's philosophy than his concept of freedom. He refers to "freedom realized" as "the absolute end and aim of the world" (*PR,* §129).[1] His *Philosophy of Right* is really a discussion of freedom, for he holds that "freedom is both the substance of right and its goal, while the system of right is the realm of freedom made actual" (*PR,* §4). Freedom is also the central concept in his philosophy of history: "World history," he says, "is the progress of the consciousness of freedom" (*RH,* p. 24). Hegel further terms freedom the very essence of spirit (*Geist*): "The essence of spirit—its substance—is freedom" (*RH,* p. 22). And since in his view spirit is not merely man's basic nature but also the fundamental principle of reality, freedom is suggested to be the nature of that most basic of metaphysical categories, the Notion or Concept (*Begriff*): "The Notion is the principle of freedom, the power of substance self-realized" (*LH,* §287).

As in the cases of so many of his other concepts, however, Hegel's concept of freedom is rarely clearly understood. He is frequently accused, on the one hand, of presenting a conception of freedom too abstract to have any bearing on real life and, on the other, of merely giving lip service to freedom while in reality taking a kind of quasi-totalitarian position diametrically opposed to the exercise of real freedom.[2] It is true that his understanding of freedom is not identical with that of many philosophers—not to mention men in the street. But such accusations only show that those who make them have not read Hegel very carefully. If it is true, as he remarks in the Preface to his *Phenomenology of Spirit,* that "the familiar is not known simply because it is familiar" (*PS,* p. 48), it is all the more true that the *un*familiar will never be understood as long as it remains unfamiliar. One may in the end decide to reject Hegel's idea of what true freedom involves, but one ought at least to do so for reasons relating to what Hegel actually holds.

In what follows, I shall attempt to clarify Hegel's view of freedom, and then shall briefly consider what is to be made of it. While I shall have something to say about freedom in the context of his philosophy generally, I shall concentrate upon his discussion of it in connection with the concepts of the will, personality, subjectivity, and "ethical life"—in short, his discussion of freedom in his *Philosophy of Right.*[3] Before turning to Hegel himself, however, it would be well to take notice of certain concepts and views of several of his predecessors that bear importantly upon his discussion of freedom. His insistence upon the continuity of his philosophical views with those of his predecessors is well known; and in the case of his analysis of freedom, this continuity is significant and illuminating.

I

In his *Essay Concerning Human Understanding*, Locke gives the following definition of liberty: "*Liberty* . . . is the power a man has to do or forbear doing any particular action according as its doing or forbearance has the actual preference in the mind; which is the same as to say, according as he himself wills it."[4] Hume gives a virtually identical explication of liberty in his *Enquiry Concerning Human Understanding:* "By liberty . . . , we can only mean *a power of acting or not acting, according to the determinations of the will;* that is, if we choose to remain at rest, we may; if we choose to move, we also may."[5] Concerning these characterizations of liberty, which may be taken to represent a fairly commonsensical understanding of freedom, several points should be noted. First, what is at stake is the source of determination of some particular course of action. Secondly, the decisive consideration is taken to be that of whether the individual's course of action is one that he himself had decided upon; when his will is done, his action is considered free. In other words, liberty or freedom is here conceived in terms of self-determination in the realm of action. And thirdly, both Locke and Hume consider liberty or freedom so conceived to be quite compatible with determinism; both deny that human actions that satisfy their definitions have the status of uncaused events, and hold that such actions are subsumable under general laws no less than are natural events.

Next, several Aristotelian ideas should be noted. One is the idea that things—or at least substances—have essences. "The essence of each thing is what it is said to be *propter se.* . . . What, then, you are by your very nature is your essence."[6] Not that which is peculiar to the individual but rather the trait or traits in virtue of which his species is set off from others is held to constitute his essence. So, for example, Aristotle conceives man's essence in terms of rationality, on the ground that "what is peculiar to man" is the "life of the rational element."[7]

Another relevant Aristotelian notion is that of the distinction between potentiality and actuality. Aristotle employs the distinction in connection with "coming-to-be" generally: "For coming-to-be necessarily implies the pre-existence of something which *potentially* 'is,' but *actually* 'is not'; and this something is spoken of both as 'being' and as 'not-being.' "[8] Applied to a discussion of essence, this suggests the possibility of something that exists and is potentially a thing of a certain sort but has not yet come to be actually what it is potentially. A child, for example, as a human being is according to its essence a rational being, but it may be rational only potentially rather than actually.

Finally, note should be taken of Aristotle's conception of two sorts of "originative source of change." He distinguishes between "originative source of change in another thing or in the thing itself *qua* other."[9] Both sorts may be seen to be operative in the case of an organism such as an animal. The movements of animals, which appear to be their own doing, are "not strictly originated by them," according to Aristotle; rather, the "originative source of change" here is to be found in the animals' environment.[10] When we consider not an animal's movements but its growth to maturity, on the other hand, we are confronted with a "change" that has its "originative source" in the animal itself. Of course, its growth and development require the proper environmental conditions. But when these are present, it is "through its own motive principle" that the changes in the organism constituting its growth toward maturity occur. This process might be characterized as the organism's self-realization, the actualization of its essence not through an external agency but through its own.

Spinoza's God embodies the principle of self-determination much more completely than do Aristotle's organisms, and in Spinoza this principle is explicitly associated with the idea of freedom. Spinoza gives the following definition of a free being: "That thing is called free which exists from the necessity of its own nature alone, and is determined to action by itself alone."[11] Something is free, for Spinoza, only if it contains within itself not only the originative source of all that it does once it is in existence, but also the source of its own being—in short, only if it is *sui causa*. That which "by another is determined to existence and action" is not free, but rather "compelled."[12] Freedom so conceived cannot, according to Spinoza, be a property of any particular existent, but rather only of God; thus he says, "God alone is a free cause."[13]

Since what is essential to freedom in Spinoza's view is complete and absolute self-determination, freedom is by no means incompatible with necessity. On the contrary, he often speaks of "the necessity of the divine nature" and holds that every actual attribute of God is a necessary one. Similarly, he sees no incompatibility between the notions of freedom and of law. God acts according to laws and yet is free, because "God acts from the laws of His own nature only, and is compelled by no one."[14] It is in the absence of dependence upon and determination by an external agency, rather than the absence of necessity and subjection to law, that freedom as Spinoza conceives it consists. Freedom does not even imply that one is subject only to laws of one's own making; God did not choose what "the laws of His own nature" would be. It is necessary that these laws should be what they are. What makes God free is the fact that they are not imposed upon him from without. They are not laws of his own making, laws he has given to himself, but rather "laws of His own *nature*"—of his very essence. Of course, if his nature had some external source he would not be free. But it is not determined by anything external to himself; he is *sui causa*.

Among finite things, according to Spinoza, matters are otherwise. No finite thing is *sui causa* with regard to either its nature or its existence. The human will is no exception: "The will cannot be called a free cause, but can only be called necessary." For "it requires a cause by which it may be determined to existence and action."[15] Human action thus constitutes no exception to the determinism that prevails throughout nature, in Spinoza's view. The actions of God alone are truly self-determined and therefore free.

Finally, reference must be made to several of Kant's ideas. Spinoza calls the free being he discusses "God"; he conceives this "God" not in terms of self-consciousness or will, however, but rather as "substance." Thus he speaks of "God, or substance consisting of infinite attributes, each one of which expresses eternal and infinite essence. . . ."[16] This substance consisting of infinite attributes is eternal, determined by nothing external to itself, and the cause of all finite things, but it is not a self-conscious subject. It is precisely of such a subject, on the other hand, that Kant predicates freedom: "There is in man a power of self-determination, independently of any coercion through sensuous impulses."[17] Indeed, Kant goes so far as to hold that being free involves acting under the idea of freedom or, at least, that it is the consciousness of freedom we have in being conscious of obligation that shows freedom to be more than a theoretical possibility.

In attributing freedom to a being that is not a self-caused, eternal substance consisting of infinite attributes, but rather a finite subject having the character of reason, self-consciousness, and will, Kant thus differs radically from Spinoza. He agrees with Spinoza, however, in conceiving of freedom in terms of self-determination, as the above passage indicates, though he does not conceive of it as extending to one's very existence, as Spinoza does. One can be said to be free only if one's will is not determined by any external agency but, rather, autonomously. Kant further agrees with Spinoza that nothing that is merely a part of nature is self-determined in this way; but unlike Spinoza, he does not feel that the human will falls entirely into this category. He argues that it is not self-contradictory to suggest that there is in man a faculty capable of initiating a new causal series in the world—a *causa noumenon*; or, as he says, "that causality through freedom is at least *not incompatible with* nature."[18] Kant is quite certain that reason as such is free, or self-determined: "We can *know*," he says, "that it is free, that is, that it is determined independently of sensibility."[19] The only question in his view is whether or not it can be said "to have causality with respect to appearances." That this is "at least possible" is a fact, he contends, that can be established on purely theoretical grounds. And he finds a practical confirmation of this idea in the experience of moral obligation, which he takes to be incompatible with the view that the will is not autonomous. "That our reason has causality, or at least that we represent it to ourselves as having causality, is evident from the *imperatives* which in all matters of conduct we impose as rules upon our active powers."[20]

For Kant as for Aristotle, man's reason sets him apart from all merely sensuous existence. Indeed, he regards reason as definitive of man's essential (noumenal) nature. If the determining ground of the will is reason, therefore, the will is self-determined in a way in which it is not when its motive principle is some mere natural impulse; for the determining principle of one's volition then lies in one's own rational nature, rather than in some agency external to it. If one were not essentially a rational being, action from a law prescribed by reason would not be free, for it would not in any sense be self-determined. Kant is able to term such action free, however, precisely because of his conception of man's essential nature in terms of reason. Action determined by a law prescribed by reason is free because it is self-determined—determined, that is, by a principle that is constitutive of one's own essential nature. It should be observed, however, that for Kant only the form of the law actually derives from reason; the content, on the other hand—as in the case of perception—derives from nature.

One further point remains to be noted: Kant's distinction between "negative freedom" and "positive freedom." He says of the freedom associated with reason: "This freedom ought not . . . to be conceived only negatively as independence of empirical conditions. The faculty of reason, so regarded, would cease to be a cause of appearances. It must also be described in positive terms, as the power of originating a series of events."[21] Our freedom thus has both a negative aspect and a positive aspect. To say that an action is free in the negative sense is simply to assert that it is not determined by any agency external to the will of the acting agent. It does not follow, however, that a free action is an undetermined one. Rather, it is one that has its "determining ground" in something other than "empirical conditions," namely, reason. To say that an action is free in the positive, fuller sense is to make this explicit. It is only when reason prescribes laws and action is based upon them that action is free in the positive sense. And action is not even free in the negative sense, short of this. Freedom is actual, or action is actually free, only when reason has prescribed a law and when the will is determined in accordance with it.

II

With these views of Hegel's predecessors in mind, a preliminary account of his own understanding of freedom in relation to theirs may now be given. As a first approximation, he would accept Locke's and Hume's explications of freedom in terms of the self-determination of one's actions. He would agree with Kant, however, that if what prompts one to act in a certain way is some mere impulse or inclination, one's action is not really free at all. For then the decision or choice upon which the action is based does not have its "originative source" or "determining ground" in the mind of the agent at all; rather, it is just as completely determined by the operation of laws of sensuous nature as is any other natural event. Hegel readily allows that many human actions have precisely this character: they are free in the Lockean and Humean sense that they are what the agent has decided or chosen to do, but they are not free in a deeper sense, in that what the agent decides or chooses to do is determined by natural laws.

Hegel differs from Locke, Hume, and Spinoza, however, and agrees with Kant in holding that a more significant sort of self-determination—freedom that is not the mere illusion of freedom—is possible: namely, self-determination at the level of the decision on which the action is based, or, in Hume's phrase, in "the determination of the will" itself. Like Aristotle and Kant, Hegel holds that man has an essential nature, and conceives of that essential nature in terms of thought or reason. "Thinking," he says, in a manner reminiscent of Aristotle, "is the characteristic property by which man is distinguished from the beasts, [while] he has feeling in common with them" (*PM*, §400). And like Kant, he further holds that reason is capable of providing men with laws on which practical decisions can be based, so that, when their determinant is a law of reason, these decisions are determined by a principle constitutive of the individual's essential nature. As such, they are self-determined, and are therefore free. A person is free, for Hegel as for Kant, if and only if the "determining ground" of his practical decisions is nothing external to reason, but rather is reason itself. Human freedom, therefore, is to be conceived not simply in terms of the self-determination of one's actions in accordance with one's will, but rather in terms of their *rational* self-determination, or determination in accordance with a will the principle of which is a law of thought rather than of mere nature.

It would not be entirely accurate to say simply that Hegel rejects the idea of freedom as caprice or the ability to do whatever one wants, in favor of the idea of freedom as action in accordance with a law of thought or reason. He does reject the former view of freedom, but only because he quite agrees with the determinists that actions answering to these descriptions, far from being truly self-determined, remain in the toils of nature. He adopts the latter view of freedom because he sees in action determined in accordance with laws of reason the only alternative to action governed by natural laws. In the Aristotelian notion of development in accordance with a law of one's own essential nature, and in the Spinozistic notion of freedom as action in accordance with the same, Hegel discerns the idea of a kind of action that does not require the assumption of the existence of uncaused events, but that at the same time answers to the description of independence of external agency. Such action alone, he feels, can truly be said to be self-determined and therefore free. As for Kant, then, freedom for Hegel cannot be conceived merely negatively, as "independence of empirical conditions." It must also be conceived positively, in terms of conformity to a law of reason; for action is independent of empirical conditions only where it has its "originative source" in the only other place it could have it: namely, in reason.

More remains to be said, however; Hegel holds that action is truly free only if it involves self-determination that is not only rational but also *self-conscious.* If one's self-determination in accordance with one's rational nature does not take place consciously, as in the case of Spinoza's God (whose nature was that of a substance rather than a self-conscious subject), it has the character of a blind and mindless necessity. Kant had maintained that freedom can be predicated only of a self-conscious subject, and that action is free only when it is determined not only in accordance with a rational principle but also under the idea of freedom; and it is this insight, for Hegel, which makes Kant's understanding of freedom superior to Spinoza's. To be sure, an action is not free in Hegel's view merely if it is self-consciously self-determined; it must further be determined in accordance with a law of reason. Yet it also is not truly free—though it may be said to be *implicitly* free—if its determining ground is a law of reason but is not self-consciously so determined. Freedom, for Hegel, is thus to be conceived in terms of self-conscious rational self-determination rather than in terms of self-determination *simpliciter,* though in spelling it out in this way Hegel takes himself simply to be making explicit what the idea of self-determination essentially involves when applied to a thinking being.

III

At this point it might seem that Hegel's understanding of freedom does not differ significantly from Kant's. In point of fact, however, Hegel breaks decisively with Kant on a number of counts—even while granting that Kant does have an essentially correct and adequate grasp of the concept of human freedom. Perhaps most fundamentally, Hegel rejects the Kantian notion of the thing in itself, and with it the idea that the will has a noumenal as well as a phenomenal existence, upon which Kant bases his entire discussion of freedom. It may be, as Kant argues, that it is *not self-contradictory* to suppose that there is in man a *causa noumenon,* or faculty of initiating a new causal series in the world; but for Hegel such a supposition has no cogency whatsoever. The only thing in itself of which it makes any sense to speak, in his view, is the "system of pure reason" or *Begriff* that constitutes the essential structure of all appearance. The *Begriff,* however, does not constitute a noumenal world over against the phenomenal. It does not exist at all except in so far as it is embodied in phenomena. And there are no noumenal entities of any sort—material, psychic, or divine. The experience of freedom of which Kant makes so much is taken by Hegel not to indicate that the will has a noumenal as well as a phenomenal existence, but rather to reflect the fact that what are commonly referred to as the laws of nature do not govern the whole of phenomenal reality. And Kant's real service in stressing it, in Hegel's view, is not that ,he shows it to provide a practical proof of the nonphenomenality of the will, but rather that he supplies an important corrective to Spinoza's characterization of freedom by bringing out the fact that freedom involves acting under the idea of self-determination.

Hegel further differs from Kant with respect to the law or laws of reason in relation to which self-determination may become rational. For Kant action is free only if the law on which it is based derives from reason. Actually, however, for Kant it is only the *form* of the law (universality) that derives from reason; its content derives from nature, that is, from our natural inclinations. In Hegel's view, action based on a law of this sort is still action in the toils of nature. It is only if the whole of the law—its content as well as its form—derives from reason that it truly deserves to be called a law of reason; and it is only if action is based on a law of this sort that it deserves to be called self-determined in accordance with reason, and therefore free. Hegel contends that virtually any maxim having as its origin some natural inclination can pass the test of universalizability. The requirement of reason that the maxim of one's action be universalizable, therefore, does not of itself eliminate the natural basis of the determination of action and replace it with reason. In short, if reason could do no more than impose this requirement upon us, it would follow, in Hegel's view, that rational self-determination would be but an empty phrase and freedom would still be but an illusion.

This, however, is not Hegel's conclusion, for he holds that reason is by no means so limited in what it can do. Rather, he contends that it can and does give rise to laws the essential content as well as the form of which derive from it itself. And to the extent that these laws are made the basis of one's actions, rational self-determination ceases to be an empty phrase and becomes a genuine reality; for action then ceases to have its originative source in natural inclination, and instead is rationally determined through and through. Kant failed to discover the existence of such laws, because he did not look for them in the right place or, perhaps, because he failed to grasp what Hegel takes to be the true significance of the phenomena in which they are to be found: namely, the laws and institutions of the social order.

Hegel holds that these laws and institutions, which constitute what he terms the "substance" of a "state," are by no means a mere conglomeration of practices bearing no relation to rational principles. He contends that, on the contrary, they are to be viewed as an inherently rational system—the "system of pure reason" itself in concrete form. They "are not accidental, but are rationality itself," and the state they collectively structure is "the divine Idea as it exists on earth" (*RH,* pp. 49, 53). The establishment of this thesis is one of Hegel's central aims in the *Philosophy of Right.* He holds that it is in these laws and institutions, and in them alone, that the individual can find a basis for the determination of his actions that is rational, and so in conformity with his essential nature, and that guarantees their independence of mere impulse and inclination. To the extent that the individual determines his actions in accordance with them, therefore, and only to this extent, he is rationally self-determined and thus free. "For law is the objectivity of spirit; it is will in its true form. Only the will that obeys the law is free, for it obeys itself and, being in itself, is free" (*RH,* p. 53).

Once again, however, it must be added that the individual is truly free, according to Hegel, only if he apprehends that in determining his actions in accordance with these laws and institutions he is determining them in accordance with the very reason that constitutes his essential nature, rather than something alien and external to him. His awareness of the rationality of these laws and institutions has the character of a "knowing presence to him of his own essence of rationality" (*RH,* p. 52). His actions, when in accordance with them, are rationally determined, and he is conscious of the fact that, in so acting, the only necessity he is obeying is one that derives from his own essential nature. His freedom is not the freedom of caprice; but such freedom is no true freedom at all—rather, it is merely a disguised form of subjection to natural laws. He cannot be said to have given the law of his actions to himself, since the law of his actions is determined by the nature of reason itself. But, like Spinoza's God, he is at least subject to no laws other than those of his own essential nature and therefore is self-determined. And this is the only form of freedom, in Hegel's view, that it is possible for man to enjoy. "The rational, like the substantial, is necessary. We are free when we recognize it as law and follow it as the substance of our own being" (*RH*, p. 53).

IV

Having given this preliminary characterization of Hegel's conception of freedom, and before considering his development of it in his *Philosophy of Right* in more detail, I should like to comment briefly on two of his more general and speculative contentions involving references to freedom: namely, that freedom realized is "the absolute end and aim of the world" (*PR*, § 129) and that the content of the Hegelian absolute—the *Begriff*—"is the principle of freedom" (*LH*, § 287). The former contention already becomes more comprehensible when taken in conjunction with the latter; for if there is an absolute, and if the ultimate end and aim of the world is conceived in terms of it (as would only be reasonable), and if, further, this absolute is to be conceived in terms of freedom, then it quite logically follows that the end and aim of the world is to be conceived in these terms as well.

It remains, then, to determine what could have led to Hegel to characterize the absolute in terms of freedom. And this is not difficult if one bears in mind that he understands freedom in terms of self-conscious rational self-determination, for the absolute is conceived by Hegel precisely in terms of self-determination, rationality, and self-consciousness. As "absolute," it quite obviously must be self-determined; for if either its existence or its nature were dependent upon anything external to it, it would not be absolute. Further, as Hegel states in the Preface to the *Phenomenology of Spirit*, it has a twofold nature: it is both substance and subject (*PS*, p. 28).[22] Considered as substance, it has the character of a "system of pure reason." Its specific determinations therefore are preeminently rational. At this point it is well to recall Spinoza's absolute—God or substance, conceived as a self-determined, rational system—and his characterization of it as free.

Spinoza's basic error, in Hegel's view, lay in his failure to realize that the absolute is not only substance so conceived but also subject. Self-consciousness is just as essential to it as is its substantial nature. The term *Begriff*, as a more concrete specification of the nature of the absolute, has a double appropriateness: it conveys the idea of a conceiving or conscious apprehending as well as the idea of a concept or rational system. It is only when the system of reason is grasped in consciousness—only when it achieves the form of self-consciousness—that it is something actual. Simply in itself, it lacks the form of existence—contrary to Spinoza, for whom the existence of the substance is inseparable from its pure essence. For Hegel the nature of the absolute does require that it exist, but that is because it is to be conceived not only as substance or pure essence but also as subject or self-consciousness. Just as Hegel believes Spinoza's understanding of freedom must be modified to the effect that freedom is to be conceived in terms of *self-conscious* rational self-determination, so also he contends that Spinoza's conception of the absolute must be modified in such a way that reference is made not only to its self-determined, rational structure, but also to the form it takes in its actual existence—namely, self-consciousness. The absolute is thus conceived by Hegel in terms of self-determination, rationality, and self-consciousness. And since self-conscious rational self-determination is freedom, as Hegel understands it, he employs this term to convey the general nature of the *Begriff* in a nutshell, saying, "The *Begriff* is the principle of freedom."

Hegel's use of the term "freedom" in his metaphysics may thus be seen to be both comprehensible—once it is seen how he is using this and certain other terms—and consistent with his use of the term in his less metaphysical writings, such as the *Philosophy of Right.* It is upon these writings, however, that current interest largely centers. For this reason I shall devote the remainder of my discussion to his conception of freedom as it is developed in them.

V

It is perhaps best to begin, as Hegel does in the *Philosophy of Right,* with a consideration of the question of the freedom of the will, before turning to the question of the relation of freedom to social institutions.[23] He observes elsewhere that "the term 'freedom,' without further qualification, is indefinite and infinitely ambiguous. Being the highest concept, it is liable to an infinity of misunderstandings, confusions, and errors.and may give rise to all possible kinds of extravagances" (*RH,* p. 25). At the very outset of his discussion, therefore, he undertakes to remove the misunderstandings and confusions so commonly associated with the use of the term, by considering precisely how the notion of the freedom of the will is to be understood.

The first point to be made is that the will is not to be conceived as a mental faculty distinct from thought or reason. It is essentially nothing other than "thinking reason resolving itself to finitude" (*PR,* §13R)—that is, thought in its practical employment, engaged in determining a course of action in the world, choosing and deciding what to do. In saying that the will is "the point of origin" of freedom (*PR,* §4), Hegel is not associating the idea of freedom with some extrarational principle, but rather is simply suggesting that it is thought, insofar as it is concerned with action, with which one is dealing in speaking of freedom. "As will, the mind steps into actuality; whereas as cognition it is on the soil of conceptual generality" (*PM*, §469). He continues to speak of "the will," but this doubtless is merely because it is more convenient to do so than to use such cumbersome formulations as "thinking reason resolving itself to finitude." It is important to keep in mind that this is a terminological convenience rather than a label for some mysterious faculty. Men are thinking beings who engage in action, and Hegel's talk of "the will" merely specifies that what he is considering is thought applied to action.

It is, then, necessary to distinguish the question of whether willing is something *determinate* from the question of whether it is something *determined*. The will, in Hegel's view, is both indeterminate and determinate. It is indeterminate in the sense that I have the "ability to free myself from everything, abandon every aim, abstract from everything" (*PR*, §5A). That is, willing is not to be associated with any specific course of action; no particular decision is implied by the general ability to decide. The act of deliberation involves a consideration of alternatives and, therefore, a disassociation, at least in principle, of the deliberating consciousness from the particular alternatives before it. In this sense the will contains an "element of pure indeterminateness" (*PR*, §5).

On the other hand, actual willing or deciding always involves resolving upon *some* particular course of action. In this sense an act of willing is always determinate. I cannot will without willing this rather than that; I cannot act without acting in some specific way. The will, therefore, whenever it is concretely active, is determinate. And it is something actual only when it is active. If freedom is conceived merely in terms of its "pure indeterminateness"—that is, merely negatively—then it is conceived in such a way that freedom and action exclude each other. Such freedom amounts to nothing in the world of action. It constitutes an essential moment of true freedom in that "freedom itself is to be found only in the reflection of spirit into itself" (*PR*, § 194R). That is, freedom involves a consciousness of oneself as independent of everything determinate, and such a consciousness emerges with the awareness of the "pure indeterminateness" of the will. By itself, however, such freedom is abstract and insubstantial. In this "unrestricted possibility of abstraction from every determinate state of mind which I may find in myself or which I may have set up in myself . . . we have negative freedom, or freedom as the Understanding conceives of it. This is the freedom of the void" (*PR*, § 5R). If the concretely active will is to be considered free, its freedom must be recognized to contain both an element of indeterminateness and an element of determinateness. So Hegel says: "Freedom lies neither in indeterminateness nor in determinateness; it is both of these at once. . . . Freedom is to will something determinate, yet in this determinateness to be by oneself and to revert once more to the universal" (*PR*, §7A).

So far, nothing has been said that affects the issue of whether or not the will, in settling upon some determinate course of action, is *determined* or *undetermined*. For the indeterminateness associated with the ability to disassociate oneself from everything determinate does not imply that one's decision to pursue this or that particular course of action is not determined. On the contrary, it is quite compatible with the deterministic thesis that every particular decision made and every particular action undertaken is determined by laws of nature. It is for this reason that the question of the will's determinateness and indeterminateness must be distinguished from the question of whether particular volitions and actions are determined or undetermined.[24]

Hegel is in complete agreement with the determinists insofar as they are concerned to deny that decisions are or can be undetermined by general laws and that even the most spontaneous and arbitrary decisions have the status of uncaused events. He grants that people often make decisions that may be described as arbitrary and are often accompanied by a feeling of spontaneity. He contends with the determinists, however, that this does not establish that such decisions originate solely in "the will of a single person in his own private self-will" (*PR*, §29R) and are independent of everything external to "his own private self-will." On the contrary, he holds that they are determined by inclinations and impulses that are subject to general laws of sensuous existence. As such, they are not in fact self-determined at all, and the feeling of spontaneity is but the illusion of freedom.

Determinism has rightly pointed to the content which, as something met with . . . , comes from outside. . . . Since, then, arbitrariness has immanent in it only the formal element in willing . . . while the other element [i.e., the content of the volition] is something given to it, we may readily allow that, if it is arbitrariness which is supposed to be freedom, it may indeed be called an illusion. (*PR*, §15R)

It should be observed that this is Hegel's conclusion wherever the content of a decision derives from a natural impulse or inclination, whatever its form may be. It thus applies even when the form is that of self-consistent universality. Kant, in other words, still leaves us with but the illusion of freedom.

Yet this is not the end of the matter; for, though determinate decisions are always determined in accordance with general laws, it does not follow that the only laws in accordance with which they may be determined are those governing mere sensuous existence. Decisions could still be free if the laws in accordance with which they were determined were laws deriving from the individual's own essential nature; for then they would in a significant sense be self-determined, even if not by "the will of a single person in his own private self-will." This in fact is possible, according to Hegel. The will can be free—but only in the sense that "its self-determination consists in a correspondence between what it is in its existence . . . and its Concept" (*PR*, § 23), that is, its essential nature. The will is thought in its practical employment; and thought, Hegel holds, is essentially rational. To the extent, therefore, that particular decisions are based upon laws deriving from reason, they are self-determined in the above-mentioned sense. This may not be the way in which freedom is ordinarily understood; but Hegel is saying that self-conscious rational self-determination is the only alternative to remaining subject to the laws governing all natural existence—the only sort of freedom man can have that is more than the mere illusion of freedom.

Such freedom, it perhaps goes without saying, is not a birthright, except as a potentiality. For example, "Children," Hegel says, "are potentially free and their life directly embodies nothing save potential freedom." Yet theirs is "a freedom still in the toils of nature" (*PR,* § 174). And adults no less than children remain merely potentially free and in the toils of nature, unless and until they realize their potential freedom by basing their decisions upon laws deriving from reason and apprehending themselves as obeying the law of their own essential nature in doing so. For since freedom is conceived not in terms of the ability to choose, but rather in terms of self-conscious rational self-determination of one's actions, it is not a reality in the life of an individual unless his actions are in fact so determined. Then and only then is his will free not merely potentially, and free not merely in the abstract and negative sense of pure indeterminateness, but free actually and in a concrete and positive sense.

It should be observed that though this conception of freedom does differ from the ordinary understanding of the term, it is not so far removed from the ordinary understanding of what freedom involves as to no longer deserve to be called by this name at all. For freedom is ordinarily conceived in terms of self-determination; and Hegel, starting from this idea and preserving it throughout, simply attempts to show what is involved in the only sort of true self-determination of which we are capable. It so happens that much of what we ordinarily take to be self-determined is not and that true self-determination involves acting along lines of which we are not used to thinking in these terms. But the concept of freedom itself that emerges from Hegel's discussion preserves at least the basic outlines of our ordinary concept of freedom, and therefore his retention of the term is not unreasonable.

VI

So far, I have been dealing only with Hegel's development of the *concept* of freedom—a development that is presented in the Introduction to his *Philosophy of Right*. The body of the work is devoted to a consideration of what is involved in the emergence of freedom as a reality in the world, or freedom as Idea. It consists in the presentation of a developmental sequence which, if completed, results in actual self-conscious and rational self-determination in the concrete practical life of the individual. Hegel distinguishes three basic stages in this developmental sequence. In brief, in the first, self-determination becomes a reality, in the sense that a sphere is marked out in which the actions of the individual are not subject to the direction of anyone else, but rather are determined by his own decisions and choices. In the second stage there emerges a self-consciousness in which the individual is carried one step closer to an adequate understanding of his essential nature. This is not exclusively or even primarily a matter of his particular characteristics and idiosyncrasies, but rather is to be conceived as involving above all the attainment of rationality and universality. And in the third stage, the individual's decisions and choices—and therefore his actions—are brought into line with his essential nature, acquiring the character of rationality and universality, through their determination in accordance with a set of objective laws and institutions that are rational and universal in nature. With the conclusion of this development, the practical life of the individual has the character of self-conscious rational self-determination, and thus freedom is an existing reality.

Hegel begins by observing that freedom is nothing in the absence of the opportunity to act without let or hindrance by others, and that it is the existence of things, together with the establishment of property rights in relation to them, which first of all secures for us this opportunity. He says:

> If the free will is not to remain abstract, it must in the first place give itself an embodiment, and the material primarily available to sensation for such an embodiment is things, i.e., objects outside us. This primary mode of freedom is the one which we are to become acquainted with as property, the sphere of formal and abstract right. . . . The freedom which we have here is [that of] what is called a person. (*PR*, §33A)

The sort of freedom I have when an external sphere is secured in which I can do as I please, however, is only freedom in an "abstract" sense, according to Hegel. For it is only in an abstract sense that I can be said to be self-determined in so acting. My actions are self-determined in that they are not determined by the will of anyone else. To conceive of self-determination simply in these terms, however, is to conceive it in a merely negative and superficial way. A more adequate understanding of it cannot be achieved until attention is diverted from the action insofar as it is unhindered and uncoerced by others, to the action insofar as it is determined by oneself. This involves a shift of attention from the objective (the action) to the subjective—the choice or decision determining the action and, more basically, the self making the choice or decision. The sort of freedom now before us is termed "subjective," in that it involves a consciousness of oneself as the determining source of one's decisions and choices. What has been added to freedom of the former sort is this element of explicit self-consciousness. And this is an important addition: "In this way a higher ground has been assigned to freedom; the Idea's existential aspect, or its moment of reality, is now the subjectivity of the will. Only in the will as subjective can freedom or the implicit principle of the will be actual" (*PR*, § 106).

Hegel's point is relatively simple. One cannot really be said to be free so long as he is not explicitly aware of himself as being free. The consciousness of oneself as free is not itself a guarantee of true freedom: it may be only the illusion of freedom and is compatible with determinism. But it is a necessary condition of true freedom in that if one does not grasp one's actions as deriving from decisions and choices of one's own making, these actions cannot truly be said to be one's own. To act unhindered by others, and yet to do so unselfconsciously and without explicitly viewing one's acts as one's own, is to be free at most only in principle or, in Hegel's terms, implicitly. Self-determination that is not self-conscious is a poor sort of freedom.

Thus Hegel distinguishes subjective freedom, or the freedom of the subject, from abstract freedom, or the freedom of the person, in terms of explicit self-consciousness that distinguishes the *subject* from the *person,* who lacks it: "This reflection of the will into itself and its explicit awareness of its identity makes the person into the subject" (*PR*, § 105). The individual's attention ceases to be absorbed in the things on which he acts and goes further than his freedom from coercion by others: "Its personality—and in abstract right the will is personality and no more [i.e., is not self-conscious]—it now has for its object" (*PR*, § 104). Freedom is now associated not merely with the right of the individual to do as he wants with what is his, but rather with the more fundamental "right of the subject to find satisfaction in the action" (*PR*, § 123)—"to recognize as its action, and to accept responsibility for, only those presuppositions of the deed of which it was conscious in its aim and those aspects of the deed which were contained in its purpose" (*PR*, § 117).

But now there arises the question of the content of the aim and purpose on the basis of which the subject self-consciously determines his actions, and of the origin of this content. For the subject can be said to be truly self-determined only if he himself is the origin of this content—only if the content on the basis of which he decides and chooses is itself self-determined. Initially, however, the subject differs from the person only in that the "person" has the character of unselfconscious personality. The content of the aims and purposes of the subject, therefore, still reflects the nature of personality. Personality, according to Hegel, is to be conceived in terms of "a differentiation and singling out of the modes which nature gives; we find it as the special temperament, talent, character, physiognomy, or other disposition and idiosyncrasy, of families or single individuals" (*PM*, §395). The content of the aims and purposes determining its action, therefore, is one which "the still-abstract and formal freedom of subjectivity possesses only in its natural subjective embodiment, i.e., in needs, inclinations, passions, opinions, fancies, etc. The satisfaction of these is welfare or happiness" (*PR*, §123).

The welfare or happiness of the particular self-conscious person—the subject—is the result of his self-conscious determination of his actions in accordance with such things as these. But is he thereby also free insofar as he is able to achieve such satisfaction? Hegel's answer is that, once again, we are dealing with something that can be called freedom only in an "abstract and formal" sense. Although self-consciousness has now been added to the absence of coercion, the individual whose aims and purposes are determined by factors of the sort mentioned above is still not truly self-determined. For if his aims and purposes are determined by the particular configuration of "the modes which nature gives" that constitutes his personality, they are not truly self-determined; rather, they are ultimately determined by the natural laws that govern the occurrence and interaction of these modes. The individual— his self-consciousness of self-determination notwithstanding—therefore enjoys but the illusion of true freedom or self-determination so long as the content of his aims and purposes is a function of the needs, inclinations, passions, etc., associated with his particular personality. Hegel finds a basis for the determination of action other than a configuration of "the modes which nature gives," yet one that accords with the individual's own essential self, in the objective and determinate system of "ethical life" (*Sittlichkeit*)—and only in it.

Ethical life is the Idea of freedom in that on the one hand it is the good become alive . . . while on the other hand self-consciousness has in the ethical realm its absolute foundation and the end which actualizes its effort. Thus ethical life is the concept of freedom developed into the existing world and the nature of self-consciousness. (*PR*, § 142)

The term "ethical" here has a sense rather different from the sense it ordinarily has in English usage. The German term *Sitte* means "custom"; and while Hegel does not simply have customs in mind in speaking of *Sittlichkeit*, he is thinking of something similar: namely, the laws and institutions of a social, cultural, and legal nature that inform the life of a people. It is Hegel's contention in the above passage that true freedom is to be found only in self-conscious self-determination in accordance with such laws and institutions. They constitute "a stable content independently necessary and subsistent in exaltation above subjective opinion and caprice" (*PR*, §144). Insofar as they determine one's aims and purposes, therefore, these aims and purposes have a content quite different from that which they have when they derive from the particular personality of the individual—a content, moreover, that is inherently rational:

> It is the fact that the ethical order is the system of these specific determinations of the Idea which constitutes its rationality. Hence the ethical order is freedom or the absolute will as what is objective, a circle of necessity whose movements are the ethical powers which regulate the life of individuals. (*PR*, §146)

This may seem to be rather paradoxical: the "ethical order" is said both to make freedom possible and to constitute a "circle of necessity" regulating the lives of individuals. For Hegel, however, there is no contradiction here; for he holds that an individual whose existence corresponds to his essential rational nature will be at one with an "ethical order" and its laws and institutions: "They are not something alien to the subject. On the contrary his spirit bears witness to them as to its own essence, the essence in which he has a feeling of his selfhood, and in which he lives as in his own element which is not distinguished from himself" (*PR*, §147).

In ethical life all opposition between the individual and the ethical order vanishes, for the individual perceives his essential nature to be rational and further perceives the ethical order to constitute a rational system. He thus sees that in determining his actions in accordance with the laws and institutions of the ethical order, he determines them not in accordance with an alien law, but rather in accordance with the law of his own essential nature. So Hegel says, "Duty is the attainment of our essence, the winning of positive freedom" (*PR*, §149A). Duty is not incompatible with self-determination if it is the law of one's own nature that determines one's duty. On the contrary, if this is the case then duty and true self-determination coincide:

> The bond of duty can appear as a restriction only on indeterminate subjectivity or abstract freedom, and on the impulses either of the natural will or of the moral will which determines its indeterminate good arbitrarily. The truth

is, however, that in duty the individual finds his liberation . . . from dependence on mere natural impulse. . . . In duty the individual acquires his
substantive freedom. (*PR*, § 149)

It should be emphasized that in speaking of duty, Hegel has in mind
neither the deliverances of the individual's own conscience nor the Kantian
Categorical Imperative, but rather the objective duties determined by the laws
and institutions of the ethical order. They include, and indeed culminate in,
the duties one has as citizen or member of the state. Hegel considers the state
to be "the actuality of the ethical Idea" (*PR*, § 257) because he holds that it
is only with the emergence of a state that laws and institutions informing the
life of a people acquire the character of an integrated and complete rational
system and thus that they come collectively to constitute a true ethical order.
This is the basis of his contention that "the state is the actuality of concrete
freedom" (*PR*, § 260). It should be observed, however, that Hegel's state is
not one in which the interests of the individual—even *qua* particular person—
are sacrificed to interests of the state that are inimical to those of the
individual. On the contrary, it is Hegel's view that "my interest, *both
substantive and particular,* is contained and preserved in another's, i.e., in the
state's" (*PR*, § 268; emphasis added). The state as Hegel conceives of it is so
constituted that as a member of it, I both attain the rationality in my actions
which renders them self-determined and therefore renders me free, *and* find
my personal well-being secured and enhanced far beyond what would be
possible in the absence of the state. This, at any rate, is the situation in the
"genuinely organized" state; and it is only in so far as a state is "genuinely
organized" that Hegel considers it to be "absolute rationality" (*PR*, § 258)
and "the actuality of the ethical Idea" (*PR*, § 257).

The essence of the modern state is that the universal is bound up with the
complete freedom of its particular members and with private well-being.
. . . The universal must be furthered, but subjectivity on the other hand
must attain its full and living development. It is only when both of these
moments subsist in their strength that the state can be regarded as articulated
and genuinely organized. (*PR*, § 260A)

The force of these remarks is that the state of which Hegel speaks is not
totalitarian: life in it is not so regimented that personality disappears. But this
involves no retreat from the position that one is truly self-determined, and
enjoys more than the mere illusion of freedom, only insofar as what one does
is determined in accordance with an objectively existing law or institution.
The fact that Hegel would allow much of what the individual does to be
determined by his personal desires and inclinations does not mean that he
regards the status of such actions any differently than has been suggested

above. Actions determined in this way are actions determined in accordance with "the modes which nature gives," and thus are determined in accordance with the general laws that govern these modes, rather than being truly self-determined. That there is occasion for actions of this sort is due to the fact that reason is incapable of engendering a system of laws and institutions that would govern the whole of life. Laws regulating matters that Hegel leaves to personal discretion may in fact exist. A state in which there are such laws, however, is not a "genuinely organized" state, in Hegel's view, since its laws are not strictly conformable to reason. In a "genuinely organized" state certain matters are governed by laws and institutions, and others are not. In the case of the latter the individual enjoys that sort of freedom discussed by Hegel in connection with personality and subjectivity. Such freedom, however, is not true freedom. The individual is truly free only when his actions are rationally as well as self-consciously self-determined—only, that is, when they are determined in accordance with objective rational laws and institutions.

VII

T. M. Knox, in his article "Hegel and Prussianism," suggests that Hegel's problem in the *Philosophy of Right* is this: "How is it possible to combine the individual Greek's complete devotion to his city with the modern emphasis on the paramount importance of individual freedom?"[25] No one would deny that Hegel's suggested solution captures well the first element mentioned. Many commentators question, however, whether the freedom he finds compatible with it deserves to be called freedom at all. E. F. Carrit, in his reply to Knox, gives expression to a common sentiment about the matter:

No doubt Hegel professed (as who does not?) and even persuaded himself (as who cannot?) that he was an admirer of freedom. And he managed to do this by giving the word a peculiar meaning of his own. Freedom is not the power of doing what you like (P.d.R. §15) nor what you think right (§140). He holds that those and only those are free who desire above all things to serve the success and glory of their State.[26]

Carrit, it would appear, holds that to be free is to be able to do what you like and/or what your conscience tells you to do. To be sure, one will not find Hegel's understanding of what true freedom involves appealing if one is committed to some such view of freedom. But aside from ignoring Hegel's analysis of the concept of freedom, Carrit fails to take account of the fact that Hegel thinks he has shown that what Carrit understands to be freedom is no true freedom at all. One may *prefer* to do what one likes or what one's conscience dictates—this Hegel does not deny. He agrees with the determinists, however, that to do so is not at all to be self-determined, the feeling of spontaneity notwithstanding. To the protest "But this is what we *mean* by freedom!" he replies that, rather than rest content with an understanding of freedom along lines tying the notion to something which amounts to but the illusion of true self-determination, he prefers to associate the term with a type of action that does in fact answer, to this description. This is hardly "giving the word a peculiar meaning of his own." Rather, it involves maintaining that the meaning of the word requires a different application of it from that which is customary if it is to have any true applicability at all.

This move is by no means as arbitrary and unreasonable as Carrit implies. It remains to be determined, however, whether or not Carrit is correct in asserting that in practice Hegel's reapplication of the term comes down to the following: "Those and only those are free who desire above all things to serve the success and glory of their State." This, it seems to me, is a ludicrous caricature of Hegel's actual position. To state Hegel's position as baldly as possible, those and only those are truly free who live in a rationally organized state, who desire above all things to do what their state requires of them, and who determine their actions in accordance with its laws and institutions. Even this is misleading if it is not added that according to Hegel the rationally organized state will require of its citizens only that which is in the "substantive and particular" interest of all concerned. He would reject the suggestion that such a state would pursue its "success and glory" at the expense of this twofold interest of its citizens. A state might do this; but to the extent that it did, it would not be the sort of state Hegel endorses. Even when he says that the individual must be prepared to sacrifice all when the state is threatened (PR, §324), he is not suggesting that the interests of the individual are to be subordinated to its "success and glory." Rather, his point is that the state is what makes possible both the maximum satisfaction of the individual's particular wants and needs and the realization of his essential nature and true freedom, and that he therefore must be prepared to make sacrifices to preserve the state, upon which his welfare and indeed his very humanity depend.

One may conclude that objections of the sort made by Carrit are not legitimate ones, however, and still consider Hegel's account to fall short of being satisfactory. For example, it may be that in a "genuinely organized" state the laws and institutions would be such that the individual could embrace them without reservation. But surely, few if any existing states are organized so adequately that their laws and institutions conform completely to "the ethical Idea" and have the character of "absolute rationality." Under these circumstances, one cannot be entirely happy with Hegel's disparagement of those who live in an ethical order and yet raise questions about what one really ought to do: if they were serious, he says, "they would have clung to what is substantively right, namely to the commands of the ethical order and the state and would have regulated their lives in accordance with these" (*PR*, Pref., pp. 3–4).

The basis of the individual's identification with the ethical order is supposed to be his recognition that it embodies the same rationality in terms of which his own essential nature is to be conceived. If, upon turning from Hegel's discussion of the genuinely organized state in the *Philosophy of Right* to his own state, the individual discovers significant discrepancies and further finds the fault to lie in the organization of the latter, he will have a problem. He may agree that true self-determination consists in action in accordance with a rational system of objective laws and institutions, and therefore is impossible outside of a state. But if the laws and institutions of his own state are not rational, the determination of his actions in accordance with them can hardly have the character of self-determination for him. Hegel's suggestion, therefore, that true self-determination is in fact possible in this way is conditionally true at best; and the most obvious condition on which its truth depends is by no means as adequately satisfied as the position he adopts would seem to require.

Ultimately, of course, the plausibility of Hegel's understanding of what true freedom involves depends upon the plausibility of his conceptions of man's nature and of the nature of the ethical order. Thse are matters that lead straight to the heart of Hegel's metaphysics and cannot be gone into here. It should be clear, however, that it is Hegel's understanding of the natures of man and the world—rather than the Prussianism or the totalitarian inclination so often attributed to him—that leads him to take the position he does on the nature of human freedom and the relation between freedom and the state. One who would maintain that his position is untenable cannot merely point to the prevalence of a different understanding of what freedom involves, but rather must show the untenability of one or more of the views on which his position depends.

VIII

Hegel's line of reasoning may be briefly summarized as follows. To be free is to be self-determined. Indeed, it is to be self-consciously self-determined, for it would be inappropriate to term a being "free" unless it were aware of its determinations as its own. Further, to be free is to be self-determined not only in one's actions but also in one's choosing to act in various ways. Self-determination implies not only the absence of coercion by other men but also the independence of one's choices and decisions of factors alien to one's self. In speaking of man's self, what is intended is not his merely physical or sensuous nature, but rather his true or essential self, which is to be conceived as spirit. Spirit, in turn, is to be conceived not in terms of the feelings, impulses, inclinations, and desires associated with mere physical or sensuous existence, but rather in terms of rational thought. Both sorts of phenomena are governed by laws, and all phenomena of human life are governed by laws of one sort or the other. The laws of reason, however, are not subordinate to or determined by the laws governing sensuous existence. They constitute a system determined by the nature of reason itself. One who determines his choices and decisions—and so also his actions—in accordance with laws of reason, therefore, is self-determined in a way in which one who determines them in accordance with his impulses and inclinations is not. He alone is truly free, for he alone is truly self-determined. A being who is essentially rational is self-determined only if he governs himself in accordance with the laws of his essential rational nature, and is thereby liberated from subjection to laws that are not laws of his own essential nature.

Man's essential rationality, however, does not of itself guarantee that the individual by himself is capable of governing himself in accordance with the laws of his essential rational nature, even if he should desire to do so. He has the capacity to come to think and act in accordance with reason; but he exists at least initially as a merely particular person, moved by natural needs and inclinations and having a determinate nature or personality the character of which is a function of the operation of laws of sensuous nature. So long as the aims and purposes of his actions are determined subjectively, they can have no source other than his particular personality—which, as the determinists correctly observe, is by no means self-determined. This is so even when these aims and purposes appear as the dictates of conscience or are given the semblance of rationality through being universalized. The individual can escape the condition of non-self-determined particularity only if he can find an objective basis for determination of his actions that is not subject to the influence of his particular impulses and inclinations. Such an objective basis obviously cannot be fixed subjectively, on one's own; for nothing determined in this way can have the requisite objectivity or independence of subjective influences. There is only one thing that does have this character: the ethical order, with its objectively existing laws and institutions.

Of course, action determined in accordance with these laws and institutions could not be considered free at all if, their objectivity notwithstanding, they were something utterly alien to the individual's own nature. In a properly organized state, however, they are nothing other than reason itself, concretely embodied; and as such they are not something alien to the individual's own nature at all. On the contrary they embody objectively the very rational structure in terms of which the individual's essential rational nature is to be conceived. In determining his actions in accordance with them, therefore, the individual at once escapes the toils of nature and brings his actions into conformity with the law of his own essential nature. He thereby achieves rational self-determination in the only way in which it is possible for him to do so. To be free is to be self-determined. Here, and here alone, is one truly self-determined. Here, and here alone, therefore, is one truly free. It follows, of course, that true freedom becomes possible only with the emergence of a properly organized state as an existing reality. But this is a proposition that Hegel explicitly affirms. And it is only in this light that one can see why he attaches so much importance to the state.

A number of the contentions upon which Hegel's understanding of freedom depends seem questionable, to say the least—in particular, his characterization of man and of the state as essentially rational and moreover as corresponding in their essential rational natures. Yet I wonder. Many irrationalist accounts of man's nature have appeared since Hegel wrote, and all discussions of man's nature have fallen into disrepute in recent years. It can hardly be denied, however, that human beings are capable of acquiring the capacity to think rationally; and it is quite probably both true and of considerable importance that rational thought is central to all human activity in connection with which it is tenable to speak of genuine self-determination. Further, it may be that the metaphysical underpinnings of Hegel's theory of the state are dubious or at any rate highly problematical, and that he exaggerates the rationality of the modern state. Still, I would venture to suggest that the kinds of laws and institutions of which he speaks do—or at least in principle can—provide a basis for the determination of action that raises it above the level of natural impulse and inclination and renders it more rational than it could be in the absence of such laws and institutions. Whether the elements of truth in what Hegel says about these matters—if they are such—are sufficient to establish the validity of his understanding of what freedom involves, either as it stands or in some modified form, is certainly open to question. It does seem to me, however, that a negative answer is by no means obviously indicated.

5:

The Early Marx on Hegel, Naturalism, and Human Emancipation

Contemporary opinions of Marx's philosophical stature vary enormously. In some quarters he is dismissed as having been no philosopher at all, while in others he is regarded as the most important one since Hegel, if not in the entire history of philosophy. In my opinion the latter estimation exaggerates his importance as greatly as the former underrates it. Marx devoted too little time and effort in his later life to the development of the philosophical ideas contained in his early writings to be credited with having done any more philosophically than to make some provocative and interesting suggestions and some tentative efforts at their elaboration. Yet the initial steps he took along these lines were a highly significant accomplishment, amply justifying the designation of him as one of the seminal philosophical minds of the post-Hegelian era.

In this chapter attention is focused upon the early Marx's departures from Hegel in the two general areas of philosophical inquiry under discussion in the two previous chapters. Marx takes objection to Hegel's thinking with regard to many matters, but two problems in particular are of concern to him. First, he is dissatisfied with Hegel's idealistic metaphysics and the philosophical anthropology associated with it, particularly because of what he views as Hegel's reduction of things and human activities to objects and modes of consciousness, and the consequences of this "abstraction." And secondly, he is unhappy with Hegel's treatment of the issue of human freedom and its presuppositions and, in particular, with the conclusions Hegel draws from his analysis of them as they relate to the character and adequacy of the kind of socio-politico-economic system with which he and Marx found themselves confronted.

Marx recognizes that what Hegel has to say along the latter lines is intimately related to his metaphysical and anthropological views. More generally, like Hegel, he feels that social philosophy cannot be separated from philosophical anthropology, which in turn is inseparable from ontology, and that normative issues can ultimately be resolved only by reference to conclusions established through these sorts of inquiry. He thus sees that the two general problems indicated above are interconnected, and that more specific problems such as those of the nature, significance, source, and course of action required for the overcoming of human "alienation," egoism and greed, social division, international conflict, and the like can be dealt with properly only within a larger context set by the treatment of these more fundamental problems.

For these reasons, therefore, even though his initial and subsequent interests may center largely on these more specific and concrete problems, and even though his most immediate and pressing concern at the time of (and also in) his early writings is with them, Marx attempts in these writings to set out at least the outlines of a naturalistic alternative to Hegel's metaphysics and social philosophy (and thus to his accounts of human nature and freedom), in the absence of which his challenge to Hegel's treatment of these and related pressing particular problems would have been too problematical philosophically to be at all convincing. He has more to say along these more general lines in certain of his other relatively early writings not discussed in this chapter (most notably, Part I of his and Engels' *The German Ideology*). Those to be discussed here, however, are of particular interest and value because of Marx's explicit attempts in them to come to terms with Hegel; for his confrontation with Hegel is both significant in connection with a consideration of Hegel's views and helpful in enabling one approaching Marx with Hegel in mind (as indeed it may be argued he *ought* to be approached) to gain access to his philosophical thinking.

One final word. It is by now almost a commonplace that the concern with the quality of human life so strongly expressed in Marx's early writings reveals a dimension of his thinking which may legitimately be termed a form of "humanism." What is less widely appreciated, however, is the fact that these writings also require a revision of the view that Marx's understanding of the character of human existence is to be regarded as a type of "materialism," the fundamental distinguishing feature of which is simply that it is "dialectical." Marx may be styled a "materialist" if the term is taken to be applicable to everyone who is not an "idealist." His position is much more appropriately characterized, however, as a form of "naturalism," which is to be contrasted with the ontologies and anthropologies of *both* idealism and materialism, and the distinctive feature of which is the importance attached to social (as opposed to merely biological and psychological) factors. This should become clear in the course of the present chapter. And it is for this reason that I have subtitled this part of the book "From Absolute Idealism to Socio-Naturalism."

One way of coming to grips with the philosophy of the early Marx (as it is presented in his writings dating from the early and mid-1840s) is in terms of what he takes to be sound and unsound in Hegel's philosophy. During the period in which Marx was developing his own views, Hegel was the dominant figure in German philosophy; and while Marx has a good deal to say about several men who were more nearly his contemporaries (such as Bruno Bauer and Ludwig Feuerbach), the amount of space in his early writings devoted to discussions of Hegel shows how extensively Marx was preoccupied with him during this period. However wrong Marx may have thought Hegel was in various important respects, he felt he could not pass over Hegel in silence. To Marx, Hegel's philosophy is the culmination of the whole mainstream of traditional and modern Western philosophy, and, therefore, no one who would consider himself a serious philosopher can afford to set forth his own views without both studying Hegel carefully and spelling out in detail what he takes to be the strengths and weaknesses of Hegel's philosophy.

In the early and mid-1840s, therefore, Marx devoted a great deal of time to a careful examination of Hegel's major works; and many of his writings dating from this period in a sense consist in a series of critical evaluations of these works, together with his first attempts to suggest the outlines of what he felt to be a more satisfactory philosophy. And it is clear, particularly from the last part of the third of his *Economic and Philosophical Manuscripts* of 1844, entitled "Critique of Hegel's Dialectic and General Philosophy," that in general he succeeded in mastering Hegel's philosophy far better than many of Hegel's more recent Marxist—and non-Marxist—critics. I shall begin by examining this "Critique," because in it Marx's evaluation of Hegel's general philosophical position and also his own position in relation to Hegel's are spelled out more explicitly and systematically than elsewhere in his early (and later) writings.

I

Near the middle of this "Critique," Marx says, "We see here how consistent naturalism . . . is distinguished from both idealism and materialism, and at the same time constitutes their unifying truth" (p. 206).[1] Without knowing yet precisely what Marx means by this assertion, one does get from it an indication of the way in which Marx views his own position in relation to Hegel's philosophy on the one hand and to pre- and post-Hegelian materialism on the other. He characterizes his own position as "naturalism," which is not merely a materialist reaction against idealism, but rather is to be distinguished both from idealism *and* from materialism. At the same time he feels that each of these positions contains an element of truth; and in his own philosophy he attempts to combine the elements of truth in each, while rejecting that in each of them which he takes to be wrong.

His naturalism is to be distinguished from idealism, above all, in that he rejects the fundamental thesis of idealism—namely, that reality is fundamentally "spiritual," and that *what exists* is in the last analysis to be conceived in terms of conscious events of one sort or another, and in terms of them alone. But his naturalism is also to be distinguished from traditional materialism (in spite of the fact that his philosophical position subsequently came to be characterized as "dialectical materialism") above all in that he rejects one of its most fundamental tenets: namely, that everything that exists is ultimately to be understood completely and solely in terms of the properties of material entities and the laws governing their motion and interactions.

To put the matter briefly, Marx's naturalism is at one with materialism to this extent: he holds that the "real world" is fundamentally the world of nature; that man is to be conceived first of all as a part of nature, a natural being existing alongside and among other natural objects; and that consciousness is a faculty of this natural being by means of which it is present to other natural objects and to itself (rather than that which alone exists, and in terms of which everything else is to be conceived). But Marx's naturalism also agrees with idealism in certain respects: he holds that man is what he is by virtue of having passed through a course of development which must be understood in its own special terms (and in particular, in terms of "social" categories), rather than in terms appropriate to the understanding of mere inorganic and organic nature. Man thus *is* what he has *made himself* to be, through his own activity, which—at least collectively considered and in relation to the laws governing mere things—is free and self-determined. For Marx, therefore, man as he now exists is not merely a part of nature, but rather a being which transcends the purely natural order and makes use of the rest of nature as a *means* to the realization of his distinctively human purposes.

Marx considers Hegel's great contribution to have been that he showed both that man must be conceived as having made himself to be what he is through a process of self-development, and (at least in principle) how this process of self-development has occurred and must be understood—namely, dialectically. Here he has in mind above all Hegel's *Phenomenology of Spirit,* the main fault of which, in Marx's view, is not that the course of development traced in it is fundamentally *inaccurate,* but rather that it is cast in terms which are too *abstract.* This is a point to which I shall return subsequently.

Yet it is Marx's fundamental disagreement with Hegel's idealism that comes through most repeatedly and emphatically in the "Critique." Marx feels that Hegel erred profoundly in his conceptions of man and of nature, even though he did grasp the general outlines of man's development. And whether he is right or wrong about this, he at least understands Hegel's conceptions of them. For Hegel, he observes, *things* do not exist independently of consciousness, but rather are simply objects of various kinds of conscious events, which exist only in relation to them. And *nature,* for Hegel, is not something ontologically independent of spirit, within the context of which certain beings with what might be termed a "spiritual life" (i.e., men) happen to exist. Rather, it is a certain *form* of "objectivity" that an essentially spiritual principle creates for itself as the first step in its process of self-actualization, which is nothing truly external to this spiritual principle, and whose appearance of externality to it is finally overcome, in absolute knowledge. Against Hegel, Marx maintains that things *do* exist independently of consciousness, that nature *does* exist "externally" in relation to the only "spiritual beings" there are, and that in point of fact "consciousness" and "spiritual beings" do exist and can only exist in relation to independently existing things and as parts of a natural world.

This leads to a further point. For Hegel, as Marx observes repeatedly in the course of the "Critique," man is not something either more or less than consciousness and self-consciousness, but rather simply *is* consciousness and self-consciousness. Human life is nothing either more or less than spiritual life (i.e., conscious events of various sorts). All spiritual life or activity ultimately consists in a variety of more or less adequate forms of knowing, and culminates in that final and complete form of knowing called "absolute knowledge," in which alone and as such man's essential nature is realized. And human existence is nothing other than the concrete manfestation or embodiment of a spiritual principle which is completely general or "universal" in nature, which transcends the individuals in which it is actualized, and which therefore is completely indifferent to them as individuals. And against Hegel, Marx maintains that man is not to be equated with consciousness and self-consciousness, but rather is a basically natural being, having the *characteristics* (among others) of consciousness and self-consciousness. Human life does not consist wholly of conscious events, but rather does so only in part—which part is dependent upon and developed out of kinds of activity that are basically practical in nature, and have nothing to do with knowing for its own sake at all. And individual human beings as parts of nature are transcended by nothing other than the natural world of which they are parts and the social world of which they are members.

With Hegel's contention that "man is essentially spirit" in mind, Marx repeatedly says such things throughout the "Critique" as that man is to be conceived as "real, corporeal man, with his feet firmly planted on the solid ground, inhaling and exhaling all the powers of nature" (p. 206), and that "*man* is directly a *natural being*. As a . . . natural, embodied, sentient, objective being, he is a suffering, conditioned and limited being, like animals and plants. . . . The fact that man is an embodied, living, real, sentient, objective being with natural powers, means that he has real, sensuous objects as the objects of his being" (pp. 206–07). In relation to this conception of man, the Hegelian conception of man as an essentially spiritual entity seems to Marx to be but a pale abstraction, in which certain features of actual human life and the general pattern of human development may be seen but are cut off and isolated from their basis in real life. The sort of activity which Hegel takes to constitute the very essence of the nature of spirit and therefore of man—knowing—appears in this context to be the most abstract and ephemeral (if not epiphenomenal) sort of human activity. It further seems to Marx that the sort of philosophical thinking which leads to Hegel's conclusions could not be further removed from real human life, and that the sort of thinker who would say what Hegel does could not have been more completely out of touch with what real human life is like. Marx expresses this point by characterizing this sort of thought as "alienated thought," this conception of human life as the "alienation of man's humanity," and a philosopher like Hegel as a "thinker alienated from his being, i.e. from his natural and human life" (p. 216).

In taking this position, Marx is trying to get at the root of the problem which led to the result of Hegel's idealism in what well may be the only sort of way something like this result really can be avoided: namely, by rejecting the basic assumptions of the whole tradition of modern philosophy beginning with Descartes. *If* one begins by holding that one is not justified in assuming the existence of anything which is not either immediately perceived or strictly entailed by something immediately perceived, and further assumes that the only things immediately perceived are objects of consciousness which as such exist only in relation to consciousness, and if one does not shrink from drawing the full consequences of taking this position, *then*, it seems to Marx (and indeed it seems to me quite reasonable to suppose[2]), something like Hegel's conclusions can hardly be avoided—unless, of course, one is prepared simply to abandon the entire enterprise of attempting to say anything about the nature of man and reality.

Now Marx is *not* prepared to abandon this entire enterprise, even though it is not his purpose to work out a full-fledged metaphysical scheme to rival Hegel's. He avoids Hegel's conclusions, and criticizes Hegel for maintaining them, by refusing to take the first step on the slippery slope leading to idealism and attacking Hegel for taking it: namely, the step of allowing, in the interest of achieving absolute certainty, that the Cartesian principle of methodological doubt requires us to restrict our self-conception to the conception of ourselves as thinking subjects or consciousness, and our conception of the world and the things in it to the conception of them as thought objects (i.e., perceptual contents or objects of consciousness). It may be that the quest for absolute certainty, and a consequent observance of the requirements of Descartes's methodological doubt, does lead to this result. But Marx refuses to yield because he is convinced that this result is nothing more than a shadowy abstraction in relation to the living human being and the real world in which he lives. And he feels that it is better to hold fast to human life and the real world in all their concreteness—even at the expense of the Cartesian program of a reconstruction of knowledge as a logically unshakable edifice built upon absolutely firm foundations—than to pursue this program at the cost of winding up with Hegel's metaphysics. For the latter, in his view, is compelling only given premises which immediately abstract from real life; and it constitutes a picture of reality in which the real dependence relation of spirit (or consciousness) and nature is reversed.

But Marx concedes that it is only if one is willing to abandon the basic assumptions of the whole tradition of classical modern philosophy, and to commit oneself to a form of naturalism—to which philosophers in the tradition of Descartes will of course have strong methodological objections—that one can avoid Hegelianism. For Hegel, in Marx's view, is to be given at least this much credit in the development of his idealist metaphysics: he worked out the conclusions that do in fact follow from the basic assumptions of his philosophical predecessors, which they had lacked either the perspicuity to see or the courage to affirm. And in this respect—though not only in this respect—Marx considers Hegel to be both quite brilliant and a thinker of great intellectual integrity.

II

I said, "In this respect—though not *only* in this respect." For, as I have already indicated, Marx considers Hegel to have been brilliant in another and, for him, more important respect as well. He says, with reference to the *Phenomenology,* "Hegel has . . . discovered an *abstract, logical* and *speculative* expression of the historical process, which is not yet the *real* history of man as a given subject, but [rather] only the history of the *act of creation*, of the *genesis of man*" (p. 198). In other words, what we find in the *Phenomenology* is a description and analysis of the process through which man has made himself to be what he is. The only trouble is that in it the process is presented in terms which are too abstract, and man is conceived too abstractly; and this leads to a "mystified" account of what is going on that in the end is profoundly unsatisfactory. If man is conceived more concretely, however, and if the process through which he has made himself to be what he is is also conceived more concretely, then Hegel's account in the *Phenomenology* may be seen to contain a great deal of truth and insight. So Marx says: "The outstanding achievement of Hegel's *Phenomenology* . . . is, first, that Hegel grasps the self-creation of man as a process . . . , as self-relinquishment and transcendence of this self-relinquishment, and that he therefore grasps the nature of *labor,* and conceives objective man (true, because real man) as the result of *his own labor*" (p. 202).

Marx further contends that, even though Hegel's conception of man and his presentation of the process of man's development are too abstract, and even though as a consequence of this his discussion creates a great deal of confusion and leads him into a number of serious errors, Hegel nevertheless grasps the general nature of the basic problem arising in the course of man's development, which must be resolved before man's development is completed: namely, the problem of "alienation." He states: "The *Phenomenology* is a concealed, unclear and mystifying critique; but in so far as it grasps the *alienation* of man (even though man appears only as spirit), *all* the elements of criticism are contained in it, and are often presented and worked out in a manner which goes far beyond Hegel's own point of view" (p. 202).

The problem here, according to Marx, is that, because Hegel conceives of man and the process of man's development too abstractly, he also conceives of the nature and origin of man's alienation too abstractly. And this leads him to give an account of the way in which man's alienation is to be overcome which not only is too abstract but further fails to get to the real root of the problem. For, since Hegel thinks that man's alienation is simply a matter of his failing properly to comprehend his own nature and the nature of the objects of his experience, he concludes that man's alienation is overcome when he succeeds in properly comprehending them—in other words, when he achieves "absolute knowledge," which is simply a matter of one mode of consciousness being replaced by another.

In Marx's view, however, man's alienation in point of fact is ultimately a matter of his practical activity—that is, his labor—resulting in the production of objects which do not fulfill his true needs as a genuinely human being; and therefore he holds that man's alienation can be overcome only by changing the nature of his practical activity. Further, since socioeconomic institutions are for Marx what determine the nature of man's practical activity, man's alienation cannot be overcome merely by replacing one mode of consciousness with another, but rather only by changing the prevailing socio-economic institutions. And, while this may result in a change of the way in which people think about themselves and the world, and while it may even presuppose a change in the currently prevailing "mode of consciousness," it *can happen* only through a fundamental alteration of the objective conditions under which men actually live and work—only through socio-economic revolution, that is, through the forcible overthrow of those objective conditions which are ultimately responsible for man's alienation. For these objective conditions, according to Marx, are not simply a matter of the existence of a certain way of thinking. Rather, they are a matter of "material force"; they are maintained in their existence by "material force"; and, if left to themselves, they will remain firmly established. And, as Marx says in his *Critique of Hegel's Philosophy of Right,* "Material force can only be overthrown by material force" (p. 52). Thus he goes on to speak of "the categorical imperative to overthrow all those conditions in which man is a debased, enslaved, abandoned, contemptible being" (p. 52). And so also, some years later, he concluded his *Communist Manifesto* by calling for worldwide revolution in view of the fact that the "workers of the world" have "nothing to lose but their chains"—or, in other words, their *alienation.* [3]

III

At this point it is perhaps appropriate to turn to a consideration of Marx's *Critique of Hegel's Philosophy of Right,* to which reference has just been made. In the light of the foregoing discussion, it should come as no surprise to find that Marx regards Hegel's social and political philosophy much less favorably than he does Hegel's *Phenomenology.* Hegel, after all, had been anything but a revolutionary; and his stated purpose in his *Philosophy of Right* is primarily to "understand the state as something rational" and to show that the modern Western state is at least very nearly everything a state ought to be. From his discussion in his *Critique of Hegel's Philosophy of Right,* on the other hand, one thing above all is clear: Marx does not think that any modern state—and in particular the modern (i.e., mid-nineteenth century) German state—is everything a state ought to be. And he is far from subscribing to Hegel's view that "things are as they should be" at this point in history (as they are at any other), since they are as they *must* be at this point in history (as they are at any other). [4] On the contrary, while he is sympathetic with Hegel's conservatism to the point of holding that radical change for the better cannot occur until the time is ripe for it, he holds that the time *is* now ripe for change, that therefore things no longer are as they *must* be, that they are emphatically *not* as they *should* be, and that the time thus has come to change them radically. In the last of his "Theses on Feuerbach," written in 1845, he says (obviously with Hegel in mind): "The philosophers have only *interpreted* the world in various ways; the point [however] is, to *change* it."[5]

Marx is fighting a battle on three fronts. First, he is critical of those (like Hegel) who hold that at the present time "philosophy *has been* actualized," in other words, that things now are essentially everything one could wish them to be, in relation to man's essential needs and nature. This position, in Marx's view, can scarcely be seriously maintained by anyone at all acquainted with the actual plight of the great majority of people in capitalistic society. That which Hegel terms the "social substance" might have the *appearance* of rationality in capitalistic society, and might in fact *be* rational when considered formally and abstractly; and the modern state might *be* committed— in principle—to the well-being of all of its citizens. But in existing modern societies, Marx contends, this is no more than a facade, which may absorb the attention of the speculative philosopher, but which very thinly veils the misery and dehumanization of the great majority of actually existing human beings. Moreover, according to Marx, the institutions which control the lives of men in modern societies are not those of the Hegelian "state" at all. Rather, they are those of what Hegel calls "civil society" and even, to some extent (e.g., in Russia and even in Germany in the 1840s), of feudal society.

Hegel, in Marx's view, was misled, by the nominal subjection of the institutions of civil society to the political structure of the state, and by the existence in law of a formal constitution, into thinking that feudalism and "civil society" are forms of society which actually have been transcended. Marx maintains, however, that in point of fact the *real* power in modern societies still lies with those groups which, as Hegel correctly had observed, predominate in civil and feudal society. Thus, for Marx, while Hegel had rightly seen the deplorable situation which exists in feudal and civil societies as a result of their dominance by these self-interested groups, he was wrong in thinking that their power in fact has now been broken. They may have yielded power in principle, and may give the appearance of having done so in fact; but in reality they still have it, and the deplorable consequences of this state of affairs still exist. In short, Hegel's *Philosophy of Right* goes beyond feudal society and civil society *in thought;* but, contrary to what Hegel believed, modern societies have not yet gone beyond this point *in reality.* Yet precisely because Hegel believed they had, his pronouncement that modern

Western societies at last have become essentially rational and are by and large all that one could wish them to be, has had the effect of giving philosophical sanction to the existing order, which actually falls far short of what even Hegel—let alone Marx himself—would wish it to be.

But I have suggested that Marx, in his *Critique of Hegel's Philosophy of Right,* is fighting a battle on three fronts; and I have so far mentioned only one. He also is at odds with two groups who are convinced that things are not as they should and could actually be, but who seek improvement of the existing situation in ways which he feels cannot be successful. Marx calls one group "the theoretical party"; the other, "the practical party." The trouble with the "theoretical" party, he contends, is that "it believes that one can actualize philosophy without superseding it" (p. 51). And the trouble with the "practical" party is that it fails to recognize that "you cannot supersede philosophy without actualizing it" (p. 50).

Marx's general point, briefly and rather crudely put, is that a movement to improve the existing state of affairs in the world cannot succeed if it lacks either muscle or brains. Those in the "theoretical" party, he suggests, devote themselves exclusively to working out a social and political philosophy which analyzes the existing socioeconomic situation more accurately than Hegel had done, and a philosophy of man which sets forth the basic human needs of real men more satisfactorily than Hegel had done, without giving due consideration to the fact that philosophy cannot be "actualized" without being "superseded" by *action*—in other words, without giving any thought to what is necessary in practical terms in order to bring reality into conformity with ideality. They proceed almost idealistically, as if all they must do is to have the right thoughts in order for things to fall into place in the world. They fail to see that the theory of man and society must be supplemented with a theory of revolutionary practice, and that such practice must be actually implemented before their theory of man and society can ever come to anything in reality.

Those in the "practical" party, on the other hand, are held by Marx to err in just the opposite way. They clearly recognize that there must be concrete action in the real world of actual socioeconomic and political institutions in order to improve the prevailing state of affairs, and that mere philosophizing or theorizing can never succeed in improving it. But they make the mistake of thinking that, simply because philosophizing or theorizing by itself is incapable of improving existing conditions, it is irrelevant to the program of doing so. They recognize that to change the world for the better, one must go beyond or "supersede" mere philosophizing; but their idea of superseding philosophy is simply to throw it out the window.

This, in Marx's view, is a grave error. One *can* of course act without first thinking things through and change the world by doing so; but Marx holds that one can scarcely expect any such thoughtless action to change the world *for the better,* except perhaps by mere luck. In fact in most cases, to act without any clear idea of what needs to be accomplished, what obstacles there are to be overcome, and what the conditions of successful revolutionary action are will wind up making things *worse* than they were before, by either playing into the hands of one's adversaries or leading to mere chaos. In this way, action without theory may actually be worse than theory without action. Thus Marx says, "You cannot supersede philosophy without actualizing it." In other words, you cannot *do philosophy one better except* by putting it into action, that is, by taking those actions which will lead to its actualization. And *this* cannot be done by *abandoning* philosophy altogether; rather, it can be done only when one has worked out a sound and adequate philosophy and when one keeps this firmly in mind.

In short, Marx's own position is that the existing socioeconomic world is in reality far from being what it should be, and that it *can* be changed for the better, but only by the concerted efforts of a "party" which is *both* "theoretical" or philosophical *and* "practical" or concerned with revolutionary action, and further, *only* if that party can succeed in mobilizing the strength of a substantial enough portion of the population to overthrow the real forces which support the prevailing socio-economic order. Here one can see the basic idea and rationale of the Communist Party and movement, which Marx was to found a number of years later. And it is with this thought that Marx's Introduction to his *Critique of Hegel's Philosophy of Right* concludes:

Just as philosophy finds its *material* weapons [with which to achieve the human ideal it discovers] in the proletariat, so the proletariat finds its *intellectual* weapons in philosophy. And once the lightning of thought has penetrated deeply into this virgin soil of the people, the Germans will emancipate themselves and become [true] men.... The emancipation of Germany will be an *emancipation of man. Philosophy* is the *head* of this emancipation and the *proletariat* is its *heart.* Philosophy can be actualized only by the abolition of the proletariat, and the proletariat can only be abolished by the actualization of philosophy. (p. 59)

This may be a far cry from Hegel's social and political philosophy; but it is not such a far cry from Hegel's conception of spirit as both substance and subject, and as something which actualizes itself only by relinquishing its abstract purity and becoming active. One needs to do little more than "naturalize" this general account, substituting "man" for "spirit," to arrive at Marx's basic position. Men are capable of attaining a certain form of ideal humanity, but only by descending from the contemplation of it in mere thought and engaging in the sort of practical activity at the socio-economic level required to actualize it. It should not be forgotten that Marx said that he did not repudiate Hegel but rather merely brought him down to earth.

Yet Marx is also indebted to Hegel for more than this general idea; for while he strongly objects to the general tone of Hegel's social and political philosophy and to its conservative conclusions, he finds a great deal of value in it as well. In particular, he feels that Hegel is profoundly right in what he says in the *Philosophy of Right* on such matters as the development of personality through productive activity, the shortcomings of individual conscience, the dehumanizing effect of surrendering the direction of one's practical activity to the will of another man, and the radical defects of "civil society." This last point in particular is important, for Marx's own critique of contemporary society differs little from Hegel's critique of "civil society." The main issue between them is over the question of whether societies like nineteenth-century (and, one might add, twentieth-century) Germany, France, England, and America are still at the stage of "civil society" and therefore still suffer from its defects. Hegel thinks such societies have gone beyond it, while Marx thinks they really have not, even if they give the appearance of having done so. But this difference does not prevent Marx from seeing in Hegel's *Philosophy of Right* a veritable gold mine, and he mines it very freely. (There is a moral here for those would-be Marxists today who think that those with whom they are in basic disagreement on certain fundamental issues cannot possibly have anything worthwhile to say.)

It should be clear from this discussion that Marx has some very definite ideas both about man's nature or ideal humanity and about man's present dehumanization or the respects in which he falls short of this ideal humanity, as well as on the matter of why this deplorable state of affairs exists and what needs to be done about it. These ideas are spelled out most completely in the first parts of his *Economic and Philosophical Manuscripts* of 1844, which I have discussed elsewhere and therefore shall pass over here.[6] They are also discussed at some length, however, in two of his early essays conventionally entitled *On the Jewish Question;* and to these essays (which, unlike the *Manuscripts* of 1844, were actually published by Marx, in 1843) I now shall turn.

IV

The basic issue in these essays, written in response to Bruno Bauer's treatment of "the Jewish question," is that of "emancipation" or liberation (or, one could also say, freedom). And what Marx says in them (and in particular, in the first of them) is of the greatest contemporary relevance. One need only substitute, for example, "Black," or "woman," for "Jew" in many of the things he says to realize this; for what he has to say applies to any situation in which a certain segment of the population in some modern Western society is denied equal participation in that society with the other members of it. The demand for "Jewish emancipation" in Marx's time, like those for "Black liberation" and "women's liberation," etc., today, was commonly intended by those advancing it as a demand for the treatment of Jews on a par with non-Jews, as opposed to their being kept in a position of inferiority or "second-class citizenship." And Marx feels that crusades of this sort are of questionable significance if no one has bothered to consider the desirability of that equality of treatment sought by and for the "second-class citizens," whoever they may be. He in effect asks: Under the conditions prevailing in modern societies, is *first*-class citizenship really such a desirable thing? Does it really profit one so much to achieve first-class citizenship if first-class citizens are really just as dehumanized and just as far from achieving truly human self-realization as second-class citizens? Indeed, what if first-class citizenship, in modern society, is even more thoroughly dehumanizing than anything else?

In short, in any call for emancipation or liberation, Marx suggests, it is essential to ask not merely "Who should be emancipated?" but "*What kind of emancipation* is involved?" (p. 7). For it frequently turns out that the kind of emancipation sought is "political emancipation," in a broad sense of the term. And it is a great mistake, in Marx's view, to "confuse political emancipation and universal human emancipation" (p. 8); for he suggests that, to put it mildly, in modern society "political emancipation is not the final and absolute form of *human* emancipation" (p. 10). On the contrary, although he allows that "political emancipation" may have to precede "human emancipation," he suggests that it prepares the way for "human emancipation" not by approaching it in a qualitative sense, but rather by leading to a condition of such widespread human misery and degradation that at last a revolution which will alter the very nature of modern society—and which alone can bring about true "human emancipation"—becomes a real possibility.

"Political emancipation" actually paves the way for the most intensive and exploitative form of capitalism, by removing all traditional obstacles to the treatment of men as mere means. Consequently, "political emancipation" in modern society means admission into the arena of "civil society," in which it is every man for himself, in a war of all against all. And since in "civil society" most men are in fact *slaves*—slaves of their employers, of money, of the market and the stock exchange, of the conditions produced by the economic laws that govern capitalistic economy—their so-called "emancipation" turns out merely to be the substitution of one sort of dehumanizing subjugation for another and worse sort. As the inequalities of feudal society gave way to the equality of "liberal democracy," men indeed "emancipated" themselves—out of the frying pan and into the fire.

Marx feels that the state of affairs which had prevailed in feudal societies had certain definite advantages, compared with the state of affairs prevailing in modern societies which have reached the level of "political democracy" or "civil society." Of course, most men then were certainly not free but rather were subject to the will of their lords and overlords, and so their self-realization as truly human beings was impossible. Yet they were united by bonds stronger than those which divided them socially, at least to the point that people in the same social classes felt a strong sense of solidarity and community, and that members of the upper classes more often than not felt a paternalistic but still very real obligation to care for the well-being of those whose lives they controlled. In civil society, on the other hand, all of these earlier "species-bonds" (as Marx terms them) have been lost. The individual has become a kind of "monad"; no one looks out for him, and he looks out for no one but himself. Interpersonal relations have become largely impersonal; and relations between members of the same social classes have become relations of competition and antagonism, while relations of members of the upper classes to the lower have become completely exploitative. Since everyone is theoretically equal, no one is encouraged to feel responsible for anyone else. Because each person's obligations to others are spelled out by law, but involve nothing further than refraining from certain sorts of extreme acts like direct physical violence and robbery, the notion has come to prevail that anything *not* explicitly forbidden by law in interpersonal relations is permitted. Thus Marx says: "The bonds which had restrained the egoistic spirit . . . were removed along with the political yoke. . . . Feudal society was dissolved into its basic element, *man;* but into *egoistic* man who was its real foundation" (p. 29).

In short, the "political emancipation" associated with full citizenship in modern society—which is "civil society" or capitalistic society—*has* made possible a kind of self-realization; but it has been the realization of what is *worst* in man, because it has removed most restraints upon men's egoistic tendencies. It has done nothing by way of transforming the men themselves from basically selfish to genuinely social beings, while at the same time it has permitted the flourishing of a form of economic organization which has the effect of both encouraging men and compelling them on pain of misery to act exploitatively and selfishly. "The right of property," Marx says,

[is] the right to enjoy one's fortune and to dispose of it as one will; without regard for other men and independently of society. It is the right of self-

interest. This individual liberty, and its application, form the basis of civil society. It leads every man to see in other men, not the *realization,* but the *limitation* of his own liberty. (p. 25)

None of the supposed rights of man [acknowledged by political democracies] go beyond the egoistic man, man as a member of civil society; that is, an individual separated from community, withdrawn into himself, wholly preoccupied with his private interest and acting in accordance with his private caprice. Man is far from being considered, in the rights of man, as a "species-being" [i.e., social being]; on the contrary..., society appears as a system which is external to the individual and a limitation of his original independence. The only bond between men is natural necessity, need and private interest, the preservation of their property and their egoistic persons. (p. 26)

Marx holds that men's institutions both reflect their existing desires and inclinations and also serve to further shape and condition them. The political revolution that led to the fall of feudal society and the rise of civil society was motivated by men's desire to be free from the arbitrary, irrational rule of those in power in feudal society, in order to be able to do as they wished. They therefore pared the institutions of the state down to a minimum, retaining or establishing only those which they felt were necessary in order to protect their ability to do as they wished with what they considered theirs. But this revolution undermined all bonds among men except those associated with property rights, and made it legitimate legally to treat other men as mere means to their own personal ends. In effect, the result of the alteration of their institutions was that they themselves came more and more to be creatures of those institutions which emerged from this process, caring above all for the focal point of these institutions—property—and allowing themselves to do everything the law permitted to accumulate it.

Of course, men had not really been *true* species-beings previously; for their bonds with one another had been based, not on a mutual recognition of one another's humanity, but rather on natural feelings, illusory religious ideas (such as that of the equality and brotherhood of all men before God), and equally specious nationalistic or racial myths. But they had at least been united by "species-bonds" of a sort. In "civil society," on the other hand, even though people may continue to pay lip service to them, these "species-bonds" have ceased to have any real force in everyday life. Whatever people may profess, they in fact are for the most part selfish and egoistic, and a member of civil society is even further than a member of feudal society from being what Marx terms "a real species-being" (p. 20).

It distresses Marx very much, as he reflects upon the French and American constitutions, that the political liberators reduce citizenship, the *political community,* to a mere *means* for preserving those so-called rights of man; and consequently . . . , the citizen is declared to be the servant of egoistic "man" . . . , the sphere in which man functions as a species-being is degraded to a level below the sphere where he functions as a partial being, and finally . . . it is man as a bourgeois and not man as a citizen who is considered the *true* and *authentic* man. (p. 26)

It is interesting to observe, however, that Hegel would object to this just as strenuously as Marx does. The chief difference between them on this point is that, while Hegel thought that modern societies in his time already had left mere civil society behind them in favor of a form of society in which "universality" and social solidarity would predominate and keep self-interest within modest limits, Marx contemplates the most modern of (mid-nineteenth-century) societies and concludes that they in fact represent an extreme form of mere "civil society." It seems to Marx that far from being already superseded in Hegel's time, "civil society" was then only beginning to build up a good head of steam. And in his view, it is going to take a revolution of major proportions, rather than a mere period of peaceful evolutionary development, to bring about any fundamental change in the situation. Hegel, he suggests, had been deluded on the matter of the nature of modern societies by mistaking what in fact were the dying remnants of feudal bonds in reactionary Germany—which had not even reached the stage of full-blown "civil society" when Hegel lived and wrote—for the genuinely social bonds of post-"civil" society. At least at the time of his essays *On the Jewish Question,* however, Marx does not differ very radically from Hegel in his characterization of the general sort of social end result to be desired, namely, one in which man would be "a real species-being." At the end of the first of these essays he says:

Human emancipation will only be complete when the real, individual man has absorbed himself into the abstract citizen; when as an individual man, in his everyday life, in his work, and in his relationships, he has become a *species-being;* and when he has recognized and organized his own powers . . . as *social* powers so that he no longer separates this social power from himself as *political* power. (p. 31)

Hegel undoubtedly would have expressed complete agreement with this statement—and would have hastened to add that he himself had already said essentially the same thing. All one need do is substitute the term "universal" for Marx's expression "a species-being," and the passage could easily be taken to come from Hegel himself. Marx's contention that "man is essentially a species-being" in this context is little more than a naturalized version of Hegel's contention that "spirit is essentially universal." What Marx seems to feel is at issue between himself and Hegel here is not so much a matter of the general goal to be reached; rather, it is primarily a matter of whether we have reached it yet, and of what it is going to take in order for us to reach it.

The same sort of point may be made in connection with what Marx has to say about freedom in relation to Hegel's position concerning it,[7] given that "emancipation" and "freedom" may be treated as roughly synonymous. In his essays *On the Jewish Question,* Marx is a vigorous advocate of "emancipation" or "freedom." Yet he denies that "political emancipation" and consequent membership in modern society result in the attainment of genuine freedom. Hegel would *seem* to take precisely the opposite position, for he holds that genuine freedom is to be found precisely in the broadly political context of membership in the modern state. But Hegel does *not* think that genuine freedom is to be conceived in terms of the sort of "liberty" which Marx discusses in relation to property; and he does *not* think that man qua member of civil society is truly free at all. On the contrary, he contends that man as a member of modern society (or as a citizen of a modern state) is truly free *only* because modern society has gone *beyond* the stage of "civil society" and has reached the stage of genuine "universality." And Marx's position here is virtually the same if Hegel's insistence upon the rational character of universality and the role of social institutions in achieving it is set aside; for Marx too argues that "human emancipation" will occur, and genuine freedom will be achieved, only when modern society goes beyond the stage of civil society, to the stage of genuine "species-life," in which man's egoism is tamed, his powers become "social powers," and he becomes first and foremost a "citizen" or unselfish participant in the life of the community.

In this light, it would thus appear that there is much less difference between them on this matter than is commonly supposed. They agree on the desirability and importance of "human emancipation" or "freedom," on the fact that it is to be conceived in terms of genuine self-determination and not merely in terms of license to act upon egoistic impulses, and also on the point that such self-determination has a strong "social" component and indispensable societal preconditions which are not met in "civil society." The main matters over which Marx takes issue with Hegel are those of whether these societal preconditions actually have been met and what sort of developmental process (starting from the existence of civil society) is required to meet them.

There is one fundamental difference of principle between them, however, which does not clearly emerge in these early essays but becomes increasingly important in Marx's subsequent writings. I have already mentioned it in passing, but it merits further comment since it importantly affects Hegel's and Marx's conceptions of the sort of society that is ultimately to be desired. Whereas the central category of Hegel's anthropology (indeed, of his metaphysics generally)—and therefore also of his ethical, social, and political philosophy—is rationality, the central category of Marx's anthropology (and so of his philosophy generally) is "praxis," where this is understood in the sense of conscious practical activity.

Rationality is essentially impersonal in nature; and its attainment involves subjecting oneself to the constraints of "universal"—or, at any rate, general—principles, laws, and institutions. Praxis, on the other hand, as Marx conceives of it, is always activity on the part of particular individuals, even if such activity is socially conditioned and the individuals (properly or improperly) socialized; and thus it is essentially personal (as well as generally social) in nature. Marx envisions a society organized in such a way that men are enabled and encouraged to live lives of self-directed praxis in community with one another, and thus come to be genuine *social individuals;* and this entails the minimization of the role of impersonal social laws and institutions. Hegel, on the other hand, argues for an extension of the dominion of such laws and institutions, as a means of rendering human activity more fully rational, with the result that men will emerge as genuinely "universal" beings.

In short, both Hegel and Marx conceive of freedom in terms of self-conscious self-determination, and both agree that "civil society" must be transcended if such freedom is to be realized. Because Hegel places a premium upon rationality, however, he concludes that the realization of freedom requires the further institutionalization of society (i.e., beyond the point to which it is already institutionalized at the level of "civil society"). Marx on the other hand, because of the premium he places upon (social) individuality achieved through self-directed praxis, concludes that freedom requires a kind of *de*institutionalization of society. Both look to the emergence of men as genuine "citizens," as opposed to egoistic, exploitative, self-centered "monads." But Marx's ideal "citizens" are simply social individuals, whose sociality is not mediated by conformity to sociocultural institutions, whereas Hegel's are first and foremost members of a sociocultural order, whose lives have the character of "universality" (rather than simple sociality), achieved through participation in such institutions.

Thus the "state" for Hegel is of vital and lasting importance, while for Marx it is merely an instrument of coercion, which ultimately can and should be dispensed with—or, as it was later to be put, will eventually "wither away." This fundamental difference between him and Hegel remains largely beneath the surface in the early essays presently under consideration; but it is there, even if only in germ, and cannot be ignored if his relation to Hegel and the distinctive character of the position he develops are to be properly understood.

V

Finally, a word about Marx's second essay *On the Jewish Question.* It is easy to be put off by the appearance of anti-Semitism on the part of Marx in this essay; but while the language in which he couches what has to say is extremely unfortunate, the actual point he is making really has nothing to do with anti-Semitic racism (as a moment's reflection on his own Jewish origins ought to suggest[8]). He is highly critical of "the Jew," but what he really is opposed to is *egoism.* Like generations of Europeans before him, however (including many others of Jewish extraction), and like many people today, he accepts the cliché that Jews as a sociocultural group are the very embodiment of egoism in their practical affairs; and so he attacks them rather than the disposition in question, even though it is the latter, rather than the former as a portion of the human race, that is his actual target. And one need not endorse his practice, or even forgive him completely for engaging in it, to see what he is driving at and to appreciate his point, which has nothing to do with any racial or ethnic group as such.

Marx seems not really to have thought the matter through very carefully; for, on the one hand, he speaks of the Jews as responsible for the egoism which prevails in modern societies or "civil society"; and, on the other hand, he says, "It is from its own entrails that civil society ceaselessly engenders the Jew" (p. 36). He does have a point worth considering seriously, however; for the central claim he is concerned to advance in this essay is that it is the socioeconomic organization of "civil society" that is responsible for egoism and selfishness and the consequences in terms of misery and dehumanization which follow in their train, and that therefore egoism and selfishness can be eliminated, and with them the misery and dehumanization to which they give rise, only by altering the conditions which prevail in civil society. This becomes clear as soon as one substitutes the term "egoist" for "Jew" and "egoism" for "Judaism," in passages like the following:

An organization of society which would abolish the preconditions and thus the very possibility of huckstering, would make the [egoist] impossible . . . . On the other hand, when the [egoist] recognizes his *practical* nature as invalid and endeavours to abolish it, he . . . works for general *human emancipation* and turns against the supreme practical expression of human self-aliena- tion [i.e., the economic exploitation of others]. (p. 34)

As soon as society succeeds in abolishing the *empirical* essence of [ego-ism]—huckstering and its conditions [i.e., the institution of private prop-erty]—the [egoist] becomes *impossible,* because his consciousness no longer has a [possible] object. The subjective basis of [egoism]—practical need—assumes a human form, and the conflict between the individual, sensuous existence of man and his species-existence, is abolished. (p. 40)

In short, Marx's contention is that it is necessary to change the prevailing organization of civil society in order to make possible true human emancipa-tion, the overcoming of man's alienation, and genuine human self-realization; and that if the right changes are made, these ends can and will be achieved. However greatly Marx may later have modified his terminology and even though his "mature" writings differ greatly in nature and tone from these early essays, he never lost this faith. And I would suggest that nothing less than this vision of a new and better form of human existence, to be made possible by a fundamental reorganization of society, animates the whole of his subsequent activity, from writing *Das Kapital* to organizaing the Commu-nist party and calling and working for world revolution.

It is interesting, in this connection, and in conclusion, to take note of a passage from Rousseau which Marx cites near the end of the first essay *On the Jewish Question:*

Whoever dares undertake to establish a people's institutions must feel himself capable of changing, as it were, *human nature* itself, of transforming each individual who, in isolation, is a complete but solitary whole, into a *part* of something greater than himself, from which in a sense, he derives his life and his being. (p. 30)

This theme in Rousseau greatly influenced Hegel, in his discussion of the relation of the individual to society in the *Phenomenology of Spirit.* Neither Hegel nor Marx undertook "to establish a people's institutions"; but they both appreciated Rousseau's suggestion of the role of such institutions in shaping human nature as it is concretely manifested at various times and places, and therefore saw such institutions as the key to the transformation of human life, to the extent that it falls short of true humanity. They differed in their conceptions of what true humanity involves and consequently in the value they assigned to various social institutions; and from these general differences, many others of a more specific nature followed. Yet the fact that Marx, like Hegel, took this theme as his point of departure would seem to say a good deal about the nature of his ultimate concerns and basic orientation.

PART III

<hr>

Individuality, Life, and Truth:
Shaken Foundations and New Directions

6:

Kierkegaard on "Truth Is Subjectivity" and "The Leap of Faith"

Kierkegaard's standing as a philosopher and the philosophical significance of his writings are the subjects of disagreement at least as great as
that which one encounters in the case of Marx. He is primarily a
religious thinker, whose philosophical concerns are subordinated to and
dictated by his Christian convictions, and whose philosophical efforts
are motivated by his desire both to lead his readers to an apprehension
of the poverty of life without faith and to induce them to embrace
Christianity as he understands it. This circumstance has led many
philosophers to conclude that, while Kierkegaard may warrant serious
consideration in theological circles and by the religiously inclined, he
need not—and indeed cannot—be regarded as a philosopher to be
reckoned with by other philosophers as such.

This conclusion, however, is questionable, not only because of
Kierkegaard's influence upon a number of important philosophical
developments in the present century, but also because his challenge to
the views of other philosophers (Hegel in particular), is philosophical as
well as religious. It involves an attempt to meet these philosophers on
their own ground in their treatment of a variety of issues, rather than a
mere retreat into a redoubt of rationally inaccessible dogma. Kierkegaard's "leap of faith" may carry him beyond the bounds of philosophical intelligibility; but even when it does, he endeavors to set the stage
for this move through a number of critical analyses and substantive
inquiries intended to be not only comprehensible but also compelling
to philosophical readers. Further, his conception of truly human existence in terms of "subjectivity" may owe more than a little of its
inspiration to his religious beliefs, but it is set forth in language and
with arguments intended to persuade philosophers unwilling to presuppose the validity of any tenet of Christianity. It also constitutes a

genuinely philosophical analysis that is both original and quite interesting in its own right, Kierkegaard's use of it for his broader, extraphilosophical purposes notwithstanding.

Kierkegaard's confrontation with Hegel is in many respects much more violent than Marx's. Whereas Marx holds Hegel in the highest esteem despite his rejection of most of Hegel's views and conclusions, Kierkegaard views him with contempt and ridicules him mercilessly (and often, it might be added, quite unfairly). He frequently borrows Hegelian terminology, as will be seen in both this chapter and the next; but he does so largely in order to be able to dispute the substantive claims of Hegelians in language they would find comprehensible. Hegel's demythologization of the God of Christianity, his reduction of religion to the status of a mere forerunner of philosophy which the philosophically sophisticated can do quite nicely without, and his analysis of human nature in terms of categories pertaining primarily to objective and impersonal qualities and activities move Kierkegaard alternately to rage and to scorn. He has many other, more specific disagreements with Hegel; but he considers these to be the matters about which Hegelianism is most profoundly and importantly mistaken—the nature of God, the nature of religious faith, and the nature of man. And were Kierkegaard to return today and contemplate the ways in which philosophers since his death have dealt with these matters, he undoubtedly would contend that most of them—in this respect, at least—have differed little from Hegel, erring as grievously as he does and along much the same lines.

Philosophy, in Kierkegaard's view, is no substitute for faith, and can accomplish neither the achievement of one's essential humanity nor the attainment of an adequate understanding of and satisfactory relationship with God. It can, however, perform a valuable function in connection with these vital tasks, by combatting misunderstandings in these areas arising from the tendency of philosophers preoccupied with knowledge and the objective to fall into certain sorts of confusions and errors, and by directing one's thinking about the issues involved along more appropriate lines. The present chapter is concerned with certain of Kierkegaard's more important efforts to do this, and thus both indicates something of the nature of the positions he seeks to advance and constitutes a kind of case study of one of the main forms of philosophical inquiry he engages in. It is not his only mode of inquiry, however, as shall be seen in chapter 7.

One of the things for which Kierkegaard is both best known to English and American philosophers and most criticized by them is his contention that "truth is subjectivity." His discussion of "truth" and "subjectivity" occupies a considerable part of his most important philosophical work *Concluding Unscientific Postscript,* and his contention that "truth is subjectivity" is the pivotal claim around which virtually the entire work revolves. Yet few of Kierkegaard's assertions have been more frequently misunderstood, and a misinterpretation of this claim has led many philosophers wrongly to dismiss him as unworthy of serious consideration.

He is sometimes taken to be saying that "subjectivity" is the criterion of "truth" *in general,* at least where human beings are concerned—in short, that propositions uttered by human beings are true if and only if those who utter them passionately affirm or believe them. He also is sometimes interpreted as saying that "subjectivity" is the criterion of a certain *kind* of "truth" and the necessary and sufficient condition of the attainment of a certain kind of *knowledge* ("subjective knowledge"). As I read the supporting discussion in which his assertion that "truth is subjectivity" occurs, however, neither of these interpretations is correct. It is my contention that his claim is a claim of a different sort, and does not bear at all upon the issue of the conditions under which "truth," in the sense of some sort of knowledge, may be attained. His question, at least for the purpose of understanding his point, is: What does it mean to exist as a human being? And his contention that "truth is subjectivity" occurs in the course of his attempt to answer this question. His concern is with something quite different from knowledge—either in general or of some special sort—and the conditions of its attainment; but the common tendency to think of "knowledge" when the word "truth" is used leads those astray who do not resist it here. Few modern interpreters of Kierkegaard have been able to resist it, and as a consequence few of them properly understand what Kierkegaard means by "truth" when he asserts that "truth is subjectivity."

On the other hand, it is not my intention to deny that Kierkegaard anywhere either sets forth a notion of "subjective knowledge" or maintains the essential "subjectivity" of all (human) knowledge. That he is committed to such a notion and/or doctrine may or may not be the case, and whether sense can or cannot be made of either or both is yet another question. Neither issue, however, is of concern to me here. The claim I wish to advance—to repeat it once more—is only that *in asserting and arguing that "truth is subjectivity,"* Kierkegaard is committing himself to no such notion, but rather is addressing himself to a different *sort* of issue altogether.

In what follows I shall indicate what Kierkegaard in fact means when he makes this contention and, more generally, what he means when he speaks of "truth" in this context. In the course of my discussion, I shall refer extensively to Hegel; for however greatly Kierkegaard may differ from Hegel on substantive issues, his special uses of the term "truth" are basically Hegelian ones. Then, in the last part of the chapter, I shall briefly consider his discussion of the related question: Why make "the leap of faith"?

I should add that I am deliberately begging an important question in Kierkegaard scholarship by imputing views expressed in *Concluding Unscientific Postscript* to Kierkegaard himself. He did publish the work under a pseudonym ("Johannes Climacus"), and he does say (in *A First and Last Declaration*) that "in the pseudonymous works there is not a single word which is mine."[1] One who feels that Kierkegaard should be taken at his word here may feel that I should have entitled this discussion "Johannes Climacus on 'Truth Is Subjectivity' and 'The Leap of Faith,' " and that I should have spoken of "Climacus" rather than of "Kierkegaard" throughout. I have not done so because the views with which I am concerned are more commonly associated with the name "Kierkegaard" than with the name "Johannes Climacus," because I would consider anyone who insisted on using the latter name rather pedantic, because Kierkegaard did in fact develop these views (whether or not they really are his own), and because my concern is to make clear precisely what they are and what is to be made of them, rather than to determine whether or not Kierkegaard himself is actually committed to them. The book in which these views figure so centrally is sufficiently important, and they themselves have been so influential and are of such intrinsic interest, that an examination of them requires no further justification. Even if Kierkegaard scholars all were to conclude that these views should not actually be imputed to him, this would not render an examination of them any less worthwhile.

I

Kierkegaard's great lament in the *Postscript* (and elsewhere) is that his contemporaries have "forgotten what it means to exist" (e.g., p. 223). He feels that they (or at any rate the intellectuals among them) have come to think that man is to be viewed primarily as a *knower* and that his most important capacity is that of attaining knowledge. For the attainment of knowledge, an attitude of objectivity is required; and the cultivation of an attitude of objectivity involves the suppression of personality and the transcendence of individuality. And in the attempt to rise above and leave behind one's individuality and personality, which can be partly if not completely successful, Kierkegaard sees a kind of self-annihilation, to which he objects in the strongest possible terms. Against the tendency to applaud and encourage this development, he argues that men are essentially finite, subjective, particular individuals, rather than unlimited, objective, impersonal knowing minds. He asks:

Is [one] a human being? . . . If he is a human being then he is also an existing individual. Two ways, in general, are open for an existing individual: *Either* he can do his utmost to forget he is an existing individual, by which he becomes a comic figure. . . . *Or* he can concentrate his entire energy upon the fact that he is an existing individual. It is from this side . . . that objection must be made to modern philosophy; not that it has a mistaken presupposition, but that it has a comical presupposition, occasioned by its having forgotten, in a sort of world-historical absent-mindedness, what it means to be a human being. Not, indeed, what it means to be a human being in general . . . ; but what it means that you and I and he are human beings, each one for himself. (p. 100)[2]

Kierkegaard is determined to remind us "what it means to be a human being." Of course, he grants that we can be knowers, but "the knower is an existing individual, and . . . the task of existing is his essential task" (p. 185). Existing—in inwardness, as finite, particular individuals—is what he holds to be our "essential task" as human beings. And so, using the term "truth" in one of the ways Hegel does, he says that for a human being "existing, the process of transformation to inwardness in and by existing, is the truth" (p. 184). In other words, a man is in a *state of truth* with reference to his essential nature qua human being (or, he is "truly human") when he is living in such a way that his actual condition corresponds to his essential nature— when he is in actuality as he ought (essentially) to be. Man's essential nature is conceived by Kierkegaard in terms of "existing" in the above sense. "Every man," he says, "is a spiritual being, for whom the truth consists in nothing else than the self-activity of personal appropriation" (p. 217).

Perhaps to stress the extent of his substantive departure from Hegel, for whom objectivity and universality are of paramount importance, Kierkegaard commonly characterizes man's nature in terms of "subjectivity." "The task of becoming subjective," he says, "may be presumed to be the highest task, and one that is proposed to every human being" (p. 146). A man is thus in a state of truth when he is fully subjective. Subjectivity is his "truth," the state he must attain to be true to his essential nature. In a word, for a human being "subjectivity is truth"—a phrase actually employed much more frequently by Kierkegaard than "truth is subjectivity." Stated either way, however, the point is exactly the same. And it is essential to observe that the point is one Kierkegaard is making solely *about human beings,* and about their essential nature *as* human beings, rather than about what it is for a mathematical or scientific or historical proposition to be true. "The reader will observe," he says, "that the question here is about essential truth, or about the truth which is related to existence" (p. 178n). Unfortunately, this is something too few readers *have* observed, in spite of his explicit statement to this effect.

Further, there is, as one might expect, another side to the coin. To the extent that a person exists in some other way, he is not being true to his essential nature; he is "untrue" to it. One may be in a state of truth; but one may also be in a state of "untruth." So Kierkegaard says that one is in "untruth if one refuses to understand that subjectivity is truth but, for example, desires to become objective" (p. 185). "The truth" as Kierkegaard conceives it here—that is, man's true, essential nature—is treated primarily as something to be *actualized.* What is important for Kierkegaard is nót that one should simply come to *know* what one's essential nature qua human being is, but rather that one should *actualize* it by achieving the appropriate inner state. And while thought plays a very considerable role in this process, what is called for is not objective, ratiocinative, impersonal cognition, but rather what Kierkegaard calls "subjective reflection." "The subjective reflection turns its attention inwardly to the subject, and desires in this intensification to realize [i.e., actualize] the truth" (p. 175).

It is important to recognize that Kierkegaard does not conceive of "subjectivity" in terms of "the accidental, the angular, the selfish, the eccentric, and so forth" (p. 117). He realizes that it can be and often is conceived in these terms—and that it was in part because Hegel conceived it in this way that he depreciated its importance. Indeed, far from endorsing *this* sort of subjectivity, Kierkegaard agrees with Hegel that it is to be superseded: "Nor does Christianity deny that such things should be gotten rid of. . . . But the difference is, that philosophy [i.e., Hegel] teaches that the way is to become objective, while Christianity teaches that the way is to become subjective . . . *in truth*" (p. 117)—that is, to become *genuinely* subjective. In short, Kierkegaard contends that an existing human being in point of fact can never become a completely rational, objective, impersonal knower. But he also holds that one can be subjective in a variety of ways, one of which is the unsatisfactory way just mentioned, and that it is only if one achieves the *proper sort* of subjectivity that one is true to one's essential nature. And Kierkegaard conceives this sort of subjectivity, not in terms of selfishness and eccentricity, but rather in terms of an intensified "inwardness," passionate personal committment, and personal decision and responsibility for what one is and does.

This, then, is one sense of "truth" as Kierkegaard uses the term, and one meaning of his assertion that "subjectivity is truth," or "truth is subjectivity." This use of the term "truth," once again, is a basically Hegelian one, which derives in an interesting way from the traditional correspondence theory of truth. In this theory of truth, a thought is true if it corresponds to an actual state of affairs—or, as Hegel puts it, "Truth is supposed to be the agreement of Thought with its object, and in order to bring about this agreement ... thinking must accommodate and adapt itself to its object."[3] While Hegel finds this view of the matter unsatisfactory, he does speak of knowledge as a "harmonious unity" of thought with "its substance," and says that "this identity, when arrived at, is truth."[4] But he contends that in point of fact that which genuine knowledge is knowledge *of* is not anything radically distinct from thought, but rather is identical with the essential structure of thought or reason itself. "In the philosophical sense of the word," therefore, "truth may be described, in general abstract terms, as the agreement of a though-content with itself."[5]

Hegel further holds, however, that it is not really appropriate to speak of "truth" in connection with particular "thought-contents" considered piece-meal, but rather only in connection with "objectivity" as a whole; and that "thought" here should properly be construed, not in terms of what some particular person is thinking, but rather in terms of the essential structure of reason—the "Concept" or "Notion" (*Begriff*). So he says, "Truth in the deeper sense consists in the identity between objectivity and the *Begriff*," or in "the correspondence of objectivity with the *Begriff*," rather than merely in "the correspondence of external things with my conceptions."[6]

Having modified the concept of "truth" in such a way that it refers to the correspondence of "objectivity" and "*Begriff*," Hegel proceeds to refer to objects as "true" or "untrue" depending on whether they do or do not adequately realize their *Begriff* or essence. He says: "It is in this deeper sense of truth that we speak of a true state, or of a true work of art. These objects are true, if they are as they ought to be, i.e., if their reality corresponds to their *Begriff*."[7] So, for example, in the *Philosophy of Right,* speaking of the will, he says that when it is "related to nothing except itself, [it] is then true ... , because its self-determination consists in a correspondence between what it is in its existence ... and its *Begriff*."[8] On the other hand, he states, "in this sense ... untruth may be said to consist in the contradiction subsisting between the function or *Begriff* and the existence of the object."[9] So, for example, he suggests that a man "is an untrue man" if he "does not behave as his *Begriff* or his vocation requires."[10] In short, for Hegel, if (and only if) one's actual spiritual state corresponds to his essential nature, one is in a state of "truth." And with this, Kierkegaard—following Hegel's usage—agrees.

This is an abstract formula, however, which Hegel and Kierkegaard fill in quite differently. Hegel construes man's essential nature above all in terms of "universality"—and, consequently, in terms of objectivity. For him, there-fore, "truth"—the truth of human existence—is objectivity and universality. Subjectivity, in his view, is not without importance; but it is not the "truth" of man's nature. It is held to refer to "the absolute unity of self-consciousness with itself . . . , the pure certainty, as distinguished from the truth, of individuality."[11] Hegel rejects "that way of looking at the matter . . . according to which what is fundamental, substantive, and primary is supposed to be the will of a single person in his own private self-will, not the absolute or rational will, and spirit [*Geist*] as a particular individual, not spirit as it is in its truth."[12]

For Kierkegaard, on the other hand, the "truth" of human existence is to be conceived precisely in terms of particularity, subjectivity, and inwardness. To attempt to achieve Hegelian universality and objectivity is, in his view, both folly and oversight; for it is both to attempt the impossible and to fail to grasp that "to be a particular individual . . . is the only true and highest significance of a human being" (p. 134). Kierkegaard and Hegel thus differ radically with regard to what the "truth" of human existence is. But they both use the term "truth" in the same basic sense in speaking of it.

II

This is not, however, the only special sense in which they both use the term. Each also uses it in two other special senses. Here, too, Kierkegaard's uses of the term may best be understood in relation to Hegel's. First, Hegel uses the term to refer to "the absolute." In the famous passage in the Preface to the *Phenomenology of Spirit* in which he contends that the absolute must be conceived both as substance and as subject, what he actually says is that "everything depends on grasping and expressing the true not [merely] as substance but as subject as well."[13] When, in place of "the absolute," he introduces the somewhat more explicit expression "the Idea," he likewise asserts, "The Idea is the truth."[14] The content of "the Idea" is the "system of pure reason" or *Begriff* proper, in its totality, which is the essential structure of reality generally; and "absolute knowledge," or knowledge of the nature of the *Begriff*, is for Hegel a knowledge of "the truth," which is absolute, ultimate, and eternal. "Logic," he says, is "to be understood as the System of Pure Reason, as the Realm of Pure Thought. *This realm is the Truth as it is, without husk in and for itself.*"[15] In short, the term "truth" is used by Hegel to refer to that which he regards as the ultimate reality (hence, "the absolute").

Kierkegaard also refers to the ultimate reality, as he conceives it, as "the truth," only that which *he* takes to be the ultimate reality is not Hegel's "system of reason" (in connection with which the term "truth" has an obvious application). Rather, it is the God of Christianity. In this context too, therefore, while the term "truth" has the same basic sense for him as it does for Hegel, Kierkegaard gives it a different application. He refers, for example, to the fact "that the eternal truth has come into being in time, that God has come into being [in time]" (p. 188). He speaks of the God relationship as a relationship in which "the eternal truth is related to an existing individual" (p. 180). And he again uses the expression "the eternal truth" interchangeably with "God" when he introduces the notion of the "paradox," saying: "By virtue of the relationship subsisting between the eternal truth and the existing individual, the paradox came into being. . . . The eternal truth has come into being in time: this is the paradox" (p. 187).

Of course, Hegel too identifies "the truth" (which in this sense he likewise considers "eternal") with "God." In both religion and philosophy, he says, "the object is Truth, in that supreme sense in which God and only God is the Truth."[16] And, after having asserted that the "system of pure reason" is "the Truth as it is, without husk in and for itself," he says that one could also put the matter in this way: "This content *shows forth God as he is in his eternal essence before the creation of Nature and of a Finite Spirit.*"[17] But Hegel can speak of "God," as well as of the *Begriff,* as "the truth," only because he identifies the two—an identification which involves a denial of something Kierkegaard emphatically asserts: God's radical transcendence of the world. Both speak of the ultimate reality as "the truth," but they differ about how the ultimate reality is to be conceived.

Secondly, it has been observed that, while Hegel modifies the traditional construal of "truth" as "the correspondence of external things with my conceptions," he does speak of it as the "harmonious unity" or "identity" of thought with "its substance."[18] For him, therefore, the thinking subject may be said to be "in the truth" to the extent that his thought is in a relation of "unity" or "identity" with that which is the proper content or "substance" of knowledge. In his view, however, the proper content or "substance" of knowledge is the "system of pure reason," which comes to light through the discipline of Hegelian logic. "Now though when one begins to study it," he says, "Logic is not present to the mind in all this recognized power, yet none the less the mind of the student conceives from it a power which will lead him into all truth."[19] He rejects the view that "truth exists merely in what . . . is called at one time intuition, at another immediate knowledge of the Absolute," and contends rather that "truth finds the medium of its existence in *Begriffe* [or Concepts] alone."[20]

Here, therefore, Hegel speaks of "truth" in connection with a relation of "unity" or "identity" with that which is at once the proper content or "substance" of knowledge and also the ultimate reality as he conceives it—namely, the "Idea," and the "system of pure reason" which is its essential content. And this relation of "unity" or "identity" is absolute knowledge, the attainment of which thus involves achieving the highest degree of objectivity and rationality.

Kierkegaard too speaks of one who "exists in the truth" (p. 222). And, like Hegel, he considers it appropriate to say of someone that he is "in the truth" just in the event that he exists in a relation of unity with the ultimate reality, and precisely in virtue of the fact that "a unity of the infinite and the finite" (p. 176) then obtains. But for him, once again, the ultimate reality is not Hegel's *Begriff*, but rather the God of Christianity. And it is his contention that a human being cannot achieve a relation of unity with God through becoming objective and rational, but rather only through a "leap of faith" which is completely nonrational. For an existing human being, he maintains, it is not Hegelian logic which "will lead him into all truth"; and it is not through the attainment of Hegelian absolute knowledge that an existing human being can achieve "unity with the infinite." Rather, one can be "in the truth" only when one is in the state of faith. So Kierkegaard regards "the venture which chooses an objective uncertainty with the passion of the infinite" not only as "faith," but also as "truth" (p. 182).

In short, for Kierkegaard as for Hegel, one who achieves a relation of unity with the ultimate reality may be said to be in a relation of "truth" to it. But whereas for Hegel one may thus be said to be "in the truth" only to the extent that one's thought corresponds to the *Begriff*, for Kierkegaard one is "in the truth" only in the state of faith.

If "truth" is construed in this sense, Kierkegaard may be seen to be making yet another point in asserting that "truth is subjectivity," in addition to that indicated in section I above: namely, that "truth" so conceived (as a relation of unity with the ultimate reality, i.e., God) is not attainable by adopting an objective, rational, cognitive orientation, but rather only by becoming radically subjective. Hegel had said: To attain unity with the ultimate reality, become objective! For it is only through the attainment of absolute knowledge that this unity can be achieved; and absolute knowledge can be attained only by becoming objective. In reply, Kierkegaard says: No—to attain unity with the ultimate reality, you must become subjective! Hegel, he holds, was mistaken both about the nature of the ultimate reality and about the way in which a finite, existing individual can attain unity with it. The ultimate reality is God, and a person can place himself in a relation to this ultimate reality only by suspending his reason and making a "leap of faith." Making a "leap of faith" requires, not objectivity and rationality, but "passion." And passion is something essentially nonrational and subjective. Kierkegaard, as has been observed, accepts the Hegelian notion of "truth" as the "unity of the infinite and finite"; but he holds that for an existing individual "this unity is realized [only] in the moment of passion" (p. 176). because it can be achieved only through a "leap of faith."

In short, Kierkegaard uses the term "truth" in three special senses, all of which are derived from Hegel. They refer (1) to a person's essential nature as a human being, (2) to the relation of unity a person may achieve with the ultimate reality (God), and (3) to this ultimate reality itself. Putting them all together, one might say that, for Kierkegaard, only a person who actualizes his essential "truth" (i.e., who is actually what he is essentially) can achieve a relation of "truth" (i.e., a relation of unity) with the eternal "truth" (i.e., the ultimate reality, God). And Kierkegaard asserts that "truth is subjectivity," or "subjectivity is truth," because he holds that a person actualizes his essential "truth," and can achieve a relation of "truth" to the eternal "truth," only if he becomes genuinely subjective.

III

Why make "the leap of faith"? To make this "leap," for Kierkegaard, is to affirm "that God has existed in human form, has been born, grown up, and so forth" (p. 194). Kierkegaard's advocacy of making "the leap of faith" is the culmination of his analysis of human existence. It has encountered even more resistance among philosophers than his contention that "truth is subjectivity," not because it has been misunderstood, but rather because (as he himself is at pains to point out) the "leap" involves the affirmation of a proposition which not only is rationally unjustifiable but moreover is radically repellent to the rational understanding. This proposition asserts what Kierkegaard takes to be "the absolute paradox," namely, that an infinite and eternal being existed as a particular and finite being. It is paradoxical because of "the absolute difference between God and man," which, he holds, "consists precisely in this, that man is a particular existing being . . . , while God is infinite and eternal" (p. 195). Kierkegaard thus not only grants but even insists upon the irrational nature of this proposition, and acknowledges the fact that its affirmation is not possible without a suspension of rational thought. Even for him, however, rational thought is not something to be lightly abandoned, just as Abraham's "suspension of the ethical," in Kierkegaard's *Fear and Trembling,* is represented as being anything but casual. Why then does Kierkegaard defend and advocate "the leap of faith"?

Man, for Kierkegaard, is a being whose most profound desire is for what he calls an "infinite" or "eternal happiness"—one which is in no way dependent upon external circumstances and which therefore cannot be shaken by the loss of anything finite. But man is also a being the "truth" of whose nature, he contends, is "subjectivity." He further holds that it is only through "the leap of faith" that a being whose "truth" is "subjectivity" can attain "an eternal happiness." The question therefore arises: What is the connection between "becoming subjective," "the leap of faith," and "an eternal happiness"?

It seems to me that two different answers to this question may be distinguished in Kierkegaard's discussion in the *Postscript,* although he himself does not explicitly distinguish between them. One answer presupposes that "an eternal happiness" is possible for a man only if it is possible for him to relate himself to God. A man, however, is a being who exists in time; and it would not be possible for such a being to enter into a "God relationship" if God had not also at some point existed in time. Through "the leap of faith," in which one affirms the proposition that God *did* exist in time, one is able to enter into a "God relationship"; and it thereby becomes possible for him to attain "an eternal happiness."

The proposition that God has existed in time, however, is radically paradoxical. Indeed, to the rational understanding, it is "absurd." If it is to be affirmed, therefore, this can only be done through a "leap of faith." And what is required to make such a "leap" is not the employment of one's reason, but rather "passion"—indeed, because of the radical nature of the paradox involved, "an infinite passion." "Passion" is not something rational and "objective," but rather something intensely "subjective." To make "the leap of faith," therefore, one must "become subjective." It is only by doing so that one can attain the degree of passion necessary to enter into a God relationship and thereby to achieve "an eternal happiness."

Several points may be observed in connection with this line of thought. First, the conclusion conforms closely to the position expressed in the statement that, for Kierkegaard, only a person who is in a state of "truth" can be in a relation of "truth" with the eternal "truth." Secondly, while this line of thought does constitute a break with the tradition of rational theology, it suggests that Kierkegaard occupies a position well within the bounds of the Pauline-Augustinian-Lutheran tradition. Indeed, if he had had nothing more to say than this, he could hardly be credited with any significant degree of originality. And the fact that he frequently asserts that he really is not saying anything new about Christianity, but rather is simply attempting to restore it in its true and original form, is an indication of the prominence of this line of thought in his own mind.

Thirdly, it should be noted that if this line is taken, passion and subjectivity have no *intrinsic* significance and are not valued for their own sake. Rather, they are *means* to the attainment of something else—means dictated by man's nature, through which alone a human being is capable of entering into a God relationship and thereby achieving the "eternal happiness" which (it is here suggested) the God relationship alone can make possible. If men were beings of a different sort—beings, for example, who could enter into a God relationship through the intensive development and employment of reason—then passion and subjectivity could be dispensed with. And if men were beings who could enter into this relationship *only* through the use of reason, then it would follow that passion and subjectivity *must* be eliminated if the goal of "an eternal happiness" is to be achieved.[21] Kierkegaard, of course, maintains that men are not beings of this sort, but rather are beings who can enter into a God relationship only through a passionate "leap of faith." The point, however, is that according to this line of reasoning the fact that human beings are essentially subjective only serves to indicate what a person must do to enter into such a relationship.

At other times, however, Kierkegaard would appear to reason along other lines. Here the importance of "the leap of faith" is suggested to lie, not in the God relationship which it alone makes possible, but rather in the intensification of passion which it requires and in the heightened and purified subjectivity to which it thereby gives rise. A man, for Kierkegaard, is a being the "truth" of whose nature is "subjectivity." The more intensely subjective one is, therefore, the more profound and complete is one's realization of one's essential nature. And, Kierkegaard says, "correspondingly, the highest reward, an eternal happiness, exists only for those who are subjective; or rather, comes into being for the individual who becomes subjective" (p. 146). This seems to suggest that the "eternal happiness" man seeks is attained just when one realizes one's essential subjectivity completely, and is a function of the attainment of a state of radical subjectivity as such.

Here the *content* of "the absolute paradox" which is affirmed in "the leap of faith" is a matter of relative indifference—as is, for that matter, the attainment of a God relationship. What counts is the fact that the paradox one affirms is "absolute"—that it is the greatest paradox imaginable. The function of the paradox here is to stimulate the individual to reach the greatest possible state of passion; for since Kierkegaard holds subjectivity to be a function of passion and passion to be "the highest expression of subjectivity" (p. 178), he further holds that the height of subjectivity is achieved precisely through the attainment of the height of passion. So he says, "Passion is the culmination of existence for an existing [i.e., essentially subjective] individual" (p. 176).

In this context, therefore, Kierkegaard's argument for making "the leap of faith" runs something like this. The task of the individual, determined by his essential nature as a human being, is that of intensifying and purifying his subjectivity. If this task is to be accomplished, he must attain a spiritual state of "infinite passion." But, according to Kierkegaard, "Faith is the highest passion in the sphere of human subjectivity" (p. 118). And, since he further holds that "without risk there is no faith" (p. 182), and that indeed the possiblity of faith is directly proportional to "objective uncertainty," it follows that the greater the objective uncertainty of that which one believes, the greater the faith must be on the part of the one who believes it. The greatest degree of objective uncertainty, however, is that which is associated with the paradoxical. There is, therefore, no greater stimulus to passion than paradox, since it is through passion alone that the paradoxical can be deliberately affirmed. The greatest conceivable paradox thus would provide the greatest possible stimulus to passion.

But, Kierkegaard contends, the greatest conceivable paradox is the central thesis of Christianity—namely, that God became a man. Nothing, therefore, is better suited to the intensification of subjectivity than Christianity. If one can achieve the "infinite passion" necessary to affirm this central thesis of Christianity, thereby making "the leap of faith," one will have effected the greatest possible intensification of one's subjectivity, and so will have accomplished one's essential task. So Kierkegaard says, "Subjectivity culminates in passion, Christianity is the [absolute] paradox, paradox and passion are a mutual fit" (p. 206). Hence "the necessity of the paradox" (p. 191) for the intensification of subjectivity and thereby for the attainment of "an eternal happiness."

Kierkegaard regards this as a kind of argument for Christianity deriving solely from considerations pertaining to man's nature as an essentially subjective being and to the connection between subjectivity, passion, and paradox. To argue in this manner, however, is to depart quite radically from traditional Christian theology; for as has been observed, this approach stresses the *form* of the central thesis of Christianity, rather than its content. Given the way the argument is structured, it is only in virtue of the fact—or what Kierkegaard takes to be the fact—that the central thesis of Christianity constitutes the greatest paradox imaginable that "the leap of faith" and Christian belief are indicated. If some greater paradox were to be conceivable, however, then some greater stimulus to passion and to the intensification of subjectivity would exist, and something other than Christian belief would be indicated.

And, in point of fact, greater paradoxes *would* appear to be conceivable, even within the context of Kierkegaard's own discussion. He says, "That God has existed in human form, has been born, grown up, and so forth, is surely the . . . absolute paradox" (p. 194). But it would seem even more "paradoxical," given his views, to claim that this happened and further that God grew up to be a speculative philosopher who forgot completely that he was an existing, essentially subjective individual—in short, that Hegel, not Jesus, was God. Or that God grew up to be a Nazi and was responsible for the deaths of millions of Jews—in short, that Hitler, not Jesus, was God.[22] Or, even more absurdly, that God has existed, not in human form, but rather as a worm, or a bicycle, or a stone.

If all that counts is the paradoxicality of the claim, then any of these claims surely would do better than the Christian one. For if it is paradoxical to claim that a being which is *a, b, c, d,* and *e* has existed as a being which was $-a$ and $-b$, it surely would be still more paradoxical to claim that it has existed as a being which was $-a$, $-b$, $-c$, $-d$, and $-e$. If God is the being in question, the truly absolute paradox would seem to be the claim that God has existed as a being whose properties included the opposites or negations of every one of God's purported properties. And, after all, the God of Christianity supposedly is not only infinite and eternal (the attributes Kierkegaard mentions) but also omniscient, omnipotent, and supremely good. And surely there are (and have been) numerous entities which fall at least as short of being infinite and eternal as Jesus did, and which moreover are much less powerful, knowing, and good than he was, or which indeed are utterly devoid of power, knowledge, and goodness, as he most certainly was not. In contending that the central thesis of Christianity is "the absolute paradox," therefore, Kierkegaard displays a rather uncharacteristic lack of imagination.

Kierkegaard may be correct in suggesting that a certain sort of subjectivity is possible only through the heightening of passion, that "paradox and passion are a mutual fit," and that therefore the greater the paradox one can muster the passion to affirm, the more complete one's subjectivity of this sort will be. His contention that this sort of subjectivity is *desirable,* however, and that it constitutes the fullest possible realization of man's essential nature, is questionable, to say the least. Kierkegaard may be right in claiming that the attainment of a state of complete objectivity and rationality is neither possible nor desirable for an existing human being, but one can accept this point without going as far as he does in the opposite direction. It may also be true that it is not possible for an existing human being to achieve "an eternal happiness" in this life unless something seemingly paradoxical is true—or at least is accepted as true—through a "leap of faith": namely, that God has existed as a man. But this would indicate only the necessity of affirming a particular paradoxical proposition if this end is to be attained, and not the desirability of affirming the greatest paradox imaginable, simply because it *is* the greatest paradox imaginable.

This does not of itself constitute a criticism of the substance of Kierkegaard's contention that a man is a being whose "truth" is "subjectivity." It may be possible to fill in the notion of "subjectivity" more satisfactorily, in a way which does not give so prominent a position to "passion" and "paradox" in the process of "becoming subjective." Yet the fact that they do come to have such a position in the course of Kierkegaard's discussion suggests that his conception of man's nature suffers from a one-sidedness that is no less unfortunate—and indeed is a good deal more dangerous—than Hegel's.[23] His radical protest against Hegel's overly objectivized and rationalized conception of man's nature may have been needed, or at least useful, as a corrective; but a more balanced view of man's nature than either of theirs may be required if it is to constitute an adequate analysis of what it is to be genuinely and fully *human*. In his fascination with the paradoxical, Kierkegaard would seem to have done, in a different way, the very thing he accuses Hegel of doing: he would seem to have lost sight of what it means to exist as a truly human being.

7:

Kierkegaard's Phenomenology of Spiritual Development

Kierkegaard may have a highly specific and rather narrow conception of what it means to exist as a human being, where this is understood to refer to the sort of thing that *genuinely* human existence involves; but he is by no means blind either to the possibility of living other than along these lines or to the variety of alternative ways in which people may live their lives. On the contrary, he both recognizes that most people very definitely do *not* achieve the specific sort of "existence" he has in mind, and devotes a great deal of attention to the examination of what he takes to be the various most common and most interesting modes of existence which they can and do adopt. Indeed, he does more than this; for he not only describes these modes, but also subjects them to scrutiny with reference to what might be termed both their existential tenability and their essential adequacy. Further, he presents them not merely as so many different and isolated alternatives, but rather in a way which suggests that they collectively constitute a discernible (although not rigidly ordered) developmental sequence. Kierkegaard may or may not have been influenced by the examples of Hegel's "phenomenology of spirit" and Socrates' "ladder of love"; his "stages" certainly differ from those of both and moreover are not set forth with programmatic explicitness and systematic orderliness. Nonetheless, it is helpful in approaching the considerable portion of Kierkegaard's writings devoted to the discussion of various life orientations to view them in this light.

It is not easy to assign to inquiries of this kind a specific location on the usual map of philosophical problem areas, or even to give a characterization of their methodology in conventional terms. With regard to the latter, Kierkegaard's discussions may loosely be described as "phenomenological," given Hegel's employment of this term to characterize his procedure in the course of a similar endeavor; but it should be recognized that what Kierkegaard does and the ways in which he does it have little to do with the "phenomenological" program and method of Husserl. And with regard to the former, while Kierkegaard's explorations may be viewed as containing contributions to a wide range of areas of philosophical inquiry—for example, the theory of value, ethics, philosophical psychology, the philosophy of religion, and philosophical anthropology—they neither fall primarily into any one of them nor are adquately classifiable by reference to their relevance to any such list of them.

Putting the matter in very general terms, Kierkegaard's concern here is with the meaning of human life and with the various ways in which people may try to structure their lives in an attempt to achieve a personally satisfying and meaningful existence; and he avails himself of a wide variety of styles and forms of discourse and analysis as he tries to make clear what each of these possible ways of structuring one's life involves, and to enable one to get a feeling for as well as an intellectual comprehension of them and their ultimate tenability and adequacy. This chapter consists in a consideration of what Kierkegaard has to say and attempts to convey along these lines, drawing together analyses to be found in a number of his works.

Kierkegaard's concern with the general issue indicated is one which relatively few contemporary English-speaking philosophers share, either because they find it too nebulous to admit of coherent discussion and cogent argument, or because they consider that philosophers as such have no special credentials entitling them to make pronouncements concerning it. Whatever one may ultimately think of the content of his particular claims and specific conclusions, Kierkegaard's attempts to come to terms with this large and admittedly very imprecisely formulatable problem should be taken seriously by anyone inclined for either reason to exclude the issue from the domain of philosophy. For they make a strong case for the view that it is too important a matter to be ignored, that attempts to deal with it philosophically are by no means invariably incoherent or idly speculative, and that a philosophical approach to it, while neither the only possible one nor perhaps an entirely adequate and definitive one, can contribute significantly to its treatment. To be sure, this depends upon a significant broadening of the conventional notion of the form an inquiry must take to have philosophical significance, but that is something for which Kierkegaard's writings in this area also offer strong support.

It is often thought that there are three basic modes of human existence or spiritual life distinguished and dealt with in Kierkegaard's various writings, which he regards as exhaustive, as mutually exclusive (thus confronting individuals with a kind of "either/or/or"), and as developmentally ordered: the "aesthetic," the "ethical," and the "religious." In point of fact, this represents a considerable oversimplification of the matter. Taken together, his various writings do contain a kind of survey of what he takes to be the various possible modes of spiritual life, which for the most part may be subsumed under the three headings mentioned above and which may be arranged in something like a developmental sequence. The result is what might be termed a "phenomenology of spiritual development" (albeit one that is set forth piecemeal rather than systematically), which bears a certain resemblance to Hegel's "phenomenology of spirit"; although allowances must be made for the considerable substantive philosophical differences dividing the two men, and also for the fact that Hegel takes the underlying impulse which drives the development onward to be a striving for the attainment of genuine, trans-personal, "absolute" knowledge, whereas Kierkegaard takes it to be the desire to achieve true personal happiness and selfhood.

The common view of the "stages on life's way" which Kierkegaard would mark and distinguish represents an oversimplification of the matter, however, in that they do not consist merely in *an* "aesthetic" mode of existence, *an* "ethical" one, and *a* "religious" one. Rather, he describes and analyzes a number of distinct modes of existence in each of these general categories, and several others which do not really fall into any of them. Commentators have often recognized some of the further distinctions which must be made, but few have dealt with the matter systematically and exhaustively. I shall attempt to do so here, in the hope of facilitating the understanding of the rather remarkable and extremely insightful general analysis of human spiritual life which is contained in the confusing array of Kierkegaard's many works. In doing so I shall often elaborate extensively on suggestions he makes, and shall make extrapolations which go some distance beyond his actual remarks; but I shall do so only when this seems necessary to render clear what he is getting at (as I understand it), and shall try to remain faithful to his thinking throughout.

I

The most obvious place to begin is with that mode of existence which Kierkegaard considers less adequate to the ideal of true personal happiness and selfhood than any other. In spite of the fact that he also considers it to be far more common than any other, many commentators pass over it completely, taking the "first" mode of existence in Kierkegaard's developmental sequence to be the form of "aesthetic" existence discussed in the first volume of *Either/Or*.[1] I have in mind the mode he analyzes most extensively in *The Present Age*,[2] and associates with the notion of "the public"—for which reason I shall refer to it as the "public" mode of existence. The neglect of this mode as distinguished from the "aesthetic," the "ethical," and the "religious" ones may be due in part to the fact that in the rest of his "phenomenological" works Kierkegaard devotes his attention primarily to these others. He does so, however, not because he considers the "public" mode to be of negligible significance, but rather because he finds the others both more interesting and worth taking more seriously as candidates for the most satisfactory form of human spiritual life. And there can be no doubt that he regards the "public" mode as the predominant one in "the present age"—a circumstance he finds dismaying, since he considers those who never rise above this level to be the most pathetic representatives of mankind, compared with whom even an unscrupulous sensualist like Don Juan comes as a welcome relief.

The fact that this mode of existence is seldom distinguished from the others may also be due in part to the fact that, in various respects, it superficially resembles several of them. It shares certain features with the "aesthetic" mode, for example, such as an undercurrent of sensuality and a craving for the "interesting," for diversion, distraction, something to occupy the attention. And outwardly, at least, it resembles certain forms of "ethical" and "religious" existence, in that in each case the individual in question presents the same appearance of social adjustment and respectability. It is fundamentally different from each of them for Kierkegaard, however; and on this point he is explicit, saying of those who exist at this level, "They do not live aesthetically, but neither has the ethical manifested itself in its entirety" (p. 107).[3]

They do not live "aesthetically" because they by no means allow their hedonistic desires and inclinations a free rein. On the contrary, these are largely repressed because their indulgence would endanger the preservation of that which those under consideration value above all else—social solidarity. Indeed, the efforts of people of this sort to achieve and maintain social acceptance have the effect of reducing any tension which might be thought to characterize this situation, for they become so completely socialized that not only their behavior but also their very feelings and dispositions come to conform with prevailing standards of social acceptability. Those who live "aesthetically," on the other hand, live very differently indeed; for (to anticipate) they pay no more heed to social conventions than is necessary to enable them to pursue their own ends, and they willingly sacrifice social solidarity for the sake of personal gratification.

Those who exist in the mode of "publicness" also fall far short of attaining any of the forms of "ethical" and "religious" existence Kierkegaard distinguishes, above all in that each of the latter involves the attainment of a dimension of personal "inwardness" of some sort, whereas the inner life of the "public" person—to the extent that he may be said to have one at all—is nothing more than a reflection of his outward, "public" existence. He not only does what others do, but also unselfconsciously thinks, feels, and desires as others do. He is a particular human being, but he has no real personality of his own and is no true "individual" in any meaningful sense of the term. He is what others have made him to be, through their presentation to him of roles, customs, and conventions of thought and action, which he unthinkingly adopts and internalizes. He is committed to the social community around him; but his commitment to it, while complete, has no depth. It represents no real choice or decision on his part, but rather is the result of a continuous yielding to social pressures, which initially may be interrupted by occasional episodes of adolescent rebellion, but which eventually is adopted as the course of least resistance and which ultimately comes to be entirely habitual. Such a person is a mere cipher—an anonymous, other-directed, soulless additional face in the crowd. He is completely "socialized," completely "acculturated," completely "adjusted"—contemporary expressions referring to a process which Kierkegaard calls "leveling" and concerning which he could not be more emphatic: "Leveling," he says, "is *eo ipso* the destruction of the individual" (p. 261).

In this mode of existence, one does not act on the basis of any personal commitment, and therefore feels no responsibility for what one is and does. One lacks a personal "center"; and therefore there is nothing to prevent one from being swept up in mass crazes, fads, hysteria, and mob action. Having no personal sense of direction, one's attention flits about seeking something to absorb it when direction is not being supplied by others. Novelties, distractions, spectacles—something to gossip about, something that does not strain one's capabilities, something to divert one's attention from one's own emptiness, something to relieve the boredom of one's own insipidity, and above all something conducive to solidarity with "the others"—these are the kinds of things one who exists at the level of "publicness" seeks.

If this mode of existence was widespread in Kierkegaard's time, it could be argued that it is at least as common today. And Kierkegaard is moved by his conviction of its pervasiveness both to anger and to sorrow. He finds it a "really terrible thing" that so "many lives are wasted," and both despises and mourns for "the many who are helpless, thoughtless, and sensual, who live superior lazy lives and never receive any deeper impression of existence than this meaningless grin" (p. 268).

II

In the mode of "publicness," it has been observed, while there is an undercurrent of the sensual, sensuality is by no means indulged in freely. On the contrary, sensual desire and the passions generally are kept in close check, and are allowed expression only in ways that are socially sanctioned. The true sensualist, on the other hand, who exists at the first level of what Kierkegaard terms the "aesthetic" mode of existence, rejects any such limits upon his indulgence of his sensuous nature. Kierkegaard's paradigm case of the sensualist is one who devotes himself to the satisfaction of his sexual desires; but he has in mind here those who give themselves over to the pursuit of any of the pleasures of the senses—in short, hedonists and epicureans generally. (He uses the term "aesthetic" in this connection because of its traditional use in connection with the senses.)

The life of the senses is not to be ignored; Kierkegaard felt this himself, even where sexuality is concerned. He would appear never to have had any actual involvement in affairs of the flesh; but no one could write about the matter as he did in the first book of *Either/Or,* who does not know—at least in terms of his desires—what he is talking about. And he certainly had a real appreciation for the life of the senses at a less basic level, being no stranger either to the banquet table or to the concert hall. He can fairly be said to have felt the pull of epicureanism, particularly in its more refined forms. And whatever his ultimate position with respect to the "aesthetic" mode of existence may have been, it is clear that he regards it as indicative of very powerful forces in man's nature, and indeed of a whole dimension of man's nature, to which Hegel, in his view, had not given sufficient consideration.

Kierkegaard's attitude toward the kinds of involvements associated with mode of "publicness" is unambiguous: it is emphatically negative. His attitude toward the sensuous in its various forms, on the other hand, is far from unambiguous. He seems to alternate between feeling that the life of the senses is something positive which may and perhaps even should be a part (though by no means the whole) of life, and feeling that it represents a danger to be avoided, since concessions to it tend to ensnare one in its toils and incline one to neglect or forget about those things which are of more importance. Of course, as the title of his book *Either/Or* suggests, one must choose between the modes of existence he analyzes in it, just as he suggests in other works that one must choose between the "ethical" and the "religious." But this does not necessarily mean that when one chooses a higher mode, the lower ones are thereby excluded altogether; for while it does imply that one must choose between the "ultimate concerns" associated with each, it is still conceivable that a commitment to one of them might allow one to sustain a degree of involvement in matters associated with the others, where they do not conflict with this commitment or anything entailed by it. Kierkegaard sometimes does suggest that something like this is possible, but he also sometimes seems to think that there are no "neutral" contexts of this sort. While his attitude toward the senses is thus ambiguous, however, there is nothing ambiguous in his judgment concerning the satisfactoriness of life lived solely on the "aesthetic" plane. That judgment is clearly negative, for reasons which shall emerge shortly.

I have been speaking of "the aesthetic" mode of existence as though it referred to a single attitude or stance. But now a variety of distinctions must be noted. The fundamental orientation associated with "aesthetic existence" is that of devotion to the life of the senses and to the pleasures they afford. For Kierkegaard, in the analysis of the various possible basic modes of existence "the question is under what determinants one would contemplate the whole of existence and would live himself" (p. 107). And the person who lives "aesthetically" is one who views life and lives his life "under the determinants" of pleasure and pain. The satisfaction of sensuous desires of one sort or another is what guides and gives meaning to the actions of those who live at the level of the "aesthetic." But while the "aesthetic" individual may begin by savoring the pleasures of his immediate situation, there are too few situations in which pleasure is immediately obtainable and in which his desires may immediately be satisfied. Thus an "aesthetically" oriented life becomes one characterized by the pursuit of or search for pleasure. Don Juan is a classic example of a person who lives in this way; he devotes his life to sexual satisfaction, going from one affair to another in the pursuit of sensuous gratification.

Kierkegaard suggests the basic shortcoming of life lived in this way in his "Diary of a Seducer" (pp. 36–80). The Seducer is shown going through a long series of intricate preparations and maneuvers; yet when he finally succeeds in his project of seduction, he experiences no enduring satisfaction but rather only emptiness. What he desired—gaining possession of the girl he had decided to pursue—was something that had meaning for him only before he satisfied the desire, since to desire something one must want it but lack it. Before he gained possession of her he was unsatisfied, because he lacked what he desired; yet after he gained possession of her he felt empty, because he could neither desire that which he no longer lacked, nor extend the fleeting moment in which desire is still present while being "consummated"—an expression most suited to Kierkegaard's point. The state of unsatisfied desire is one which can persist over a considerable period of time, but it is hardly a pleasant state. The moment of satisfaction, on the other hand, may be pleasant; but it almost immediately gives way to a state of indifference, which (like the first) can persist for some time, but once again is hardly very pleasurable.

If this is the pattern of existence at the sensuous level, it is clear that—at least in the case of a being having the capacity of reflection—a repetition of the pattern is likely to lead to a loss of immediacy. One can neither remain in a state of ecstasy, nor proceed directly from one ecstatic moment to another, nor remain oblivious to the fact that such moments tend to be few and far between. One must choose between relying upon luck and attempting actively to bring about pleasurable episodes; but the fates are seldom generous in this regard, and in the perspective of hindsight few such episodes seem to justify the effort required to bring them about, even in cases in which one's designs have not been thwarted. Even the most intensely pleasurable things begin to lose their luster when experience makes one aware of their ephemerality and the letdown that invariably follows in their wake.

It need not be only when this realization impairs one's ability to take pleasure in anything at all that doubts begin to emerge about the "aesthetic" enterprise as a way of living which is sufficiently satisfying to sustain one devoted exclusively to it. And once this process of disillusionment begins, it rarely can be reversed. Childlike immediacy gives way to hopeful persistence, and then to desperate determination, until at length one reaches a state in which one clings to the ideal of finding genuine satisfaction in a succession of pleasurable moments, but without any longer really expecting to be able to do so. Finally, one's efforts to find satisfaction in this way are coupled with a skepticism concerning the possibility of doing so. Faust constitutes a paradigm case of one who has reached this stage. He still longs to be able to have an experience which will be sufficiently pleasurable to enable him to want to say: "Remain; thou art so fair." But he doubts of ever doing so, to the point that he is willing to wager his soul that even the devil cannot bring it about.

Kierkegaard distinguishes one further stage in the unfolding bankruptcy of the "aesthetic" mode of existence, which also derives its character from an initial adoption of an "aesthetic" orientation toward life. That stage is one of complete despair. Such despair differs from Faust's pessimism in that here one ceases even to long for the pleasurable moment. One has given up. One takes the view that such moments—and only such moments—*would* make one's life meaningful, but that they are quite unattainable any longer, and that therefore there is no point in even wishing for them. To such a person, life seems intolerable on the only conditions it offers, and death appears as the only possible salvation. Once this stage has been reached—and for Kierkegaard it is the logical and eventual outcome of adopting an "aesthetic" attitude toward life—the untenability of this orientation clearly emerges; and it becomes evident that man is simply not the kind of being that can find enduring satisfaction on this plane alone.

This raises the question of whether there are any other, more enduringly satisfying possible modes of existence and, if so, what they are. Kierkegaard suggests that there are; and with this we leave the "aesthetic" plane—with its succession of stages beginning with immediacy and proceeding through optimistic calculation to pessimism and finally despair—and turn to the "ethical." Kierkegaard uses the term "ethical" to refer to several quite distinct modes of existence. In each case, however, the individual orients himself toward something that transcends the realm of particular desires and momentary pleasures and does not have the unstable, ephemeral character they do.

III

Kierkegaard does not always attach the same meaning to the expression "the ethical." In *Fear and Trembling,* the term is to be understood in the Hegelian sense, in which it refers to *objective* spirituality or sociocultural integration. Thus Kierkegaard says that "the ethical as such is the universal," and that a person's "ethical task is to . . . abolish his particularity in order to become the universal."[4] In the *Concluding Unscientific Postscript,* on the other hand, the realm of "the ethical" is that of inwardness and *subjectivity;* and this is a radically different use of the expression. Here the "ethical" task is said to be "the task of becoming subjective."[5] "The ethical," Kierkegaard writes, "is a correlative to individuality." The person who exists at the "ethical" level is held to be one who has an "infinite interest" in "his own reality."[6] And it is clear that Kierkegaard considers this second type of "ethical" existence to constitute a higher stage of spiritual development than the first; thus he says, "The individual as the particular is higher than the universal."[7] (The conception of "the ethical" developed in the long section of *Either/Or* entitled "Equilibrium" is closer to the latter than to the former. The emphasis there is upon the development of a stable and unified "personality" rather than "the task of becoming subjective," but the two are clearly related.)

It is important to distinguish these two modes of existence, because they are very different indeed and because the difference between them is of great importance for Kierkegaard. Both are to be distinguished from the "public" as well as the "aesthetic" modes, in that each involves a firm and self-conscious commitment to something which transcends the plane of the life of the senses no less than that of mere conformity for the sake of social acceptance and solidarity. In the first case, however, the commitment made is to what Hegel calls "the social substance," regarded as a "universal" system of institutions (at least in the context of the society in which one lives) which structures one's life in a way that gives it objective and enduring significance. Thus this mode of existence is much like that which Hegel describes in his discussion of "ethical life" in his *Philosophy of Right*[8] —whence Kierkegaard's characterization of it as "ethical." In the second case, on the other hand, the commitment made is to something intensely personal, chosen without taking anything like "the social substance" into consideration; and the result is a mode of existence that is highly individualistic rather than "universal" and a life the significance of which is to be characterized in terms of the attainment of "subjective" uniqueness rather than "objective" identity. This mode of existence is very different from Hegelian "ethical life," and calls to mind the existentialist notion of "authenticity," which to a very considerable extent is modeled upon it.

It is unfortunate, therefore, that Kierkegaard characterizes both modes of existence as "ethical," even though he is to some extent justified in doing so, in that the "determinants" under which life is viewed and lived in both cases transcend those of "aesthetic" existence and yet are essentially different from those of "religious" existence. Faced with a somewhat similar problem, Hegel takes two terms which are often used interchangeably—"ethical" and "moral"—and distinguishes sharply between them, reserving each to one specific sort of post-"aesthetic" orientation, in an attempt to minimize confusion. Kierkegaard might have done better to follow suit. Since he does not do so, however, I shall not abandon his terminology; but I shall modify it, speaking in the one case of an "objective-ethical" mode of existence and in the other case of a "subjective-ethical" mode. To do so is admittedly awkward, but considerations of clarity render it imperative to adopt some such procedure.

The connection between Kierkegaard's conception of "objective-ethical" existence (as it is developed in *Fear and Trembling*) and Hegel's notion of "ethical life" is made clear by Kierkegaard's explicit references to Hegel and by his use of Hegelian expressions in characterizing it. "The ethical" is said to be "the universal"; the individual "has his end in the universal"; his "ethical" task is "to abolish his particularity in order to become the universal." He feels that he commits a wrong when he "asserts himself in his particularity over against the universal." And he fights the temptation to do so, "penitently abandoning himself as the particular in the universal."[9]

When Kierkegaard speaks of "particularity" here, he is thinking—as Hegel does—of a person's sensual impulses, his egoistic tendencies, his inclination to give free reign to his desires, and his disposition to do whatever he feels like doing, whenever he pleases. This is basically the animating principle of "aesthetic" existence. There is no question in Kierkegaard's mind in *Fear and Trembling* (or elsewhere) about the fact that "particularistic" (or "aesthetic") existence represents a lower developmental stage of spiritual life than "universal" (or "objective-ethical") existence. The question he raises is that of whether the latter is "the highest thing that can be said of a man and of his existence."[10] And he clearly feels that if there is a mode of existence higher than the latter, it is not the "particularism" which must be relinquished if "universality" is to be achieved. In comparison with living at the level of mere particularity, he says, "it is beautiful and salutary to be the individual who translates himself into the universal . . . , who has the universal as his home, his friendly abiding-place."[11]

While Kierkegaard's conception of "objective-ethical" existence is similar to Hegel's notion of "ethical life," there are some points of difference between them. For example, while Hegel does subsume family relations under the general heading of "ethical life," his greatest emphasis is on social institutions of a broader sort and the obligations they define for the individual, whereas Kierkegaard lays his main emphasis upon family relations and obligations (Abraham's relation to his son and to his wife) and states, "The ethical had for Abraham no higher expression than the family life."[12] In doing so, he departs from Hegel's view that participation in the life of the "state" is the type of "objective-ethical" relation that is to be regarded as the highest manifestation of "ethical" existence.

It does not seem, however, that he would go so far as to restrict the domain of such relations to family relations alone, excluding social institutions from consideration. After all, to say that "the ethical has no higher expression than the family life" is to suggest that it *does* have other expressions, even if they are not on a par with this one. Kierkegaard's failure to bring them into the discussion may be attributed to design: if there are cases in which even the highest of "objective-ethical" relations are to be subordinated to other considerations, then in such cases the same will be true of the others as well. It is therefore sufficient for the purpose of establishing his general point to focus on this one example—not confusing the issue by bringing in other relations. Precisely because Kierkegaard does not go into the matter, however, it is not clear whether (in addition to family life) he would include participation not only in social and cultural institutions but also in political and civil ones in the "objective-ethical" mode of existence which he places above existence at the level of mere particularity. Thus while there can be no doubt that he agrees with Hegel in regarding "objective-ethical" existence as a higher form of spiritual life than mere particularity, one cannot confidently assert that it includes everything for him that it does for Hegel.

"Objective-ethical" existence for Kierkegaard is a mode of existence in which one chooses to live in accordance with a system of "ethical" norms of generally acknowledged validity in the society in which one lives. The "determinants" in terms of which one judges and acts are those of "duty," "good," and "right," as opposed to "pleasure" and "pain"; and the content of these determinants is ascertained "objectively," rather than being fixed "subjectively," by consulting conventional wisdom on normative and evaluative matters instead of one's private conscience or personal inclinations. A person who lives at this level does not merely think and act as those around him do; he attempts to conform to those normative and evaluative ideals which are generally acknowledged as such but often ignored in practice by others. And he does not do so for the sake of social acceptance and solidarity, or even to win the esteem and admiration of others. Rather, he does so because he feels he *ought* to do so in virtue of what he takes to be the unconditional validity of these ideals and because life lived in this way seems to him to be better and more meaningful than life lived on a merely "aesthetic" plane.

In doing so, one's life acquires a kind of stability and orderliness (Hegel would say a degree of rationality) and also of dignity and significance which is not possible so long as one remains immersed in the flux of the life of the senses or blindly follows the crowd. The individual places his obligations to his family, his responsibilities as a citizen, and in general his duties as a member of an "ethical" order ahead of both sensuous gratification and considerations of expedience. He does not devote himself to the pursuit of pleasure, and is not concerned to achieve the dull comfort of immersion in the mass; but he is able to achieve a kind of happiness, which is both greater than that associated with the latter and more enduring than that attainable at the "aesthetic" level. It might best be described as satisfaction of the sort taken in virtue when one is conscious of it and feels it to be its own reward.

The shortcomings of this mode of existence, while perhaps less obvious than those of the modes discussed previously, are for Kierkegaard nonetheless quite serious. First, even though this mode would seem to make possible the attainment of an enduring happiness, it in fact is capable of doing so (according to Kierkegaard) only if it is more than a merely secular affair, in which case it ceases to be a purely "ethical" mode of existence and becomes a "religious" one. Kierkegaard takes this position on the ground that "fundamentally every duty is a duty toward God. . . . Duty becomes duty by being referred to God."[13] His point is that unless one believes one's obligations to be divinely ordained, there is nothing to prevent one from beginning to question them; that there is no purely rational way of establishing their validity; and that once one comes to regard them as problematical at best and possibly merely conventional, one can no longer derive that satisfaction from living in accordance with them which is associated with confidence in their validity.

Hegel had attempted to establish the claim of the "ethical order" upon the individual in a nonreligious way by arguing that it is a concrete manifestation of the "system of pure reason" which is both the ultimate principle of reality and the essence of the human spirit. For Kierkegaard, however, Hegel's case for the sort of metaphysical scheme which would yield this conclusion is less than compelling, to say the least. In his view, reason cannot establish the claim of any set of "ethical" obligations upon the individual. A nonreligious individual may not question the validity of some such set for an extended period of time; and as long as he does not think to question it, he may remain at the level of purely "objective-ethical" existence. It may become problematical for him at any time, however; and when it does, he will be driven from this mode of existence, since he will no longer be able to achieve satisfaction in it. He may regress to the "aesthetic" plane, or he may advance to a further form of "ethical" or even "religious" existence; but he will be unable simply to carry on as before, except perhaps in a purely mechanical way that yields no real satisfaction and is associated with a kind of inward despair similar to that accompanying disillusionment with "aesthetic" existence.

It does not follow, however, that transcendence of the "objective-ethical" plane necessarily involves abandoning "objective-ethical" life altogether. On the contrary, while Kierkegaard speaks of a "teleological suspension of the ethical" which may at times be necessary in connection with certain "religious" modes of existence, he does not regard this "suspension" as something permanent. "Objective-ethical" life, he contends, is ultimately to be "reduced to a position of relativity." But, he says, "from this it does not follow that the ethical is to be abolished."[14] Rather, even—and indeed especially—for one who has acheived the highest of the modes of ("religious") existence, it is generally to be adhered to; for Kierkegaard would seem to feel that, except in unusual circumstances (e.g., when God is testing one's faith), it may very well represent God's will. In short, Kierkegaard does not mean to suggest that "objective-ethical" life is intrinsically objectionable, but rather only that a purely "objective-ethical" mode of existence cannot be sustained and does not as such make possible the attainment of an enduring happiness.

This mode of existence as such does suffer from a further defect, however; for its strongly "objective" character also has the consequence that it does not enable the subjectivity and personality of the individual to develop sufficiently. And, given the importance Kierkegaard attaches to their development, this defect is even more crucial than the first. For Kierkegaard would attach little importance to the attainment of an enduring happiness if it were achieved while the development of the individual *as* an individual were neglected. A person is what he ought to be as a human being, according to Kierkegaard, only if he becomes genuinely *subjective*—a genuine individual, with a personality that is both unique and unified, who thinks, acts, chooses, decides, and believes as a responsible self dependent upon no other men for guidance and direction.

Kierkegaard expresses this by saying that for a human being "subjectivity is truth"—the "truth" or essence of his nature.[15] And he distinguishes genuine subjectivity from the mere particularity of the person who devotes himself to the life of the senses (at which level true individuality obviously is not to be found), from the anonymity and impersonality of mere "public-ness," and also from the "universality" of the "objective-ethical" mode of existence. The attainment of genuine subjectivity is held by Kierkegaard to involve personal commitment; and while the "objective-ethical" individual does make a commitment, it is a commitment to something objective and impersonal in nature and therefore does not suffice to "individuate" him. On the contrary, it in a sense leaves him without even the semblance of individ-uality which the independently minded "aesthetic" man achieves. His com-mitment does serve to stabilize his existence (as long as he maintains it), and results in his attainment of a definite unified personality of a sort; but it is an impersonal personality in that it does not differ significantly from that of any other person committed to the same form of "objective-ethical" life.

Since this mode of existence leaves much to be desired in terms of what Kierkegaard takes full human self-realization to involve, therefore, he regards it as fortunate that it suffers from the basic instability discussed above; for if it did not, human spiritual development might simply halt at this point, in which case the "truth" of the individual's human nature would never be actualized. One would simply rest content once one reached this stage of spiritual life—as Hegel had thought one would and should, except to proceed within its context to develop that higher mode of "objective" consciousness which he calls absolute knowledge.

IV

It may seem curious that there is no place for anything like this latter type of consciousness—which Hegel represents as the culmination of the whole process of spiritual development—in the developmental sequence of stages Kierkegaard explicitly identifies; for while he argues that Hegelian absolute knowledge is unattainable by finite human beings, he does allow that it is possible for men to become preoccupied to a considerable extent with the attainment of objective knowledge. If a kind of existence conceived along these lines were to be recognized, it would be subsumable neither under any of the general modes discussed to this point, nor under any of those to be discussed below. It would be characterizable in terms of "objectivity," but "objectivity" of a sort very different from that which is the hallmark of "objective-ethical" existence; for the commitment it would involve would be a commitment to the goals and methods of cognitive inquiry, rather than a commitment to a form of "ethical life."

The fact that Kierkegaard does not give explicit recognition to this as a separate and distinct mode of existence, along with the others which he treats as such, may reflect a rather perverse inclination on his part to snub Hegel by not even deigning to recognize as worthy of consideration an orientation so dear to him. Another explanation is possible, however: namely, that since his concern is with orientations bearing more or less directly on the down-to-earth *living* of life, and since a philosopher's or scientist's theoretical endeavors have little bearing on the way in which he lives when he is not pursuing them, his endeavors along these lines may be disregarded in an analysis of the ways in which human life may be lived. Thus it might be maintained that the philosopher or scientist *as a human being* always exists in one or another of the modes Kierkegaard distinguishes. And if this is so, one might argue that Kierkegaard does not need to make room for an "objective-cognitive" mode of existence in his phenomenology of spiritual development; for it is only with the various ways in which people *as human beings* may exist that this phenomenology is concerned.

This explanation is quite plausible, and it certainly is more satisfying than the first suggested. It also has some force as a justification of Kierkegaard's failure to make room for a distinct mode of existence of this sort somewhere between the "aesthetic" and "religious" modes he discusses. It seems to me, however, that it is not a completely persuasive justification. There are people who find refuge from the despair which accompanies the collapse of both the "aesthetic" and the "objective-ethical" modes of existence in cognitive endeavor, and derive sufficient satisfaction from it both to sustain them and to keep them from feeling the need to seek further alternatives—at least for a considerable time. And there are people so involved in their cognitive pursuits that they really have no life apart from them and are largely oblivious to the things which are of "ultimate concern" to those at the various levels of spiritual life which Kierkegaard distinguishes. They may be vulnerable to a form of eventual disillusionment no less devastating than (and in some ways similar to) those encountered at the "aesthetic" and "objective-ethical" levels of existence; and they may be no closer to genuine self-realization (as Kierkegaard conceives it) than those whose mode of existence is "objective-ethical," for essentially the same reason. But these shortcomings obviously do not suffice to exclude from consideration other modes of existence and so should not do so here.

In short, I would argue that Kierkegaard ought to have given explicit recognition to the possibility of an "objective-cognitive" mode of existence which is on all fours with the various "ethical" modes he distinguishes, which like them is neither "aesthetic" (nor merely "public") nor "religious," but which is quite distinct from each of them. Developmentally considered (within the context of Kierkegaard's general scheme of spiritual development), this mode would seem to be roughly on a par with "objective-ethical" existence and might be viewed as an alternative to it, since it has essentially the same virtues and defects as the latter and differs from the other modes of existence in essentially the same ways. While Kierkegaard's developmental sequence of stages does not include such a mode of existence, his writings—and in particular his *Concluding Unscientific Postscript*—contain a wealth of analytical material pertaining to it and especially to its shortcomings. The theme to which he constantly returns in his attack upon Hegel indicates one of these: a person who devotes himself completely to "objective-cognitive" endeavor never actualizes his essential "truth" as a human being by becoming genuinely "subjective," but rather strains in precisely the opposite direction and so is at the furthest remove from achieving true humanity.[16]

Kierkegaard is willing to grant to Hegel that only "absolute knowledge" is genuine knowledge, and that nothing short of it can truly satisfy one who strives to achieve genuine knowledge; but he turns this point against Hegel and uses it to bring out what he takes to be a second and fatal shortcoming of what I would term "objective-cognitive" existence. He maintains that while God may have absolute knowledge, it is utterly impossible for human beings ever to achieve or even closely approximate it, for reasons rather similar to those which many subsequent philosophers have given. Consequently, one who lives "objective-cognitively" and seeks an enduring happiness through the attainment of genuine knowledge is doomed to frustration and ultimately to despair.

Such a person may derive satisfaction for some time from the hopes he may have of attaining it and from what he takes to be his progress in that direction. The more sophisticated concerning the nature of his endeavor he becomes, however, the more clearly he recognizes the elusiveness of the goal he seeks, and the less confident that he is making real progress toward it he becomes, until philosophical criticism at length reveals to him that his goal of genuine (i.e., absolute) knowledge is unattainable, and he is reduced either to rehearsing the reasons for his ultimate ignorance (if he is a philosopher) or to describing and arranging—and redescribing and rearranging—collections of merely phenomenal data in terms of provisional hypotheses (if he is a scientist). Either task may keep one busy; but to one who is aware of what he is doing and its lack of ultimate significance, keeping busy in this way can hardly afford much real satisfaction and ultimately ceases to be an effective refuge from despair. And so, once again, we are brought to the bankruptcy of an "objective" mode of spiritual existence—and thus to the consideration of Kierkegaard's analysis of a different post-"aesthetic," pre-"religious" mode, which I have termed "subjective-ethical."

V

The "subjective-ethical" mode of existence might be viewed as the natural successor to the "objective-ethical" and the "objective-cognitive" modes on the part of a nonreligious person for whom both the validity of the "objective-ethical" order and also "objective-cognitive" endeavor have become too problematical to enable him to continue to find satisfaction in commitment to them, and who further has come to recognize that distinctness of personality, true individuality, and genuine subjectivity are of greater importance than the "objectivity" and "universality" of either thought or practical life. This is the mode of existence designated as "ethical" in the *Postscript* and in the latter part of the first volume of *Either/Or,* and it differs markedly from that designated as "ethical" in *Fear and Trembling.* Both kinds of "ethical" existence involve a break with "aesthetic" existence. Different aspects of the "aesthetic" mode of existence are negated, however; and (as Hegel might say) different definite negations give rise to different positive conceptions. In *Fear and Trembling* "ethical" existence is conceived in terms of superseding mere "particularity" and attaining "universality." In the other two works, on the other hand, "ethical" existence is held to involve a passionate personal commitment to a way of living of one's own choosing, and thus is conceived not in terms of "universality" but of personality, individuality, and subjectivity (which are not to be confused with mere "particularity").

The difference between this mode of existence and the "aesthetic" is brought out most clearly in the section of *Either/Or* entitled "Equilibrium," in which Kierkegaard argues explicitly that one does not live "ethically" if one lives "aesthetically," and vice versa. This is put in terms of an "either/ or," but, of course, these are not the only two alternatives. The main point being made here is that the development of personality requires a definite commitment to something of one's own choosing, for only such a commitment can both unify and individuate it. Without such a commitment a definite personality never emerges out of the multiplicity of possibilities which we are. Under these circumstances Kierkegaard says that one lacks "the inmost and holiest thing of all in a man, the unifying power of personality" (p. 121). "The choice itself is decisive for the content of personality.... When it does not choose it withers away in consumption" (p. 102). What is important for the development is less *what* one chooses than *how* one chooses: "In making a choice it is not so much a question of choosing the right as of the energy, the earnestness, the pathos with which one chooses. Thereby . . . the personality is consolidated" (p. 106).

The trouble with the "aesthetic" individual (or at least, the trouble singled out here) is that "he who lives aesthetically does not choose"—and thus fails to "consolidate" his personality (p. 107). However, this requires qualification. In a sense, such a person does choose: he dabbles first in this and then in that, and this involves his *choosing* to do first this and then that. But, according to Kierkegaard, these are not real choices. For here one "chooses only for the moment"; and one makes a real choice, for Kierkegaard, only when one "chooses absolutely"—that is, makes an enduring commitment to something. One who lives "aesthetically" may busy himself with various projects—for example, the Seducer undertaking to seduce the girl who captures his fancy at the moment. But this is not the sort of commitment around which one can build one's whole life; it is only an episode.

There is a sense, however, in which one who lives "aesthetically" *does* "choose absolutely." He commits himself or devotes himself completely to the pursuit of pleasure in one form or another; and this general commitment—to be distinguished from some particular project (e.g., of seduction)—can be an enduring and unconditional one. It thus would seem that it *does* make a difference what one chooses after all. Kierkegaard's move at this point apparently would be to suggest that one's commitment will lead to the consolidation of personality only if it is to something which is more *capable of sustaining* an absolute commitment than the pursuit of pleasure— something which will not land one in frustration and despair should one try to build one's life around it.

To be confronted with the kind of "either/or" Kierkegaard has in mind, once again, is to be confronted with the question of the "determinants" under which "one would contemplate the whole of existence and would himself live" (p. 107). One possibility is that of approaching life in terms of pleasure; this is the "aesthetic" alternative. What other way is there? Kierkegaard suggests approaching life in terms of good and evil, right and wrong. And it is this alternate way of life that he really has in mind, in speaking of an "either/or" here. He is not saying that one must choose between the good (which is the "ethical") and the evil (which is the "aesthetic"). He is saying that one must choose between an "ethical" mode of existence in which one makes distinctions of this sort and an "aesthetic" one in which one does not. His point would seem to be that making an enduring commitment, of the sort that the consolidation of personality requires, entails that one employ the categories of "good" and "evil" in judging things which impinge on one's commitment, rather than the categories of "pleasurable" and "unpleasurable." Making an enduring commitment to a certain way of living and employing the categories of "good" and "evil" go hand in hand.

At this point the distinction between the "objective-ethical" and the "subjective-ethical" modes of existence might seem to be in danger of collapsing. The difference between them emerges, however, when one observes that here the content of the commitment (and of the attendant applications of the judgment "good") is not supplied from without, by reference to "objective-ethical" norms and institutions. Kierkegaard is explicit about this: "He who chooses the ethical chooses the good, but here the good is entirely abstract, only its being is posited" (p. 107). This is related to the fact that in *Fear and Trembling* the emphasis is on the notion of "universality," whereas here it is on the notion of "personality." There Kierkegaard starts with a notion of the "ethical" which derives from Hegel's discussion of "ethical life." Here, on the other hand, he is concerned with the presuppositions of the consolidation of personality—of becoming a genuine "self." This involves committing oneself unconditionally and enduringly to something beyond the level of the merely pleasurable. This in turn involves judging things in terms of the categories of "good" and "evil." These are commonly considered "ethical" categories, and so Kierkegaard speaks of this mode of existence as an "ethical" one. In this case, however, these categories are devoid of any content until supplied with it by a commitment on the part of the individual to a specific way of living. Nothing is determined in advance—"objectively"—except the necessity of *some* such commitment for the consolidation of personality. In the case of "objective-ethical" existence, on the other hand, the content of "the good" is regarded as antecedently determined and "objectively" valid; and the choice made by the individual is not one which affects it, but rather is simply a decision to live in accordance with it.

It thus emerges that, whereas one who lives "objective-ethically" makes only a single, general choice, which consists of his opting for an independently determined "universality" (thereby relinguishing his autonomy), one who lives "subjective-ethically" must make a twofold choice, which asserts and maintains his autonomy: a choice of a life of "subjective-ethical" commitment *and* a choice of something specific to which to make that commitment. A choice of the former sort requires a choice of the latter sort, since one cannot be "committed" without being committed to something specific. But a choice of the former sort does not entail any particular choice of the latter sort; it only makes some such choice necessary. And it is this further choice, which the individual makes entirely on his own, that individuates as well as consolidates his personality.

In the *Postscript*, as I have suggested, the key concepts in terms of which this mode of existence is conceived are those of "subjectivity" and "inwardness," rather than "personality." "The ethical," Kierkegaard says, "is the inwardness of spirit."[17] Man's "ethical" task is held to be the task of "becoming subjective," or becoming an "individual subject." That which is of utmost importance for one who lives "subjective-ethically" is his own existence: "The ethical demand is that he become infinitely interested in existing," that is, in existing as a subject, as an individual.[18] The use of the phrase "infinitely interested" conveys the element of passionate intensity which is also emphasized in connection with the consolidation of personality in "Equilibrium."

What does this involve? "The true ethical enthusiasm," Kierkegaard maintains, "consists in *willing* to the utmost limits of one's powers," without being concerned with the objective significance of that which is willed. "A truly great ethical personality would seek to realize his life in the following manner. He would strive to develop himself with the utmost exertion of his powers."[19] He is unconcerned with the impact which his "exertions" may (or may not) have upon the world and society around him, for the only thing that counts for him is his attainment of genuine individuality or selfhood. Thus Kierkegaard says that he "ethically strives to further the development of his own self."[20] What others may think of him is of no importance to him. The life of the senses is also of little concern to him, since individuality cannot be achieved through the satisfaction of desires deriving from the sensuous nature which is common to all men. And he is indifferent both to "objective-ethical" norms and institutions and to "objective-cognitive" pursuits, since neither stand in any relation to the accomplishment of his task of "becoming subjective." His mode of existence also is non-"religious," however, in that "the sole ethical interest is the interest in one's own reality"; and "the believer differs from the ethicist in being infinitely interested in the reality of another," that is, God.[21]

Here, too, the way in which the "subjective-ethical" individual attempts to "become subjective" and "develop his own self" is suggested to be through a commitment to something of his own choosing. Kierkegaard does not get much more specific than this; but his refusal to be more specific is quite reasonable, since it is a part of the very notion of "subjective-ethical" existence that there is no one particular choice that one is supposed to make. What counts is simply that one make some such choice on one's own and commit oneself to living one's life in accordance with it.

The notion of "subjective-ethical" existence with which we are dealing here may be illuminated by a comparison with Kant's conception of morality. What makes an action moral, for Kant, is neither its conformity to prevailing norms (as for conventionalists), nor its conformity to universally applicable substantive moral laws (as for absolutists), nor the goodness of its results (as for utilitarians). Rather, it is its satisfaction of a criterion (viz., accordance of the maxim of the action with the Categorical Imperative) which itself is purely formal and void of substantive content. Essentially the same is true where "subjective-ethical" commitment is concerned.

Of course, the general criterion under consideration by Kierkegaard is quite different from Kant's. The principle that one should act in such a way that one could endorse the idea of everyone acting in that way is far from identical with the principle that one should live one's life on the basis of a commitment to something of one's own choosing. But there is a formal similarity between the two which distinguishes both of them from the sort of principle governing Hegelian "ethical life" and Kierkegaard's "objective-ethical" mode of existence. For even though a general statement of the latter may make no reference to any specific set of substantive norms, an individual existing within the framework of an "ethical" order is not called upon to decide for himself what he ought to do; that is determined in advance, by the "objective" content of the "ethical" order, and he is directed simply to act and live accordingly. In the cases of both Kantian morality and Kierkegaardian "subjective-ethical" existence, on the other hand, the "objective" content of the "ethical" order in which the individual lives does not settle the question of what he is to do. That is something which he must decide for himself.

Any shortcomings of the "subjective-ethical" mode of existence will obviously be very different from those associated with either of the "objective" modes of existence discussed above. This mode does constitute a definite step in the right direction for Kierkegaard. Yet he feels that it too falls short of enabling one to achieve either the ultimate in subjectivity and individuality or a truly enduring happiness. Consider first the matter of individuality. If (as is the case for Kierkegaard) it is conceived as a function of the uniqueness of the relation obtaining between a person and his "ultimate concern," then it is clear that commitment to something of one's own choosing does not as such guarantee radical individuality. It does guarantee a greater degree of individuality by far than is to be found in any of the modes discussed previously, in each of which the "determinants" in terms of which one thinks and acts are essentially general and impersonal in nature. But it by no means precludes the possibility that that to which one commits oneself is something to which others may happen to have committed themselves as well, in which event one's individuality would not be complete.

Such a commitment also does not involve one's becoming as "subjective" as it is possible—and, according to Kierkegaard, desirable—for one to become, given the way in which Kierkegaard conceives of "subjectivity." "Subjectivity," as he conceives of it, is a function of *passion,* of the sort involved in commitment.[22] He further considers intensity of passion to be a function of the tenuousness (from the standpoint of rationality) of that to which commitment is made. And while "subjective-ethical" existence involves committing oneself to something one simply chooses on one's own, for which choice one neither has nor seeks a rational justification (thus making it a kind of "leap" analogous to "the leap of faith"), such commitment requires a lesser degree of passion than certain other forms of commitment do. For it merely involves commitment to something *neutral* from the standpoint of rationality—something the choice of which is not rationally justifiable, but is not rationally objectionable either.

Such a commitment does require a degree of passion, since that to which commitment is made is rationally tenuous (because it has no specific rational justification), and since passion is required in order for one to commit oneself to something rationally tenuous. But a commitment of this sort requires less passion than a commitment made to something rationally *objectionable*— something which is *not* merely "neutral" from the standpoint of rationality. Hence one who makes a commitment of this sort is not impelled to achieve the greatest possible degree of passion in order to be able to make it, and thus falls short of attaining that intensity of passion which Kierkegaard maintains is required to achieve the ultimate in "subjectivity." And since he considers nothing less than this to be necessary in order for a human being to be what he ought (essentially) to be, he thus regards "subjective-ethical" existence as an unsatisfactory mode of existence.

There is also another shortcoming of this mode of existence, and it is the one which Kierkegaard holds ultimately renders this mode sufficiently dissatisfying to one who has reached it to impel him to further spiritual development. This shortcoming consists in the fact that it is difficult for one to derive enduring satisfaction from a commitment of the sort under discussion. The problem is not that encountered in connection with the "objective" modes of existence discussed above; for since there is no belief in the objective validity or tenability of that to which one commits oneself to begin with, there is no possibility of disillusionment along these lines. Instead, the problem is, at least in part, that it is difficult to sustain one's commitment to something over an extended period when there is nothing more to be said for it than the fact that at some previous time one simply happened to choose it and committed oneself to it.

It is possible to derive considerable satisfaction from such a commitment for some time, in spite of a recognition of the intrinsic meaninglessness of that to which the commitment has been made. The sense of autonomy associated with charting one's own course can be initially exhilarating; and, especially after having felt oneself to be merely adrift, following the collapse of a previous mode of existence, the sense of direction one thus acquires may be satisfying temporarily—even though one knows that the path one is following really leads nowhere—simply because one is doing something *definite*. These are charms, however, which are not very lasting, and therefore hardly can serve to make possible a truly enduring happiness.

A further possible source of satisfaction for one who lives "subjective-ethically," which is at least somewhat more substantial, is that of accomplishment, when that to which one has committed oneself is a project of some sort. In cases in which such satisfaction is possible, however, another equally serious problem is encountered. Circumstances often interfere with one's attempts to carry out one's projects; and even when they are not an immediate problem, the fact that almost any course of action to which one may commit oneself is susceptible to frustration from this quarter must sooner or later occur to the "subjective-ethical" individual. When it does, he cannot but begin to question the wisdom of any attempt to achieve an *enduring* (not merely temporary) happiness by means of a commitment to something that may at any time be adversely affected by forces beyond his control. And since virtually nothing to which one might commit oneself in this world is both completely within one's control and capable at least in principle of affording one a sense of accomplishment, one who desires to achieve an enduring happiness (as Kierkegaard thinks all men do) is sooner or later forced to recognize that it cannot be achieved through the sort of commitment associated with the "subjective-ethical" mode of existence.

Kierkegaard holds that in point of fact the shortcomings of this mode of existence can only be made good through a form of commitment which involves the transcendence of all forms of merely human and worldly relations, and thus through an advance to the plane of "religious" existence.

Before turning to the "religious" modes of existence he distinguishes, however, reference must be made to one further form of non-"religious" existence he discusses, which represents a kind of last resort on the part of one
who despairs of achieving an enduring happiness in any of the ways dealt with
up to this point, but who nonetheless is not yet persuaded that it simply
cannot be achieved through his own efforts on a purely secular plane. Because
it is non-"religious" and because it is strongly reminiscent of stoicism (which
is generally regarded as an ethical orientation), it might also be considered an
"ethical" mode of existence, although Kierkegaard himself does not refer to
it as such.

VI

This mode of existence, which (for the reason just alluded to) I shall term
the "stoic-ethical" mode, is that which Kierkegaard speaks of in the first part
of his discussion of the"knight of infinite resignation" in *Fear and Trembling.*
(In the latter part of this discussion, it seems to me that a different—"religious"—mode of existence is described, which I shall consider subsequently.)
Kierkegaard distinguishes the "knight of infinite resignation" (whom I shall
henceforth speak of as one who exists "stoic-ethically") from the "knight of
faith"; but the mode of existence of the former is also different from any of
those discussed previously, for it is characterized neither by other-directed-
ness, nor by devotion to the life of the senses, nor by adherence to an
"ethical" order, nor by dedication to cognitive endeavor, *nor* by the sort of
commitment associated with "subjective-ethical" existence.

Indeed, the point of departure for one who exists "stoic-ethically" is the
recognition that it is not within one's power to ensure that any state of affairs
in the world shall either be brought about or preserved, that anyone who
builds his life around a commitment to the attainment or preservation of any
such state of affairs thus lays himself open to devastation, and that an
enduring happiness is not achievable under such conditions. A commitment
to anything finite or worldly produces more anxiety than satisfaction even in
the absence of actual frustration, once the vulnerability of everything finite
or worldly to forces beyond one's control is recognized. The only hope of
achieving an enduring happiness on a nonreligious plane thus would seem to
involve resigning oneself to the necessity of adopting an attitude of indifference to everything finite and worldly, and refraining from making any of the
sorts of commitment discussed above. The "stoic-ethical" individual therefore
refrains from building his life around anything which forces beyond his
control might affect, and places no value on anything in the realm of
objectivity and action. It is for this reason that Kierkegaard characterizes him

as the "knight of infinite resignation"; and it is in this sense that he is to be understood when he says, "In resignation I make renunciation of everything."[23]

The traditional stoic term for this state of cultivated indifference to everything finite and worldly is *ataraxia,* and it is through the attempt to achieve this state that the "stoic-ethical" individual strives to attain an enduring happiness. In this state one achieves a peace of mind and a freedom from anxiety and frustration which are not possible for those who leave themselves exposed to the possibility of disillusionment and the vicissitudes of fate—a kind of Olympian calm which enables one to accept whatever may befall one with equanimity and which is satisfying simply in virtue of the awareness of one's transcendence of fate and fortune that it involves. Kierkegaard goes so far as to say that a kind of eternity is thereby achieved, and he would seem to feel that this is as close as one can come to an enduring happiness on a nonreligious plane.

The "renunciation of everything" which this mode of existence involves is not carried to the point of strict asceticism, for it is not a condition of the attainment of ataraxia that one must rigorously abstain from any activity not absolutely required to sustain one's existence. As Hegel observes, the stoic is equally at ease on the throne or in chains. His external condition is a matter of indifference to him; but precisely for this reason, he can accept it as he finds it. He can live a "normal" life—only there are very definite limits on what he will do for the sake of anything finite he possesses or might possess. He allows himself to enjoy the use of things and the company of others where opportunity allows, but he is unperturbed by material deprivation and social isolation. He does not shun participation in the life of the community in which he lives and may engage in cognitive inquiry, but he sets no great store by either "ethical life" or knowledge as such. Whatever may happen in any of these contexts ultimately makes little difference to him, for his happiness is not at stake in any of them. His happiness is strictly and solely a function of the tranquility he achieves by taking care never to become seriously involved in any such affairs and concerning himself only with the preservation of his fundamental independence in relation to all of them. Thus Kierkegaard says, "He who has made the act of infinite resignation is sufficient unto himself."[24]

This mode of existence might seem at first glance to be very similar to that final stage of "aesthetic" existence characterized by despair concerning the possibility of achieving happiness on the "aesthetic" plane. It seems to me, however, that the two are quite distinct; for despair of this sort is something very different from "infinite resignation." Despair has nothing of the peacefulness and calm about it which characterizes the latter; it tends to be bitter, resentful, and angry and thus not at all like quiet resignation.

This mode is further characterized by a stance which, if not incompatible with that associated with "subjective-ethical" existence, would at least be rather out of keeping with it. For it is difficult to imagine someone with an attitude of infinite resignation toward everything finite committing himself passionately to *anything* on this plane. And more importantly, one would expect that, generally speaking, someone who is "infinitely resigned" would not be "infinitely interested" in anything like the attainment of genuine individuality. Thus these two modes of existence are distinct, even if perhaps not quite mutually exclusive. Roughly the same thing can be said about "infinite resignation" and the "objective-ethical" and "objective-cognitive" modes of existence.

The moving force which underlies the act of "infinite resignation" is the same as that which underlies both the adoption and the ultimate rejection of the "aesthetic" mode of existence: the longing for happiness. This longing initially leads one to devote oneself to the enjoyment and pursuit of pleasurable moments; but it also leads one to abandon this orientation when one realizes that the only true happiness is an enduring happiness, and that an enduring happiness cannot be founded on so ephemeral a basis as momentary pleasures. Similarly, the act of infinite resignation is made on the basis of a recognition that an enduring and secure happiness cannot be grounded in attachment to anything finite—anything which fortune's vicissitudes or human changeability can take away, or anything which claims rational validity but succumbs to critical analysis—and that, in fact, an enduring happiness cannot be secured so long as one is not able to contemplate with stoic calm the lack of possession or validity of any such thing. The hope is, however, that through this self-elevation above attachment to things of the world, one will be able to achieve an enduring happiness—in the self-sufficient state of ataraxia itself.

Now, I have been treating the mode of existence characterized by "infinite resignation" as, in Kierkegaard's terms in the early pages of his discussion, "a purely philosophical movement"[25] which expresses a purely "worldly wisdom."[26] It is important, however, to distinguish between this form of resignation and renunciation, which is quite independent of any notion of or relation to a God of any sort, and one in which it is a desire for unity with an infinite and transcendent God that leads one to renounce everything finite and worldly—any attachment which would bind one to this world and thereby keep one from achieving this unity. The latter is associated with a mode of existence that is no longer merely "ethical"; the introduction of the notion of God into the picture makes it a "religious" one.

The moving force giving rise to this new mode is, as elsewhere, the desire to achieve an enduring happiness. Here, however, this happiness is sought not simply in a state of ataraxia, but rather in a relation to an eternal reality other than both the world and oneself. The difference between the two modes of existence should be clear: one is characterized by self-sufficiency, the other by a relation of dependence upon a reality which most emphatically transcends oneself. One is characterized by a primary negative attitude toward the world; the other is characterized by a primary positive attitude toward something otherworldly.

Unfortunately, Kierkegaard does not clearly distinguish between these two modes in *Fear and Trembling;* he begins by talking about the former sort of infinite resignation and ends by talking about the latter. Where Hegel had clearly distinguished between the stoic mode of consciousness and the otherworldly consciousness exemplified by the monasticism of the Middle Ages, [27] Kierkegaard makes no such explicit distinction. Yet it is not the monk but rather the stoic who takes self-sufficiency as his aim; and it is the monk, not the stoic, of whom it may be said that he "concentrates his soul in a single glance toward heaven. . . . Then he will calmly put on the motley garb." And it is the monk (but not the stoic conceived as the embodiment of the ultimate in strictly "wordly wisdom") who would say, "It is more to me than my earthly happiness that my love of God should triumph in me." [28] Yet Kierkegaard attributes both the aim of self-sufficiency and the latter sentiments to the "knight of infinite resignation." The fact that he does so, however, would not seem to me to require that both be regarded as attitudes associated with a single mode of existence. Since they quite clearly reflect two very different basic orientations—one still "ethical," the other obviously "religious"—I consider it necessary to distinguish two different modes of existence here and to suppose that Kierkegaard simply felt it unnecessary for his purposes in *Fear and Trembling* to deal with them separately.

Before turning to this "religious" mode of existence, I shall refer briefly to the shortcomings of the "stoic-ethical" mode, which render it unsatisfactory, both in Kierkegaard's eyes and also eventually (according to Kierkegaard) to one who attempts to achieve an enduring happiness through adopting the sort of stance associated with it. First, Kierkegaard considers it profoundly unsatisfactory in that it constitutes a definite step away from, rather than toward, what he regards as true human self-realization. It is a highly impersonal mode of existence, since by its very nature it involves a repudiation of that through which alone (for Kierkegaard) individuality can be achieved and subjectivity intensified, namely, commitment. The "stoic-ethical" individual is no real individual at all, since he deliberately abstains from the sort of commitment which might render him a unique personality, and thus is essentially indistinguishable from any other. Moreover, the very tranquility and calm achieved in the state of ataraxia could not be further removed from the passion required to reach the ultimate in Kierkegaardian subjectivity. In short, this mode of existence is characterized by a degree of "objectivity" and impersonality greater than that encountered in any of the other modes of existence he discusses. And since he takes true human self-realization to involve the attainment of genuine individuality and the intensification of subjectivity, it is obvious that "stoic-ethical" existence falls far short of it.

This mode of existence also suffers from another shortcoming: like all the others encountered up to this point, it too proves incapable of yielding the enduring happiness it seems at first to promise. Initially, it may indeed yield considerable satisfaction, akin to the relief one feels when liberated from some torment or worry. With the passage of time, however, this feeling of satisfaction begins to pale, just as one ceases to feel relief as the threat of some danger to which one had been exposed and from which one then had been delivered recedes into the past. The more secure one comes to feel in relation to anything which might befall one, the less satisfaction is derivable from one's achievement of invulnerability. Precisely because the kind of self-sufficiency attained through the act of "infinite resignation" is essentially negative in character, consisting simply in a systematic abstention from all commitments and involvements which would have the effect of making one dependent upon forces and factors beyond one's control, it lacks any positive feature which could serve as a source of intrinsic satisfaction.

The closer one comes to achieving a state of pure ataraxia, therefore, the duller and emptier the peace of mind associated with it becomes; and the duller and emptier the peace of mind, the less capable it is of yielding any real happiness. Thus Kierkegaard contends that one cannot escape the conclusion that an enduring happiness cannot be achieved in any of the non-"religious" modes of existence, for each of them is seen upon examination to culminate in despair.

VII

The mode of "religious" existence referred to above is one of a number Kierkegaard discusses, and is to be sharply distinguished both from that represented by Abraham in *Fear and Trembling* and from the Christian mode as he presents it. I shall refer to the first of the three as the "ascetic-mystical" mode of existence, to mark it off as clearly as possible both from the modes I have been discussing (and in particular from the "stoic-ethical" mode) and from the other "religious" modes to which I shall turn subsequently (neither of which involves either an ascetic stance in relation to things of this world or a mystical type of religious consciousness).

This mode of existence is by no means to be associated with historical Christianity in any special way. Indeed, although an "ascetic-mystical" tendency has characterized certain variants of both Judaism and Christianity almost from the time of their appearance in history, Kierkegaard seems to feel that this tendency represents an orientation importantly different from those of both true Judaism and true Christianity. At any rate, the orientation under consideration is clearly "religious" as opposed to merely "ethical" or "aesthetic," in that what is central to it is the attempt to achieve unity with a transcendent "eternal reality." This orientation may be termed "mystical," in that the achievement of such unity is felt to be possible only through the attainment of a kind of consciousness which is utterly different from those associated with sensuous, social, and rational life and in which both subjectivity and objectivity are left behind as the "ascetic-mystic" becomes one with something transcending the world of men and things altogether. And it may be termed "ascetic" in that a precondition of the achievement of such unity is thought to be a life of physical and spiritual discipline and self-denial, through which alone one may hope to break free of the hold of the finite and worldly and to attain the kind of state in question.[29]

The terms "renunciation" and "resignation," if used to characterize both the "stoic-ethical" and the "ascetic-mystical" attitudes toward everything worldly and finite, conceal an important distinction. As has already been suggested, the "stoic-ethical" mode of existence is a mode in which one can accept with tranquility the loss of anything of this sort, but in which one also can enjoy the possession of the same if and when one has it. One is able to take it or leave it, but feels under no constraint to leave it when it is there to be taken. The "ascetic-mystic," on the other hand, regards enjoyment of anything finite and worldly as a definite obstacle to the achievement of unity with the "eternal reality"; for him, therefore, such enjoyment must be set aside altogether. In order for "my love of God [to] triumph in me," as Kierkegaard puts it (speaking for the "ascetic-mystic"), "my earthly happiness" is something I must deny to myself. After my "single glance toward heaven," I must "calmly put on the motley garb" of one who has taken the vow of poverty. (It should be observed, for future reference, that asceticism of this sort is something Kierkegaard considers to be no part of either true Judaism or true Christianity.)

Another crucial difference between the "stoic-ethical" and "ascetic-mystical" modes of existence is to be found in the form of transcendence of the finite associated with each. In both an enduring happiness is sought, and in both it is seen that this cannot be found by building one's life around anything finite. The "stoic-ethical" individual, however, seeks happiness in pure self-sufficiency; it is this aim which keeps him from becoming committed to relations to anything outside of himself. The "ascetic-mystic," on the other hand, seeks it by attempting to achieve a relation to an eternal reality which transcends him, with the idea that a truly enduring and unlimited happiness can only be found through the achievement of a relation of this sort.

In this respect Kierkegaard would seem to think that the "ascetic-mystical" orientation constitutes an advance over the "stoic-ethical," for he feels that the attempt to achieve an enduring happiness through the attainment of self-sufficiency overlooks the fact of man's essential finitude. Self-sufficiency would be possible as a foundation for an enduring happiness only for a being not subject to the limitations of finitude (for God, in other words, but not for man), and only if the state in which it is attained is not merely negative—as the state of ataraxia essentially is. When these facts are recognized, the ultimate untenability of the "stoic-ethical" mode of existence as one in which an enduring happiness can be achieved clearly emerges. It follows, therefore, that if one is to carry the quest for an enduring happiness any further, one must seek it in a relation of some kind which is neither to anything worldly nor simply to oneself. This suggests the idea of a relation to something beyond both, and the "eternal reality" with which the "ascetic-mystic" attempts to become one is something precisely of this sort.

The "ascetic-mystical" mode of existence (or "religiousness A," in the terminology of the *Postscript*) is the highest mode of existence that Kierkegaard considers men to be capable of attaining by their own efforts. It is the highest mode, in other words, that "has only human nature in general as its assumption" (in addition to the existence of the "eternal reality," or God, with whom unity is sought), as opposed to some sort of divine initiative. [30] Kierkegaard refers to it as the outcome of "the dialectic of inward transformation." [31] He says, "If the individual is inwardly shaped by self-annihilation before God, then we have religiousness A." [32] The realm in which God—and eternal happiness—is to be found is viewed as distinct from the world in which we have our finite, particular existence. It is a realm to which we have a degree of access, but only on a limited basis and only on the condition that we transcend the plane of finite, particular existence. Thus everything associated with our finite existence is repudiated; self-denial and even self-abnegation at the level of particularity and individuality are practiced and sought; and death is welcomed as the only complete liberation of the soul from the bondage of finitude.

While Kierkegaard does consider this mode of existence to constitute an advance beyond "stoic-ethical" existence, these last remarks indicate several important respects in which it falls short of being satisfactory. First, far from

making possible the attainment of genuine individuality, it involves a pervasive self-annihilation which precludes the attainment of even a semblance of
individuality. Indeed, if an "ascetic-mystic" were to succeed completely in
becoming one with the transcendent "eternal reality" he seeks, he would
cease to exist as an individual at all. And this, for Kierkegaard, is by no means
what the attainment of true humanity involves.

Secondly, the "ascetic-mystical" mode of existence is held to suffer from
the now familiar defect that an existing human being cannot achieve an
enduring happiness by adopting such an orientation; for while Kierkegaard
holds that an enduring happiness can be achieved only through the attainment of a relation to an "eternal reality," the "ascetic-mystic" sets about
trying to attain a relation of this sort in a way that involves doing everything
in his power to become something other than a finite, existing human being.
In fact, if it is the case that death is the only complete liberation of the soul
from the bondage of finitude, and that short of death the only unity with the
"eternal reality" one can attain is merely temporary and partial, it follows
that the happiness the "ascetic-mystic" achieves so long as he lives is anything but complete, and indeed is as ephemeral as the moments in which
he is able to transcend his finite worldly existence. What is sought is an
enduring happiness that *an existing human being* can achieve, not an enduring
happiness that can be achieved only when one ceases to be an existing human
being; and it is above all for this reason that Kierkegaard feels this mode of
"religious" existence must ultimately give way to some other, in which both
this defect and that discussed previously are remedied.

VIII

In all of the works in which Kierkegaard discusses this mode of "religious"
existence—most notably, *Fear and Trembling, Philosophical Fragments,* and
the *Postscript*—he contrasts it with another which he feels must be both
distinguished from it and placed above it. It is not the same alternate mode in
all three cases, however. In the latter two works it is Christianity he has in
mind, whereas in *Fear and Trembling* that which is in question is the
religiousness of Abraham—who not only was not but obviously could not
have been a Christian. And while there is certainly a connection between the
two modes, there is also a very essential difference. The very heart of
Christianity, according to Kierkegaard, is a belief in the paradox that God,
who is "eternal" and "infinite," has entered the realm of the temporal and
finite and has assumed the form of human existence—that is, the paradox of
the Incarnation. And clearly, that is not—cannot be—what is definitive of
Abraham's religiousness.

This is an obvious distinction, yet commentators rarely make it. Abraham's religiousness is not of the Christian sort, but neither is it "ascetic-mystical." The distinction between it and the latter should be obvious; indeed, the whole point of the preliminary investigation early in *Fear and Trembling* is to distinguish the "knight of faith"—exemplified by Abraham—from the "knight of infinite resignation," who initially represents the "stoic-ethical" stance and then becomes the "ascetic-mystic." In this section I shall discuss the mode of existence of the "knight of faith" as epitomized by Abraham in *Fear and Trembling*, before turning in the next to that which Kierkegaard associates with Christianity. Since I shall be characterizing the latter as "Christian," and since the former is modeled on Kierkegaard's depiction of the religiousness of a personage who is commonly regarded as quintessentially Jewish, I shall characterize this "religious" mode of existence as "Jewish." It may be historically (and perhaps also theologically) questionable to do so; but some relatively general and yet revealing designation is desirable, and I can think of no other that would better meet both requirements.

For the Abrahamic "knight of faith," as for the "ascetic-mystic," the key to the attainment of an enduring happiness is the achievement of a relation to an "eternal reality" (God) who does not number among the things of this world. And he places this relation before all others. He renounces all claim to everything finite, in the sense that he is prepared to give up anything and everything in this world if God should require him to do so—even to the extent of taking the life of his only son. Unlike the "ascetic-mystic," however, Kierkegaard's Abraham neither denies himself all enjoyment of things of this world, nor feels that the achievement of the proper relation to God requires that he abandon all concern with such things. Here he even differs from the "stoic-ethical" individual; for he not only enjoys such things when they come to him, but moreover retains a strong—if limited, in relation to his commitment to do God's will—attachment to certain of them. He is not "ultimately concerned" with anything worldly and finite; but it is part of his faith in God that he believes not only that God will not require him actually to sacrifice everything along these lines, but moreover that God both can and will see to it that things go well with him in this world. Thus, for example, even though he is prepared to obey God's command to sacrifice his beloved son Isaac, he believes that God will not really require it of him, when it comes right down to it, or, at any rate, that if God really does require it of him, then God will bring Isaac back to life again, or will give him a new Isaac, or will do *something* to make things turn out well in the end.[33]

God is not utterly remote and indifferent to Kierkegaard's Abraham personally, and Abraham does not expect "eternal happiness" only in another world than this or only by transcending this world altogether. He feels that God will bestow an enduring happiness upon him in *this* world, if only he believes in Him unconditionally and obeys Him completely, subordinating to God's will absolutely everything—including his personal inclinations and his "objective-ethical" obligations. For this reason he does not feel that he must lead a life of self-denial and achieve "self-annihilation" in order to achieve the happiness he seeks. Nor is his happiness a function of his attainment of a state of ataraxia; for he does not resign himself to the view that life is by and large a pretty grim affair, subject to the vicissitudes of fate and fortune. He believes that God will see to it that his life is better than that, even when this looks impossible in human terms. He does not transcend the finite by cultivating an attitude of indifference toward it; rather, he does so by placing his relation to God above his attachment to the finite.

In short, "Jewish" religiousness (as Kierkegaard analyzes it in *Fear and Trembling*) is characterized by a subordination of absolutely everything else to God's will and the belief that no matter how impossible the situation may look, "with God all things are possible." Abraham is willing to accept the loss of anything finite if God should require it; but he believes that God will not require it, if he can only satisfy God that he is prepared to part with it. He lives in accordance with the "objective-ethical" order under ordinary circumstances, but is prepared to depart from it should God demand this of him. This is the issue in Kierkegaard's discussion of the "teleological suspension of the ethical" (i.e., the suspension of "ethical" considerations for the sake of something more important). Abraham's enduring happiness is sought neither in the pursuit of pleasure, nor in the attainment of "universality" as such, nor in anything else he may achieve solely through his own powers, nor in a mystical, otherworldly, self-annihilating union with God; rather it is sought— and apparently achieved—in this world through his relation of complete faith and obedience as a particular existing individual to his God for whom all things are possible.

This serves to distinguish the "Jewish-religious" mode of existence from those discussed previously. A further point to be noticed, with the "Christian-religious" mode in mind, is that no reference is made to the Incarnation of God in human form. From Kierkegaard's discussion in *Fear and Trembling,* it would seem that God was able to make clear to Abraham that He comes above all else and to imbue him with the faith that with Him all things are possible, without resorting to such extreme measures. Unless Abraham's faith is still defective (in some respect that only the Incarnation can remedy), however, it is not clear why Kierkegaard should consider the Incarnation to be so important. And certainly no indication of any such defect is given in *Fear and Trembling.*

If the "Jewish-religious" mode of existence exemplified by Kierkegaard's Abraham leaves little to be desired in Kierkegaard's eyes, it follows that it must be at least largely free from those shortcomings Kierkegaard detects in the modes discussed previously. And in fact, as Kierkegaard represents it, it involves both a high degree of "subjectivity" and a relation that promotes and sustains individuality. It involves a high degree of subjectivity in that a belief in a God with whom all things are possible requires a great deal of "passion," since such a belief cannot be sustained by a rational consideration of what the probable outcome of many situations will be. And it is clear that if "subjectivity" is a function of "passion," a person like Kierkegaard's Abraham will have attained a much higher degree of "subjectivity" than one who believes and commits himself to nothing which it runs counter to "rationality" to believe and commit himself to.

Kierkegaard would also seem to think that one who is related to God as Abraham is achieves a degree of individuality which surpasses that of anyone who is not, in spite of the fact that there is nothing about the nature of his faith which is radically individuating. This is because Kierkegaard regards the sort of relation to God that Abraham achieves as itself radically individuating. He contends that to stand before God is to stand before him as this particular individual, interchangeable with no other. For God each person is utterly unique; and in the case of one who makes his relation to God the focal point of his existence, the uniqueness which is his in the context of his relation to God constitutes him as one whose existence is utterly unique. By coming to be thus related to God through faith, he is *endowed* with an individuality he could not otherwise achieve. And if God's concern for him is the ultimate basis of his individuality, it follows that his individuality is grounded in something infinitely more stable and trustworthy than anything finite and worldly. One's faith may falter; but as long as it does not, the individuality attained through it is secure. For nothing that may happen at the level of the finite and worldly can affect it.

Finally, Kierkegaard would appear to suggest that a happiness that is both genuine and enduring is achieved by one who is related to God as Abraham is. It is genuine in that it does not consist merely in that relief which accompanies the achievement of freedom from anxiety in the face of any circumstances which might possibly affect one adversely, but rather consists in positive satisfaction. And it is enduring in that there is nothing that can happen to one (short of a loss of faith) which can undermine the God relationship upon which it depends. For everything that happens to one is accepted as being the will of God for whom all things are possible and who never ceases to be concerned with one personally, and therefore one's happiness is unshakable as long as one keeps the faith. Of course, if one loses faith, one may be plunged into despair; but Kierkegaard is not concerned with that (very real) possibility. His interest is in discovering whether there is some possible mode of human existence in which one's nature as a human being *may* be realized and an enduring happiness *may* be achieved, not in answering the question of whether most people will or will not be able to sustain such a mode of existence once they have achieved it.

In "Jewish-religiousness" Kierkegaard would appear to have found a mode of existence of this sort. Yet he was not a Jew, but rather one of the strongest advocates of Christianity in modern times. Thus if this mode of "religious" existence does not suffer from any serious shortcomings in his view, it must at least be the case that he regards Christianity as a type of religiousness which does the religiousness of Abraham one better in one or more of the respects discussed above. It is with this suggestion that I now turn to the final stage in Kierkegaard's phenomenology of spiritual development, the "Christian" mode of "religious" existence.

IX

One might begin by asking, In what respect does Christianity (as Kierkegaard understands it) differ from Abraham's faith? In his discussion of Christianity, Kierkegaard places great emphasis upon the Incarnation; and thus the answer to this question would seem to be that the difference has something to do with this event. Since Kierkegaard is not concerned with doctrinal differences as such but rather with differences in types of belief or faith, however, the problem becomes that of determining what difference of the latter sort is involved in cases in which the Incarnation is and is not an article of faith. One thing this might affect is the idea that with God all things are possible—and with it, the syndrome of faith, passion, and subjectivity.

Kierkegaard seems to feel that there is nothing more paradoxical—and therefore nothing seemingly more impossible—than the idea that God (who is infinite and eternal) should have become man (and thus temporal and finite) without ceasing to be God. If this is so, therefore, and if God has done this, then he has shown in the most radical way that with him absolutely anything is possible. And at least one point of making the doctrine of the Incarnation central to Christianity, for Kierkegaard, is that one's willingness to accept the idea that God existed as man is the ultimate test of one's faith that with him all things are possible. Next to this test Abraham's does not look so difficult. All God had to do in that case was to rescind his command that Abraham sacrifice Isaac. And the most Abraham had to be able to believe was that God was capable of bringing Isaac back to life or to give him a new Isaac. Here, however, something seemingly much more impossible is in question, since it apparently involves the occurrence of an event that is more than merely miraculous. Even one with a faith as strong as Abraham's might have second thoughts about what is possible with God when the issue is carried this far, for a greater faith than Abraham's is required for one to affirm that God can do the *logically* (and not merely humanly) impossible.

The significance of this point is not difficult to see. It is one thing to believe that God can intervene in the world and bring about some state of affairs which would not occur in the ordinary course of events; but it is another to believe that God can do something which, rationally considered, ought to be utterly impossible. The latter is clearly much more "unreasonable" than the former, and thus it involves the mustering of a greater amount of passion than the former. Since "subjectivity" is held by Kierkegaard to be a function of "passion," however, this means that one who believes in the fact of the Incarnation attains a greater degree of "subjectivity" than one who simply believes in a God who has the power to work miracles. And it is for this reason that Kierkegaard can maintain that, with respect to "subjectivity," the "Christian" mode of "religious" existence constitutes an advance over the "Jewish."

The Incarnation is also of great significance for Kierkegaard in connection with the possibility of attaining an enduring happiness, given that a genuinely enduring happiness is attainable only through achieving a relation to something eternal, in the very world in which we live, and under the conditions of actual human existence. Kierkegaard seems to feel that such a relation was made possible through the Incarnation in a way in which it was not possible previously. In the "ascetic-mystical" view such happiness is possible only by transcending this world, since the relation to God which it presupposes is thought to be attainable only in this way, on the grounds that an "eternal reality" cannot be encountered within this world. According to Kierkegaard, however, a happiness of this sort is possible *in this world* for those who are able to accept the paradox of the Incarnation, which involved the appearance of God in the realm of the finite and temporal and so eliminated the necessity of a transcendence of the finite and temporal on the part of those who wish to relate themselves to him.

If the occurrence of the Incarnation (or at least, if a belief in its occurrence) is so decisive for the attainment of such a relation, however, what then are we to say about Abraham? His relation to God is not mediated by a belief in the fact of the Incarnation. It would seem, therefore, either that his relation to God is in fact defective or deficient in some respect or that the Incarnation does not have such great importance for the possibility of attaining a relation to God after all. Since Kierkegaard's insistence upon the importance of the Incarnation in this matter would appear to rule out the latter alternative, the former is indicated. Yet it is by no means easy to see any respect in which Abraham's relation to God is defective.

If there is a solution to this problem, it would seem to be along the following lines. The possibility of an existing human being's attaining a relation to God is a function of the extent to which God makes himself accessible to existing human beings. By addressing himself directly to a particular person, God makes himself accessible to him to some degree. By taking the form of an existing human being, however, God makes himself much more accessible—even though centuries may separate a given person from the event; for the access that an existing human being has to something which actually exists (or has existed) on the plane of the finite and temporal is much greater (humanly speaking) than it is if what he must attempt to relate himself to is something which addresses itself to him from on high but remains completely "other," that is, "infinite" and "eternal."

Through the Incarnation, therefore, in which God made himself more accessible to man than he had been before, by taking the form of a man, God made it possible for men to relate themselves to him in a way which previously was not possible. And in doing so, he laid a firmer foundation for the attainment of genuine individuality and an enduring happiness on the part of existing human beings than exists for one whose faith is simply that of Abraham. The difference is more quantitative than qualitative; but even if it is only a difference of degree, Kierkegaard regards the difference as sufficiently great to render the "Christian" mode of religiousness a significant advance over the "Jewish" mode with respect to both individuality and the attainment of an enduring happiness.

There is something more to the distinction between the two modes of existence than this, however. The happiness of Kierkegaard's Abraham is at least to a considerable extent a function not merely of his relation to God and his faith in God's ability to cause things to turn out well for him in his worldly existence, but moreover of things *actually* turning out well. If in point of fact they often do *not* do so, it would not be surprising to find the happiness of a man like Abraham greatly diminished, in relation to that which Abraham himself enjoyed. For Kierkegaard's Abraham is by no means indifferent to the circumstances of his worldly existence, even though he places his relation to God above them and his faith in God's omnipotence and benevolence above any temporary reverses he might suffer. And precisely because his happiness is not solely a function of his God relationship, it is vulnerable in no small degree in a way that the happiness of one whose *only concern* is with his God relationship is not.

Here the Kierkegaardian Christian may have an advantage over one whose mode of existence is "Jewish-religious," where the attainment of an infinite and enduring happiness is concerned. He does not merely place his relation to God above all other things, to which he nonetheless retains a considerable attachment. Rather, he is quite prepared, in the words of the Lutheran hymn, to "let goods and kindred go"; for his concern with his God relationship is so great that it reduces all else to utter insignificance in his eyes. He does not worry about whether or not God will exercise his omnipotence to cause things to turn out well for him in his worldly existence; for he does not really care about such things at all, actively concerning himself with them only insofar as he believes it to be God's will that he do so. To be sure, many (perhaps most) of those who consider themselves Christians do not satisfy this description, but rather resemble Abraham in this respect; but to Kierkegaard this would only mean that they are less than true Christians. The true Christian's happiness is complete even in the face of the greatest worldly adversity, because it is not even partially dependent upon the circumstances of his worldly existence, and is as great as it can possibly be if only his God relationship is secure.

If this account is a correct representation of Kierkegaard's view of Abraham and of the true Christian, then it is indeed not difficult to see why he finds the "Christian-religious" mode of existence to be superior to the "Jewish-religious" mode in at least one respect, given the criteria of evaluation he employs. One may find his portrait of Abraham more appealing than that of the true Christian (in spite of Abraham's readiness to slay his son at what he took to be God's command); but that, for Kierkegaard, is an irrelevant consideration, which, if raised against him as a purportedly decisive criticism, would have undoubtedly prompted him to suggest that his critic was suffering from a case of arrested spiritual development (rather as Hegel would have responded to a naive realist who objected to his metaphysical conclusions in the name of common sense).

X

Kierkegaard feels that it can be demonstrated philosophically—and indeed, that he has done so—that the ultimate in subjectivity can be attained only through belief in the paradox of the Incarnation,[34] and that genuine individuality and a truly enduring happiness cannot be attained by an existing human being unless one who is an existing human being succeeds in relating himself to God. He recognizes, however, that it is one thing to understand this philosophically and quite another actually to make "the leap of faith" and thereby enter into a God relationship. And he further recognizes and stresses that the reality of God and the fact of the Incarnation are matters which cannot be demonstrated philosophically and moreover are highly questionable philosophically (i.e., rationally), to say the least. It follows from this that, while he has elucidated three different modes of "religious" existence, he has *not* shown that the God relationships on which they depend are actually (as opposed to merely hypothetically) possible; for to do so, he would have had to establish the reality of God. Consequently, he also has not shown that that sort of individuality and that genuinely enduring happiness which presuppose the attainment of a God relationship are actually possible. He feels he has shown that in the absence of the attainment of an adequate God relationship, human life must eventuate in despair; but he knows that he has not given anything like an argument that despair can actually be avoided in this way, since its central presupposition is neither provable nor demonstrably probable.

He presents for our consideration descriptions and analyses of three purportedly possible modes of "religious" existence, all of which involve God relationships of some sort, as well as descriptions and analyses of a considerable number of possible modes of existence which do not. He *claims* these modes are possible and asks us to consider the consequences for human self-realization (as he understands it) and human happiness on the assumption that they are, as well as the consequences if one does not (or cannot) advance to them. He further in effect invites us to take "the leap of faith" ourselves, by suggesting that nothing less will enable us to become both truly human and truly happy. But he offers no guarantee that the madness of such a "leap" from the standpoint of rationality and everything worldly is merely apparent. If there is no God, the "leap" is ridiculous, and the result is a life that is both ludicrous and pathetic. It is for this reason that Kierkegaard's title for the book in which he presents his analysis of the "knight of faith" is *Fear and Trembling.* The "leap" cannot be made with confidence but rather only in "fear and trembling," since it involves staking everything on something that is not only uncertain but improbable and even (in the case of Christianity) "absurd."

It is obvious that one who does not attach the importance Kierkegaard does to the intensification of subjectivity, the achievement of radical individuality, and the attainment of a truly enduring happiness will not accept his evaluation of the various modes of existence he analyzes in his phenomenology of spiritual development. And since his evaluation of them in terms of these factors is essential to his ordering of them, one who rejects his criteria of evaluation will undoubtedly reject his construal of them as ordered stages of spiritual development, and indeed the entire pattern of spiritual development as he understands it. Even if one does so, however, it seems to me that his discussions of the various modes of existence with which he deals are of considerable value; for, like Hegel's in his *Phenomenology of Spirit,* they contain a great many insights concerning the nature of different possible ways of arranging our lives, which are by no means inextricably bound up with his own particular philosophical and theological orientation and convictions. It is no doubt at least in part for this reason that his writings have exerted so great an influence upon subsequent philosophers, in spite of the fact that few if any have embraced the form of Christianity to which he was so completely committed.

8:

Nietzsche and Nihilism

Nietzsche shares a number of the basic concerns of Marx and Kierke-gaard—and also their fundamental dissatisfaction with the modern phil-osophical tradition proceeding from Descartes to Kant and culminating in the idealism of Hegel. In his analysis of various human "types" and dispositions, one may discern a persisting interest in something like the sort of problem with which Kierkegaard deals in his exploration of the various possible modes of human existence. In Nietzsche's attempt to show how the whole of reality can be understood in terms of the operation and manifestation of a single, non-"spiritual," dynamic prin-ciple the basic character of which is to be conceived as "will to power," one can recognize an attempt similar to Marx's to set forth a viable naturalistic alternative to Hegel's idealist mestaphysics. And in Nietzsche's extended effort to develop a philosophical anthropology in which all aspects of human life are analyzed as particular instantiations and expressions of this same fundamental principle, one can see him making common cause with both Kierkegaard and Marx against the tendency of both Hegel and many of his predecessors to construe man's nature primarily in terms of consciousness, reason, and cognitive en-deavor—even though his substantive views in this area, as also with respect to the other matters indicated, differ very considerably from both of theirs.

To ascertain the positions he takes and his reasons for doing so, however, on these and most of the other issues with which he deals is by no means easy. This is partly because both his writing style and the structure (or apparent lack of structure) of most of his works pose problems for philosophical readers. But it also is partly because some of Nietzsche's more celebrated remarks have given rise to the impression that he repudiates the very possibility of "truth" and "knowledge"

175

conceived other than in terms of the conduciveness of various beliefs to the survival and increase of power of one or another type of human being and that, consequently, he rejects the possibility of achieving any sort of genuine philosophical understanding of ourselves and reality, beyond a recognition of the cognitive insignificance and merely pragmatic value of anything we may happen to think. One who takes this position would be a philosophical nihilist, unable consistently to go on to propose substantive answers to most of the questions with which philosophers generally have been and continue to be concerned. To place oneself in a position to understand and evaluate much of what Nietzsche has to say, therefore, one must first come to terms with the question of whether he does in fact subscribe to these nihilistic principles; and it is the initial aim of the present chapter to do so—and to make it clear that he does not.

This chapter also has another purpose, however, which is both broader and more constructive than that of merely establishing this negative conclusion. For in the course of doing so, the chapter is also intended to indicate the nature of a number of the more important views Nietzsche advances on a variety of major philosophical issues pertaining to the nature of the world we live in, the kind of being a human being is, values, and moralities. As such, it may be conceived both as an attempt to remove a major obstacle to the consideration of Nietzsche's positions on these and related matters, and as an introduction to his thinking about them. And, by bringing some of the main themes of his philosophy into focus, it should further serve to provide the reader with some assistance in coping with the problems, alluded to above, arising from the very unsystematic, rather disjointed character and frequently aphoristic, metaphorical, and hyperbolical style of many of his writings. Nietzsche is too important a philosopher—not only historically but also where ongoing philosophical inquiry is concerned—for his writing style to be allowed to stand in the way of understanding his works and coming to terms with him.

Through a kind of guilt by association, the popularity of certain of Nietzsche's works (notably *Thus Spoke Zarathustra*) with large numbers of young and philosophically unsophisticated readers since the turn of the century in many parts of the Western world has led more than a few philosophers to write him off as a kind of Pied Piper of modern youth, to be set aside (along with other childish things) when one achieves intellectual maturity. This estimation of him and his writings as shallow, superficial, and simple-minded is profoundly mistaken—although it is difficult to say which misapprehension is greater: this one or that involved in the romanticization of him by those youthful devotees who project into him their own longings and sentiments. Both do Nietzsche a great injustice. To be properly understood, he must be approached unemotionally, carefully, and rigorously—as every philosopher who is any philosopher at all must be. And none of those discussed in this book is more deserving of serious consideration than Nietzsche, or can more richly reward the effort that studying him in this way requires.

Was Nietzsche a nihilist? It is widely thought that he was; and Arthur Danto, in an influential study,[1] subscribes wholeheartedly to this view (unlike such earlier commentators as Jaspers, Löwith, Morgan, and Kaufmann). Indeed, Danto claims that "Nihilism" is "the central concept of his philosophy."[2] He attributes to Nietzsche "a deep and total Nihilism"[3]—one which "is not an ideology but a metaphysics."[4] Nietzsche, he states, makes "unbridled claims in behalf of this extreme Nihilism";[5] and he asserts that "Nietzsche's philosophy is a sustained attempt to work out the reasons for and the consequences of Nihilism . . . ."[6] In short, according to Danto, "Nietzsche's is a philosophy of Nihilism."[7] It seems to me that it is quite illuminating to approach Nietzsche's philosophy by considering whether Danto is right—not because Danto's analysis is of exceptional interest in its own right, but rather because, in doing so, many of the main themes of Nietzsche's thought come to light and may be seen to form a more coherent whole than is initially apparent in his various writings.

There are several ways in which one might attempt to answer this question. First, one might examine Nietzsche's own assertions about the nature of nihilism and see whether he explicitly subscribes to it as he himself conceives of it. Secondly, one might consider the way in which "nihilism" as a philosophical doctrine is generally to be understood, and then determine whether or not the definition is applicable to Nietzsche's philosophical views. "Nihilism" in the philosophical sense of the term may be defined either as the doctrine that there is and can be no such thing as "truth" where reality is concerned, since reality is such that nothing whatsoever—except this fact—is true about it (metaphysical nihilism); or, more narrowly, as the doctrine that normative and evaluative principles have no objective basis in reality (axiological nihilism). Nietzsche might thus legitimately be termed a "nihilist" if it is the case that he subscribed to either or both of these doctrines. (Danto claims that he subscribes to both.)

It is my contention that, whichever way one chooses to approach the question, the answer is that Danto is wrong. Nietzsche may perhaps be said to have embraced a highly restricted form of "nihilism," namely, one which consists simply in the denial of any realm of "true being" apart from this world and of any transcendentally grounded system of values. At least from

Thus Spoke Zarathustra (1883) onward, however, he was not a "deep and total" nihilist, either as he himself conceived of "nihilism" or in either of the senses (metaphysical and axiological) mentioned above. I shall attempt to establish this first by considering what Nietzsche himself has to say about nihilism and then by showing that his actual views are such that the term "nihilism" cannot be applied to them in either of these senses.

I

"At times," Danto says, Nietzsche "spoke of his philosophy as Nihilism."[8] Is this true? And is it true, moreover, that Nietzsche makes "unbridled claims in behalf of this extreme Nihilism"?[9] Nietzsche does write: "—That it is the measure of strength to what extent we can admit to ourselves, without perishing, the merely *apparent* character, the necessity of lies. To this extent, nihilism, as the denial of a truthful world, of being, might be a divine way of thinking" (*WP*, §15).[10] He does say: "Nihilism . . . can be a sign of strength: the spirit may have grown so strong that previous goals . . . have become incommensurate" (*WP*, §23). He does speak of "nihilism as the necessary consequence of our valuations so far" (*WP*, § 69n). He does suggest that "it could be the sign of a crucial and most essential growth . . . that the most extreme form of pessimism, genuine *nihilism,* would come into the world" (*WP*, § 112). He does say, in a note of 1887, "That I have hitherto been a thoroughgoing nihilist, I have admitted to myself only recently" (*WP*, § 25). And, in a passage intended to serve as the preface to a work he planned to entitle *The Will to Power,* he does refer to himself as "the first perfect nihilist of Europe" (*WP*, Pref., § 3).

But can these remarks support the weight of Danto's claim? Two facts ought to give one pause at once. First, they are very nearly the only passages in the entire corpus of Nietzsche's writings which could be cited in direct support of these claims. And secondly, all of these statements are to be found in Nietzsche's notebooks, which he himself never published. In his published writings, he never refers either to himself as a "nihilist" or to his philosophy as "nihilism." In *Ecce Homo,* in which he is nothing if not candid about himself, he refers to himself not as a "nihilist" but as an "immoralist"—an expression which itself actually applies to him only in a restricted sense, since he does not repudiate all forms of morality but rather only certain ones, associated primarily with the Socratic-Judeo-Christian tradition.

Further, even in the passages cited above, Nietzsche may scarcely be said to make "unbridled claims" in behalf of an "extreme Nihilism." On the contrary, most of his remarks either are quite tentative or are qualified by subsequent observations. In the last passage cited, for example, after referring to himself as "the first perfect nihilist of Europe," he goes on to speak of himself as one "who, however, has even now lived through the whole of nihilism, to the end, leaving it behind, outside himself" (*WP*, Pref., § 3). And he immediately proceeds to characterize the relation of his philosophy to nihilism as follows: "For one should make no mistake about the meaning of the title that this gospel of the future wants to bear, '*The Will to Power: Attempt at a Revaluation of All Values*'—in this formulation a *countermovement* finds expression, regarding both principle and task; a movement that in some future will *take the place of* this perfect nihilism" (*WP*, Pref., §4).[11]

Finally, in the earlier note of 1887 (*WP*, §25), Nietzsche does not assert that he *is* a nihilist, but rather only that he has "hitherto been" one. And, while this consideration does not rule out the posibility that he *might* still have thought himself to be one, his wording provides little support for this interpretation; indeed, it would seem to weigh against it.

Thus the case for the mature Nietzsche's having conceived his position as one of nihilism is weak, to say the least, even if one considers only those passages which provide the strongest support for it. It becomes completely untenable, however, when one considers the sustained critical analysis to which "nihilism" is subjected in the large body of notes which make up the first book of *The Will to Power*. It is to this analysis that I now shall turn.

Consider, first, the following remarks: "A nihilist is a man who judges of the world as it is that it ought *not* to be, and of the world as it ought to be that it does not exist" (*WP*, § 585A). Again, "Nihilism represents a pathological transitional stage (what is pathological is the tremendous generalization, the inference that there is no meaning at all)" (*WP*, §13). Again, "It is in one particular interpretation, the Christian-moral one, that nihilism is rooted" (*WP*, §1). Again, "The nihilistic movement is merely the expression of physiological decadence" (*WP*, §38). Again, "We can abolish either our reverence [for traditional values] or ourselves. The latter constitutes nihilism" (*WP*, § 69*n*). Again, "The belief in . . . aim- and meaninglessness, is the psychologically necessary effect once the belief in God and an essentially moral order becomes untenable. Nihilism appears at that point. . . . One interpretation has collapsed; but because it was considered *the* interpretation, it now *seems as if* there were no meaning in existence at all" (*WP*, § 55).[12]

And from Nietzsche's published writings: "There may actually be puritanical fanatics of conscience who prefer even a certain nothing to an uncertain something to lie down on—and die. But this is nihilism and the sign of a despairing, mortally weary soul" (*BGE*, §10). Again, "Some have dared to call pity a virtue. . . . To be sure—and one should always keep this in mind—this was done by a philosophy that was nihilistic and had inscribed *negation of life* upon its shield" (*AC*, p. 573). Again, "Nihilism and Christianism: that rhymes, that does not only rhyme" (*AC*, p. 650). And finally:

This man of the future, who will redeem us not only from the hitherto reigning ideal [i.e., the "Christian-moral" one] but also from that which was bound to grow out of it, the great nausea, the will to nothingness, nihilism; this bell-stroke of noon and of the great decision that liberates the will again and restores its goal to the earth and his hope to man; this antichrist and antinihilist; this victor over God and nothingness—*he must come one day.* (*GM,* p. 96)

In the light of these and other similar passages, it is difficult indeed to see how anyone could conclude that Nietzsche considered himself a nihilist. For in them nihilism is regarded as a phenomenon deriving from and related to others which he associates with "decadence" and also as a danger, against which he directly and strongly reacts and which he considers it imperative to overcome. What requires an answer is the question: Given that these passages express his basic stance in relation to nihilism, how is one to understand those of his other remarks pertaining to nihilism which have led Danto and others to conclude that he embraced it? In some of these remarks, Nietzsche attempts to show that "the advent of nihilism" is at hand and is indeed inevitable, and to explain why. In others, he suggests that while nihilism may prove disasterous, its advent may also in certain circumstances be a good sign; and to this extent he regards it positively. In neither case, however, do his remarks imply an unqualified affirmation of nihilism, which would conflict with the attitude expressed in the passages cited above. This I shall now attempt to show.

"Nihilism," Nietzsche says, "stands at the door" (*WP*, §1). The advent of nihilism is inevitable. What is this nihilism of which he speaks? "What does nihilism mean? *That the highest values devaluate themselves*" (*WP*, §2). "*Radical nihilism* is the conviction of [the] absolute untenability of existence when it comes to the highest values one recognizes" (*WP*, §3). Why is the advent of nihilism held to be inevitable? Because "we have measured the value of the world according to categories that refer to a purely ficticious world" (*WP*, §12B). When this is recognized—as it is coming to be—the world is bound to appear valueless and meaningless to those who cannot conceive of its value and meaning in any other terms. When it is recognized that the world cannot be understood in terms of the categories which traditionally have been applied to it, those who cannot conceive of it in any other terms will despair of being able to comprehend it at all. This is only natural; indeed, according to Nietzsche, it is psychologically unavoidable. And those in question include all of us—not excepting Nietzsche himself—at least for a time. "The categories 'aim,' 'unity,' 'being' which we used to project some value into the world—we *pull out* again; so the world looks valueless" (*WP*, §12A).

The world *looks* valueless. But that does not mean that it *is* valueless and essentially incomprehensible. With the collapse of our traditional world view, a period of nihilism must follow. But that is not, for Nietzsche, the end of the line. "The universe seems to have lost value, seems 'meaningless'—but that is only a *transitional stage*" (*WP*, §7). For it is not the intrinsic meaninglessness and incomprehensibility of the world itself that he holds to be the source of the coming nihilism. Rather, its source is held to be the collapse of an (erroneous) *interpretation of* the world: "It is in one particular interpretation, the Christian-moral one, that nihilism is rooted" (*WP*, §1). Nietzsche goes on to observe that "the untenability of one interpretation . . . awakens the suspicion that *all* interpretations of the world are false" (*WP*, §1). The nihilist, after all, does not stop with a repudiation of the previously accepted interpretation of the world; he generalizes, denying the possibility of any alternative. This generalization, however, is not only not logically warranted but is also, according to Nietzsche, "pathological"; nihilism, in his view, is not simply a transitional stage, but moreover is "a pathological transitional stage (what is pathological is the tremendous generalization, the inference that there is no meaning at all)" (*WP*, §13).

Of course, the logical illegitimacy of this generalization by itself does not serve to establish that some other interpretation of the world is in fact either possible or correct, and it remains to be seen what Nietzsche intends to propose along these lines. But it should be clear that, in his prophecy and explanation of the advent of a period of nihilism, he does not commit himself to the position that nihilism is a doctrine which is both final and correct.

Given that Nietzsche holds a period of nihilism to be inevitable following the collapse of "the Christian-moral" interpretation of the world, the question of his attitude toward it arises. The answer to this question is twofold, because his attitude toward it depends on whether it has the character of epilogue or prologue. He considers it necessary to distinguish between two types of nihilism, only one of which is transitional in a positive direction. It, however, is held not to be the "expression" of "decadence," as the other is, but rather a symptom of the fact that the fictions of the traditional world view are no longer *needed:* "Nihilism . . . can be a sign of strength: the spirit may have grown so strong that previous goals . . . have become incommensurate" (*WP*, §23). Thus Nietzsche writes: "Nihilism: It is *ambiguous:* A. Nihilism as a sign of increased power of the spirit: as *active* nihilism. B. Nihilism as decline and recession of the power of the spirit: as *passive* nihilism" (*WP*, §22).

Nietzsche is profoundly contemptuous of nihilism of the latter sort, as, for example, in the note, "*The perfect nihilist.* – The nihilist's eye idealizes in the direction of ugliness" (*WP*, §21). Still, it deeply worries him. He thinks of "the nihilistic catastrophe that finishes Indian culture" (*WP*, §64), and fears that a similar fate may be in store for the West. So, for example, in the paragraph in which he speaks of "the advent of nihilism," he states, "For some time now, our whole European culture has been moving as toward a castastrophe" (*WP*, Pref., §2). And in the Preface he added to the *Genealogy of Morals,* he says: "I understood the ever spreading morality of pity . . . as the most sinister symptom of a European culture that had itself become sinister, perhaps as its by-pass to a new Buddhism? to a Buddhism for Europeans? to–nihilism?" (*GM*, p. 19).

Nietzsche's attitude toward nihilism of the former sort, on the other hand, is quite different. He says: "It could be the sign of a crucial and most essential growth, of the transition to new conditions of existence, that the most extreme form of pessimism, genuine *nihilism*, would come into the world" (*WP*, §112). For this reason he does not view "the advent of nihilism" as an unmitigated disaster. It must come, as the traditional world view must go, if a new world view is to take its place; and the fact that it is coming may be due at least in part to the fact that some feel strong enough to try to do without the traditional world view.

Still, Nietzsche considers "nihilism as the necessary consequence of our valuations so far" to be "*the danger of dangers*" (*WP*, §69*n*). And he regards it as "the danger of dangers" because he holds that no one can do without *any* world view indefinitely. Unless we are able to achieve a new world view in relation to which we may orient ourselves–one which is more tenable than the traditional one–even the strongest will not be able to endure. "The time has come," he writes, "when we have to pay for having been Christians for two thousand years: we are losing the center of gravity by virtue of which we have lived; we are lost for a while" (*WP*, §30). The question is, Are we to remain lost, or can we find a *new* "center of gravity"?

Faced with the advent of nihilism, Nietzsche found this question profoundly worrisome; and his great anxiety in the face of the former possibility was the source of the urgency with which he attempted to realize the latter. He felt it to be imperative, if at all possible, not merely to avoid "passive nihilism" but moreover to go beyond the stage of "active nihilism" which must be expected to follow the demise of the traditional world view, "leaving it behind" in favor of "a countermovement . . . [which] will take the place of this perfect nihilism" (*WP*, Pref., §§ 3–4). And in fact he holds not only that this *is* possible, but moreover that in his philosophy–and more specifically, in his conception of "the will to power"—this "countermovement finds expression" (*WP*, Pref., §4).

While Nietzsche does see something positive in one type of nihilism, therefore, he is far from embracing it unreservedly and unconditionally. He does at times speak highly of it in *The Will to Power*—as, for example, when he says that it can take the form of a courageous denial of the existence of any "true world" apart from this one, and that "to this extent, nihilism ... might be a divine way of thinking" (*WP*, §15). But he qualifies his approval even as he gives it, with the words "to this extent." A nihilism of strength compares favorably in his eyes with the blind acceptance of what he regards as the lies and deceptions associated with the traditional world view. Further, it constitutes progress; it is a step in the right direction, in relation to the traditional world view. But it is *only* that—*only* a "transitional stage." Nietzsche himself does not want to stop there, with a "No" to traditional morals and values and a denial of traditional metaphysics; and he is anxious that *we* do not stop there either. He wants us to see that they are untenable and that they are going to have to be abandoned, whether we like it or not. But he is just as concerned—indeed, more so—that something else should take their place. "My style," he says, "is *affirmative,* and deals with contradiction and criticism only as a means" (*TI*, p. 511).[13]

II

It remains to be determined, however, whether or not the affirmations Nietzsche makes are sufficient to refute the claim that he *in fact* was a nihilist. For, to be sure, it does not refute *this* claim simply to show that he did not consider himself to be one, and that he regarded his philosophy as a "countermovement" to nihilism, which went beyond it. I shall now attempt to show that this claim too is wrong, and that Nietzsche does not hold, as Danto contends he does, that "there is nothing about reality to be said (or, about reality, there is only *that* to be said)."[14] I shall argue that, on the contrary, he holds that there *are* positive general truths, both about the nature of reality and in the matter of value, which can be stated and which ought to be recognized, at least by those who are strong enough to live with an awareness of them.

Nietzsche's views on these matters do entail a rejection of the basic tenets of most traditional metaphysical and axiological systems; but they are of such a nature that he could be termed a nihilist only if it were to be arbitrarily stipulated that everyone is a nihilist who is not a Platonist, a Christian, a rationalist, or an adherent of some other such traditional philosophical or religious world view. If, on the other hand, nihilism is understood (as I believe it should be) to involve the claim that neither the world nor values are such that anything both positive and objectively true may be said about them, then Nietzsche most emphatically is *not* a nihilist. In support of this contention, I shall first consider some of his basic views about reality generally and about man's nature, and then some of his main points concerning axiological matters.

According to Danto, "if we take 'true' in [the] conventional sense of expressing what is the case," then it is Nietzsche's position that "nothing is true and everything is false."[15] He takes Nietzsche to be saying that men have not discovered "the truth" about the world, not because anything has kept them from it, but rather because "there is none to discover."[16] Consider, however, the following passages from *Ecce Homo:* " 'We strive for the forbidden': in this sign my philosophy will triumph one day, for what one has forbidden so far as a matter of principle has always been—truth alone" (*EH,* p. 219). Again, "I was the first to *discover* the truth by being the first to experience lies as lies" (*EH,* p. 326). Again, "The truth speaks out of me.— But my truth is *terrible;* for so far one has called *lies* truth" (*EH.* p. 326). Again, "How much truth [can] a spirit *endure,* how much truth does it *dare?* More and more that became for me the real measure of value" (*EH,* p. 218).[17]

In *Ecce Homo,* Nietzsche also frequently speaks of "truth" in connection with both the person and the message of his Zarathustra. He refers to his work *Thus Spoke Zarathustra* as "born out of the innermost wealth of truth" (*EH,* p. 219). "Zarathustra," he says, "is more truthful than any other thinker. His doctrine, and his alone, posits truthfulness as the highest virtue; this means the opposite of the cowardice of the 'idealist' who flees from reality" (*EH,* p. 328). And he writes, "What Zarathustra wants: this type of man that he conceives, conceives reality *as it is,* being strong enough to do so" (*EH,* p. 331). Innumerable similar passages could be cited, from this and other published works, as well as from *The Will to Power.* They clearly indicate that, far from holding that "nothing is true," Nietzsche in fact holds that there *is* such a thing as "truth"—truth about the nature of things and about man, and not only that it *may* be discovered, but moreover that it *has* been discovered, and that he himself has discovered it.

But what is it that he has discovered, which he refers to repeatedly as "the truth"? Many things, as shall be seen, but most importantly, in his eyes, one thing in particular. In the last lines of the last section of *The Will to Power,* he states his fundamental "discovery" and his most profound metaphysical "truth" as follows: *"This world is the will to power—and nothing besides! And you yourselves are also this will to power—and nothing besides!"* (*WP,* §1067). Nietzsche is by no means prepared to regard his conception of the world as "will to power" as merely one more world interpretation alongside others—the Platonic, the Christian, the Kantian, the Hegelian, the mechanistic, etc.—which is no less but also no more ultimately valid than they are. On the contrary, he argues at length that each of the others is untenable; and he further argues at length that his is sound. In *Beyond Good and Evil*, for example, it is set forth, not as a poetic vision but rather as a serious hypothesis, the validity of which is to be determined by its explanatory power. "Suppose," he says,

> we succeeded in explaining our entire instinctive life as the development and ramification of *one* basic form of the will—namely, of the will to power, as *my* proposition has it; suppose all organic functions could be traced back to this will to power and one could also find in it the solution of the problem of procreation and nourishment ... —then one would have gained the right to determine *all* efficient force univocally as—*will to power*. The world viewed from inside, the world defined and determined according to its 'intelligible character'—it would be 'will to power' and nothing else.— (*BGE*, §36)

In this passage the matter is stated hypothetically; but it is quite clear, from other passages in this work and elsewhere, that Nietzsche is quite convinced of the correctness of his hypothesis. "Life itself," he states categorically in *Beyond Good and Evil*, "is will to power" (*BGE*, §13, also §259). And, in *The Will to Power:* "But *what is life?* Here we need a new, more definite formulation of the concept of 'life.' My formula for it is: Life is will to power" (*WP*, §254). All of the phenomena associated with life, according to Nietzsche, from the "lowest" to the "highest," are to be understood in these terms. "In the case of an animal," he says, "it is possible to trace all its drives to the will to power; likewise all the functions of organic life to this one source" (*WP*, §619).[18]

Nietzsche also extends the application of this concept beyond the phenomena associated with life. "Life," he states, "is merely a special case of the will to power" (*WP*, §692). He refers to the "will to power" as that "in which I recognize the ultimate ground and character of all change" (*WP*, §685). "The victorious concept 'force,'" he says, in terms of which science has come to understand all things, "still needs to be completed: an inner will must be ascribed to it, which I designate as 'will to power'" (*WP*, §619). He even goes so far as to say that "the innermost essence of being is will to power" (*WP*, §693). These and other similar passages make it clear that Nietzsche is committed to a definite if rather unorthodox metaphysical world view, and that he intends his statements of it to be taken, not as false, but as true—and as true not merely in a relative or perspectival sense, but in the sense of expressing the way the world really is.

He further holds a number of other, though related, metaphysical propositions to be true. The one for which he is perhaps best known is the proposition that all events recur eternally. Even Danto is compelled to admit that Nietzsche commits himself to the truth of his doctrine of the eternal recurrence of the same events. At times, to be sure, Nietzsche seems less concerned with the truth of the doctrine than with the cultivation of an affirmative attitude toward life so great that one not only could *endure* the thought of an eternal recurrence of the same series of events which has produced and is the existing world, but moreover could *desire* such a recurrence. To *will* the eternal recurrence of the same events is for Nietzsche the ultimate expression of an affirmative attitude toward life. So, for example, in *Beyond Good and Evil*, he puts forward "the ideal of the most high-spirited, alive, and world-affirming human being who has not only come to terms and learned to get along with whatever was and is, but who wants to have *what was and is* repeated into all eternity" (*BGE*, §68).[19]

At other times, however, that with which Nietzsche is concerned is the demonstration of the *truth* of the proposition that the same series of events which has occurred must recur eternally. And that he should have both concerns is not unreasonable. After all, there is nothing contradictory in both maintaining the truth of a doctrine and desiring that people should have an attitude toward life so positive that they can embrace it gladly. Indeed, it is only reasonable that once Nietzsche had come to be convinced of the truth of the doctrine of eternal recurrence, he would become all the more concerned with the problem of our responses to the idea of eternal recurrence, and that he would continue to regard one's reaction to the idea as a decisive test of one's attitude toward life; for he knew, from personal experience, that the idea could appear terrible indeed. In moments of pessimism and weakness, he found the idea unendurable, while in moments of exuberance and strength, he embraced it enthusiastically. And this suggested to him both that he himself was still "human-all-too-human" and what a better man than himself would in part be like. He undoubtedly had the doctrine of eternal recurrence in mind when he wrote the passage in which he asks: "How much truth [can] a spirit *endure*, how much truth does it dare?" (*EH*, p. 218).

That Nietzsche does hold this doctrine to be true is clear. One of the notes in *The Will to Power* consists of an outline of a projected discussion of it, which reads in part: "*The eternal recurrence.* . . . 1. Presentation of the doctrine and its *theoretical* presuppositions and consequences. 2. Proof of the doctrine" (*WP*, §1057). He never completed, let alone published, the systematic discussion which he contemplates here; but his basic line of reasoning is indicated clearly enough in a number of other notes in *The Will to Power*. In one he states, "The law of the conservation of energy demands *eternal recurrence*" (*WP*, §1063). In another, "Our presuppositions: no God; no purpose; finite force" (*WP*, §595). Nietzsche does not think it necessary to argue for the first of these "presuppositions." He spells out and argues for the second as follows: "If the world had a goal, it must [already] have been reached. If there were for it some unintended final state, this also must have been reached" (*WP*, §1062). He takes it to be obvious, however, that no such goal or final state *has* been reached. This argument itself supposes, first, that an infinite time has preceded the present moment—a supposition Nietzsche considers incontrovertible—and, secondly, that the third presupposition cited above ("finite force") is sound. In this connection he says, "The world, as force, may not be thought of as unlimited, for it *cannot* be so thought of; we forbid ourselves the concept of an infinite force as incompatible with the concept 'force' " (*WP*, §1062). Assuming the validity of these presuppositions, Nietzsche thus states his argument for the truth of the doctrine of eternal recurrence as follows:

If the world may be thought of as a certain definite quantity of force and as a certain definite number of centers of force—and every other representation [of it] remains indefinite and therefore useless—it follows that, in the great dice game of existence, it must pass through a calculable number of combinations. In infinite time, every possible combination would at some time or another be realized an infinite number of times. And since between every combination and its next recurrence all other possible combinations would have to take place, and each of these combinations conditions the entire sequence of combinations in the same series, a circular movement of absolutely identical series is thus demonstrated: the world as a circular movement that has already repeated itself infinitely often and plays its game *in infinitum*. (*WP*, §1066)

Now, it is by no means my intention to argue for the validity either of Nietzsche's presuppositions or of his reasoning from them; on the contrary, I would argue that several of his presuppositions are in fact questionable at best and that his reasoning is fallacious. I would only contend that these passages clearly show him to be convinced of the truth of the doctrine of eternal recurrence and of its demonstrability, and that this provides a further illustration of the fact that, whatever the merit of the specific positions he takes may be, his philosophy cannot be considered nihilistic in the sense under consideration.

Innumerable other illustrations of this fact may be found in his extensive discussions of the many more specific phenomena to which he directs his attention, both in his published writings and in the notes which make up *The Will to Power*. I shall not develop any others at length; but perhaps it would be well to cite a few, simply in order to indicate some of the other matters about which he considers it possible to discover and state facts and truths, and to uncover and refute illusions and falsehoods. First, on life and living things: "Physiologists should think before putting down the instinct of self-preservation as the cardinal instinct of an organic being. A living thing seeks above all to *discharge* its strength—life itself is *will to power;* self-preservation is only one of the indirect and most frequent *results*" (*BGE,* § 13). Again, "The influence of 'external circumstances' is overestimated by Darwin to a ridiculous extent: the essential thing in the life process is precisely the tremendous shaping, form-creating force working from within which *utilizes* and *exploits* 'eternal circumstances' " (*WP,* §647). Again, "A *species* comes to be, a type becomes fixed and strong, through the long fight with essentially constant *unfavorable* conditions" (*BGE,* §262). And finally:

Life itself is *essentially* appropriation, injury, overpowering of what is alien and weaker; suppression, hardness, imposition of one's own forms, incorporation and at least, at its mildest, exploitation. . . . "Exploitation" does not belong to a corrupt or imperfect society; it belongs to the *essence* of what lives, as a basic organic function; it is a consequence of the will to power, which is after all the will of life. . . . If this should be an innovation as a theory—as a reality it is the *primordial fact* of all history: people ought to be honest with themselves at least that far. (*BGE,* §259)

Next, on man, Nietzsche writes: "In man *creature* and *creator* are united: in man there is material, fragment, excess, clay, dirt, nonsense, chaos; but in man there is also creator, form-giver, hammer hardness, spectator divinity, and seventh day: do you understand this contrast?" (*BGE,* §225). And, "man is the *as yet undetermined* animal" (*BGE,* §62). Again, "I distinguish between a type of ascending life and another type of decay, disintegration, weakness" (*WP,* §857). And, "What determines rank, sets off rank, is only quanta of power, and nothing else" (*WP,* §855). Again, "For it is our energy that disposes of us; and the wretched spiritual game of goals and intentions and motives is only a foreground—even though weak eyes may take them for the matter itself" (*WP,* §995). And, "All 'purposes,' 'aims,' 'meaning' are only modes of expression and metamorphoses of one will that is inherent in all events: the will to power" (*WP,* §675).

Further, "We think that . . . everything evil, terrible, tyrannical in man, everything in him that is kin to beasts of prey and serpents, serves the enhancement of the species 'man' as much as its opposite does. Indeed, we do not even say enough when we say only that much" (*BGE,* §44). In this connection Nietzsche says, "Today's ears resist such truths" (*BGE,* §202); and he speaks of the emergence of a new breed of "investigators and microscopists of the soul"—to whom he is clearly sympathetic—"who have trained themselves to sacrifice all desirability to truth, *every* truth, even plain, harsh, ugly, repellent, unchristian, immoral truth. —For such truths do exist" (*GM*, p. 25).

When one considers passages such as these, and Nietzsche's many other substantive assertions and denials in connection with issues in philosophical psychology and the philosophy of mind and on such matters as the nature and origin of conventional morality, religious belief, and social and political institutions, it is difficult to believe that Danto is talking about the same person when he attributes to Nietzsche the view that "if we take 'true' in [the] conventional sense of expressing what is the case," then "nothing is true and everything is false."[20] These passages make it quite evident that Nietzsche does *not* hold this view. If, therefore, a nihilist is one who takes this position, then Nietzsche clearly is not a nihilist.

At this point one might begin to wonder what possibly could have led Danto and others to attribute this position to Nietzsche. The reason would appear to be that Nietzsche does say some things that might seem to warrant this attribution which commentators like Danto have seized upon and have used to support their interpretation of him. In fact, however, Nietzsche does not mean what they have taken him to mean when he says these things; and, consequently, their interpretation of him is based on a misconstrual of his actual points. For example (and most importantly, for present purposes), Nietzsche says, quite a number of times both in his published writings and in his unpublished notes, that there is no "true world" in connection with which the term "truth" has an application (which application moreover has often been held to be its only proper philosophical one). In saying this, however, he does *not* mean that it is meaningless to speak of "reality" at all or that nothing true can be said about it. Rather, what he means is that there is no world or reality or realm *which transcends* that in which we live and with reference to which *this* world is unreal, illusory, a mere apperance, or merely phenomenal.

Philosophers and religious thinkers throughout history, according to Nietzsche, have been led, by their distaste for the conditions of life and their longing for stability and order, to invent the idea of a world other than the one we live in that is more conformable to their desires, and to assert that this other world is the *true* or *real* world. Further, in their hands "truth" has come to be understood in such a way that it has application only to such a world or only under conditions which could not obtain except in such a world. And since, by traditional metaphysical and theological convention, the expressions "true world" and "truth" have become associated with this "other world," one of the ways in which Nietzsche feels it appropriate to deny the existence of such an "other world" is to assert that there is no "true world" and thus no "truth"—*in this sense*. But *only* in this sense; and the fact that Nietzsche intends his denial of the existence of a "true world" and of "truth" to be understood as subject to this restriction is to be seen in the fact that he usually either places the expressions in scare quotes, italicizes them, or else links them explicitly with such expressions as "other world," "thing-in-itself," "world of forms," and "metaphysical world" (the last mentioned referring to what is represented as "reality" in traditional metaphysical systems).

His denial of the existence of a "true world" and of "truth" in this sense, however, is by no means tantamount to the assertion that it is meaningless to speak about "reality" at all or that there are no fundamental truths about reality which may be discovered and expressed. In *Twilight of the Idols,* for example, Nietzsche writes: "*First proposition.* The reasons for which 'this' world has been characterized as 'apparent' are the very reasons which indicate its reality; any other kind of reality is absolutely indemonstrable. *Second proposition* . . . : the 'true world' has been constructed out of contradiction to the actual world" (*TI,* p. 484). And at the conclusion of the next section, entitled "How the 'True World' Finally Became a Fable," he states: "The true world—we have abolished. What world has remained? The apparent one perhaps? But no! *With the true world we have also abolished the apparent one*" (*TI,* p. 486). That is, with the abolition of the idea of a "true world" apart from the actual world, the actual world ceases to seem merely to be an apparent world and comes to be recognized as reality; for it was only by contrast to the fictitious other world which was regarded as the "true world" that the actual world was taken to be merely apparent.

Nietzsche recognizes that nihilism is the natural first response to the discovery that the "true world" of traditional theology and metaphysics is a mere fiction: "The untenability of one interpretation of the world, upon which a tremendous amount of energy has been lavished, awakens the suspicion that *all* interpretations are false" (*WP,* §1). It "awakens the suspicion"—but does it *follow* that "*all* interpretations are false"? Obviously not. And, more importantly for present purposes, is it Nietzsche's conclusion that it follows? Clearly, no. In this same note he speaks of the "rebound from 'God is truth' to the fanatical faith 'All is false' "—a "fanatical faith" which Danto seems to think Nietzsche shares but which it should be obvious he does not from the very way in which he refers to it. And, if that is not decisive, his attempt to establish that reality can and should be understood in terms of the concept of "the will to power" is.

In short, Nietzsche can be considered a metaphysical nihilist only if his remarks about the untenability of conceptions of "the true world" of the sort associated with traditional theology and metaphysics are taken to apply to all possible interpretations of the world, his own included, and only if he is held not to have gone beyond the nihilistic reaction which he describes as the "rebound" or natural initial response to the discovery of the untenability of these traditional conceptions and world views. It seems to me, however, that to understand him in this way is to misunderstand him completely, and that the passages cited in this section demonstrate this conclusively.

III

To show that Nietzsche is not a metaphysical nihilist, of course, is not to show that he is not an axiological nihilist; for one who cannot be considered a nihilist with reference to his views on the nature of reality might nonetheless quite consistently hold that there is no objective basis in reality for value determinations. The question therefore arises: Is Nietzsche a nihilist in the latter respect? Danto claims he is, asserting that it is "Nietzsche's view" that "values have no more application to the world than weights do to numbers."[21] And on this point the consensus of popular opinion is if anything more strongly behind Danto than on the previous one.

In the light of the foregoing, Danto's argument for this conclusion has little force; for it consists, in effect, in merely pointing out that if Nietzsche is a metaphysical nihilist, he must a fortiori be a nihilist with reference to values. If nothing true can be said about reality, then obviously there can be no substantive and positive assertions pertaining to values which have an objective basis in reality. Danto's reasoning is sound; but since, as I believe I have shown, his major premise is false, his argument does not establish his conclusion. Of course, the falsity of his major premise does not suffice to establish the contrary conclusion; the matter must be settled by looking at what Nietzsche actually has to say about value. It is my contention, however, that Danto is wrong here too, and that Nietzsche is no more an axiological nihilist than he is a metaphysical nihilist.

It must be admitted at the outset that Nietzsche does frequently characterize himself as an "immoralist," that he openly declares war on what he often simply terms "morality" and "the moral interpretation of the world," and that he denies the existence of any divinely ordained moral principles or self-contained "moral facts." Yet it does not follow from this that he therefore holds all values to be completely conventional and without any objective basis in reality. Indeed, a quite different conclusion is suggested by such remarks as these: "One has deprived reality of its value, its meaning, its truthfulness, to precisely the extent to which one has mendaciously invented an ideal world" (*EH*, p. 218). Again, "To us the democratic movement is . . . a form of the decay, namely the diminution of man, making him mediocre and lowering his value" (*BGE,* §203). Again, "All . . . ways of thinking that measure the value of things in accordance with *pleasure* and *pain,* which are mere epiphenomena and wholly secondary, are . . . naivetés on which everyone conscious of *creative* powers . . . will look down not without derision, nor without pity" (*BGE,* §225). Again, "My problem . . . : under what conditions did man devise these value judgments good and evil? *and what value do they themselves possess?*" (*GM,* p. 17).

Again, "The world does not have the value we thought it had. . . . [But] the world might be far more valuable than we used to believe; . . . and while we thought that we accorded it the highest interpretation, we may not even have given our human existence a moderately fair value" (*WP,* §32). Again, "Destruction of the world of being: intermediary period of nihilism: before there is yet present the strength to reverse values and to deify becoming and the apparent world as the only world, and to call them good" (*WP,* §585A). And, "*Fundamental innovations:* In place of 'moral values,' purely naturalistic values" (*WP,* §462). Again, in connection with the idea that all events are transitory, "To me . . . everything seems far too valuable to be so fleeting: I seek an eternity for everything" (*WP,* §1065). And finally, Nietzsche speaks of "a Dionysian value standard for existence" (*WP,* §1041), and says: "Dionysus is a *judge!*–Have I been understood?" (*WP,* §1051).

Unfortunately, Nietzsche has not been understood by all too many writers who—in spite of these and many other similar passages—maintain that he is a nihilist and a complete relativist in the matter of value. In point of fact, he holds that there is a single, ultimate, absolute value, by reference to which the value of everything else can and should be determined: namely, the quantitative and qualitative enhancement of life and, in particular, of what he frequently refers to as "the type 'man'," culminating in the ideal of a "union of spiritual superiority with well-being and an excess of strength" (*WP,* §899). And he further holds that this absolute value is grounded in the very nature of things. It is not divinely ordained but neither is it a mere human convention or invention. It derives directly from a consideration of the very essence of life as Niezsche conceives it, namely, as "will to power." He writes: "For this is the doctrine preached *by life itself* to all that has life: the morality of development. To have and to want more—*growth,* in one word— that is life itself" (*WP,* §125).[22] And because of the connection Nietzsche envisages between this absolute value and the essential nature of things, there is, in his view, an objective basis for his particular value determinations. He says, "There is nothing in life that has value, *except the degree of power*— assuming that life itself is the will of power" (*WP,* §55).[23]

Nietzsche thus is far from holding, as Danto says he does, that "values have no more application to the world than weights do to numbers."[24] On the contrary, he holds that the fundamental nature of things and their ultimate value are to be conceived in precisely the same terms; and the values of actions, practices, institutions, and the like are to be determined, in his view, precisely in terms of the extent to which they enhance or detract from the (quantitative and qualitative) degree of power of the beings under consideration—their "quanta of power" being just what they essentially *are* for Nietzsche. He thus is a naturalist in the matter of value, as he himself states he is; but he clearly is no nihilist. Indeed, it is difficult to imagine any stronger version of the thesis that value determinations have an objective basis in reality than his.

On the more general level there are several basic considerations which ought to suggest, even to the casual reader, that Nietzsche is not an axiological nihilist. The first concerns his program of a "revaluation of values," of which he constantly speaks and to the implementation of which he devotes a great deal of attention. The point may be stated quite simply. Nietzsche could not have undertaken such a project—indeed, he could not even have envisioned it—if he himself did not hold that there is some value standard by reference to which the traditional values he proposes to consider could be "revalued."

He does not propose simply to show that traditional values are nothing more than conventions, with no objective basis in reality. It is not his intention merely to *devalue* these values, while maintaining that there are no others that have been overlooked which ought to be set in their place. On the contrary, his contention is that certain things have been regarded as absolute values whose actual value is only derivative, or even (in some cases) precisely the opposite of what it has been taken to be, and that there is an ultimate value, which ought to be recognized, by reference to which the actual value of these traditional values can and should be determined. And it is on the basis of this conviction that he proceeds to pose and consider "the problem of the value of truth," in the first part of *Beyond Good and Evil* (*BGE*, §1), and the question of the value of such things as religion, conventional morality, social institutions, knowledge, and art in subsequent writings.

On these issues he states his general point as follows: "Man has repeated the same mistake over and over again: he has made a means to life into a standard of life; instead of discovering the standard in the highest enhancement of life itself" (*WP*, §354). When he speaks of "the highest enhancement of life," once again, what he has in mind is a "union of spiritual superiority with well-being and an excess of strength" (*WP*, §899). And with this standard of value in mind, he proceeds to assess the actual value of traditional values—and also of men. Thus he says, "if [an individual] represents the ascending course of mankind, then his value is in fact extraordinary . . . [while if] he represents the descending course, decay, chronic sickening, then he has little value" (*WP*, §373).

The second consideration is even more general. It pertains to Nietzsche's basic concern, which led him to undertake the investigations and write the things he did; and I would suggest that no one with any feeling for this basic concern of his could possibly consider him a nihilist in the matter of value. Few philosophers have been motivated in their philosophical efforts by a stronger fundamental concern, and few have felt that more depended upon the success of their philosophical enterprises.

It seemed to Nietzsche that Western man—and indeed mankind generally—is at the crossroads. The fundamental assumptions about ourselves and the world associated with our Judeo-Christian-Socratic heritage, which have given structure and meaning to life in the Western world for the past several millennia, are being called into question. Indeed, he claimed, they have been undermined by the spirit of truthfulness, which has exposed their foundations and has made them no longer tenable. And Nietzsche felt that unless a new world interpretation could be developed, in terms of which life could once again be seen to be meaningful and desirable, the West would go the way of the East, and mankind thus would sink into a degenerate and ultimately moribund condition. He regarded Schopenhauer as the first modern European to exhibit and explicitly embrace this latter sort of development; and while Schopenhauer was not taken seriously by most of his contemporaries, Nietzsche viewed him as the herald of things to come, if no one could show any other way.

If Nietzsche had been a nihilist where values are concerned, one would expect him to have been content simply to describe this situation. For what would it matter to someone holding that nothing really has any value anyway, if growth and development were to give way to stultification and decline? In fact, however, Nietzsche hardly regarded the situation he contemplated with indifference. On the contrary, he viewed it with alarm, at least as great as that with which Plato viewed the collapse of traditional values in the Greece of his day. He sensed impending disaster, and the increasing urgency with which he wrote and the relentlessness with which he drove himself were expressions of the intensity of his concern. He did not sit down, in a cool hour, and say to himself: "Values have no more application to the world than weights do to numbers. And now, there is this matter of the enhancement versus the decline of life: shall I simply describe the situation and let things take the course they appear to be taking? Or shall I take sides, on one side or the other, even though there is really nothing to choose between the two?"

This was not at all the way in which Nietzsche approached the matter. He could allow that weak souls like Schopenhauer will quite naturally find life too disagreeable to be worth living on the only terms it offers them. But he was far from indifferent to the possibility that the whole human race might come to be like Schopenhauer and that Schopenhauer's ideal of the termination of all life might become a reality. He was not content merely to observe that the strong will be able to find life endurable and even desirable in spite of its hardships, while the weak will not, and that if no one is strong, then the human race will cease to develop and ultimately to exist. Rather, he held that *this must not happen;* that life ought to flourish, ought to be enhanced, ought to continue to develop; that there ought to be strong, creative men, able to take the hardships of life in their stride; and, moreover, that there ought to come to be men who are stronger and more creative than any now or previously existing—he himself included. And he did not regard these as his own personal, subjectively determined, objectively groundless imperatives, but rather as imperatives with an objective basis in reality, deriving from "the doctrine preached by life itself to all that has life" (*WP,* §125). The use of the term "objective" in this context is not mine but Nietzsche's. He writes: "What is the objective measure of value? Solely the quantum of enhanced and organized power" (*WP,* §674).

"Nihilism," in the axiological sense, is characterized by Nietzsche as "the radical repudiation of value, meaning, and desirability" (*WP,* §1). In the same note in which this characterization occurs, he describes his own position in the following terms: "Against 'meaninglessness' on the one hand, against *moral* value judgments on the other."[25] His formulation of the byword of nihilism is: " 'Everything lacks meaning' " (*WP,* §1). But this byword is certainly not his own. "Now that the shabby origin of [traditional] values is becoming clear," he says, "the universe seems to have lost value, seems 'meaningless'—but that is only a *transitional stage*" (*WP,* §7). His own pronouncement, which he places in the mouth of Zarathustra, is very different: "Behold, I teach you the overman. The overman is the meaning of the earth."[26] For Nietzsche, "the earth" and life *have* a "meaning"—a meaning deriving from the value he takes to be associated with the realization of the ideal of a "union of spiritual superiority with well-being and an excess of strength," the symbol of which is the "overman."

In taking this position, Nietzsche does not consider himself merely to be indicating a personal preference or giving expression to his own feeling of strength and vitality. He is not saying that he, Friedrich Nietzsche, has chosen to regard the enhancement of life affirmatively, even though nothing is of any intrinsic value. He is not saying that the "overman" is the meaning of the earth *for him,* although others, who have conceived its meaning differently, and Schopenhauer, for whom life lacked any positive meaning, have been on equally firm—or weak—ground since the question of the general validity of such claims does not even arise. Rather, he is saying that Schopenhauer and Plato and Christianity and the rest have *missed* the *true* meaning of the earth, just as they have missed the fact that the enhancement of life *is* an absolute value, and is the only absolute value which does not rest upon illusion but rather has an objective foundation in the nature of life itself. For him, these things are so quite independently of his assertions to this effect and regardless of whether Schopenhauer or Plato or St. Paul or most men or even anyone at all would concur. Indeed, he recognizes that these men and most others most definitely would *not* concur, but that, for him, does not count against the truth of his claims or render them merely subjective and personal.

Here it is illuminating to refer again to *Thus Spoke Zarathustra.* Nietzsche has Zarathustra attempt to *"teach"* men that "the overman is the meaning of the earth." The fact that he calls this a "teaching" implies that he does not regard it merely as an expression of a purely personal value determination. When he has Zarathustra say, "This is *my* way; where is yours?" and *"the* way—that does not exist,"[27] he does not mean this to apply to Zarathustra's basic teaching, but rather to the ways in which particular individuals are to live in light of it. Zarathustra's pronouncements would be absurd—and the work itself would have been an absurdity—if Nietzsche had not been convinced that it mattered whether or not life flourished and developed. And this could not have mattered to him—as it did, so obviously, and so greatly—if he had felt that the world actually is utterly devoid of meaning, and that there is nothing more to be said for the ultimate value he proposes than there is for the traditional values whose ultimacy and objective validity he denies.

The claim that Nietzsche is an axiological nihilist is thus quite clearly wrong. Like the claim that he is a metaphysical nihilist, it reflects a profound misunderstanding of him. And also like this other claim, it reflects a misunderstanding that derives from a misconstrual of a number of things he does say about values and morality. There are, for example, many passages in his writings which, taken by themselves, would seem to support the view that he is a relativist in the matter of values, holding that all values are merely creations of those whose interests they serve. Nietzsche does frequently speak of changes of values, of differences of values, and, most notably, of the "creation of values." For example, he says that the true task of the genuine philosopher "demands that he *create values*" (*BGE,* §211). And he also often says things like: "In valuations are expressed conditions of preservation and growth" (*WP,* §507). But passages like these should not be taken to imply that he holds that even the basic value he affirms, and in terms of which he proposes to "revalue" traditional values, has no objective standing, and reflects nothing more than his own needs or disposition.

To understand these and other similar passages properly, it is necessary to distinguish between two sorts or orders of values, which Nietzsche treats quite differently. One consists of values which are the creations of particular individuals or groups of men, whose physiological conditions and natural and social circumstances lead them to esteem certain qualities and to condemn others. These conditions and circumstances vary greatly and so, consequently, do the valuations to which they give rise. It is values so conceived that Nietzsche has in mind when he discusses those which prevail among the great masses of men, on the one hand, and when he urges higher men to create their own values, answering to their own distinctive powers and abilities, on the other.

These values are not thought by Nietzsche to be completely arbitrary or strictly conventional, for he contends that they are strongly correlated with the psychological and ultimately the physiological characteristics of those who affirm them. But he also holds that they are not absolute, that men differ profoundly with regard to the psychological and physiological characteristics to which they are related, and that consequently it is improper to claim universal validity for any set of values which "express conditions of preservation and growth" of one particular individual or group of men, or to ask which of several competing sets of such values is the "true" or "right" one.

The matter is different, however, with regard to the value by reference to which Nietzsche proposes to carry out his program of a "revaluation of values." This value is one which he regards as objective and unconditional, being grounded in the very nature of things. It is held not to be the value of some particular individual or group of men, but rather that "preached by life itself to all that has life" (*WP*, §125). It does not "express conditions of preservation and growth" of some one individual or group, but rather pertains to the general *desirability of* "preservation and growth," that is, of the quantitative and qualitative enhancement of life and in particular of "the type 'man,' " conceived in terms of the emergence of a union of the greatest possible physical well-being and strength with the greatest possible spiritual development.

Given this as the ultimate value, and since one man's meat is sometimes another man's poison, it follows that different lower-order valuations of various particular things by different types of men are entirely in order and indeed are quite necessary, and that it will further be appropriate for men of exceptional ability to "create" their own particular "values" as a way, and as a means, of enabling themselves—and through them, "the type 'man' "—to attain the highest possible degree of spiritual development. It should thus be clear that this lower-order relativism in the matter of values, upon which Nietzsche insists, is by no means incompatible with the idea of an ultimate and nonrelative standard of value, to which he is equally firmly committed.

There are, to be sure, passages in Nietzsche's writings like the following, from *Twilight of the Idols:* "Judgments, judgments of value, concerning life, for it or against it, can, in the end, never be true; they . . . are worthy of consideration only as symptoms; . . . *the value of life cannot be estimated*" (*TI*, p. 474). Passages like this one may seem to pose a serious problem for the interpretation of Nietzsche that I am suggesting. It seems to me, however, that they in fact do not. It is quite true that Nietzsche regards judgments about or estimations of the value of life not as propositions which—at least in principle—might be true, but rather as indications of the sort of stuff the person is made of who makes them. So, for example, in the same section of *Twilight of the Idols*, he observes, "Concerning life, the wisest men of all ages have judged alike: *it is no good*," and then says, " 'At least something must be *sick* here,' *we* retort" (*TI*, p. 473). And he goes on to suggest that "the great sages are *types of decline.*"

Again, he states, with reference to philosophers according to whom "no ultimate meaning is posited except the appearance of pleasure or displeasure," that "for any healthier kind of man the value of life is certainly not measured by the standard of these trifles" (*WP*, § 35). Yet his language in these and other similar passages is significant; for his characterization of certain estimations of the value of life as expressions of "sickness," "decadence," and "decline" certainly suggests that he does not consider them to be on a par with that of "any healthier kind of man." At the very least, the way in which he speaks of them clearly indicates that he thinks there is *something wrong* with them.

However, this does not yet touch the central point, which concerns Nietzsche's meaning in asserting that "the value of life cannot be estimated." In this connection it is of interest that he goes on to say, "For a philosopher to see a problem in the value of life is thus an objection to him" (*TI*, p. 474). I take him to mean that one is mistaken to think that the value of life is *something problematical*—an issue which remains open after the essential nature and conditions of life have been determined and which is to be resolved by seeing how life fares when measured against a standard of value which has some other derivation. He holds, on the contrary, that the value of life is *not* problematical in this sense. For him the ultimate standard of value is to be conceived in terms which derive directly from a consideration of the essential nature of life itself; and if the former is given and determined by the latter, then the question of the value of life cannot arise, and the value of life cannot become a problem. Thus "the value of life cannot be estimated," in his view, not because life is without value, but rather because its essential nature itself determines the ultimate standard of value, and because it itself, in its highest form of development, *is* the ultimate value, and therefore because there is no conceptually distinct value or standard of value in terms of which *its* value can be "estimated."

Similarly, when Nietzsche says that "judgments" concerning the value of life "can . . . never be true," even when they are positive, his point concerns judgments in which life is asserted to be of value *because* it happens to contain certain features to which a conceptually distinct standard of value attributes positive significance. Nietzsche denies that any such judgments are true because he denies the objective validity of any standard of value of this sort. His contention that life, in its highest form of development, is the ultimate value, on the other hand, is a judgment of a quite different sort—if, indeed, it is even a *judgment* at all. For it does not involve passing judgment upon the extent to which life is capable of satisfying certain antecedently determined conditions, but rather merely accepting it on its own terms, as he understands them.

In short, life, for Nietzsche, is not something the value of which can be judged or determined by reference to any independent criteria. Rather, it is, so to speak, a game, which exists because the world as "will to power" of necessity gives birth to it, in which all of us, however well or poorly we can and do play, are by our very natures engaged. It has rules set not by us, nor by mere chance, but by the essential features of the "will to power" that is constitutive of reality generally. And it is a game the very nature of which delineates an ideal that both constitutes the ultimate value and determines the standard of value for everything falling within its compass. When Nietzsche's assertion that "the value of life cannot be estimated" is viewed in this light, it seems to be quite evident that it is not to be construed as a profession of axiological nihilism.

Next, it is necessary to consider Nietzsche's denunciations of what he often refers to simply as "morality" and "the moral interpretation of the world," and his characterization of himself as an "immoralist." These have often been taken to provide a clear indication of the fact that he is a nihilist. In fact, however, this interpretation involves a misunderstanding of his meaning, though it is a misunderstanding for which his frequent failure to qualify his use of the terms "moral" and "morality" is partly responsible. Just as what he means to repudiate in his denunciations of "metaphysics" are those metaphysical systems which traditionally have prevailed in Western thought, rather than the possibility of any metaphysics at all, so also, what he means to repudiate in his denunciations of "morality" are those moralities which have prevailed in Western culture up to the present time, rather than morality as such.

Nietzsche is harshly critical of the claims of Christian morality, and, more generally, of what he terms "slave" morality or "herd" morality, to absolute and universal validity. He also rejects the similar claims of Plato, Kant, Hegel, and the utilitarians for their moral theories. He is opposed to so much of what has passed and currently passes for "morality" that he often uses the term descriptively to refer to it, and so refers to himself as an "immoralist." It does not follow, however, that he is opposed to every possible morality in principle. Indeed, the contrary is suggested by the famous passage in which he says that when he speaks of "Beyond Good and Evil," this "... does *not* mean 'Beyond Good and Bad' " (*GM*, p. 55). And it is indicated even more clearly when he states: "*Morality in Europe today is herd animal morality*—in other words, as we understand it, merely *one* type of human morality besides which, before which, and after which many other types, above all *higher* moralities, are, or ought to be, possible" (*BGE*, §202).

Even if Nietzsche is not really an "immoralist" in a strict or absolute sense, however, questions still remain. What, for example, is to be made of his assertion that "there are no moral phenomena at all, but only a moral interpretation of phenomena" (*BGE*, §108)? It might seem to follow from this that Nietzsche holds there is no objective basis for the assessment of particular moral claims and purported moral principles. In fact, however, all that follows is that Nietzsche rejects the complete *autonomy* of moral principles. That is, he rejects the view that moral principles express a special kind of facts—"moral facts"—which are ultimate in the sense of being independent of facts of any other sort, neither logically presupposing them nor depending upon them in any other way.

It is quite consistent with this position to hold, however, that there *are* moral principles for which there *is* an objective basis, in virtue of their relation to certain *non*moral "facts." And this, I submit, is precisely Nietzsche's position. Certain moral principles, in his view, may be derived from his standard of value, even if they have no objective status independent of it. So, for example, he refers to "the doctrine preached by life itself to all that has life" as "the morality of development" (*WP*, §125).

Nietzsche's morality might fairly be characterized as naturalistic, but naturalism in morality surely is something quite different from nihilism. Thus he asserts that his "fundamental innovation" in this area in the "naturalization of morality" (*WP*, §462), and the "naturalization" of morality is by no means equivalent to the complete repudiation of it. Once again, it would be well to recall Nietzsche's exclamation: "Dionysus is a *judge!*—Have I been understood?" (*WP*, §1051). This is not the place to spell out his own morality in detail; but its outlines may be grasped by taking his characterization of it as a "morality of development" together with the statement: "I teach No to all that makes weak—that exhausts. I teach Yes to all that strengthens, that stores up strength" (*WP*, §54). And it bears emphasizing that Nietzsche does not say, "I propose" or "I will" or "I affirm" but "I *teach.*"

Finally, there is the problem of the interpretation of those passages in which Nietzsche seems to commit himself to a moral relativism. The problem here is similar to that which arises in connection with his apparent commitment to a form of relativism in the matter of values, for he says many of the same sorts of things in this context. For example, "I understand by 'morality' a system of evaluations that partially coincides with the conditions of a creature's life" (*WP*, §256). And he maintains that, since men differ radically in terms of what he calls "order of rank," and so have different "conditions of life," a concrete morality which will be appropriate for one sort of men will differ from that which will be appropriate for another. Thus he says, "Moralities must be forced to bow first of all before the *order of rank*" (*BGE*, §221). And he explicitly denies that he is proposing a single sort of practical morality—a morality of individualism—for adoption by all men, saying, "My philosophy aims at an ordering of rank: not at an individualistic morality" (*WP*, §287).

As in the case of his remarks on values, however, no real difficulty is posed by these and similar passages. The solution to the problem they seem to raise once again is to be found by distinguishing between the basic moral principle to which Nietzsche is committed and the differing lower-order "moralities" which are indicated by it when the differing capacities of men are taken into consideration. In brief, Nietzsche's "morality of development" is a consequence of his identification of the greatest possible enhancement of strength and spirituality of "the type 'man' " as the ultimate standard of value. He further holds, however, that men are far from equal where the relevant capacities are concerned, and that therefore the enhancement of "the type 'man' " would not be served if all men were to live individualistically and self-assertively.

For those who would be unable to endure an existence unstructured by conventions, therefore, and for those whose acts of self-assertion would not be creative, there is indicated one type of concrete "morality" which reflects the only sort of contribution they are capable of making to the enhancement of the "type." It is what Nietzsche likes to refer to as "herd morality," which corresponds quite closely to prevailing and traditional conventional morality, and the desirability of which he suggests when he says, "A high culture can stand only upon a broad base, upon a strong and healthily consolidated mediocrity" (*WP*, §864). On the other hand, for those who are strong enough to live a life of their own and who have the capacity to be truly creative, another type of concrete "morality" is indicated. It is an individualistic, self-assertive morality, which reflects the much greater and more direct contribution *they* are capable of making to the enhancement of the "type."

Neither type of "morality" is right or appropriate for all men, according to Nietzsche, and neither is wrong or inappropriate for all; but it is important to observe that he further holds that each is right for one type of men and wrong for another. And that this is so is something which is determined by reference to the general "morality of development" to which he is committed, and to the basic standard of value which underlies it. In this way, it is possible for Nietzsche to take a position of moral relativism at one level, while maintaining his commitment to a nonrelative morality at another, more fundamental level.

In short, the widespread view, endorsed by Danto, that Nietzsche was a "nihilist" and that his philosophy is a philosophy of "radical nihilism" is wrong. A careful analysis of his writings shows that he neither considers himself to be a nihilist nor deserves to be termed one, either metaphysically or axiologically. Far from considering nihilism to be the last word, he actually regards it as a mere "transitional stage"—a natural consequence of the discovery of the untenability of a certain traditional metaphysical and axiological views—which, however, he himself goes beyond and to which his own philosophy is a "countermovement." Far from holding that there are no truths about reality which may be discovered and stated, because there is no actual nature of things to discover and describe, he in fact holds the contrary and has a good deal to say of a substantive nature in this connection. And far from denying objective validity to all value judgments and moral principles as such, he in fact maintains that a certain standard of value and a certain morality have an objective basis in the very nature of things.

To show this, of course, is not at all to show that the substantive positions Nietzsche takes on these matters are correct. I have not been concerned in this chapter either to defend or to criticize them, and do not propose to turn to this task now. This task is an important one—much more important, indeed, than that of merely showing that he does take such positions, and what they are. Yet philosophers will not turn to such an undertaking, because they will not even see the need for it, if the erroneous view prevails that Nietzsche is a nihilist and, therefore, takes no substantive metaphysical and axiological positions which require evaluation.

PART IV

Between Subjectivity and Objectivity:
Responses to a Century of Philosophical Upheaval

9:

Husserlian and Heideggerian Phenomenology

Hegel's system was a hard act to follow. Marx, Kierkegaard, and Nietzsche in effect recognized that topping it was out of the question, and proceeded by reacting to it and striking out in quite different directions. In doing so, they did manage to follow Hegel's act after all, in ways which collectively have appeared to many European philosophers in the present century to fix the other basic points of the philosophical compass, leaving little room for further radical reorientation of philosophical inquiry into ontological, anthropological, axiological, epistemological, and ethical matters—and thus constituting even harder acts to follow than Hegel's had been. Consequently, much of European philosophy in this century has taken the form of responses to these developments in the previous one. These responses generally have consisted either in mediations between the conflicting stands taken by some of these four figures, or in renewals of lines of thought initiated by them or their predecessors.

If there is any recent development which might appear to constitute a genuine innovation against this background, it is the emergence of phenomenology. Edmund Husserl, who may fairly be said to have initiated this development, certainly regarded it in this way, conceiving it as a revolution and a new beginning in philosophical inquiry which would put an end to the kinds of "unscientific" and inconclusive endeavors in which his various predecessors had engaged and of which they had taken philosophy to consist. Yet, in a number of respects there is more than a passing resemblance between his explicitly avowed idealism and some earlier idealisms (including Hegel's); and as Husserl himself admits, his enterprise in general and also his initial point of departure are fundamentally Cartesian. One can also discern distinctly Kantian elements in his thought. Indeed, Husserlian phenomenology is very much in the tradition of classical modern philosophy from Descartes to Kant and Hegel, departing significantly from the form and substance of the thought of later philosophers only to renew with certain modifications the philosophical undertaking and orientation they had abandoned.

These modifications are by no means insignificant; but they are, as it were, essentially moves made *within* a game long since begun, rather than specifications of the ground rules of a radically new one. Husserlian phenomenology is a vigorous response to the various forms of naturalism (and the relativism commonly associated with them) developed in reaction to Hegelian idealism in the nineteenth century and contributing to the emergence of a kind of naturalistic orthodoxy in the twentieth. It constitutes a counter attack against these varieties of naturalism, mounted with a view both to the establishment of their untenability and to the demonstration of the possibility of complete and adequate knowledge of the natures of things and ourselves, and resulting in the resurrection of idealism. The first half of the present chapter, consisting in an account of the main programmatic, methodological, and ontological themes which emerge in the course of several of Husserl's most important works, should serve to make these points clear and to indicate some of the more noteworthy respects in which his thinking is similar to as well as different from that of his classical modern predecessors.

Heideggerian phenomenology, discussed in the second half of this chapter, is a rather different sort of case. One of the main purposes of this chapter is to show that it differs considerably from Husserlian phenomenology in many important ways. This being so, it is not surprising that the former stands in quite a different relation to the efforts of earlier philosophers than does the latter. Husserl's concern, in effect, is to try to improve upon what philosophers from Descartes to Kant and Hegel did by approaching the same general problems in a somewhat different way than they had. Heidegger's concern, on the other hand, is to direct our attention to a rather different set of problems and range of phenomena, and to get at these problems by subjecting the phenomena in question to a modified form of the kind of analysis Husserl advocates. He shares Husserl's antipathy to naturalism, but is strongly opposed to the idealisms of both Hegel and Husserl, and indeed is as unsympathetic to the entire classical modern tradition (and its revival in Husserl) as Marx, Kierkegaard, and Nietzsche had been.

Like Husserl, but with some greater warrant, Heidegger considers his approach to ontology to constitute a major philosophical innovation, his expressions of indebtedness to Husserl for his methodology notwithstanding. To the extent that this is so, however, this innovation applies more to his attempt to recast and rethink the problem of what he calls "the meaning of 'Being' " than it does to his relatively more intelligible analysis of the nature of human existence. For here, at least, his thinking may be viewed as a development of certain themes and suggestions of some of his post-Hegelian nineteenth-century predecessors, stripped of their original theological and naturalistic colorings— even though these are reformulated, elaborated, integrated, and then interpreted in a way that is sufficiently distinctive to render inappropriate the characterization of Heidegger as a mere neo-Kierkegaardian or eclectic. One who would achieve an understanding of what Heidegger is doing and saying in the "phenomenological-ontological" analysis of *Dasein*—in which the main portion of his most influential work *Being and Time* consists—may find it difficult to do so and to comprehend the reasons for his departures from Husserl, if one's knowledge of the history of philosophy prior to the present century extends no further than Kant or Hegel. One's task is made somewhat easier, however, if one brings to it not only an acquaintance with Husserl but also an awareness of post-Hegelian and pre-Husserlian treatments of human reality, and of the procedures employed as well as the contentions advanced in them.

Phenomenology is associated above all with the name of Edmund Husserl. Husserl is acknowledged on all hands to be the founder of what has been referred to as "the phenomenological movement,"[1] and it is in his writings that the program of phenomenology and the method of phenomenological analysis find their classical expression. But phenomenology is also associated with the names of a number of the most influential "existentialists," so-called, who make much of the fact that the method they employ is "phenomenological." In this connection the names of Jean-Paul Sartre, Gabriel Marcel, and Martin Heidegger immediately come to mind. Because these writers characterize their method in these terms and because they express indebtedness to Husserl, it is commonly assumed that "phenomenology" is pretty much the same thing for them as it is for Husserl.

Particularly in the case of Heidegger, the circumstantial evidence seems to support this view. During the last years in which Husserl held his chair at Freiburg, Heidegger was closely associated with him, serving as the editor of a series of Husserl's lectures published under the title *The Phenomenology of Internal Time-Consciousness*[2] and even on occasion collaborating with him. Heidegger succeeded to Husserl's chair at Freiburg upon the latter's retirement, much to Husserl's initial satisfaction. Heidegger's most famous work, *Being and Time,* which contains his most systematic discussion and his most explicit employment of the phenomenological method as he conceives of it, is dedicated "to Edmund Husserl, in friendship and admiration"; and the book was first published as an issue of the *Jahrbuch für Phänomenologie und phänomenologische Forschung,* of which Husserl was the founder and editor.

Circumstantial evidence, however, is often misleading; and the fact that two writers use the same term to describe what they are doing does not necessarily mean that they are doing the same thing. An examination of Husserl's and Heidegger's actual discussions of the nature of phenomenology and phenomenological method, and of their actual practice, seems to me to support a conclusion contrary to that which appearances suggest. In fact, it is my contention that Husserlian phenomenology and Heideggerian phenomenology are radically different and have virtually nothing to do with each other.

Heidegger does follow Husserl to the extent of restoring subjective experience to a position of prominence in philosophical inquiry, in opposition to the Hegelian tendency to depreciate the subjective in favor of the objective. To regard this "subjective turn" as the defining feature of phenomenology, however, would be to conceive it in so loose a fashion that it would virtually cease to have any identity at all; for, so conceived, Descartes, Hume, and Kant, together with quite a few others in the history of philosophy and many early twentieth-century analytic philosophers as well, would then qualify as "phenomenologists."

It is what one does once one makes this turn to the subjective that is decisive for Husserl and for Heidegger as well, and what Husserl does is very different indeed from what Heidegger does. In fact, they even differ with regard to precisely what it is that is to be focused upon when one makes this turn. In this respect Heidegger's profession of indebtedness to Husserl, his retention of Husserl's label, and his use of Husserl's motto ("To the things themselves!") are less significant than is the fact of Husserl's disappointment with Heidegger. Husserl began to have doubts about Heidegger soon after the appearance of *Being and Time,* writing to Roman Ingarden at the time that "Heidegger has not grasped the whole meaning of the phenomenological reduction."[3] His doubts culminated in his embittered feeling, in his later years, that Heidegger neither practiced nor understood phenomenology as he conceived it at all.

It seems to me that Husserl was quite right to feel that what Heidegger was doing and calling "phenomenology" was entirely different from what he, Husserl, was doing under the same name. I shall attempt to show this to be so first by characterizing phenomenology as Husserl conceives of it in *Ideas Concerning a Pure Phenomenology* (published in English as *Ideas*[4]) and *Cartesian*

Meditations;[5] and then by characterizing phenomenology as Heidegger conceives of it in *Being and Time.*[6] The question of the relative merit of the two versions of phenomenology, however, is one which I shall not undertake to discuss here. Nor, for that matter, shall I be concerned with their intrinsic strengths and weaknesses or with parallels to both of their positions in recent Anglo-American philosophy, which are more numerous than one might think. The task of establishing what Husserlian phenomenology and Heideggerian phenomenology are and how they radically differ is large enough for one undertaking, and is of sufficient interest and importance in its own right to require no such supplementation for its justification.

I

Husserlian phenomenology is first of all an epistemological enterprise. Husserl's *Cartesian Meditations* is an explicit attempt to renew Descartes's program of a systematic reconstruction of knowledge which would render it immune to skeptical doubt. Descartes's aim, which Husserl characterizes as "a complete reforming of philosophy into a science grounded on an absolute foundation" (*CM,* p. 1),[7] is also Husserl's own: "That aim," Husserl says, "shall indeed continually motivate the course of our meditations" (*CM,* p. 8). Accordingly, the first order of business for the Husserlian phenomenologist is to identify "those cognitions that are first in themselves and can support the whole storied edifice of universal knowledge," with a view to "constructing on their basis a science governed by the idea of a definitive system of knowledge" (*CM,* p. 14). The epistemological character of Husserlian phenomenology is not merely implicit in the program Husserl sets for himself; it is also explicitly acknowledged. "Phenomenology seems rightly to be characterized," he says, "as transcendental theory of knowledge" (*CM,* p. 81).

Like Kant, however, Husserl considers the theory of knowledge to be inseparable from the philosophy of mind or, more precisely, from a philosophical account of the ego qua knowing subject. Husserlian phenomenology thus is not only "transcendental theory of knowledge" but also "a science of concrete transcendental subjectivity"; it is not only epistemology but also, at the same time, "a pure egology" (*CM,* p. 30). Here, too, Husserl considers himself to be following the lead of Descartes' *Meditations,* attempting "to renew with greater intensity the radicalness of their spirit . . . , [and] to uncover thereby for the first time the genuine sense of the necessary regress to the ego" (*CM,* p. 6).

It is important not to overlook Husserl's use of the terms "transcendental" and "pure," which are to be understood in a Kantian manner. The "transcendental subjectivity" or "transcendental ego," of which Husserlian phenomenology is ultimately the science, is not the "I" of ordinary experience; rather, it is "the ego as subject of one's pure *cogitationes*" (*CM*, pp. 2–3), which is "the underlying basis on which all objective cognition takes place" (*CM*, p. 27) and which is the same in all of us. And Husserlian phenomenology is "a *pure* egology" in that it is concerned only with this "pure ego of [our] *cogitationes*" (*CM*, p. 3) and is "an *a priori* science," in Husserl's terms, that "sets out . . . the indissoluble essential structures of transcendental subjectivity, which persist in and through all imaginable modifications" (*I*, p. 6).

Husserlian phenomenology is "radical" in the sense in which the philosophy of Descartes is "radical": it is intended to be entirely "presuppositionless." "There lies embedded in its meaning," Husserl says, "a radicalism in the matter of foundations, an absolute freedom from all presuppositions, a securing for itself [of] an absolute basis" (*I*, p. 20). Nothing is to be accepted which is not free from the slightest possibility of doubt—nothing, in Husserl's terminology, which is not completely "evident." Husserl's first principle is very much like Descartes'. I "must neither make nor go on accepting any judgment as scientific *that I have not derived from evidence*" (*CM*, p. 13), that is, from experiences the content of which has the character of being completely and indubitably evident.

Husserl thus initially proceeds in a spirit that is decidedly Cartesian and Humean, rather than Kantian. He does not take it to be given from the outset that we know various things, and then inquire into the conditions of the possibility of such knowledge. Rather, he begins by assuming that there can be no knowledge worthy of the name which does not rest upon completely certain foundations, and asks what we can in this light be said to know or to be able to come to know. None of our ordinary judgments are to be accepted unless they "carry with them an absolute certainty" (*CM*, p. 14). Those which do not are to be "bracketed," or set aside as problematical, at least until such time as they are seen to be justified on the basis of judgments which *are* "absolutely certain," or receive a "reinterpretation" in the light of subsequent investigation.

This is the *epoché* of Husserlian phenomenology. The best-known example of such a judgment, for Husserl, is that of "the existence of the world," where "the world" is conceived as something ontologically independent of consciousness; another is that of one's own existence as a natural entity with various empirically observable characteristics (*CM*, pp. 16, 25). These judgments are not absolutely indubitable, as Descartes observed, and are therefore to be "bracketed." And it turns out that for Husserl they never emerge from their "brackets," except in a radically altered form in which their ontological independence of the transcendental ego is denied.

Husserl thus is led to maintain a form of transcendental idealism. His conclusion with regard to the ontological status of the world is that "the real worlds exists, but in respect of essence is relative to transcendental subjectivity, and in such a way that it can have its meaning as existing reality only as the intentional meaning-product of transcendental subjectivity" (*I*, p. 14). (He takes the same position with regard to "the more special apperceptions through which I take myself to be a man with body and soul, who lives in the world with other men, lives the life of the world, and so forth" (*I*, pp. 10–11). "Now as ever," he says in his 1930 Preface to *Ideas*, no doubt with a glance toward Heidegger, "I hold every form of current philosophical realism to be in principle absurd" (*I*, p. 12). He is equally unequivocal in *Cartesian Meditations:* "The attempt to conceive the universe of true being as something lying outside the universe of possible consciousness, possible knowledge, possible evidence . . . is nonsensical" (*CM*, p. 84).

Husserl denies both that transcendental phenomenology is devised as a buttress of idealism and also that it is separable from the latter. Rather, he contends, it is "a science founded in itself, and standing on its own basis" (*I*, p. 13)—but one which leads inescapably in the direction of transcendental idealism. "Carried out with . . . systematic concreteness," he states, "phenomenology is *eo ipso* 'transcendental idealism' " (*CM*, p. 86). Thus the nature or meaning of "being" generally constitutes no problem for him: "The predicates being and non-being," he says, "relate . . . not to objects *simpliciter* but to . . . our pure meaning and to the meant, purely as meant" (*CM*, p. 56). In other words nothing remains to be understood about the meaning of "being" once one sees that "being" is simply the intentional correlative of consciousness or, more strictly speaking, of the transcendental ego.

Husserlian phenomenology is eidetic, that is, its concern is with the description of essences (*eidoi*) or essential structures of consciousness and essential types of things. "Phenomenology," Husserl states, "aims at being a descriptive theory of the essence of pure transcendental experiences" (*I*, p. 191). He refers to it as an "eidetic science," like mathematics and unlike the natural sciences, not to mention history and biography; but it is said to be a "material eidetic science," whereas the different branches of mathematics are "formal" ones (*I*, p. 185). For it is concerned with the qualitative differences among the various possible modes of experience and types of intentional objects, rather than with mere quantitative considerations; and it starts not from arbitrary definitions and axioms, but rather with "the flow of experience" in its "whole wealth of . . . concreteness" (*I*, p. 192). Moreover, it does not proceed deductively, but rather in a quite different manner, which shall be described shortly.

Like mathematics, however, Husserlian phenomenology is not concerned with what is unique, either in a particular experience or in a particular individual. "Whatever facts present themselves," Husserl says, "serve only as examples" (*I,* p. 5). Husserlian phenomenology "is restricted . . . to the realm of pure eidetic 'description,' " which is to say, to the description of pure "essences" (*I,* p. 7). To be sure, Husserl holds that "transcendental phenomenology must proceed in two stages" and that "in the first stage the realm accessible to transcendental self-experience . . . must be explored—and at first, with simple devotion to . . . the harmonious flow of such experience." But he goes on to say that this is not phenomenology proper—rather, it is "a stage that is not yet philosophical in the full sense"—because it is concerned merely with the accurate apprehension of particulars, rather than with the discernment of "essences" (*I,* p. 29).

Husserlian phenomenology essentially involves the performance of what Husserl terms a "phenomenological reduction," and it further involves distinguishing between ordinary experience and "transcendental experience" and also between the "natural standpoint" and the "phenomenological standpoint." Phenomenology proper is characterized by Husserl as "the critique of transcendental experience" (*I,* p. 29). "Transcendental experience" is said to be "a new kind of experience" (*I,* p. 27), distinct from ordinary experience; and the "phenomenological reduction" is held to be the operation through the performance of which this "new kind of experience" becomes accessible to us.

Husserl observes that when I occupy the natural standpoint, as even the phenomenologist does during most of his life, "I experience myself . . . as 'I' in the ordinary sense of the term, as this human person living among others in the world" (*I,* p. 7). I take for granted my embodied existence "in an objective, spatio-temporal Nature" (*I,* p. 8). I may, however, adopt a different standpoint. I may determine to set aside all judgments which are not absolutely certain, and this means that I must at least for the time regard everything I experience as nothing more than phenomena in my "flow of experience." In short, I may "bracket" all judgments involving explicit or implicit reference to existence independent of my "flow of experience," and restrict myself to the consideration of the phenomena which constitute my "flow of experience" qua phenomena.

This, very briefly, is what the "phenomenological reduction" involves. Having made this reduction, I leave the natural standpoint and adopt the phenomenological standpoint; and my experience, thus reduced, becomes what Husserl terms "transcendental experience." It is only at this point that Husserlian phenomenology proper begins. Husserlian phenomenology is nothing if not the exploration of "transcendental experience," and the important point for present purposes is that for Husserl "transcendental experience . . . becomes available only through a radical . . . readjustment of viewpoint which . . . is called 'phenomenological reduction' " (*I*, p. 5).

In *Ideas*, Husserl suggests that the systematic investigation of human existence "at the natural standpoint" is a task "of extraordinary importance, although so far scarcely noticed" (*I*, p. 95). And he makes a number of remarks intended to indicate the outlines of such an investigation. Most obviously, he observes, this standpoint, in which "I find myself related . . . to the fact-world which is constantly about me," is the one I occupy "*for the most part*" (*I*, p. 94).[8] At this standpoint, Husserl says, "real objects are there for me, definite, more or less familiar, agreeing with what is actually perceived without being themselves perceived." He continues: "I find myself . . . set in relation to a world which, through its constant changes, remains one and ever the same. It is continually 'present' for me, and I myself am a member of it" (*I*, p. 91). This holds, he observes, for my "world of values" as well as for the world of objects. Further: "Things in their immediacy stand there as objects to be used. . . . These values and practicalities, they too belong to the constitution of the 'actually present' objects as such, irrespective of my turning or not turning to consider them" (*I*, p. 93). The world I thus perceive is also one in which I find other men to be present, and "I apprehend the world-about-them and the world-about-me objectively as one and the same world" (*I*, p. 95).

Husserl goes on at some length on themes such as these, with considerable sensitivity. What is important for present purposes, however, is that he considers all of this to be "a piece of pure description *prior to all 'theory*' "– scientific or speculative *or phenomenological*. While he states that the investigation of such matters is a task "of extraordinary importance," he goes on to say that "it is not ours to attempt" (*I*, p. 95). For Husserl the task of phenomenology lies elsewhere; it consists in "transcendental theory of knowledge" and "the science of transcendental subjectivity," rather than in the exploration of human experience as it is met at the natural standpoint. "Instead now of remaining at this standpoint," he says, "we propose to alter it radically" (*I*, p. 96). It is only if one adopts the different standpoint indicated previously, via the phenomenological reduction of ordinary experience, that one can be said to be doing Husserlian phenomenology.

While Husserlian phenomenology has for its ultimate aim the ascertainment of the "essential structures of transcendental subjectivity," that is, of the transcendental ego, it cannot proceed directly to the description of these structures; for they are not subject to direct observation. They can be discovered only indirectly, by means of a kind of transcendental argument in the Kantian sense, subsequent to the determination of their counterparts in the realm of intentional objectivity. In other words, Husserl's "pure egology" is based upon his "transcendental theory of knowledge." Discoveries in the latter domain serve as "clues" to the structure of the transcendental ego.

Transcendental phenomenology thus consists in a number of related enterprises, all of which presuppose that the phenomenological reduction has been made. The first involves the careful description of "the stream of experience" or "the phenomena of consciousness," precisely as experienced. As has been observed, Husserl does not consider this to be phenomenology proper. The second enterprise is epistemological; and because it is eidetic, it is a part of Husserlian phenomenology proper. It consists in the analysis of intentional objects, with a view to the discernment of the essential types of intentional objects of which particular ones are instantiations. While "the realm of phenomena of consciousness is truly the realm of Heraclitean flux," Husserl says, "*an essentially necessary conformity to type* prevails and *can be apprehended in strict concepts*" (*CM*, p. 49). The task of "transcendental theory of knowledge," as he conceives of it, is to "explicate systematically . . . this set of structural types" (*CM*, p. 51). These "types" are the *eidoi*—the rather Platonistic "ideas" or "essences" which are the only *objects* with which Husserlian phenomenology, as an eidetic discipline, is concerned.

The third enterprise is "egological," in Husserl's phrase. It is the other part of Husserlian phenomenology proper, and it too is eidetic in that it is concerned with the "essential structures" of the transcendental ego. Here one turns from the investigation of the "ideas" or "essences" in the sphere of intentionality to the ascertainment of their subjective counterparts, namely, the essential structures of the ego which they presuppose. "Any 'objective' object," Husserl says, meaning any "idea" or "essence" (*eidos*), "points to a structure, within the transcendental ego, that is governed by a rule" (*CM*, p. 53). In this way what Husserl calls "the critique of all transcendental cognition" gives rise to a theory of the nature of the transcendental ego, or a "pure egology" (*CM*, pp. 29–30).

Husserl's use of Kantian terminology is calculated to indicate the Kantian character of his program and procedure at this stage of "phenomenological research." It is *only* at this stage, however, and *only* in connection with the "ideas" or essential types of intentional objects, that he makes use of a kind of "transcendental method" in the Kantian sense. It is the "ideas" alone which are held to serve as "transcendental clues" to the nature of the transcendental ego. Once they are grasped, however, he proceeds to ask *what they necessarily presuppose.* And as in the case of Kant, his answer is that the necessary condition of their possibility is that the transcendental ego is structured accordingly.

Given that the method Husserl employs in moving from a knowledge of the "ideas" to a knowledge of the essential structures of the pure ego is transcendental, the nature of the prior procedure he proposes, through the application of which a knowledge of the "ideas" is to be achieved, remains to be determined. As a Husserlian phenomenologist, I direct my attention to "the pure stream of my *cogitationes*" (*CM*, p. 21)—"the universe of 'phenomena,' " regarded solely as such (*CM*, p. 20). I am thus confronted with a great multitude of "pure conscious events." My task is "to bring them to complete clearness, and within this zone of clearness to subject them to analysis and the apprehension of their essence" (*I*, p. 174). Not every "conscious event" has the character of clearness or evidence; on the contrary Husserl holds that "evidence is only an occasional occurrence in conscious life" (*CM*, p. 57).

Unfortunately, he himself is far from clear in his characterization of that which distinguishes the evident from the nonevident. He says, "Evidence denotes . . . the quite preeminent mode of consciousness that consists in the self-appearance, the self-exhibiting, the self-giving, of an affair" (*CM*, p. 57). But this does not tell us how to distinguish a "conscious event" which has the character of being "self-exhibiting" and "self-giving" from one which does not. The problem is similar to that associated with Descartes' concept of the "clear and distinct," to which Husserl's concept of the "evident" is obviously related. The latter is associated with the notions of heeding mindfully what one is experiencing, paying close attention, and concentrating. These notions themselves are far from transparent. Still they serve to convey at least a rough idea of what Husserl has in mind. The first step is to attend closely to the stream of phenomena of which one is conscious, with a view to discerning similarities and differences between these phenomena.

In doing this, one may discover that some of one's intentional objects are sufficiently similar that they seem to be instances of a general type. The next step is thus to attempt to form a rough idea of the characteristic features of these general types, by considering what features the particular objects of that type have in common in one's experience. Ordinary language supplies us with a large number of type-concepts, such as "animal," "tool," and "law," which (once phenomenologically reduced) may provide us with points of departure, though they are no more than that and need not be relied upon at all. I may have had a great variety of "tool-experiences," for example; and on the basis of these experiences, I might then attempt to determine what features the intentional objects which I ordinarily call "tools" share.

At this stage the procedure of the Husserlian phenomenologist might be characterized as a kind of inductive generalization, on the basis of one's various past and present experiences. One should not base one's idea of what it is for something to be a "tool" on a single "tool-experience," for this might lead one to regard some accidental feature as essential. By taking into consideration a wide range of "tool-experiences," one has a better chance of seeing what is and what is not an essential feature of what might Platonistically be called "tool-hood." In this way one moves from what Husserl calls "eidetic singularities" to "essences at a higher specific level" (*I*, p. 192).[9]

Inductive generalization is for Husserl a step in the direction of a knowledge of essences, but he holds that by itself it does not give us such knowledge. "Inferences," he says, "have only the methodological meaning of leading us toward facts which it is the function of an ensuing direct essential insight to set before us as given" (*I*, p. 193). A further step is necessary—another operation must be performed—before we can be reasonably sure that we have grasped the *eidos* in question.

This operation might be characterized as that of imaginative variation. "Research in the region of the essence," according to Husserl, "necessarily demands that one should operate with the help of fancy" (*I*, p. 183). For while generalization may serve to eliminate many inessential features from one's notion of what a given *eidos* involves, there is no guarantee that all such inessential features have thereby been eliminated. As long as my idea of "tool-hood" is conditioned by the fact that it is based on a limited number of actual "tool-experiences," I may have a distorted understanding of the essence of "tool-hood."

It is for this reason that Husserl says that "*free fancies* assume *a privileged position over against perceptions*" (*I*, p. 182).[10] I must try to imagine things that lack the various features which I have tentatively concluded, on the basis of my inductive generalization, to be common to all tools; and it is only those which cannot conceivably be subtracted without the object's ceasing to be a tool which I can conclude belong to the essence of "tool-hood." It is only when I thus come to see what features something *must* have in order to be something or other—for example, a tool—that I grasp the essence.

The "direct essential insight" of which Husserl speaks thus presupposes a process of inductive generalization; but such "insight" is not achieved until one carries out a further operation of imaginative variation, which Husserl characterizes as "intuitive," rather than inductive *or* deductive—or, for that matter, purely descriptive. And if this operation is carried out properly, he says, "such presenting under the form of fancy can . . . be so perfectly clear as to enable us to see and apprehend perfectly the essential nature of things" (*I*, p. 181).

In short, through the performance of the phenomenological reduction, the careful exmination of "the stream of experience," the process of inductive generalization, and the operation of systematic imaginative variation, "each singly selected type is . . . elevated from its milieu within the empirically factual transcendental ego into the pure eidetic sphere" (*I*, p. 71). The Husserlian phenomenologist then proceeds, in the transcendental manner discussed previously, to determine what sorts of essential structures of the transcendental ego are thus presupposed. When this has been done comprehensively and systematically, and all the phenomena of consciousness have been thus analyzed and accounted for, the task of the Husserlian phenomenologist has been completed.

II

Heideggerian phenomenology is not a program in its own right at all. Heidegger's program is fundamentally an ontological one, both in *Being and Time* and subsequently. Phenomenology for him is the method he employs, most explicitly in *Being and Time*, in his attempt to achieve an understanding first of all of man's nature and secondarily of the world in which man lives, with the ultimate intention of ascertaining the nature of "Being" generally. The question he poses at the outset of *Being and Time* is the question of "the meaning of Being" (*BT*, p. 21), where "Being" refers not to any particular entity but rather to what it is for anything at all *to be*. (A more accurate rendering of his title, *Sein und Zeit*, would be: '*To Be' and Time.*) And "the question of the meaning of Being [or 'To Be']," he says, "is one that must be treated *phenomenologically*" (*BT*, pp. 49–50).

For Husserl, it may be recalled, this question is answered fairly easily: "being" is simply the intentional correlative of consciousness. "To be" is to be an object of consciousness, and the criterion of "true being" is the possibility of integration of such an object with such others as are "harmoniously combinable" (*CM*, pp. 62–63). All being is relative to consciousness and is grounded in some structure of the transcendental ego—all, that is, save the "being" of the transcendental ego itself, which Husserl regards as the sole absolute and ultimate reality (*I*, p. 14). Heidegger, however, rejects Husserl's transcendental idealism and with it Husserl's transcendental ego. For him, it is an irreducible and ultimate fact that man exists in a world which transcends him and in which he finds himself. He *is there* in it; hence Heidegger's characterization of man as "Dasein"—"there-being," "*da-sein*," or (as it is customarily rendered) "being-there." It follows, in Heidegger's view, that the question of what it is for something *to be* must be raised again, since the idealist (and phenomenalist) answer purportedly will not do. The question of man's nature must also be raised again for the same reason. We may have little more to go on at the outset, as we inquire into this matter, than that man is "in-the-world"; but this, according to Heidegger, we must suppose (since it can never be *proved*) or else deny the obvious, with disastrous philosophical results.

Heidegger feels that Husserl was led to take the latter course—and so to misinterpret radically both man's nature and the meaning of "Being"—because of his misguided attempt to achieve "an absolute freedom from all presuppositions." "If," Heidegger says, "we 'take our departure' from a worldless 'I' in order to provide this 'I' with an Object and an ontologically baseless relation to that Object, then we have 'presupposed' not too much, but *too little*" (*BT*, p. 363). The notion of "the [pure] ego as subject of one's pure *cogitationes*" is to him an empty abstraction. The only real "I," in his view, is that which Husserl speaks of in connection with "the natural standpoint"; and the only actual experiences open to investigation are those of this "I," which has the fundamental essential character of "being-in-the-world."

Heidegger therefore rejects the "regress to the [pure] ego," which is the *sine qua non* of Husserlian phenomenology, and along with it the related view that phenomenology is "a pure egology." And he also rejects Husserl's ideal of presuppositionlessness and his program of the reconstruction of knowledge on an absolutely certain foundation as well, with which this ideal is associated. Quite aside from the fact that Heidegger's concerns are largely non-epistemological and the fact that the adoption of the ideal of presupposition lessness has consequences which he takes to be most unfortunate, he shares the skepticism of many Anglo-American philosophers with regard to the very possibility of carrying out such a Cartesian reconstruction.

Phenomenology, he says, in his most definitive statement concerning it,

does not subscribe to a 'standpoint' or represent any special 'direction.' . . . The expression 'phenomenology' . . . signifies primarily a *methodological conception*. This expression does not characterize the *what* of the objects of philosophical research as subject-matter, but rather the *how* of that research. . . . [It] is removed from what we call "technical devices," though there are many such devices even in the theoretical disciplines. (*BT*, p. 50)

This passage is of great importance, for in it Heidegger departs radically from Husserl on a number of crucial issues. In saying that phenomenology "does not subscribe to a 'standpoint,' " he is rejecting Husserl's idea of a "phenomenological standpoint" which differs profoundly—and crucially, for philosophical purposes—from the "natural standpoint." In saying that phenomenology "does not characterize the *what* of the objects of philosophical research as subject-matter," he is rejecting Husserl's contention that phenomenology *does* have a distinctive twofold subject matter—namely, a very special kind of experience, "transcendental experience," and the "transcendental ego" which is its ground. In saying that phenomenology "is removed from . . . 'technical devices,' " he is rejecting Husserl's contention that phenomenological analysis presupposes the performance of a special technical operation—namely, the "phenomenological reduction." And in saying that phenomenology does not "represent any special 'direction,' " he is rejecting Husserl's view that phenomenology *does* inescapably lead in a definite direction—namely, toward transcendental idealism.

Heidegger does seem to be following Husserl when goes on to say, "The term 'phenomenology' expresses a maxim which can be formulated as 'To the things themselves!' " (*BT*, p. 50). For this maxim is Husserl's and is the watchword of Husserlian phenomenology. But Heidegger's endorsement of Husserl's maxim conceals a profound difference between them; for the "things themselves" with which Heidegger is concerned are not Husserl's phenomenologically reduced "pure conscious events" but rather "entities," the existence of which may be quite independent of the consciousness in which they are apprehended. The "phenomena" with which Heidegger is concerned are not conceived simply as the contents of the observer's stream-of-consciousness experiences, purely as experienced; rather, he says, "the 'phenomena' are the totality of what lies in the light of day *or can be brought to* the light—what the Greeks sometimes identified simply with τὰ ὄντα (entities)" (*BT*, p. 51).[11]

While for Husserl the "phenomena" to be analyzed have the status of appearances in the consciousness of the observer, Heidegger states that "phenomena" as he conceives of them have "nothing at all to do with what is called an 'appearance' " (*BT*, p. 51). "Phenomena," he says, "are *never* appearances, though on the other hand every appearance is dependent on phenomena" (*BT*, p. 53). He conceives of "the 'phenomena' of phenomenology" as "what thus shows itself *in itself*" (*BT*, p. 55);[12] and this in effect is to identify "phenomena" with something like things in themselves, insofar as they show themselves to us as they are, rather than in some other way. "An entity can show itself," Heidegger says, "in many ways, depending . . . on the kind of access we have to it. Indeed, it is even possible for an entity to show itself as something which in itself it is *not*" (*BT*, p. 51).

Nothing could be less Husserlian than to speak of entities in this way; for doing so commits one to some form of realism, in the modern sense of the term—a position which Husserl holds to be "in principle absurd" (*I*, p. 12). Yet it is precisely with the investigation of the nature of entities so conceived that Heideggerian phenomenology is concerned. "In the phenomenological conception of 'phenomenon,' " Heidegger says, "what one has in mind as that which shows itself is the Being of entities." And as he conceives of it, "Phenomenology is our way of access to what is . . . the theme of ontology," namely, the just-mentioned "Being of entities" (*BT,* p. 60).

Husserl, it has been observed, acknowledges that the "natural standpoint" is the "standpoint" which the individual occupies "for the most part," and that the investigation of both human existence and the world as they are experienced at this standpoint is a task "of extraordinary importance." But it has also been pointed out that he does not take this to be the task of phenomenology. On the contrary phenomenology as Husserl conceives of it requires the transcendence of this standpoint for the duration of one's phenomenological investigations and, with it, the suspension of concern with human existence and the world as they are experienced "for the most part."

For Heidegger, on the other hand, it is precisely with such matters that the phenomenologist must begin—with things as they are experienced "for the most part," with other people as we are related to them "for the most part," and with the way people live "for the most part." And when he goes beyond the description of the way people live "for the most part," it is not to leave the "natural standpoint" at all, but rather to describe a different way in which it is possible to live and to relate to things and other people *at* that standpoint.

Heideggerian phenomenology is not transcendental but rather existential. Husserl's "transcendental ego," "transcendental experience," and "pure essences" are for Heidegger pure abstractions; and he considers it an illusion to regard them as either more real or more fundamental than the self, the experience, and the things of concrete everyday existence. For Heidegger, if the phenomenologist is to grasp the true natures of things, he must *not* perform Husserl's phenomenological reduction, and he must *not* concern himself with anything like Husserl's "transcendental theory of knowledge" and "pure egology." Rather, he must undertake a careful analysis of the *Umwelt, Mitwelt,* and *Eigenwelt* of *Dasein*—that is, of the concretely existing human being. In short, Heideggerian phenomenology is concerned with matters pertaining to concrete existence, the analysis of which Husserl explicitly asserts to be prephenomenological (as *he* conceives of phenomenology). And Husserlian phenomenology is concerned with transcendental matters to which Heidegger denies any real significance.

Nor do the differences between them stop here. They further extend to the general method or pattern of analysis which each of them employs and terms "phenomenological." If allowances are made for their differences with regard to that which it is the preliminary task of the phenomenologist to describe, both do hold that phenomenological analysis begins with the careful description of experience in language which is as un-theory-laden as possible. For Heidegger, however, nothing like the performance of Husserl's operations of inductive generalization and imaginative variation follows. Rather, he proceeds directly from such description to what he calls "interpretation" or "hermeneutic" analysis, consisting in the attempt to uncover the basic structures of that which has been described, which are presupposed by the features noted in the course of its description. Such a "hermeneutic" analysis is necessary because, first, it is assumed that things *have* such basic structures, which are definitive of their "Being," and because, secondly, Heidegger holds that (generally speaking) their "Being," is "something that lies *hidden*, in contrast to that which proximally and for the most part does show itself" (*BT*, p. 59).

Heidegger's method of "interpretation" or "hermeneutic" analysis does resemble the method Husserl employs, in moving from the knowledge of essences to the ascertainment of the essential structures of the pure ego, at least to some extent; for it too is a kind of transcendental method in the Kantian sense. That is, here too one is to proceed by attempting to determine what fundamental structures are necessarily presupposed by that which one has already observed. In Heidegger's words, one "aims at ascertaining the *a priori* conditions . . . for the possibility" of observable states of affairs (*BT*, p. 31). But this is a Kantian procedure, rather than a distinctively Husserlian one. And the things which Heidegger proposes to subject to transcendental "interpretation" are not Husserlian "essences," apprehended through the operations of inductive generalization and imaginative variation, but rather states of affairs which come to light in the course of one's analysis and description of ordinary experiences.

In short, Heidegger not only replaces Husserl's program of the analysis of the "essential structures of transcendental subjectivity" with the program of the analysis of the "structures which are essential to Dasein's state-of-being" (*BT*, p. 421), but also abandons Husserl's view that a detour through "transcendental theory of knowledge" is necessary in order to carry out this program. He proceeds directly from "ontical" inquiry, or the description of observable states of affairs, to "ontological" inquiry, or the determination of the fundamental structures of the entities in question, by means of a kind of transcendental "interpretation." For Husserl it is the *eidoi* or essences which are the "transcendental clues" enabling us to determine the essential structures of the ego. Heidegger also speaks of "clues," only they are clues enabling us to determine the fundamental structures of concrete human existence. And they are to be found among the directly ascertainable matters of fact pertaining to concrete human existence which are "given" in ordinary experience, if only we have the eyes to see them.

Heidegger does not confine himself to the phenomenological investigation or "interpretation" of the basic structures of human existence alone; he also considers "things," which he concludes have the fundamental character of being "ready-to-hand." But his attention centers largely upon the question of the ontological characteristics of Dasein, and so I shall make reference to the way in which he deals with this issue to illustrate phenomenological inquiry as he conceives and practices it. Given the task of an "interpretation" of the basic structures of human existence, he asks, "Where does this Interpretation get its clue, if not from an idea of existence . . . which has been 'presupposed'?" (*BT,* p. 361). And the "idea of existence" to which Heidegger refers derives from a number of rather commonplace observations; the warrant for "presupposing" it is precisely their purported obviousness. A number of what he takes to be obvious features of human existence are mentioned in the following passage:

Without any ontological transparency, it has nevertheless been revealed that in every case I am myself the entity which we call Dasein, and that I am so as a potentiality-for-being for which to be this entity is an issue. Dasein understands itself as Being-in-the-world, even if it does so without adequate ontological definiteness. . . . [Further], Dasein is not just present-at-hand but has already *understood itself* [in some way or another], however mythical or magical the interpretation which it gives may be. (*BT,* p. 361)

In more ordinary language, Heidegger is observing that each instance of the entity under investigation is "I" to itself and thus has a dimension of subjectivity, that this entity is one which must to a considerable extent determine the course of its own life, that it is further an entity which finds itself in a world and which moreover has the capacity and the need to understand itself and the world in which it finds itself, and finally that it is an entity which tends to understand itself differently from the ways in which it understands the objects with which it is confronted. These are examples of what Heidegger terms "ontical" characteristics of human existence—features of it which are ascertainable simply by attending carefully to ordinary experience. They, together with a number of others (pertaining to death and to possible ways of relating to other men and to things), provide Heidegger with "clues" for his "interpretation" of the fundamental structures of human existence. The transcendental character of his method of "interpretation" is evident when he writes, "Can ontological Interpretation do anything else than base itself on *ontical possibilities* . . . and project these possibilities upon their *ontological possibility?"* (*BT*, p. 360). And since he contends that "only as phenomenology is ontology possible" (*BT*, p. 60), it follows that phenomenology as he construes it consists in proceeding in just this manner.

It is not my purpose here to characterize in detail the fundamental structures which Heidegger takes these "ontical possibilities" to presuppose, for my concern is with the nature of his program and of the method he employs and not with the results he achieves. It remains to be observed only that he subjects the structures which first come to light—such as "being-ahead-of-itself" and "being-towards-an-end"—to further "interpretation." For he regards them not as absolutely fundamental, but rather as having a further, still more basic, structural presupposition. "We shall point to temporality," he says, "as the meaning of the Being of that entity which we call 'Dasein.'" He continues, "If this is to be demonstrated, those structures of Dasein which we shall provisionally exhibit must be Interpreted over again as modes of temporality" (*BT*, p. 38). His phenomenological method of "interpretation" thus proceeds in a number of stages, in the course of which ever more fundamental structures are progressively revealed.

In short, Heideggerian phenomenology is a method employed with a view to ascertaining the fundamental structures of entities of various sorts and, ultimately, with a view to ascertaining "the meaning of Being" generally. It consists of "interpreting" the features of things which we observe them to have in ordinary experience, by determining what basic structures these things *must* have in order for them to have these immediately observable features, and by subjecting the structures which first come to light to a similar "interpretation," if and when this is possible.

While it has been customary since Kant to refer to this sort of procedure as "transcendental," the use of this term should not obscure the fact that Heideggerian phenomenology is anything but "transcendental" in the sense in which Husserlian phenomenology is "transcendental phenomenology." The experience to be analyzed is not "transcendental experience," in the sense of phenomenologically reduced experience, but rather ordinary experience; the "self" which is the focal point of investigation is not the "transcendental ego," but rather the "I" of concrete human existence; and nothing even resembling Husserl's "transcendental theory of knowledge" is undertaken, either in the course of attempting to ascertain the basic structures of this "self" or at any other point in the Heideggerian program. The radical difference between Heideggerian and Husserlian phenomenology extends even to their uses of the term "phenomena"; the "phenomena" to be investigated are not at all for Heidegger what they are for Husserl.

The only similarity of any substance between Heideggerian and Husserlian phenomenology—other than a common insistence upon the primacy of subjective experience, which by no means sets Husserl and Heidegger apart from nonphenomenologists generally—is that at some point in each version use is made of what I have called "transcendental" argument in the Kantian sense. Because Husserl does not hold the patent on this sort of argument, however, this similarity is not particularly significant—especially in view of the fact that the use made of this sort of argument occurs in quite different contexts in the two cases.

It is not my intention to maintain that Heidegger, by his radical departure from Husserl on the matter of the nature of phenomenology, presents us with a kind of phenomenology that is either superior or inferior to Husserl's. In point of fact, many of the features of Husserlian phenomenology which Heidegger rejects are features which I find questionable to say the least; yet while I find Heidegger's program more attractive, I am far from being persuaded either of the validity of all his conclusions or of the soundness and adequacy of his method. These are issues, however, which go beyond the scope of this discussion; and I shall not pursue them here. But it is not necessary to do so to show that Husserlian phenomenology and Heideggerian phenomenology are related in little more than name and motto, and that there is scarcely even a remote family resemblance between them.

By way of a kind of postscript, I would like to take note of an increasingly common use of the terms "phenomenology," "phenomenological," and the like, and to offer a suggestion concerning it. In recent years many philosophers have begun to employ these terms in connection with the careful description—simply as such—of particular phenomena of various sorts, exactly as they are immediately encountered or experienced. Husserl and Heidegger would be the first to insist upon the importance of such description in philosophical inquiry. If there is one thing which they agree upon, however, it is the fact that phenomenology proper begins only with the attempt to *go beyond* such description in some way or other, in order to ascertain the *logos* of the "phenomena" immediately encountered or experienced. Thus for Husserl one cannot be said to be doing phenomenology unless one is engaged in "eidetic" analysis, and for Heidegger one can be said to be doing phenomenology only if one is engaged in "hermeneutic analysis" or "interpretation." It seems to me that it would be well to restrict the use of the term "phenomenology" and its derivatives to contexts in which something of this sort—as opposed to the kind of mere description of particular experiences mentioned above—is attempted; for if it is not, the confusion of such description with phenomenology proper (and vice versa) can hardly be avoided. And such confusion is highly undesirable, since it easily leads to a misunderstanding of what Husserl and Heidegger—and with them, many subsequent European philosophers—are up to.

One may object that, while this is true, we lack any better terms than "phenomenology," etc., with which to refer to the sort of careful description under consideration, and that it is desirable to have at our disposal expressions which enable us to refer economically and transparently to such description. I agree to both points; but I would suggest that rather than yield to the growing practice to which I have referred, the best thing to do is to introduce a new set of terms to be employed in this connection. My candidates are "phenomenography" and "phenomenographical" (etc.). They satisfy the requirements of economy and transparency (cf. "biography," "biographical," etc.), and are no more—if admittedly no less—pretentious and cumbersome than "phenomenology" and its derivatives. And they would serve to mark an important distinction.

It may be that artificial technical terms ought not to be introduced when there is no real need for them. However, this seems to me to be a case in which such a need clearly exists. And while philosophers may have no right to prescribe and proscribe in the realm of ordinary language, they surely have the right to adjust the terminology to be used to refer to their own philosophical activities. I would very much like to see generally adopted either the convention I propose or something like it; for it is difficult enough to get straight what phenomenology proper is—or rather, what the major variants of phenomenology proper are—without the term and its derivatives being used to refer to a much more restricted sort of analysis undertaken by a great many philosophers with widely differing programmatic orientations. Indeed, I fear that unless some such practice gains general acceptance, the term "phenomenological" will go the way of the term "existential," and, through promiscuous employment, will achieve great popularity at the cost of its integrity. Philosophers may not be able to prevent the corruption of the term, but they need not and ought not encourage such a development by using it loosely themselves.

10:

Existentialism, Existenz-*Philosophy, and* Philosophical Anthropology

Previous chapters of this book have dealt with men whose thought has profoundly influenced the various main currents of contemporary European philosophy. The present chapter identifies certain of these currents and thus brings into focus the nature of the concerns and endeavors of some of the more important recent writers attempting in different ways to come to terms with this legacy. Whether any of these writers are comparable in philosophical stature to those discussed up to this point is not yet clear; for while a few, like Sartre, are widely known and very popular and others, like Karl Jaspers, Maurice Merleau-Ponty, and Helmuth Plessner, are highly regarded by smaller readerships, it remains to be seen whether the efforts of any of them will prove to represent the accomplishment and to have the enduring interest of those of Kierkegaard and Marx, or of Husserl and Heidegger. (That any of them will one day be generally recognized as belonging in the select company of Hegel and Nietzsche, however, is scarcely conceivable.) This is one reason why none of them has been singled out here for the kind of special attention that has been devoted to these other (for the most part earlier) figures, although another is that, because they do deserve careful consideration and because the number of those deserving it is so large, it is simply beyond the scope of this book to do more than briefly indicate something of the character of their thought.

It also remains to be seen whether any of the philosophical tendencies and movements with which these more recent writers are associated will prove to be more than passing episodes or transitional developments, and what directions contemporary European philosophy will take as these currents intermingle with one another—and also with those constituting the main orientations of present-day Anglo-American philosophy (of which there is a growing awareness on the Continent).

There is much more to twentieth-century European philosophy than existentialism, and with the passage of time even the relatively large role which the latter at one point played in the domain of the former has greatly diminished and continues in its decline. In the course of the past several decades attention has shifted strongly toward such related and different enterprises as *Existenz*-philosophy, phenomenology, neo-Marxist philosophy, hermeneutics, structuralism, and philosophical anthropology, which in some cases are pursued independently and in others in various combinations. Never homogeneous even before the Second World War, European philosophy since the war has been characterized by an increasing heterogeneity reminiscent of its state a hundred years ago. Any fear or suspicion English-speaking philosophers may have, deriving from an impression of the complete ascendancy of Heidegger and Sartre, that philosophy on the Continent is too narrow and rigid to be capable of either receiving or producing anything of general philosophical interest is utterly unwarranted.

In the present chapter, which should serve to help correct any such misapprehension (at least to the extent that its main purpose is to sort out and characterize the three developments indicated in the title), some suggestions are made concerning the lines along which a partial integration of some of these various enterprises may be under way and certainly might be brought about. No grand synthesis is to be expected, however, as long as Continental philosophers continue to respond in such varied ways to their radically differing predecessors of the past several centuries, as well as to one another and to other contemporary influences. The richness of European philosophical thought from Kant and Hegel to Nietzsche virtually guaranteed that its twentieth-century sequel would be a very lively affair, provided only that the former were encountered and taken seriously; and this European philosophers in the present century generally have not neglected to do.

"Existentialism" is by now a household word. Indeed, as long ago as 1947, Sartre felt moved to complain (to a French audience, to be sure), "The word is now so loosely applied to so many things that it no longer means anything at all."[1] Still, this circumstance did not induce him to abandon the term as a convenient label for his views. And it is not difficult for almost anyone who has kept abreast of postwar literary and intellectual developments to state the basic tenets of "existentialism" in a rough-and-ready way, for they have been so extensively popularized in recent years that they are by now familiar to almost everyone who has any contact with the printed word.

The same is by no means true, on the other hand, of "*Existenz*-philosophy" and "philosophical anthropology"—expressions referring to two very important general European philosophical developments of the past half century, which should be distinguished both from "existentialism" and from each other. My purpose here is to draw these distinctions and to indicate something of the nature of each of these philosophical tendencies, focusing primarily upon *Existenz*-philosophy and philosophical anthropology. I shall begin, however, with a brief consideration of existentialism as it is commonly conceived and as it is characterized by various commentators, in order to provide the subsequent discussion with a familiar point of departure.

I

As it is generally understood, the term "existentialism" refers to a certain comprehensive world view, which is in striking contrast to what might be termed the traditional Judeo-Christian world view and also to most traditional philosophical interpretations of reality, from the idealistic to the materialistic; and an "existentialist" is one who subscribes to this understanding of the ways things are. He is thought to maintain that there is no God of any sort and no absolutes in the realms of value and morality. There are only men and things. Men find themselves thrown into a cold and hostile world, condemned to an existence that is ultimately meaningless and fundamentally absurd, in which the only certainty is that of striving, suffering, and final oblivion.

Unlike mere things, the story continues, men are free in a most radical sense, the acknowledged limitations placed upon them by historical and social circumstances, heredity, mortality and the like notwithstanding; for they are always confronted by a range of alternatives, and within that range the choices they can and must make are neither psychologically determined nor governed by objectively valid normative principles. Men thus are what they make themselves to be through the choices they make—or, as the saying goes, their existence precedes their "essence" (i.e., their determinate character)—and so they are completely responsible for the lives they lead. This may be an exhilarating prospect; but it is also accompanied by the greatest anguish, since choice in the absence of fixed and objective guidelines of any sort is not an easy affair, particularly when the shape of the only life one has is at stake. There are, of course, other men with whom one shares one's human lot of condemnation to absurd freedom; but no lessening of one's freedom and responsibility for one's choices is to be found in this fact. Indeed, while men share a common ontological constitution and a common human condition, they are radically isolated from one another, never being capable of achieving more than the most superficial sort of unity and constantly struggling against one another except when temporarily making common cause in some struggle against still others.

In short, in the "existentialist" view (as this is usually understood), each person exists as a kind of monad, locked into his own subjectivity and yet continuously confronted with objective realities—such as things, others, institutions, and his own "facticity"—with which he must deal without ever being able to achieve any real unity or even harmony with them. He may minimize his conflicts and his choices by making a general decision to follow the line of least resistance and take his cues from others, but he only deceives himself if he thinks that in this way he relieves himself of all responsibility for what he is. And one who does this further surrenders that possible authenticity or integrity which is the source of the only nonillusory sort of dignity attainable by man, in return for nothing more than a false sense of security and significance. He exists as a truly human being only if he recognizes his situation for what it is, in all its insecurity, meaninglessness, and absurdity; if he acknowledges his radical freedom and responsibility, resolutely accepting the inevitability of that anxiety which is inseparable from this acknowledgment; and if he charts a course of his own choosing, without any illusions of thereby rendering his existence less intrinsically absurd and more ultimately meaningful than it otherwise would be.

This is more or less the sort of thing that "existentialism" is ordinarily taken to involve—with considerable justification. And, if understood along these lines, the term is by no means a meaningless one, although to say this much is of course to say nothing about the plausibility and relative merit of the world view in question. Problems arise, however, not so much from the fact that this characterization of the position is oversimplified and incomplete (as it admittedly is), as from the fact that the term "existentialist" is also commonly used to refer to a considerable number of rather diverse philosphers of European origin and recent vintage who would themselves take issue with this world view on a variety of counts. Indeed, the situation is further complicated by the fact that in the English-speaking world "existentialism" and "recent Continental philosophy" are at least very widely regarded (even in philosophical circles) as virtually coextensive expressions. The latter notion is grossly inaccurate, as I shall shortly show by indicating something of the nature of another recent philosophical development in Europe, which cannot be assimilated to existentialism so conceived by any stretch of the imagination.

The former practice, on the other hand, of lumping together a large but *restricted* group of recent European philosophers under the rubric of "existentialism" presents a different sort of problem, at least where intelligent commentators who know what they are talking about are concerned. They realize that the position outlined above is by no means adhered to by all of those to whom the term "existentialist" has come to be applied (*viz.,* not only Sartre and Camus but also Heidegger, Jaspers, Marcel, Kierkegaard, Nietzsche, and a number of others). Rather than attempting to restrict its application to those who do adhere to it (or to something close to it), however, they by and large have chosen to try to modify the description of what being an "existentialist" involves in such a way that the label may *accurately* be applied to all of those in question, however fortuitously it may initially have come to be applied to many of them.

There is something to be said for this move, given the difficulty of removing a brand once it has been burned in. It seems to me, however, that it would be greatly preferable to allow the term to retain its well-established and by no means illegitimate association with the general sort of world view indicated above (thereby enabling it to retain its utility as a descriptive term with definite content), and to adopt an alternate way of referring to those philosophers to whom it is frequently applied but whose substantive views differ significantly from those outlined, as well as to most of those who do subscribe to this world view. This procedure might be just as questionable as the above-mentioned alternative to it, if it were the case that this would require an arbitrary terminological innovation. In fact, however, it would merely involve adopting a practice which has long been customary in Europe and in Germany in particular—and thereby making a very useful distinction. In the following section of this chapter, I shall develop this suggestion and shall elaborate upon my reasons for advancing it, before going on to discuss several related matters.

II

The term "existentialism" derives primarily from certain recent French philosophers—most notably Sartre (although Camus may also be mentioned in this connection). And it has become associated above all with a particular body of doctrine, namely, that which is set forth in Sartre's works written prior to his conversion to a form of Marxism in the early 1950s. This is not unusual. Terms ending in "-ism" generally refer to some set of views. But precisely for this reason, not many other philosophers—and very few who are not closely associated with Sartre—will admit to being "existentialists."

For example, Heidegger and Jaspers (the two most important German philosophers associated with the so-called "existentialist movement" in this century, as everyone knows) and the French philosopher Gabriel Marcel are vehement in their rejection of the label. And they are quite justified in rejecting it, considering the significant differences between their views and those of Sartre and Camus and their followers. To classify them under the rubric of "existentialism" is as inaccurate as it would be to term Kant's moral philosophy a type of utilitarianism simply because he is interested in ethics. Utilitarianism represents one particular philosophical position one can take in relation to various ethical questions, but ethics itself is simply a general problem area; "ethics" refers only to the problems to be dealt with and not to any particular answers to them. In the terms of this analogy, "existentialism" corresponds not to the latter (ethics) but rather to the former (utilitarianism).

Some commentators try to save "existentialism" as a general umbrella-term covering the positions not only of Sartre and Camus but also of Heidegger and Jaspers, Kierkegaard and Nietzsche, and Marcel and others, by looking for a common element in all their writings. Upon finding (or thinking they have found) something of this sort, these commentators then proclaim that this common element is the essence of "existentialism," and that a philosopher may be considered an "existentialist"—his objections notwithstanding—if this thematic common demoninator is to be found in his works.

This is the approach of Blackham, for example, in his well-known book *Six Existentialist Thinkers;* he justifies his selection of the six philosophers with whom he deals (*viz.*, those mentioned in the above paragraph minus Camus) by maintaining that "together they develop the content of certain common themes." What are these themes? Blackham says that the "existentialist movement" led by those he singles out "appears to be reaffirming in a modern idiom the protestant or the stoic form of individualism, which stands over against the empirical individualism of the Renaissance or of modern liberalism or of Epicurus as well as over against the universal system of Rome or of Moscow or of Plato."[2] And at another point he says, "The peculiarity of existentialism, then, is that it deals with the separation of man from himself and from the world."[3]

Generalizations such as these, however, usually turn out to be only half true at best and are more misleading than they are accurate and informative. They certainly do not provide satisfactory criteria for the inclusion of the writers popularly styled "existentialists" and for the exclusion of others who most definitely are *not* so regarded. Blackham's second statement above, for example, suggests that Hegel should be considered an "existentialist"; for no philosopher has been more concerned than Hegel—who is usually viewed as the exact opposite of an "existentialist"—with "the separation of man from himself and from the world." And on the other hand, this statement does not apply very well to Heidegger, for he is much more concerned with our everyday *absorption in* the world of others and things and institutions than he is with any problems associated with separation from it.

Similar problems arise in connection with Blackham's first suggestion. If advocacy of "the protestant or the stoic form of individualism" in some form or other is made the criterion of being an "existentialist," then it would appear that Kant, Marx, and Bertrand Russell are as entitled to inclusion among the "existentialists" as are any of Blackham's six. On the other hand, the use of this criterion would seem to render the inclusion of Nietzsche highly questionable, for reasons I shall indicate toward the end of this chapter; and while it may be applied to Jaspers, this characterization of his position is grossly one-sided and distorted since he draws heavily not only on Nietzsche, but also on Hegel (as well as on Kierkegaard).

A different kind of attempt to find a common denominator is made by Walter Kaufmann, who finds the essence of "existentialism" not in any particular doctrine, but rather in the individualism of the various writers *themselves*—as thinkers and as human beings—and their critical attitude toward philosophical schools and systems generally. "Certainly," says Kaufmann,

existentialism is not a school of thought nor reducible to any set of tenets. The three writers who appear invariably on every list of "existentialists"— Jaspers, Heidegger, and Sartre—are not in agreement on essentials. Such alleged precursors as Pascal and Kierkegaard differed from all three men by being dedicated Christians; and Pascal was a Catholic of sorts while Kierkegaard was a Protestant's Protestant. If, as is often done, Nietzsche and Dostoevsky are included in the fold, we must make room for an impassioned anti-Christian and an even more fanatical Greek-Orthodox Russian imperialist. By the time we consider adding Rilke, Kafka, and Camus, it becomes plain that one essential feature shared by all these men is their perfervid individualism.

The refusal to belong to any school of thought, the repudiation of the adequacy of any body of beliefs whatever, and especially of systems, and a marked dissatisfaction with traditional philosophy as superficial, academic, and remote from life—that is the heart of existentialism.[4]

Now, some of those Kaufmann mentions may have been perfervid individualists; but this is hardly true of two of the three "who appear invariably on every list," namely, Heidegger and Jaspers. Heidegger may have become mildly eccentric in his later years; but both were professors whose lives (at least for their times and circumstances) could hardly be said to be unconventional and who never approached the individualism and anti-establishmentarianism of a Kierkegaard or a Nietzsche—or even of a Russell or a Wittgenstein. And the repudiation of systems and the dissatisfaction with traditional philosophy of which Kaufmann speaks are common to many contemporary philosophers whom no one would think of terming "existentialists," such as Wittgenstein, G. E. Moore, A. J. Ayer, and J. L. Austin.

More importantly, it is hard to see why the general sort of orientation

Kaufmann has in mind should be called "existentialism." The only conceivable reason would seem to be that it suggests a desire on the part of those in question to make philosophy "relevant" to human existence. But this desire is far from being the special property of the men Kaufmann names, and has been shared (if such a desire can be meaningfully spoken of at all) by such diverse philosophers as Socrates, Hegel, and Marx. If the philosophers Kaufmann names have nothing more than this in common, there ceases to be any point in even grouping them together, let alone in speaking of something called "existentialism" in connection with what they wrote and thought.

In Germany the terms *Existentialismus* and *Existential Philosophie* are used, but only in connection with the philosophy of Sartre and those whose views are closely associated with his. Another term, which stands to *Existentialismus* as epistemology does to positivism and ethics to utilitarianism, is used to refer to the general philosophical problem area. This term is *Existenzphilosophie*. Heidegger and Jaspers are not lumped together with Sartre as *Existentialisten* ("existentialists"); rather, they all are considered to be (at least part-time) *Existenzphilosophen*—philosophers who take human "*Existenz*" for their theme (or at least for one of their themes). No attempt is made to define *Existenzphilosophie* in terms of certain fundamental doctrines, or a pervasive basic mood (as Mary Warnock does[5]), or a particular attitude toward traditional philosophy, or a shared personality trait. Rather, it is defined in terms of its *subject matter:* a certain distinctive (purported) dimension of actual or possible human "being," which I shall attempt to characterize in a general sort of way later in this chapter. And concern with this subject matter is the criterion for determining whether someone deserves to be considered an *Existenzphilosoph*. To my way of thinking, it is extremely valuable to be able to distinguish between "existentialism" as an "-ism" and "*Existenz*-philosophy" as a branch of philosophical inquiry, concerned with the analysis of human *Existenz*. The two are only too often confused in the English-speaking world, and this confusion easily leads to a misunderstanding of the general nature of an important part of European philosophy since the First World War.

"*Existenz*-philosophy" is an expression commonly associated primarily with Jaspers by English-speaking commentators; and "*Existenz*" is often treated as a term central to his analysis of human reality but so distinctly *his* that reference to it is best restricted to discussions of his views. In fact, however, this very term is given an equally central place in Heidegger's "hermeneutic of *Dasein*," which he himself characterizes as an "analytic of *Existenz*."[6] In one of Heidegger's most categorical and definitive pronouncements concerning the nature of Dasein (his technical term for human reality), he asserts, "Das 'Wesen' des Daseins liegt in seiner Existenz."[7] He further remarks, in this connection, that "when we choose to designate the being of this entity as *'Existenz,'* this term does not and cannot have the ontological signification of the traditional term *'existentia.'* . . . The term *'Existenz,'* as a *Seinsbestimmung* [i.e., designation of (a way of) being], will be allotted solely to *Dasein.*"[8] And when he refers to aspects of the *"Existenzstruktur"* of Dasein, he terms them *"Existenzialien"* in order to emphasize their fundamentally different character from the "categories" applicable to "entities whose character is not that of *Dasein.*"[9] In short, it is quite appropriate to speak of *"Existenz*-philosophy" in connection with Heidegger as well as Jaspers.

Much the same sort of case can be made with respect to Sartre, once one takes into account the language difference. To be sure, Sartre uses the same term (in French, as in English, *"existence"*) in connection with both human reality and nonhuman entities. But he is at pains to point out that human "existence" is a very different affair from that of mere things, having the character not of determinate *being* but rather of the *transcendence of* determinate being (albeit limited by the latter, in the form of one's situation and "facticity") and thus, in a manner of speaking, of "nothingness" and freedom. It is held to consist in a process through which one "encounters himself, surges up in the world," and comes to be "what he makes of himself"—this being Sartre's gloss on his dictum that "existence precedes essence,"[10] alternatively expressed (in *Being and Nothingness*) in the proposition that "consciousness" is an entity "whose existence posits its essence."[11] (Or again, it is said to consist in "a perpetual project of founding itself *qua* being and a perpetual failure of this project."[12]) Thus, he writes: "With man the relation of existence to essence is not comparable to what it is for things of the world. Human freedom precedes essence in man and makes it possible. . . . What we call freedom is impossible to distinguish from the *being* of 'human reality.' "[13]

The details of Sartre's analysis of the distinctive character of human "existence" are not of concern here. The point is simply that his entire "phenomenological ontology" centers around his analysis of its distinctive character, and that he himself supplies the warrant for referring to his discussion of "the being of 'human reality' " as an investigation of human "existence" in a special sense of that term. While Sartre (writing in French) does not actually use the German term *Existenz,* therefore, the legitimacy of subsuming his analysis of human reality under the general rubric of *"Existenz*-philosophy" can hardly be denied.

In short, it seems to me that it would be pointless for anyone to insist that these expressions should be restricted to discussions of Jaspers and avoided in discussions of Heidegger and Sartre (and others), merely because Jaspers is the only one of the three who actually refers to what he is doing as "*Existenz*-philosophy." It might be argued that it would be preferable to use more neutral language here and simply to speak of "existence" and "the philosophy of existence." This, however, would be (and is) a dubious practice since it would tend to obscure the very distinction—between a certain special (opaquely subjective) dimension of human reality and garden-variety non-human existence generally—which these and other such writers are concerned to draw and to clarify and explicate. As Heidegger suggests, in the passage cited above, a term to mark this distinction is precisely what is needed here; and I am simply proposing, as a designation of this general enterprise, an expression fixing upon the term which both he and Jaspers actually employ for this purpose.

Actually, I believe that another distinction should be drawn here as well. An *Existenz*-philosopher, I have suggested, is simply one who is concerned with the analysis of *Existenz*. As such, he need make no special claims for *Existenz*, such as attributing to it greater significance than any other dimension of human life or maintaining that human self-realization is exclusively a matter of its cultivation. Philosophers who concern themselves with the issue of man's nature, however, often feel obliged to take a position (either explicitly or implicitly) on this second issue. Most of those historically associated with *Existenz*-philosophy—including Jaspers, Heidegger, and Sartre, as well as Kierkegaard—have made such claims. But this does not establish that there is no point in characterizing *Existenz*-philosophy formally, as I have done. It only shows that these writers were interested not merely in analyzing the nature of *Existenz*, but also in making further claims for it. And it should be observed that one is not *eo ipso* an existentialist even if one does so. Perhaps another term is needed here, such as "*Existenz*ist"; and if I may be allowed to use this inelegant term, I can make my point by saying that existentialists as I have characterized them are only one tribe of "*Existenz*ists," and that there are other such tribes of equal interest and significance, who generally regard the tribe of "existentialists" either with dismay or with hostility or with pity.

It should also be observed that the *Existenz*-philosophy of Jaspers, Heidegger, and Sartre (not to mention existentialism) would not stand as the only significant and interesting recent philosophical development in Europe, even if attention were to be confined to the works of these three men alone; for it would be misleading and inaccurate to characterize any of them simply as an *Existenz*-philosopher. And *Existenz*-philosophy would be as seriously misunderstood if it were to be identified with their philosophical efforts generally as it is when it is identified with existentialism as characterized at the beginning of this chapter. This may come as no news to those familiar with the complete range of their philosophical efforts, but it is worth emphasizing here.

Heidegger, for example, is primarily an ontologist and is only secondarily (or preliminarily) an *Existenz*-philosopher. The basic question for him is not that of the nature of man, but rather that of the nature of "Being" generally. His analysis of *Existenz* does not stand or fall with his reflections on "Being" and may be considered quite independently of them; but he never tires of repeating, in *Being and Time* and elsewhere, that his analysis of human existence is a mere "preliminary analysis," undertaken simply in order to prepare the way for an analysis of the nature of "Being" as such. And so, while he has never carried out this long-promised analysis of "Being" in any systematic way, most of his later writings are related more directly to his ontological interests than to the question of the nature of *Existenz* as such, and thus cannot be considered part of the literature of *Existenz*-philosophy.

Similarly, Jaspers' interests are by no means confined to the nature of *Existenz*. Originally a psychologist of great importance in Germany, he gradually shifted his interest to many of the questions of traditional metaphysics. In his writings he neither raises nor answers these questions in traditional ways, and uses a vocabulary which tends to disguise the fact that he is dealing with them. Yet he expressly states that the three volumes of his *Philosophy* correspond to the traditional threefold division of metaphysics into speculation concerning the world, the soul, and God; only he finds it preferable to speak instead of world interpretations, *Existenz*, and Transcendence. Thus the second volume of this work, which contains the most complete statement of his *Existenz*-philosophy that he has published, is only one of three; and the other two—not to mention many of his subsequent writings—deal at length with themes which cannot be subsumed under the category of *Existenz*-philosophy.

As for Sartre, since the publication of *Being and Nothingness*, he has moved steadily in the direction of Marxism; and in his more recent *Critique of Dialectical Reason*, he has developed a position which has more in common with the thought of the early Marx and various neo-Marxists than it does with Heidegger's *Being and Time* and his own earlier work. He therefore cannot simply be regarded as an *Existenz*-philosopher and advocate of the existentialism which he had developed in that earlier period. To be sure, a shift in the direction of a Marxist conception of man's nature and human life does not preclude *Existenz*-philosophical concerns. Indeed, whereas Sartre may be said to have left his erstwhile existentialism behind him, setting it aside in favor of a rather different world view, the same cannot be said with reference to his commitment to *Existenz*-philosophy. He has not abandoned it, but rather has broadened his approach to the understanding of human reality in a way that incorporates it and at the same time complements it with an objectivity-oriented Marxian philosophical anthropology; and thus in his own particular way he has attempted an integration of these two rather different concerns (about which I shall have something to say shortly). But precisely to the extent that this is true, it follows that in his more recent work he deals extensively with matters falling outside the scope of *Existenz*-philosophy proper.

A word is in order here about the relation between *Existenz*-philosophy and ethics. Sartre's particular version of the former, to which the term "existentialism" may justly be applied and in terms of which existentialism is generally conceived, is often regarded as a type of ethical orientation. This is in no small measure due to Sartre himself, for it is in effect treated as such in his popular lecture entitled "Existentialism Is a Humanism."[14] From what I have said about the nature of *Existenz*-philosophy, however, it should be clear that the philosophy of *Existenz* as such is a general program involving commitment to no particular set of doctrines and therefore entailing no particular moral imperatives or axiological conclusions. There is only one way in which the question of such consequences can arise within the context of this program, and that is if some such consequence were in some way entailed by a particular analysis of *Existenz*. Sartre and Jaspers both seem to take this to be the case, whereas Heidegger does not (proclaiming his "authenticity-inauthenticity" distinction to be purely descriptive and to have no evaluative significance). It is an open question, however, whether any such consequences actually are entailed by the analyses Sartre and Jaspers give, and indeed whether an analysis of this sort can have such consequences even in principle.

III

At this point I wish to draw attention to another recent European philosophical development; for I want to attempt to correct the mistaken idea that *Existenz*-philosophy even in this broader sense (let alone existentialism) has completely dominated European philosophy or constitutes the sole important development in European philosophy in the past half century. And here I do not simply have in mind the survival of Catholic philosophy and the revival of Marxist philosophy, although the former is taken much more seriously by secular European philosophers than it is by most of their Anglo-American counterparts, and the latter is of much greater genuine philosophical interest than most of what passes for Marxist philosophy originating in English. The existence and autonomy of both (in relation to the tendencies I have been discussing) are generally known, even if the works and the identity of the more important proponents of each are unfamiliar to most English-speaking readers.

Nor do I have in mind the attempt to achieve a kind of synthesis of Marxism and Sartrean existentialism, in which there is now a great deal of interest in both Eastern and Western Europe, although this development is not to be taken lightly by admirers of Sartrean existentialism, since Sartre himself went over to such an "existentialist Marxism," giving it one of its earliest and weightiest expressions in his *Critique of Dialectical Reason.*[15] I do think it important to point out that Heidegger and Sartre have no monopoly on phenomenology, that phenomenology is by no means merely the methodology of existentialism or even of *Existenz*-philosophy, and that in fact the phenomenology of Husserl could hardly be further removed from that of either of the other two in terms of focus, method, and content. However, I shall not go into this matter here, since I have done so at length elsewhere.[16] I would merely call attention to these other developments.

There is another philosophical movement, however, which is perhaps more important than any of these other developments and which emerged contemporaneously with both phenomenology and *Existenz*-philosophy. In fact, the two works which marked the emergence of this movement, as Heidegger's *Being and Time* did in the case of *Existenz*-philosophy, appeared almost simultaneously with the latter. This movement is commonly referred to as "philosophical anthropology." Despite its importance in European philosophy (and its considerable intrinsic philosophical interest), it is virtually unknown in the English-speaking world, although it has a good deal in common with what is called "philosophy of mind" (which however has long had a much wider compass than this label would indicate) in this part of the world.[17] Its neglect on this side of the English Channel may be partly due to the fact that existentialism is much more sensational and conducive to literary exposition, and therefore has completely overshadowed it. Another reason, however, may be that philosophical anthropology draws heavily on human biology and the social sciences, and therefore strikes philosophers anxious to avoid overstepping the boundaries between philosophy and the sciences as a questionable commodity. European philosophers generally seem to be less concerned with the boundary than with the subject matter—which is, as its name taken quite literally indicates, the biological, social, cultural, and intellectual being, man.

Before proceeding to discuss "philosophical anthropology" further and contrast it with *Existenz*-philosophy, I should perhaps indicate a few of the more important and influential men and books I am talking about. There is, first of all, Max Scheler, earlier a phenomenologist, whose book *Die Stellung des Menschen im Kosmos* (1928)[18] set out the program of a philosophical anthropology and, through the interest it aroused, provided the initial impetus toward the actualization of this program (although Scheler himself died before he could make any further contributions to it). Next, there is Helmuth Plessner, whose early book *Die Stufen des Organischens und der Mensch* (1928)[19] is a classic in the field and who has more recently written a good, short introduction to it entitled *Conditio Humana* (1964).[20] And finally, I would mention Arnold Gehlen, whose early book *Der Mensch* (1940),[21] which focuses largely upon the biological nature of man and its behavioral consequences, is complemented by later writings which deal extensively with the essential functions of social and cultural institutions in human life.[22] (Unfortunately, due to the unclear standing of philosophical anthropology and its elipse by other philosophical movements, almost none of the works of either Plessner or Gehlen have been translated into English.[23])

The "structuralism" of Claude Levi-Strauss in France may also be considered at least a kind of near relation to this development. And much of the work of Ernst Cassirer, who emigrated to the United States from Germany after philosophical anthropology had begun to achieve some recognition in his homeland, may be viewed as yet another contribution to it. Indeed, in his book *An Essay on Man,*[24] he expressly associates himself with this movement; and this book, together with his monumental *Philosophy of Symbolic Forms,*[25] constitutes the most important such contribution presently available in English.

At first glance the programs of philosophical anthropology and *Existenz*-philosophy would seem to be identical; for the one is concerned with the nature of man, and the other with human *Existenz;* and at the very least the two would appear necessarily to be closely connected. Indeed, I would suggest that it is pointless to insist upon the incompatibility and hence ultimate irreconcilability of the two, as some of the adherents of each have done; for however different their starting points and methods may be, their conclusions will be suspect unless they can be integrated into a single, unified account of what it is to be a human being.

They *have* developed along different lines, however, in part because each has focused upon a different aspect of man's nature. The philosophical anthropologists have been concerned with what might be termed the "universal" in man—in other words, that which all men have in common in virtue of their common biological nature and sociocultural existence. They concern themselves with the general *forms* or *patterns* of human life, which can be discovered through the objective study of the human body, human behavior, and human institutions. Philosophical anthropology is by no means necessarily or even generally naturalistic or behavioristic, but its leading proponents have tended to characterize man's nature in terms which do not make essential reference to any irreducibly subjective dimension of human life or to the uniqueness of personal existence and experience. (I shall have more to say about it in the concluding section of this chapter.)

It is precisely this sort of subjectivity and uniqueness, however, which has been the focus of the investigations of the *Existenz*-philosophers. When they speak of *Existenz* (or the same thing in other terms), they are not referring to *all* dimensions or levels of human life, but rather to this one in particular. The term *Existenz* (or rather, its Danish equivalent) was first used in this special, narrower sense by Kierkegaard; and many *Existenz*-philosophers have followed him in this. These philosophers have tended to focus upon this dimension in presenting their characterization of what it is to be a human being, and to take the position that man's essential nature or true humanity is to be conceived in terms of the uniqueness and subjectivity of the individual person. Philosophical anthropologists for the most part have not; and so there is a major disagreement between the two groups (generally speaking) on this substantive issue.

But this difference is not a difference which precludes the possibility of any integration of the general programs of philosophical anthropology and *Existenz*-philosophy; for one does not have to take this position in order to be properly characterized as an *Existenz*-philosopher (nor do philosophical anthropologists have to take some other, fundamentally different position to be philosophical anthropologists). Strictly speaking, an *Existenz*-philosopher is any philosopher who investigates the basic structures of human *Existenz* (or explores the meaningfulness of the notion), regardless of whether he conceives man's essence or true humanity in terms of it. Moreover, an interest in the nature of *Existenz* is by no means incompatible with the general program of philosophical anthropology. In fact, it would be quite reasonable to view *Existenz*-philosophy as a subdivision of a comprehensive philosophical anthropology, devoted to the analysis of one particular dimension of human "being" among others. (This, I might note, is precisely the position of a growing number of Western European philosophers today. They feel that the traditional antagonism between the two is pointless, that earlier *Existenz*-philosophers and philosophical anthropologists both offered one-sided and therefore inadequate accounts of what it is to be a human being, and that only something like an attempt to integrate the two is likely to yield anything approximating an adequate understanding of human reality.)

IV

I shall now turn briefly to the question, What is to be understood by the term *Existenz?* Since the influence of Kierkegaard upon the development of this notion has been so great, I shall couch my initial remarks in terms of his approach to the matter as contrasted with the traditional philosophical treatment of the question of man's nature; and then I shall suggest a certain sort of basic problem subsequent philosophers have encountered as they have attempted to appropriate this notion from him, outside of the context in which he develops it, and some of the matters at issue between them.

Kierkegaard repeatedly poses the question, What does it mean to exist as a human being?[26] Initially the question had for him a quite general meaning; the term "exist" had not yet been given a special sense. It was only as Kierkegaard undertook to answer the question that the term came to have a special, restricted meaning. In the writings of subsequent philosophers, the dimension of human life upon which Kierkegaard focused, and in terms of which he concluded that *truly* human "being" is to be conceived, has come to be associated with the term *Existenz*. The term can be employed in this connection, however, regardless of whether one agrees with Kierkegaard concerning its importance.

Thus where there was only one question for Kierkegaard—What does it mean to exist as a human being?—it is necessary for us to distinguish two quite independent questions: (1) What is the nature of that actual or possible (purported) dimension of human life to which Kierkegaard drew attention? and (2) Is this a privileged, uniquely important dimension, in terms of which alone man's essential nature or true humanity is to be conceived? (*Existenz*-philosophy, as I have characterized it, is the attempt to answer the first question. No affirmative answer to the second question is presupposed.)

Now, speaking very generally, it has been traditional in Western (not to mention Eastern) philosophy to conceive of man's nature in terms of characteristics or qualities which are such that what is unique and opaquely subjective about the individual cannot be expressed in terms of them. This implies (whether or not the implication is always explicitly acknowledged) that in these conceptions of man the subjectivity and uniqueness of the individual as such are inessential, if indeed there is anything at all in the existence of a human being to which such notions are to be granted actual application. Consider, for example, the classical Aristotelian definition of man as a "rational animal." Here man is conceived in terms of two things: his reason and his animate nature. Reason is something entirely impersonal and universal. What is true in geometry or physics, or what is true as a matter of historical fact, is true for everyone if it is true at all, whether or not everyone actually recognizes it. In the realm of objective truth, idiosyncrasies have no place and must be set aside. It is this position which led to the conclusion, on the part of some classical philosophers, that while the mind might survive the death of the body, there would be no survival of personality in conjunction with it.

If one focuses instead upon Aristotle's other well-known definition of man, as a "social (or political) animal," the implications are similar. For, after all, social and political existence—existence and activity qua citizen or member of a sociopolitical order—is something just as impersonal and general in its own way as is intellectual activity. Here again, personal idiosyncrasies and subjective feelings and dispositions are out of place and must be set aside; for in the realm of institutionally structured sociopolitical interaction, what counts is conformity to general norms and observance of established rules and conventions.

Similarly, man's fundamental animate nature is something universal among men. It is constituted essentially by certain basic physiological structures associated with such general functions as nourishment, reproduction, movement, and perception. Characteristics which individuate one animate being from another of the same species are recognized by Aristotle to exist, but they are explicitly relegated to the realm of the inessential. (Not that one could characterize the uniqueness of the individual human being satisfactorily in such terms anyhow.)

Or consider Descartes' self-conception, set forth in his *Meditations.* He explicitly sets aside Aristotle's definition of man as a rational animal—and implicitly sets aside his definition of man as a sociopolitical animal as well—only to substitute the simpler definition of himself as a thinking being. ("I am not," he asserts, "this assemblage of members which is called the human body.") Thus, in the *Meditations* we read the following: "Thought is an attribute that belongs to me; it *alone* is inseparable from my nature. . . . I am therefore, to speak precisely, *only* a thinking being, that is to say, a mind, an understanding, or a reasoning being."[27] All else is relegated to the category of the dubitable and thus, for Descartes, to the realm of the inessential, where the nature of the self is concerned.[28] But as Descartes' critics have been fond of pointing out, there is nothing that identifies this thinking being as "I"—that is, as a particular, unique individual self. If I am essentially nothing more than this, I am essentially nothing more than an instance of something quite general in nature.

Finally, consider the position taken by Hegel, who is of particular importance in connection with the emergence of *Existenz*-philosophy. Hegel does depart from the philosophical tradition to which I have been referring, at least to some extent. He argues that one essential trait of man is that of particularity; and he acknowledges the existence and ineliminability of a dimension of subjectivity in human life, in addition to its objective and impersonal dimensions. But while he thus does recognize that particularity—and its manifestations and transformations in conscious life in the form of "subjective will" and personality—cannot be neglected in forming an adequate conception of man's nature, he does consider this dimension of human existence to be of merely secondary importance in relation to that of "universality."

Man, according to Hegel, is essentially "spirit"; and spirit is necessarily, and above all else, "universal." "Universality," in practical terms, means thought and action in accordance with universal principles—principles binding either upon the whole of a group of men (as in the case of laws and customs) or upon men generally as thinking beings (as in the case of the sciences, logic, etc.).[29] And it should be observed that while Hegel recognizes that there is more to human life than such "universality," the Hegelian categories of particularity, personality, and subjectivity are conceived in such a way that they do not refer to anything opaquely inward or radically unique or intrinsically private about the individual and his experience. For Hegel denies the meaningfulness of speaking of an inwardness that cannot be outwardly manifested and of a privateness that is not publicly accessible, and he has no principle in his system which even renders the radical uniqueness of the individual intelligible as a possibility.

Kierkegaard reacts strongly against this whole tradition and against Hegel in particular. As he sees the matter (and as most *Existenz*-philosophers, following him in this, see it as well), Hegel grasps neither the nature nor the importance of a kind of human individuality and subjectivity which is at least a possibility in human life, even if not a reality in most men's lives. Kierkegaard cannot abide the idea of the subordination of everything particular to the socially and intellectually "universal"; for in his understanding of man's nature, each person's uniqueness and subjectivity—his individual *soul*—are of paramount importance. He more than reverses Hegel: for him, in relation to this dimension of human existence, all others pale into virtual insignificance.

What Kierkegaard has in mind, however, is by no means mere empirical, objectively ascertainable differences between men. He emphatically does not conceive of the radical individuality of which he speaks in terms of physical characteristics; nor does he conceive of it in terms of habits and abilities and dispositions and preferences. He is ultimately thinking of the individual standing alone before a personal God who calls him to judgment and looks into the innermost recesses of his soul, completely stripped of the comfort and anonymity of the universal and laid bare to his very depths—in which context the observance of general customs, laws and rules, and intellectual attainments as well no longer have any positive significance. Thinking of oneself as related at every moment, by and as oneself alone, to a God concerned with what one has done with the particular life and freedom He has given to one gives to all of one's thoughts and actions, and indeed to one's existence generally, a dimension of radical uniqueness, and at the same time bestows the greatest significance precisely upon what is unique about one. It is in terms of this possible dimension of human experience that Kierkegaard answers his question, "What does it mean to exist as a human being?"

To be sure, neither Heidegger nor Jaspers nor Sartre (nor, for that matter, virtually any other important philosopher associated with *Existenz*-philosophy, with the exception of Marcel) retains Kierkegaard's conception of God and the individual's personal, radically individuating confrontation with Him. And this has meant that they have had to expend a good deal of effort attempting to come up with, and to establish the satisfactoriness of, some substitute—one, that is, which does not presuppose the validity of Kierkegaard's religious stance but which nonetheless performs the same function of radical individuation as does his "God relationship." For Jaspers, who remains closer to Kierkegaard than either Heidegger or Sartre, the place of Kierkegaard's confrontation with God is taken by what Jaspers terms an encounter with "Transcendence" (a kind of demythologized version of the God of Judeo-Christianity and Kierkegaard); while for Heidegger its place is taken by the individual's recognition of his "thrownness" into the world and of the inevitability and possible imminence of his own death; and for Sartre its place is taken by the individual's awareness of his "condemnation to freedom" and of the absence of any objectively and universally valid guidelines which might direct him in the exercise of his freedom.

In all cases, however, an attempt is made to direct attention to the possibility and nature of a mode of existence in which a person is radically individuated (inwardly, though by no means necessarily in any objectively observable manner) in some such way. None of these writers deny that a great deal of what people are and do can and indeed must be understood in other terms; on the contrary, they generally insist that this is so. But as *Existenz*-philosophers their interest in these other actual and possible modes or dimensions of human existence is only secondary and derives from the light which may be shed upon *Existenz* by a contrasting consideration of them. All are convinced that there is—or at any rate can be—more to human existence than can be expressed in terms of such impersonal notions as rationality, sociality, and animality; and also that there is more to it than anything which an observer could ever record, however closely he might attend to a person's appearance and behavior. And it is with this "more"—in virtue of which subjectivity can not strictly be correlated with objectivity, and individuality is not to be conceived merely as particularized universality or as the sum of various general forces converging on one point—that they, as *Existenz*-philosophers, are concerned.

This being the case, one may begin to wonder how it is that I could feel justified in my earlier contention that these men differ among themselves too greatly to be held to have anything more in common than an interest in a certain subject matter, except for the fact that those I have mentioned tend to be "*Existenz*ists" (in the sense indicated in section II above) and so to be more than merely noncommittal analysts of *Existenz*. To make this clearer, I shall briefly indicate some of the kinds of differences which divide *Existenz*-philosophers—and thereby also *Existenz*ists—at the level of their analyses of human *Existenz*. At the level of their general world views, their differences could hardly be greater; for they take up a wide variety of positions on a broad range of the most basic philosophical issues, concerning, for example, the existence and nature of some sort of divine transcendent being or principle, the possibility and nature of a universally binding scheme of moral principles and values, the nature and limits of human knowledge, the status of nonhuman objects, and the kinds of interpersonal relationships of which people are capable. However, differences at this level are relatively easily detected once one ceases to assume that there are none and goes looking for them. Moreover, they are only indirectly related to the issue of the nature of *Existenz*-philosophy. For these reasons I shall restrict myself to suggesting a few of the issues over which *Existenz*-philosophers as such often find themselves at odds.

First, there is the matter, to which I have already referred, of what these philosophers take to perform the function of radical individuation, when the proper or appropriate relation to it is achieved. Few of them are at all in agreement about this, their proposals ranging from God to the prospect of one's own death. But this is by no means the only question over which they differ greatly. Another concerns the issue of the ways in which one's relationships with other men affect the realization of *Existenz*. Some contend that the realization of *Existenz* essentially involves engagement in a certain sort of interpersonal relationship; others consider all such relationships to be entirely inconsequential to it; and still others regard all interpersonal relationships as a threat to it if not actually incompatible with it.

Another concerns the more fundamental issue of whether *Existenz* is something which *requires* to be realized at all. Some clearly hold that it does and indeed that the realization of it is a very arduous process which can never be accomplished once and for all. Others maintain that it is a permanent structure of human "being," to which we may remain oblivious but which we ignore only at the cost of deceiving ourselves. Further, among the former some contend that it is within our power to realize *Existenz* entirely on our own, while others hold that its realization is possible only through something like the extension of an act of grace from some source beyond ourselves, in addition to our own best efforts.

Another question concerns the issue of the nature of *Existenz* in relation to what is often summed up under the label of one's "facticity"—that is, all of the "given" circumstances involved in one's being as one is in a particular situation. For some writers *Existenz* is simply a matter of the transcendence of one's facticity, in the sense that one is neither identical with it nor determined by it to any specific future course, but rather is always capable of taking up a variety of stances in relation to it. For others, on the other hand, *Existenz* essentially involves a certain sort of positive appropriation of one's facticity. This difference is related to (and may to some extent be clarified by) another, which concerns the issue of whether the personal uniqueness associated with *Existenz* in the life of a particular individual is completely acquired through, or in some sense and to some extent given independently of, the choices he makes. Is one's *Existenz* the sort of thing the specific "filling" of which is in a significant way *at stake* in the particular choices one makes? Or is it unaffected by what these choices happen to be except insofar as they move one toward or away from the realization of it? Putting the question somewhat differently, is one's *Existenz* to be regarded as a kind of predetermined personal "essence," to which one may or may not *be true* (in which case it may be associated with the idea of "becoming what one is")? Or is it simply to be conceived in terms of a fundamentally indeterminate general capacity of choosing on one's own, in a kind of void in the sense that there is nothing more specific in the nature of one's self to be true to (in which case it may be associated with the idea of "existence preceding essence")?

Existenz-philosophers differ on this issue too, and on others as well; indeed, a complete enumeration and explication of their differences would require a good deal of space. What has already been said, however, should suffice to show that while they agree that there is a peculiar, opaquely subjective dimension of human life that philosophers previously have tended to overlook, the analyses of it they propose render it advisable to characterize their efforts collectively in terms of the area of their concern, rather than in terms of their general substantive agreements.

The fact that their substantive agreements are few indeed—in fact, virtu-ally nonexistent—may of course be seized upon by those skeptical of the soundness of the notion of *Existenz* and the enterprise of *Existenz*-philos-ophy as providing ample grounds for concluding that their skepticism is well-founded. It seems to me, however, that to leap from this fact to that conclusion would be rather hasty, for this state of affairs is by no means unique to the philosophy of *Existenz*. One has only to reflect upon the problem one would encounter upon undertaking to ascertain areas of substantive agreement among philosophers of stature who have been concerned with the philosophy of mind, or of morality, or of value, or of language or knowledge or the world of things and events, to conclude that a stronger case than this would have to be made to establish that the philosophy of *Existenz* deserves to remain beyond the pale of serious philosophical concern.

V

I shall conclude with a few further remarks about philosophical anthropology, in an attempt to make somewhat clearer both its nature and the distinctness of the "philosophical space" it occupies (particularly vis-à-vis *Existenz*-philosophy as characterized above). It seems to me to be best viewed as an outgrowth of the confluence of two philosophical traditions. One of them is that against which *Existenz*-philosophy emerged as a kind of reaction—namely, the tradition of which the most notable post-Kantian representative is Hegel, to whose approach to and understanding of man's nature reference has already been made. The second was itself a kind of reaction against the first—namely, what is known in Germany as *Lebensphilosophie* (the "philosophy of life," i.e., of the nature of life). This second tradition is often traced to Schopenhauer, and Bergson may also be mentioned in this connection. Most relevant for present purposes, however, is Nietzsche; and partly for this reason and partly because he is frequently thought to be among the precursors of "existentialism" and *Existenz*-philosophy, I shall introduce my remarks about philosophical anthropology by saying a few words about him.

In my view, it is a mistake to associate Nietzsche at all closely with *Existenz*-philosophy. To be sure, various *Existenz*-philosophers, such as Heidegger and Jaspers, have been greatly influenced by him; but then, they have also been greatly influenced by Kant and Hegel, who do not thereby also qualify as *Existenz*-philosophers. And that in Nietzsche which attracts them is something quite different from an analysis or even a conception of anything like *Existenz*. (In the case of Jaspers it is primarily Nietzsche's style of philosophizing, while in the case of Heidegger it is above all his purported ambiguous relation to traditional metaphysics, as both its culminator and destroyer.)

The reason I take it to be a mistake to associate Nietzsche with the philosophy of *Existenz* is partly that I believe he would be highly unsympathetic to the very notion of *Existenz,* and would regard it merely as a late, dying echo of Christian "soul-atomism" (in his phrase), which continues to sound only because the full implications of "the death of God" have not yet been adequately recognized. But it is partly also because he is as firmly committed as is Hegel to the idea of correlativity of "inward" and "outward" and, further, because his preoccupation is with something altogether different from anything like *Existenz.*

Nietzsche's basic questions are of the following sort:[30] What is the fundamental nature of *life* in general? What is conducive and detrimental to it and its development? And, more specifically, in terms of what basic principle(s) are we to conceive of man's nature and of the quantitative and qualitative differences between men as these are exhibited in their lives and actions? And what would the "enhancement" of "the type 'man' " (in his words) involve? He simply is not interested in the idea of some sort of opaque subjectivity and radical uniqueness which every individual might be supposed to have or to be capable of achieving, even if it were granted that he does not absolutely rule out the possibility of such a thing.

In some respects Nietzsche is closer to Kierkegaard than he is to Hegel (e.g., in his reservations concerning the possibility of men attaining anything that might be properly called absolute knowledge). However, he is in many ways closer to Schopenhauer (hardly an *Existenz*-philosopher) than he is to Kierkegaard—particularly in his general understanding of the nature of both reality and man. Schopenhauer broke with philosophical tradition when he took something nonrational—namely, "will"—to constitute man's essence and, indeed, to express the nature of reality generally. Yet he adhered to the tradition of employing a principle in characterizing man's nature in terms of which it is no more possible to express the individual's uniqueness than it was in the case of any of those who focused upon reason. Indeed, Schopenhauer even insisted upon the ultimately illusory character of any *principium individuationis,* not only in nature but also among men. And in this matter Nietzsche's position is similar to his. Thus it is with good reason that in Germany, Nietzsche is usually considered to be one of the first and most important representatives of so-called *Lebensphilosophie* rather than of *Existenz*-philosophy.

It by no means follows, however, that Nietzsche therefore is not as significant a figure philosophically as he is taken to be by those who associate him with the tradition of *Existenz*-philosophy. It only follows that his significance is at least largely to be conceived in other terms. If Kierkegaard provided the initial impetus for the emergence of *Existenz*-philosophy in the present century, Nietzsche may be said to have done the same for the subsequent emergence of philosophical anthropology, and also to have contributed a great deal to the discussion of those issues with which philosophical anthropologists in this century have been concerned. Both were convinced that the cognitive and intellectual activities of which men are capable have been greatly overemphasized in most previous philosophical accounts of man's nature. But whereas Kierkegaard proposed displacing "mind" and "reason" in favor of the more subjective, personal, inward aspects of spiritual life, Nietzsche proposed displacing both in favor of the more objective manifestations of human life—and in particular, the human body and human conduct.

Like Hegel, but most emphatically unlike Kierkegaard and most subsequent *Existenz*-philosophers, Nietzsche contended that the only reliable guide to the inward is the outward, and that the key to what man may be said to *be* is what he may be observed to *do*. Hegel placed more emphasis upon social and "spiritual" expressions than Nietzsche, who in turn placed more emphasis on the body than Hegel; and this undoubtedly accounts for the fact that until relatively recently philosophical anthropologists have tended to divide into two camps, one focusing more upon human biology and the other more upon human culture. But in virtue of their subscription to this same basic methodological principle, their convergence was only a matter of time; and it is no longer easy to discern a greater affinity to the one or the other, even in the cases of writers like Gehlen and Plessner, whose biological orientation initially was quite pronounced.

Perhaps the best way to give some more concrete indication of the nature of philosophical anthropology in a very brief space is simply to indicate some examples (1) of what various philosophical anthropologists have taken to be human phenomena having significance for the understanding of the kind of being we are, (2) of what concepts figure importantly in the thinking of some of the more important of them, and (3) of what some of the issues are which are a matter of disputation between them.

In the case of (1), a great deal of attention has been focused upon what might be termed biological differences between man and other zoological species, such as man's upright posture (and related characteristics), the unique development of certain parts of the human brain (and associated functions), and the underdeveloped state of the human organism at the time of birth, although in the more recent literature attention has tended to center upon those distinctive human biological characteristics which are closely associated with elements of human sociocultural life, either by way of facilitating or necessitating them. In addition, much discussion has been devoted to the consequences of the fact that while human beings may be said to have certain general needs and drives, they lack highly specified instincts and are capable of conditioning and adaptation to a degree far surpassing that characteristic of any other species. And finally (to mention only one more example), much has been made of a great variety of highly developed human behavioral phenomena, including not only the more obviously significant ones (e.g., toolmaking, language use, symbol formation, the institutionalization of various levels of human interaction, and need satisfaction), but also such more commonly overlooked ones as aggression and war, tradition and habit, asceticism and self-destructiveness, luxuriation and boredom, and laughing and crying, as well as some which have recently become the objects of concern of quite a few English-speaking philosophers, for example, emotion, punishment, "knowing how," and promising.

Examples of (2), as might be expected, are generally related in one way or another to (1). To be rendered comprehensible, let alone adequately explicated, these examples would require a good deal of discussion, which is impossible here. But they are much more than mere, vague catchwords, and the literature associated with them is well worth serious attention. They include instinct reduction and unspecialization, world-openness and ex-centricity, sublimation and acculturation, historicity and sociality, symbolization and abstraction, and many others. (A brief but comprehensive and lucid summary and discussion of many of these notions and the related literature may be found in Michael Landmann's *Philosophische Anthropologie*.[31]

As for (3), once again a few brief hints are all that can be given here. One general issue which has preoccupied and divided philosophical anthropologists is that of the extent to which various forms and aspects of human social, cultural, and ethical life are necessitated by or independent of human biological characteristics. Another is that of whether in the case of man "instinct reduction" is so complete that human life is not even informed by certain very general "instinct residues," or whether it is incomplete with the consequence that there are significant limits to the plasticity of human nature. Another issue is that of the place and significance in human life—the relative necessity and/or dispensability—of such things as tradition, myth, conflict, and social participation. And another concerns the status of the intellect and rational thought (in its various practical and theoretical forms) in the conduct of human affairs, in relation to the variety of noncognitive forces and circumstances associated with human life as we must live it.

This list of examples, like those preceding it, could be expanded at great length. Even from the little that has been said, however, several things should be clear. First, it should be evident that while some of the matters with which philosophical anthropologists concern themselves are closely connected with questions that require scientific investigation, their enterprise cannot be dismissed by philosophers as merely scientific rather than philosophical. Secondly, it should be clear that while some of these matters are of little current interest to most Anglo-American "philosophers of mind," others are at least reasonably close to some of their concerns, and that therefore the nature of philosophical anthropology is not so strange that there is no place for this enterprise within the realm of legitimate philosophical endeavor. (Indeed, one would think that it would if anything be an enterprise much more congenial than *Existenz*-philosophy to both traditionally and analytically minded philosophers.) And finally, it should be obvious that philosophical anthropology represents a very different approach indeed to the analysis of "human being" than does *Existenz*-philosophy, the interest and importance of which are at least as great as those of the latter, even if, as was suggested earlier, the two do not exclude but rather merely complement each other.

Afterword

I have attempted in this book to contribute to the understanding of a number of noteworthy developments in post-Kantian Continental philosophy. I would consider it most unfortunate, however, if they were to come to be regarded in the Anglo-American philosophical community as intellectual phenomena deserving greater attention than they have received in the past, but were at the same time to be viewed as philosophical oddities having little or no relevance to the greater part of ongoing philosophical inquiry; and it is with a few remarks along these lines that I wish to conclude.

Growing numbers of English-speaking philosophers have taken notice of the existence and efforts of European philosophers of the previous and present centuries to the point of acknowledging that philosophy in Europe did not effectively come to an end with the labors of Kant. It is symptomatic of the present understanding the former typically have of the latter, however, that a concern with nineteenth- and twentieth-century Continental philosophy is commonly taken to be either a purely historical one or an interest in some obscure set of problems related only remotely if at all to those subsumable under such familiar labels as ethics, social philosophy, the philosophy of mind, and epistemology. "Continental philosophy," in short, may no longer be regarded as "philosophy" in name only; but its relation to the various domains of *genuinely philosophical* inquiry is generally thought to be sufficiently tenuous and tangential that in practice it both requires to be treated as a thing apart and may be ignored without loss by those engaged in such modes of inquiry.

English-speaking partisans of "Continental philosophy" bear a share of the responsibility for the emergence and perpetuation of this lamentable state of affairs. They all too frequently have allowed themselves to develop and exhibit a kind of "ghetto mentality" in relation to their counterparts in the "mainstream" of Anglo-American philosophy, standing aloof from the latter, employing philosophical dialects virtually unintelligible to others, and supposing that the efforts of "non-Continentalists" need not concern them. This tendency, however, is a sociological fact rather than a reflection of something fundamental to the nature of European philosophy since Kant.

Most philosophers of whatever stature exhibit characteristics in their thinking and writing, and even in their concerns and views, which mark them as products and members of societies and historical periods distinctively different from our own. This is clearly true of Plato and Aristotle, Descartes and Spinoza, Leibniz and Kant, and even Locke and Hume; and it is also true of the philosophers dealt with in this book. Few would deny, however, that it would be both artificial and inaccurate to compartmentalize these earlier philosophers in such a way that their efforts would be considered contributions to "Greek philosophy," "early modern European philosophy," and "early modern British philosophy," but not to the various areas of ongoing philosophical endeavor. And it is no less artificial and inaccurate to regard the philosophers dealt with here in a similar way. Their thought is not so intrinsically bound up with the intellectual life of their own times and places that it is without wider philosophical significance. To the extent that English-speaking philosophers are unaware of the relevance of the efforts of the philosophers discussed here to their own general concerns, and are unappreciative of what these writers have to say relating to them, they are blinkered in a way that renders their thought less fruitful and consequential than it could be.

Recent Continental philosophy is not a floating island which once was part of the philosophical mainland but broke away after Kant and subsequently has drifted even further from it. After Kant certain migrations of the various tribes upon this mainland to separate regions of it did occur, leading to the emergence of rather different philosophical forms of life among them. But the differences between these forms of life have not obliterated the existence of common frontiers and common interests and problems; nor are they so great that they now preclude the possibility of mutually beneficial commerce and even fruitful union between the sometimes warring tribes. In recent years (to pursue the metaphor a bit further), open hostilities have largely ceased, and a policy of peaceful coexistence has come to be generally adopted, occasionally accompanied by a detached and rather bemused curiosity about one's "alien" counterparts. But this *rapprochement* need not and should not be allowed to end here, with diplomatic recognition, the courtesy of cultural exchanges, and token gestures of interest and concern veiling a continuing practice of benign neglect. For however benign the neglect, it cannot yield the rewards in which more intensive involvement would issue.

Such involvement is possible and desirable because the problems with which Continental philosophers since Kant have been and continue to be concerned are at least for most part problems relating to the same basic philosophical issues confronted and dealt with by their predecessors, and also by many of their Anglo-American contemporaries. "Post-Kantian Continental philosophy" is not something analogous to but differing from moral and social philosophy, the philosophy of mind and of language, the theory of knowledge and of value, and the rest, any more than "recent Anglo-American philosophy" is. Both designations serve merely to indicate the existence of different geographically and temporally identified groups of philosophers who, as philosophers, have attempted to contribute to the understanding of the matters indicated by these and other such labels. It may be that it is useful for certain pedagogical and scholarly purposes to treat the two separately, as is often done in the case of Continental philosophy and British philosophy in the two centuries before Kant. It further may be that the two groups of philosophers approach the matters with which they both deal in very different ways, and that they often reach markedly differing conclusions concerning them—as was also true of their pre-Kantian geographical counterparts. But as in the case of this historical parallel, both of these observations are beside the point with respect to the understanding and appreciation of the concerns and efforts of both groups.

The sooner English-speaking philosophers cease to think of the philosophical undertakings of recent Continental philosophers as "Continental" in *nature* rather than merely in geographical, linguistic, and cultural *setting* (and vice versa), the better it will be philosophically for all concerned. Provincialism and chauvinism die hard, in philosophy as elsewhere in human life; and philosophers only deceive themselves if they suppose that these "human, all-too-human" afflictions could not possibly taint *their* thought. The fact that a problem of this sort does exist, however, does not mean that it is endemic to philosophical thinking. It is a problem which can at least be very considerably alleviated. For this to be possible, however, it must first be viewed *as* a problem. It is to be hoped that the time is near when such a recognition will occur on a broad scale, and will lead to widespread and concerted efforts to combat it and to compensate for its past effects. It is not possible to predict with any confidence what the results of such a development would be. But one may be sure that they would be interesting.

Notes

Introduction

1. F. Nietzsche, *Human, All-Too-Human,* trans. H. Zimmern, Vol. 6 of *The Complete Works of Friedrich Nietzsche,* ed. O. Levy (Edinburgh: Foulis, 1909. Reissued, New York: Russell & Russell, 1964), pt. I, §621.

Chapter 1. From Hegel to Nietzsche: A Selective Overview

1. Søren Kierkegaard, *Fear and Trembling,* trans. W. Lowrie (Garden City: Double-day, 1954), pp. 49–51.
2. Søren Kierkegaard, *Concluding Unscientific Postscript,* trans. D. F. Swenson and W. Lowrie (Princeton: Princeton University Press, 1941), p. 540.
3. *Fear and Trembling,* p. 51.
4. G. W. F. Hegel, *Phänomenologie des Geistes* (Hamburg: Meiner, 1952), pp. 563–64. My translation.
5. Karl Marx, *Early Writings,* ed. and trans. T. B. Bottomore (New York: McGraw-Hill, 1963), pp. 155, 160–61.
6. *Ibid.,* pp. 124–25.
7. *Fear and Trembling,* p. 30.
8. Arthur Schopenhauer, *The World as Will and Idea,* in *The Philosophy of Schopenhauer,* ed. I. Edman (New York: Random House, 1956), pp. 334–35.
9. *Ibid.,* pp. 306–09.
10. F. Nietzsche, *The Will to Power,* ed. W. Kaufmann, trans. W. Kaufmann and R. J. Hollingdale (New York: Random House, 1967), §1067.
11. *Ibid.,* §§1041, 1050.

Chapter 2. The Philosophical Background of Hegel's Metaphysics

1. Up to this point I obviously have been drawing primarily upon Kant's *Critique of Pure Reason.* These theological arguments, however, happily do not mar that work, but

rather are set forth in Book II of his *Critique of Practical Reason.* Yet it should be observed that he is careful to argue in the first *Critique* in such a manner as to prepare the way for them; cf. his famous remark, in the Preface to the second edition, that "I have found it necessary to deny *knowledge* in order to make room for *faith,*" and his preceding answer to his question, "What sort of a treasure is this that we propose to bequeath to posterity?" (*Critique of Pure Reason,* trans. N. Kemp Smith, 2nd [corrected] impression [London: Macmillan, 1933], B, pp. xxx and xxiv–xxv.) (In citations from this work, "A" refers to the first edition, and "B" to the second.)

2. The philosophers discussed up to this point should be no strangers to most readers, but Fichte will be, at least to many. Fichte (1762–1814) would undoubtedly be recognized today as the most important of the post-Kantian idealists, and so would be much better known, had he not had the misfortune to have Hegel appear upon the scene and draw all eyes to him shortly after Fichte's death. This circumstance is reflected in the relative unavailability in English of his major works. Of those which have been translated, that which is most readable is his semipopular little book, *The Vocation of Man,* ed. R. M. Chisholm (New York: Bobbs-Merrill, 1956). Those who wish to take on something more substantial (and philosophically more rewarding) may be referred to his *Science of Knowledge,* ed. and trans. P. Heath and J. Lachs (New York: Appleton-Century-Crofts, 1970).

3. Schelling (1775–1854) is even less well known in the English-speaking world today than is Fichte (if that is possible), despite the fact that he wrote more, exerted a greater direct influence upon Hegel, received the acclaim of many more of his contemporaries than Fichte did, and lived to become a leader of the reaction against Hegelianism in the decades following Hegel's death (he outlived Hegel by twenty-three years). He underwent a number of philosophical metamorphoses, from idealist to rationalist to mystic to protoexistentialist. None of this is to say, however, that he is intrinsically more deserving of attention than Fichte; on the contrary, in my opinion he is much the less important of the two. Schelling's many works from his idealist period remain untranslated into English; but readers may gain some insight into his thinking by consulting two somewhat later works, *Of Human Freedom,* trans. J. Gutman (La Salle, Ill.: Open Court, 1936), and *The Ages of the World,* trans F. D. Bolman, Jr. (New York: AMS Press, 1942). One would perhaps do better, however, to refer to J. Watson's useful paraphrase of his most important idealist work, *System des transcendentalen Idealismus,* published under the title *Schelling's Transcendental Idealism* (Chicago: Griggs, 1882).

4. G. W. F. Hegel, *Differenz des Fichte'schen and Schelling'schen Systems der Philosophie* (Hamburg: Meiner, 1962). For a brief discussion of this work, see my *Alienation* (Garden City: Doubleday, 1970), pp. 30–33.

Chapter 3. A Commentary on the Preface
to Hegel's *Phenomenology of Spirit*

1. *Hegel: Texts and Commentary,* ed. and trans. W. Kaufmann (Garden City: Doubleday, 1966). All citations from the Preface in this commentary are from Kaufmann's translation, and all page references refer to the Anchor edition of it. In some cases, however, I have slightly modified Kaufmann's renderings.

2. Immanuel Kant, *Critique of Pure Reason,* trans. N. Kemp Smith, 2nd (corrected) impression (London: Macmillan, 1933), preface to 2nd ed. (B), p. xxx.

3. G. W. F. Hegel, *Differenz des Fichte'schen und Schelling'schen Systems der Philosophie* (Hamburg: Meiner, 1962), pp. 12–17.

4. This point will be discussed further below.

5. *Differenz,* pp. 13–14.

6. The phenomenology of spirit is distinguished from mere history, according to Hegel, by virtue of the fact that it is concerned not with particular historical facts, but rather with what might be termed the "logical development" of the human spirit which underlies—and is often quite obscured by—the particular facts of history. It is thus concerned with those features of the existential development of spirit which are essential and necessary to that development, rather than with its merely particular and accidental features. It certainly would seem, however, that Hegel does not always keep within these limits in the *Phenomenology;* for he brings in a great deal of material which cannot plausibly be considered to relate solely to the necessary and essential, even by one convinced that the progression of stages of spiritual development he describes constitutes a necessary sequence.

7. This may seem to be a coldly impersonal estimation of the value of human life and of individual human beings. But at least it is far from *nihilistic; it does assign a value* to our lives—even if it is not the value which two thousand years of Christianity has accustomed us to assume the human individual has. And one might ask oneself, If one abandons the Christian belief in the existence of a personal God who endows each individual with an immortal soul of infinite worth, how would one go about justifying the attribution of any greater ultimate significance to ourselves than that which Hegel attributes to us? And one might further ask oneself, If one rejects Hegel's view of the matter altogether—his whole metaphysics—as well as the traditional Christian one, what sort of ultimate significance—if any—*can* one justify assigning to human life and the human individual?

8. My translation. The term "God," to be sure, is not used here; but that is because Hegel is now writing from the standpoint of "absolute knowledge," rather than in the language of religious symbolization, and so speaks of "absolute spirit" instead.

It is interesting to reflect on Hegel's use of the term "Golgotha" in this passage. At first glance it seems quite bizarre, but upon reflection it turns out to be a strikingly appropriate image. The "logic" and the "phenomenology of spirit" may be compared to Golgotha, in that they, like it, contain nothing but skeletal remains until they are animated by the presence of living spirit or consciousness. And Hegel's last words upon the completion of the *Phenomenology* (referring not to the book itself, but rather to that with which it deals) are in effect the same as Jesus's last words on Golgotha: "It is finished." But in the former case as in the latter, what is finished is not life itself, but rather only merely human life—only the development of the human spirit as it rises from its lowly origins to maturity and perfection. The result is not really *death* at all; rather, it is the beginning of eternal life, in which the agonies of development are left behind and the human spirit enters into that "divine" life in which it is at one with "God" (or "absolute spirit") and lives "the life of God"—which "life," symbolically characterized, is simply "God knowing himself as God," i.e., "spirit knowing itself as spirit," or the actuality of "absolute knowledge."

Chapter 4. Hegel on Freedom

1. In identifying citations from Hegel, I have employed the following abbreviations:

LH *The Logic of Hegel* (the "Lesser Logic"), trans. W. Wallace, 2nd ed. rev. (London: Oxford University Press, 1892).

PS   *Phenomenology of Spirit*, Preface, ed. and trans. W. Kaufmann, in Kaufmann's *Hegel: Texts and Commentary* (Garden City: Doubleday, 1966). The entire work is translated by J. B. Baillie under the title *Phenomenology of Mind*, 2nd ed. rev. (New York: Macmillan, 1931).

PM   *Philosophy of Mind*, trans. W. Wallace (Oxford: Clarendon Press, 1894, reissued 1971).

PR   *Philosophy of Right*, trans. T. M. Knox (Oxford: Clarendon Press, 1942).

RH   *Reason in History*, trans. R. S. Hartman (New York: Bobbs-Merrill, 1953).

2. See section VII below.

3. Hegel covers the same ground in the third part of his *Encyclopedia* (published separately in English as *PM*), § §469–552. But the *Philosophy of Right* is more accessible, more readable, and more detailed; and, most importantly, it represents Hegel's final statement of his views on freedom and subjects relating to it.

4. John Locke, *An Essay Concerning Human Understanding* (London: Cummings & Hilliard and J. T. Buckingham, 1813), II:21:15.

5. David Hume, *An Enquiry Concerning Human Understanding* (La Salle, Ill.: Open Court, 1952), p. 103 (sec. VIII, pt. I).

6. Aristotle, *Metaphysics,* VII:4, in *The Basic Works of Aristotle,* ed. R. McKeon (New York: Random House, 1941), 1029b.

7. Aristotle, *Nicomachean Ethics,* I:7, in *ibid.,* 1098a.

8. Aristotle, *On Generation and Corruption,* I:3, in *ibid.,* 317b.

9. Aristotle, *Metaphysics,* IX:1, in *ibid.,* 1046a.

10. Aristotle, *Physics,* VIII:6, in *ibid.,* 259b.

11. Benedict Spinoza, *Ethics,* in *Spinoza Selections,* ed. J. Wild (New York: Scribner, 1930), pt. 1, df. VII.

12. *Ibid.*

13. *Ibid.,* pt. 1, prop. XVII, corol. 2.

14. *Ibid.,* pt. 1, prop. XVII.

15. *Ibid.,* pt. 1, prop. XXXII.

16. *Ibid.,* pt. 1, prop. XI.

17. Immanuel Kant, *Critique of Pure Reason,* trans. N. Kemp Smith, 2nd (corrected) impression (London: Macmillan, 1933), A534/B462.

18. *Ibid.,* A558/B586.

19. *Ibid.,* A557/B585; emphasis added.

20. *Ibid.,* A547–48/B575–76.

21. *Ibid.,* A553–54/B581–82.

22. Cf. Chapter 3, section II, above.

23. The *Philosophy of Right,* in its present form, consists of numbered paragraphs to which Hegel himself frequently appended "Remarks," and to many of which "Additions" derived from notes taken at Hegel's lectures have been added by an early editor of the work. I shall identify citations by giving Hegel's paragraph numbers, adding an "R" when the material cited appears in a "Remark" and an "A" when it occurs in an "Addition." The "Additions" obviously do not have the authority of what Hegel himself submitted to print. They are often illuminating, however; and because they are generally considered to be reasonably faithful to what Hegel actually said, I shall on occasion draw upon them. I have followed Knox's translation, except in a few instances in which a different rendering than his has seemed to me to be desirable. (See, e.g., note 24 below.)

24. In his translation of the *Philosophy of Right,* Knox confuses the issue by

employing the terms "determinacy" and "indeterminacy" both when Hegel is discussing the issue of the will's determinateness and indeterminateness and when he is discussing the issues of whether or not determinate volitions are determined and in what ways they may be determined. Knox has as an excuse the fact that Hegel uses the same German terms in both cases. But he would have done better to avail himself of the alternate English renderings of these terms, to bring out the differences between the two issues with which Hegel is dealing.

25. T. M. Knox, "Hegel and Prussianism," *Philosophy,* XV, no. 57 (1940): 53.

26. E. F. Carrit, "Discussion: Hegel and Prussianism," *Philosophy,* XV, no. 58 (1940): 194.

Chapter 5. The Early Marx on Hegel, Naturalism, and Human Emancipation

1. See Karl Marx, *Early Writings,* ed. and trans. T. B. Bottomore (New York: McGraw-Hill, 1963). All page references in the text of this chapter are to this volume. In my citations, I generally follow Bottomore's translation but depart from it slightly on occasion when my reading of the German suggests this to be desirable. Cf. Karl Marx, *Frühe Schriften,* ed. H.-J. Lieber and P. Furth, vol. I (Stuttgart: Cotta, 1962).

2. Cf. chapter 2 above.

3. For an extended discussion of Marx on "alienation," cf. chapter 3 of my book *Alienation* (Garden City: Doubleday, 1970). Cf. also chapter 2 of the same book, on Hegel.

4. Hegel had written, in an early essay entitled *The German Constitution:* "The thoughts contained in this work can have no purpose or effect . . . other than that of the comprehending of what exists, and thus of a more tranquil attitude toward it, together with a moderate toleration of it in word and deed. For it is not what *exists* that makes us vehement and causes us suffering; rather, it is what is *not* as it *should* be. But if we see that it *is* as it *must* be—i.e., that it is not arbitrary or accidental—then we also see that it *should* be as it is" (from *Schriften zur Politik und Rechtsphilosophie,* ed. G. Lasson [Leipzig: Meiner, 1923], p. 5; my translation).

5. Karl Marx, *Writings of the Young Marx on Philosophy and Society,* ed. and trans. L. D. Easton and K. H. Guddat (Garden City: Doubleday, 1967), p. 402.

6. In my *Alienation,* chap. 3.

7. On the latter see chapter 4 above.

8. Marx's parents were Jews, who converted to Protestantism when he was six.

Chapter 6. Kierkegaard on "Truth Is Subjectivity" and "The Leap of Faith"

1. Appended to Kierkegaard's *Concluding Unscientific Postscript,* trans. D. F. Swenson and W. Lowrie (Princeton: Princeton University Press, 1941), p. 551. All page references in the text of this chapter are to this volume.

2. Hegel, it should be noted, would not accept the "either/or" proposed by Kierkegaard in this passage. For him man's nature is to be conceived *both* in terms of "universality" *and* in terms of individuality, neither of which (he holds) completely

excludes the other. He writes, "Spirit is the nature of human beings generally, and their nature is therefore twofold: on the one hand, explicit individuality of consciousness and will; and on the other, universality which knows and wills what is substantive" (*Philosophy of Right,* trans. T. M. Knox [Oxford: Clarendon Press, 1942] , §264 [hereafter cited as *PR*]. I have slightly modified Knox's rendering of this passage). Again, "The will's activity consists in annulling the contradiction between subjectivity and objectivity and giving its aims an objective instead of a subjective character, while at the same time remaining by itself [i.e., subjective] even in its objectivity" (*PR,* §28).

3. G. W. F. Hegel, *Science of Logic,* trans. W. H. Johnston and L. G. Struthers (New York: Macmillan, 1929), 1:55. All citations from this work in this chapter are from the first of the two volumes of its English translation.

4. G. W. F. Hegel, *Phenomenology of Mind,* trans. J. B. Baillie, 2nd ed. rev. (New York: Macmillan, 1931), pp. 98–99.

5. G. W. F. Hegel, *The Logic of Hegel,* trans. W. Wallace, 2nd ed. rev. (London: Oxford University Press, 1892), pp. 51–52 (hereafter cited as *LH*).

6. *Ibid.,* pp. 354, 352.

7. *Ibid.,* p. 354.

8. *PR,* §23.

9. *LH,* p. 52.

10. *Ibid.,* p. 354.

11. *PR,* §25.

12. *Ibid.,* §29. It is of some interest to observe that this passage continues as follows: "Once this principle [of the supremacy of subjectivity] is adopted, of course, the rational can come on the scene only as a restriction of the type of freedom which this principle involves. . . . This view is devoid of any speculative thinking, and is repudiated by the Philosophic concept. And the phenomena which it has produced in men's heads and in the world are of a frightfulness parallel only to the superficiality of the thoughts on which they are based."

13. *Phenomenology of Mind,* p. 80.

14. *LH,* p. 352.

15. *Science of Logic,* p. 60.

16. *LH,* p. 3

17. *Science of Logic,* p. 60.

18. *Phenomenology of Mind,* pp. 98–99.

19. *Science of Logic,* p. 69.

20. *Phenomenology of Mind,* p. 74.

21. Cf. Spinoza, in the first pages of his *On the Improvement of Human Understanding,* in *Works of Spinoza,* trans. R. H. M. Elwes (New York: Dover, 1951), vol. 1.

22. Walter Kaufmann offers a similar counterexample (viz., Nero) in a critical discussion of Kierkegaard in his *From Shakespeare to Existentialism* (Garden City: Doubleday, 1959), p. 198.

23. Cf. Hegel's remarks cited in note 12 above.

Chapter 7. Kierkegaard's Phenomenology of Spiritual Development

1. Søren Kierkegaard, *Either/Or: A Fragment of Life,* trans. D. F. Swenson, L. M. Swenson, and W. Lowrie, 2 vols. (Garden City: Doubleday, 1959).

2. Søren Kierkegaard, *The Present Age and Two Minor Ethico-Religious Treatises,* trans. A. Dru and W. Lowrie (New York: Harper & Row, 1962).

3. For the convenience of most readers, I shall identify my citations from Kierkegaard by giving the location of the passages in question in *A Kierkegaard Anthology,* ed. R. Bretall (New York: Random House, 1959), whenever this is possible. All page references in the text of this chapter are to this volume. When this is not possible, the locations of the passages are indicated in the notes.

4. Søren Kierkegaard, *Fear and Trembling,* trans. W. Lowrie (Garden City: Doubleday, 1954), pp. 64–65.

5. Søren Kierkegaard, *Concluding Unscientific Postscript,* trans. D. F. Swenson and W. Lowrie (Princeton: Princeton University Press, 1941), p. 142.

6. *Ibid.,* p. 138.

7. *Fear and Trembling,* p. 66.

8. Cf. chapter 4 above.

9. *Fear and Trembling,* p. 65.

10. *Ibid.*

11. *Ibid.,* p. 86.

12. *Ibid.,* p. 121.

13. *Ibid.,* p. 78.

14. *Ibid.,* p. 80.

15. Cf. chapter 6 above.

16. Cf., once again, chapter 6 above.

17. *Postscript,* p. 128.

18. *Ibid.,* p. 280.

19. *Ibid.,* p. 121.

20. *Ibid.*

21. *Ibid.,* p. 288.

22. Cf. again chapter 6 above.

23. *Fear and Trembling,* p. 59.

24. *Ibid.,* p. 55.

25. *Ibid.,* p. 59.

26. *Ibid.,* p. 48.

27. Cf. his *Phenomenology of Mind,* trans. J. B. Baillie, 2nd. ed. rev. (New York: Macmillan, 1931), pp. 241–67.

28. *Fear and Trembling,* p. 60.

29. In Kierkegaard's *Philosophical Fragments* this mode of existence is discussed in terms of what he refers to as the "Socratic" standpoint, while in the *Postscript* it is dealt with under the designation "religiousness A." Cf. *Philosophical Fragments: Or A Fragment of Philosophy,* orig. trans. and intro. D. F. Swenson, rev. trans. H. V. Hong, new intro. and commentary N. Thulstrup (Princeton: Princeton University Press, 1962).

30. *Postscript,* p. 496.

31. *Ibid.,* p. 494.

32. *Ibid.,* p. 507.

33. *Fear and Trembling,* p. 46.

34. But cf. my criticism of Kierkegaard on this point, near the end of chapter 6 above.

Chapter 8. Nietzsche and Nihilism

1. A. Danto, *Nietzsche as Philosopher* (New York: Macmillan, 1965).

2. *Ibid.,* p. 22.

3. *Ibid.,* p. 31.
4. *Ibid.,* p. 30.
5. *Ibid.,* p. 33.
6. *Ibid.,* p. 34.
7. *Ibid.,* p. 80.
8. *Ibid.,* p. 22.
9. *Ibid.,* p. 33.
10. In identifying citations from Nietzsche, I have employed the following abbreviations:

AC *The Antichrist,* in *The Portable Nietzsche,* ed. and trans. W. Kaufmann (New York: Viking, 1954), pp. 568–656.

BGE *Beyond Good and Evil,* trans. W. Kaufmann (New York: Random House, 1966).

EH *Ecce Homo,* in *On the Genealogy of Morals: Ecce Homo,* ed. and trans. W. Kaufmann (New York: Random House, 1967), pp. 215–335.

GM *On the Genealogy of Morals,* in *On the Genealogy of Morals: Ecce Homo,* pp. 13–163.

TI *Twilight of the Idols,* in *The Portable Nietzsche,* pp. 465–563.

WP *The Will to Power,* ed. W. Kaufmann, trans. W. Kaufmann and R. J. Hollingdale (New York: Random House, 1967).

11. Emphasis added.
12. Second emphasis added.
13. It is interesting to observe that Nietzsche's own understanding of his work, as expressed in this passage, is directly at odds with Danto's contention that "he was less interested in characterizing the world as it might be in itself then he was in bringing . . . to our attention that what we believe about the world is all wrong. . . . He was less interested in stating what was true than in telling what was false" (*Nietzsche as Philosopher,* p. 98).
14. *Nietzsche as Philosopher,* p. 130.
15. *Ibid.,* p. 75.
16. *Ibid.,* p. 93.
17. Cf. *WP,* § 1041, and *BGE,* § 37.
18. Cf. also *WP,* § 658.
19. Indeed, Nietzsche may initially have conceived the significance of the idea of eternal recurrence—and the idea itself—in these terms, that is, as a *test* of the nature of one's attitude toward life. Schopenhauer, in *The World as Will and Idea,* proposes a similar test, only the result he anticipates is the exact opposite of the one Nietzsche desires. Schopenhauer suggests that one reflect upon the hard facts of life, and upon one's own experience in particular, and then ask oneself which one would choose, if offered a choice between living the same life over again and absolute annihilation; and he contends that if one is "in full possession of his faculties, he will never wish to have it to live over again, but rather than this, he will much prefer absolute annihilation" (*The Philosophy of Schopenhauer,* ed. I. Edman [New York: Random House, 1956], p. 267). Nietzsche, who was intimately acquainted with Schopenhauer's work, may initially have intended his affirmation of the idea of eternal recurrence as a response to Schopenhauer, in just the terms he proposes in his test; only Nietzsche extends them, to include not merely the events of one's own life but all events which have occurred, and to encompass a recurrence of them not merely once but infinitely many times ("eternally"), to

indicate that his response to Schopenhauer's test differs from Schopenhauer's own as radically as possible.

20. *Nietzsche as Philosopher,* p. 75.
21. *Ibid.,* p. 33.
22. First emphasis added.
23. Emphasis added.
24. *Nietzsche as Philosopher,* p. 33.
25. Emphasis added.
26. *The Portable Nietzsche,* p. 125.
27. *Ibid.,* p. 307.

Chapter 9. Husserlian and Heideggerian Phenomenology

1. See, for example, H. Spiegelberg's excellent study, *The Phenomenological Movement,* 2nd ed., 2 vols. (New York: Humanities, 1969).

2. Edmund Husserl, *The Phenomenology of Internal Time-Consciousness,* ed. M. Heidegger, trans. J. S. Churchill (Bloomington: Indiana University Press, 1964).

3. See *The Phenomenological Movement,* vol. 1, p. 281.

4. Edmund Husserl, *Ideas: General Introduction to Pure Phenomenology,* trans. W. R. Boyce Gibson (New York: Macmillan, 1931; pb. ed., New York: Collier, 1962). In addition to a translation of this work as originally published in 1913, this volume also contains a translation of a Preface written for the English edition by Husserl in 1930. Citations from this volume in the text of this chapter are identified by "*I.*"

5. Edmund Husserl, *Cartesian Meditations,* trans. D. Cairns (New York: Humanities, 1960). Citations in the text are identified by "*CM.*"

6. Martin Heidegger, *Being and Time,* trans. J. Macquarrie and E. Robinson (New York: Harper & Row, 1962). Citations in the text are identified by "*BT.*"

7. See notes 4, 5, and 6 above for an explanation of the works to which the capital letters in all such references in the text of this chapter refer.

8. Emphasis added. I stress this phrase because of its continual recurrence in Heidegger's discussion in *Being and Time.*

9. There are, to be sure, a variety of objections which might be made both to the specific procedure and to the kind of program under consideration here. I shall not consider them, not because I do not think that any of them are well taken—quite the contrary—but rather because my concern here is with the *nature* of Husserlian phenomenology as opposed to that of Heidegger, and not with the critical evaluation of it.

10. Emphasis added.
11. Emphasis added.
12. Emphasis added.

Chapter 10. Existentialism, *Existenz*-Philosophy, and Philosophical Anthropology

1. Jean-Paul Sartre, "Existentialism Is a Humanism," in *Existentialism from Dostoevsky to Sartre,* ed. W. Kaufmann (New York: World, 1956), p. 289.

2. H. J. Blackham, *Six Existentialist Thinkers* (New York: Harper, 1959), pp. v–vi.

3. *Ibid.*, p. 151.

4. W. Kaufmann, "Existentialism from Dostoevsky to Sartre," in *Existentialism from Dostoevsky to Sartre*, pp. 11–12.

5. M. Warnock, *Existentialist Ethics* (London: Macmillan, 1967), e.g., p. 57.

6. Martin Heidegger, *Sein und Zeit* (Tübingen: Niemeyer, 1927), p. 38; cf. *Being and Time*, trans. J. Macquarrie and E. Robinson (New York: Harper & Row, 1962), p. 62 (hereafter cited as *BT*).

7. *Ibid.*, p. 42; *BT*, p. 67.

8. *Ibid.*

9. *Ibid.*, p. 44; *BT*, p. 70.

10. "Existentialism Is a Humanism," p. 290.

11. Jean-Paul Sartre, *Being and Nothingness: An Essay on Phenomenological Ontology*, trans. H. E. Barnes (New York: Philosophical Library, 1956), p. lxii.

12. *Ibid.*, p. 620.

13. *Ibid.*, p. 25.

14. This lecture may be found, among other places, in Kaufmann, ed., *Existentialism from Dostoevskey to Sartre*, pp. 287–311.

15. Jean-Paul Sartre, *Critique de la raison dialectique*, pt. I (Paris: Gallimard, 1960). This work has not yet been translated into English, although Sartre's long prefatory essay has been translated and published as a volume in its own right, under the title *Search for a Method*, trans. H. E. Barnes (New York: Random House, 1963), and selections from the work are included in *The Philosophy of Jean-Paul Sartre*, ed. R. D. Cumming (New York: Random House, 1965), in the section entitled "Consciousness and Society," pp. 415–84.

16. See chapter 9 above.

17. The only extended English-language study of the writings of those associated with philosophical anthropology is Marjorie Grene's *Approaches to a Philosophical Biology* (New York: Basic Books, 1968). While far from comprehensive, this book is most useful as an introduction to and analysis of some of the more important literature of the movement.

18. Max Scheler, *Die Stellung des Menschen im Kosmos*, 6th ed. (Bern and Munich: Francke, 1962). Published in English as *Man's Place in Nature*, trans. H. Meyerhoff (New York: Farrar, Straus & Cudahy, 1962).

19. Helmuth Plessner, *Die Stufen des Organischen und der Mensch*, 2nd ed. (Berlin: de Gruyter, 1965).

20. Helmuth Plessner, *Conditio Humana* (Pfullingen: Neske, 1964).

21. Arnold Gehlen, *Der Mensch: Seine Natur und seine Stellung in der Welt*, 8th ed. (Frankfurt a.M.: Athenäum, 1966).

22. E.g., Arnold Gehlen, *Urmensch und Spätkultur*, 2nd ed. (Frankfurt a.M.: Athenäum, 1963).

23. The only exception, to my knowledge, is Plessner's *Laughing and Crying*, trans. J.S. Churchill and M. Grene (Evanston: Northwestern University Press, 1970).

24. Ernst Cassirer, *An Essay on Man* (New Haven: Yale University Press, 1944).

25. Ernst Cassirer, *Philosophy of Symbolic Forms*, trans. R. Manheim, 3 vols. (New Haven: Yale University Press, 1953, 1955, 1957).

26. See chapter 6 above.

27. René Descartes, *Meditations on First Philosophy* (New York: Bobbs-Merrill, 1960), p. 26.

28. *Ibid.,* p. 74.

29. Cf. chapter 4 above, and also my *Alienation* (Garden City: Doubleday, 1970), ch. 2.

30. Cf. chapter 8 above.

31. M. Landmann, *Philosophische Anthropologie,* 2nd ed. (Berlin: de Gruyter, 1964). See especially parts III and IV.

Bibliography

This bibliography generally follows the sequence of chapters in this book; however, single sections are provided for the two chapters dealing with Hegel (chapters 3 and 4) and for the two dealing with Kierkegaard (chapters 6 and 7). The listings are by no means exhaustive. Not all of the writings of the figures discussed are mentioned; and the literature on them and related philosophical developments, in English as well as in other languages, is vastly larger than the sampling of it which appears here. For one thing, only books—and only some of those—are listed. And for another, with certain exceptions (most notably, in the case of the writings of philosophical anthropologists), the only ones listed are English-language originals or English translations. The explanation of these facts is that this bibliography is meant primarily for English-speaking readers, and that my purpose in providing it is merely to identify some of the sources and discussions to which readers interested in pursuing the matters dealt with here. (and others related to them) might profitably turn.

The commentaries and studies listed in each section are assuredly not all of equal accuracy, insightfulness, and philosophical interest. Although I have my preferences among them, I have made no attempt to impose them upon the reader, by singling out some of them above the rest as particularly deserving of attention. Instead, I would simply offer two words of caution. First, one would do well to read rather widely—above all in the works of the philosophers under consideration—before accepting the interpretations of their thought of any particular commentators and analysts (the present writer included). And second, one should not assume, as a matter of course, that the latest interpretations are invariably the better of those which exist, or the best which can be developed.

Chapter 1: From Hegel to Nietzsche: A Selective Overview

COMPREHENSIVE STUDIES

Copleston, F. *A History of Philosophy.* Vol. 7. London: Burns, Oates & Washbourne, 1963. Pb. ed. (in 2 parts), Garden City: Doubleday, 1965.

Ewing, A. C. *Idealism: A Critical Survey.* London: Methuen, 1934; reissued 1974.

Gilson, E.; Langan, T.; and Mauer, A. A. *Recent Philosophy: Hegel to the Present.* New York: Random House, 1966.

Kaufmann, W. *From Shakespeare to Existentialism.* Garden City: Doubleday, 1959.

Löwith, K. *From Hegel to Nietzsche: The Revolution in Nineteenth-Century Thought.* Trans. by D. E. Green. New York: Holt, Rinehart & Winston, 1964. Pb. ed., Garden City: Doubleday, 1967.

Mandelbaum, M. *History, Man and Reason.* Baltimore: Johns Hopkins University Press, 1971.

Marcuse, H. *Reason and Revolution: Hegel and the Rise of Social Theory.* London: Oxford University Press, 1941. 2nd ed., New York: Humanities, 1954. Pb. ed., Boston: Beacon, 1960.

Merz, J. T. *A History of European Philosophical Thought in the Nineteenth Century.* 2 vols. Edinburgh: Blackwood, 1903–14. Pb. ed., New York: Dover, 1965.

O'Connor, D. J., ed. *A Critical History of Western Philosophy.* New York: Free Press of Glencoe, 1964.

Rintelen, J. v. *Contemporary German Philosophy and Its Background.* Bonn: Bouvier, 1969.

Royce, J. *The Spirit of Modern Philosophy.* New York: Houghton Mifflin, 1892. Reissued, New York: Braziller, 1955. Pb. ed., New York: Norton, 1967.

Solomon, R. C. *From Rationalism to Existentialism.* New York: Harper & Row, 1972.

Tatarkiewicz, W. *Nineteenth Century Philosophy.* Trans. by C. A. Kisiel. Belmont, Calif.: Wadsworth, 1973.

SPECIFIC FIGURES

HEGEL. See bibliography for chapters 3 and 4.

KIERKEGAARD. See bibliography for chapters 6 and 7.

MARX. See bibliography for chapter 5.

NIETZSCHE. See bibliography for chapter 8.

SCHOPENHAUER
Essay on Freedom of the Will. Trans. by K. Kolenda. New York: Bobbs-Merrill, 1960.
On the Basis of Morality. Trans. by E. F. J. Payne. New York: Bobbs-Merrill, 1965.
On the Fourfold Root of the Principle of Sufficient Reason and *On the Will in Nature.* Trans. by K. Hillebrand. London: Bell, 1897.
The Philosophy of Schopenhauer. Edited by I. Edman. New York: Random House, 1928; reissued 1956.
The Will to Live: Selected Writings of Arthur Schopenhauer. Edited by R. Taylor. Garden City: Doubleday, 1962.
The World as Will and Idea. 3 vols. Trans. by R. B. Haldane and J. Kemp. London:

Kegan Paul & Trench Trubner, 1883. Reissued, London: Routledge & Kegan Paul, 1964. Pb. ed., Garden City: Doubleday, 1961.

Copleston, F. *Arthur Schopenhauer, Philosopher of Pessimism.* London: Burns, Oates & Washbourne, 1947.

Gardiner, P. *Schopenhauer.* Baltimore: Penguin, 1963.

Chapter 2: The Philosophical Background of Hegel's Metaphysics

COMPREHENSIVE STUDIES

Adamson, R. *The Development of Modern Philosophy.* Edited by W. R. Sorley. Edinburgh: Blackwood, 1903. Reissued, Freeport, N.Y.: Books for Libraries, 1971.

Copleston, F. *A History of Philosophy.* Vols. 4–7. London: Burns, Oates & Washbourne, 1959–63. Pb. ed., Garden City: Doubleday, 1963–65.

Gilson, E., and Langan, T. *Modern Philosophy: Descartes to Kant.* New York: Random House, 1963.

Hegel, G. W. F. *Differenz des Fichte'schen und Schelling'schen Systems der Philosophie.* Hamburg: Meiner, 1962.

_____. *Lectures on the History of Philosophy.* Vol. 3. Trans. by E. S. Haldane and F. H. Simson. London: Kegan Paul & Trench Trubner, 1896. Reissued, London: Routledge & Kegan Paul, 1955.

Höffding, H. *A History of Modern Philosophy.* 2 vols. Trans. by B. E. Meyer. London: Macmillan, 1900; reissued in 1935. Pb. ed., New York: Dover, 1955.

Kelly, G. A. *Idealism, Politics and History: Sources of Hegelian Thought.* London: Cambridge University Press, 1969.

Kroner, R. *Von Kant bis Hegel.* 2 vols. Tübingen: Mohr, 1921–24.

Nauen, F. G. *Revolution, Idealism, and Human Freedom: Schelling, Hölderlin, and Hegel and the Crisis of Early German Idealism.* New York: Humanities, 1971.

Nelson, L. *Progress and Regress in Philosophy.* Vol. 2, *From Hume and Kant to Hegel and Fries.* Edited by J. Kraft, trans. by H. Palmer. Oxford: Blackwell, 1971.

Royce, J. *Lectures on Modern Idealism.* New Haven: Yale University Press, 1919. Pb. ed., New Haven: Yale University Press, 1964.

Windelband, W. *A History of Philosophy.* Vol. 2. Trans. by J. H. Tufts. 2nd ed., London: Macmillan, 1921. Pb. ed., New York: Harper, 1958.

SPECIFIC FIGURES

FICHTE

The Science of Knowledge. Edited and trans. by P. Heath and J. Lachs. New York: Appleton-Century-Crofts, 1970.

The Vocation of Man. Edited by R. M. Chisholm. New York: Bobbs-Merrill, 1956.

Adamson, R. *Fichte.* Philadelphia: Lippincott, 1881.

Talbot, E. B. *The Fundamental Principle of Fichte's Philosophy.* New York: Macmillan, 1906.

Thompson, A. B. *The Unity of Fichte's Doctrine of Knowledge.* Boston: Radcliffe College Monographs (No. 7), 1895.

KANT

Critique of Judgment. Trans. by J. H. Bernard. New York: Hafner, 1951.
Critique of Practical Reason. Trans. by L. W. Beck. New York: Bobbs-Merrill, 1956.
Critique of Pure Reason. Trans. by N. Kemp Smith. 2nd (corrected) impression. London: Macmillan, 1933.
Foundation of the Metaphysics of Morals. Trans. by L. W. Beck. New York: Bobbs-Merrill, 1959.
Prolegomena to Any Future Metaphysics. Edited by L. W. Beck. New York: Bobbs-Merrill, 1950.

Kemp, J. *The Philosophy of Kant.* London: Oxford University Press, 1968.
Körner, S. *Kant.* Baltimore: Penguin, 1955.
Wolff, R. P., ed. *Kant: A Collection of Critical Essays.* Garden City: Doubleday, 1967.

SCHELLING

The Ages of the World. Trans. by F. D. Bolman, Jr. New York: AMS, 1942.
Of Human Freedom. Trans. by J. Gutman. La Salle, Ill.: Open Court, 1936.

Hayner, P. C. *Reason and Existence: Schelling's Philosophy of History.* Leiden: Brill, 1967.
Jaspers, K. *Schelling: Grösse und Verhängnis.* Munich: Piper, 1955.
Watson, J. *Schelling's Transcendental Idealism.* Chicago: Griggs, 1882.

Chapters 3 and 4: Hegel

WORKS BY HEGEL

Lectures on the History of Philosophy. 3 vols. Trans. by. E. S. Haldane and F. H. Simson. London: Kegan Paul & Trench Trubner, 1892–96. Reissued, London: Routledge & Kegan Paul, 1955.
Lectures on the Philosophy of History. Trans. by. J. Sibree. Rev. ed., New York: Colonial, 1899. Pb. ed., New York: Dover, 1956.
Lectures on the Philosophy of Religion. 3 vols. Trans. by E. B. Spiers and J. B. Sanderson. London: Kegan Paul & Trench Trubner, 1895. Reissued, London: Routledge & Kegan Paul, 1962.
The Logic of Hegel (Part I of the *Encyclopedia of the Philosophical Sciences*). Trans. by W. Wallace. London: Oxford University Press, 1873. 2nd ed., 1892; reissued 1950.
The Phenomenology of Mind. Trans. by J. B. Baillie. New York: Macmillan, 1910. 2nd ed., 1931. Pb. ed., New York: Harper & Row, 1967.
The Philosophy of Fine Art. 4 vols. Trans. by F. P. B. Osmeston. London: Bell, 1920.
Philosophy of Mind (Part III of the *Encyclopedia*). Trans. by W. Wallace. Oxford: Clarendon, 1894; reissued 1971.
Philosophy of Nature (Part II of the *Encyclopedia*). 3 vols. Trans. by M. J. Petry. London: Oxford University Press, 1970.
Philosophy of Right. Trans. by T. M. Knox. Oxford: Clarendon, 1942.
Science of Logic. 2 vols. Trans. by W. H. Johnston and L. G. Struthers. New York: Macmillan, 1929.

COLLECTIONS AND SELECTIONS FROM HEGEL'S WRITINGS

Hegel's Political Writings. Trans. by T. M. Knox. With an Introductory Essay by Z. A. Pelczynski. Oxford: Clarendon, 1964.
Hegel: Texts and Commentary (principally the Preface to the *Phenomenology*). Edited and trans. by W. Kaufmann. Garden City: Doubleday, 1966.
On Art, Religion, Philosophy: Introductory Lectures to the Realm of Absolute Spirit. Edited by J. G. Gray. New York: Harper & Row, 1970.
On Christianity: Early Theological Writings. Edited by H. Nohl, trans. by T. M. Knox and R. Kroner. Chicago: University of Chicago Press, 1948. Pb. ed., New York: Harper, 1961.
The Philosophy of Hegel. Edited by C. J. Friedrich. New York: Random House, 1953.
Reason in History. Trans. by R. S. Hartman. New York: Bobbs-Merrill, 1953.

COMMENTARIES AND STUDIES

Avineri, S. *Hegel's Theory of the Modern State.* London: Cambridge University Press, 1972.
Croce, B. *What Is Living and What Is Dead in the Philosophy of Hegel.* Trans. by D. Ainslie. London, 1915. Reissued, New York: Russell & Russell, 1969.
Findlay, J. N. *Hegel: A Re-Examination.* New York: Macmillan, 1958. Pb. ed., New York: Collier, 1962. In recent printings of the Collier edition the title has been changed to *The Philosophy of Hegel: An Introduction and Re-Examination.*
Greene, M. *Hegel on the Soul: A Speculative Anthropology.* New York: Humanities, 1973.
Harris, H. S. *Hegel's Development.* Oxford: Clarendon, 1972.
Heidegger, M. *Hegel's Concept of Experience.* New York: Harper & Row, 1970.
Kaufmann, W. *Hegel: A Reinterpretation.* Garden City: Doubleday, 1966. First published as part of *Hegel: Reinterpretation, Texts, and Commentary.* Garden City: Doubleday, 1965.
_____, ed. *Hegel's Political Philosophy.* New York: Lieber-Atherton, 1970.
Kojeve, A. *Introduction to the Reading of Hegel.* Edited by A. Bloom, trans. by J. H. Nichols, Jr. New York: Basic Books, 1969.
Lauer, Q. *Hegel's Idea of Philosophy.* New York: Fordham University Press, 1971.
Löwenberg, J. *Hegel's Phenomenology.* La Salle, Ill.: Open Court, 1965.
MacIntyre, A., ed. *Hegel: A Collection of Critical Essays.* Garden City: Doubleday, 1972.
Marcuse, H. *Reason and Revolution: Hegel and the Rise of Social Theory.* London: Oxford University Press, 1941. 2nd ed., New York: Humanities, 1954. Pb. ed., Boston: Beacon, 1960.
Mure, G. R. G. *The Philosophy of Hegel.* London: Oxford University Press, 1965.
_____. *A Study of Hegel's Logic.* Oxford: Clarendon, 1950.
Pelczynski, Z. A., ed. *Hegel's Political Philosophy: Problems and Perspectives.* London: Cambridge University Press, 1971.
Plant, R. *Hegel.* Bloomington: Indiana University Press, 1973.
Reyburn, H. A. *The Ethical Theory of Hegel.* Oxford: Clarendon, 1921.
Schacht, R. *Alienation.* Garden City: Doubleday, 1970; pb. ed., 1971.
Soll, I. *An Introduction to Hegel's Metaphysics.* Chicago: University of Chicago Press, 1969.

Stace, W. T. *The Philosophy of Hegel.* London, 1924. Pb. ed., New York: Dover, 1955.
Walsh, W. H. *Hegelian Ethics.* London: Macmillan, 1969.

Chapter 5: Marx

WORKS BY MARX

The Communist Manifesto (with Engels). Trans. by S. Moore. Baltimore: Penguin, 1967.
Critique of Hegel's Philosophy of Right. Edited by J. O'Malley, trans. by A. J. and J. O'Malley. London: Cambridge University Press, 1970.
Critique of the Gotha Program. Edited by C. P. Dutt. New York: International Publishers, 1938; reissued, 1966.
The German Ideology (with Engels). Parts I and III. Edited by R. Pascal. New York: International Publishers, 1947.
The Grundrisse. Edited and trans. by D. McLellan. London: Macmillan, 1971.
Writings of the Young Marx on Philosophy and Society. Edited and trans. by L. D. Easton and K. H. Guddat. Garden City: Doubleday, 1967.

COLLECTIONS AND SELECTIONS FROM MARX'S WRITINGS

Basic Writings on Politics and Philosophy (with Engels). Edited by L. S. Feuer. Garden City: Doubleday, 1959.
Early Texts. Edited and trans. by D. McLellan. New York: Barnes & Noble, 1971.
Early Writings. Edited and trans. by T. B. Bottomore. New York: McGraw-Hill, 1963.
Selected Writings in Sociology and Social Philosophy. Edited by T. B. Bottomore and M. Rubel, trans. by T. B. Bottomore. New York: McGraw-Hill, 1956.

COMMENTARIES AND STUDIES

Althusser, L. *For Marx.* Trans. by B. Brewster. New York: Random House, 1970.
Avineri, S. *The Social and Political Thought of Karl Marx.* London: Cambridge University Press, 1968.
Berlin, I. *Karl Marx.* London: Oxford University Press, 1939; 2nd ed., 1956. Pb. ed., New York: Time, 1963.
Bochenski, J. N., et al., eds. *A Guide to Marxist Philosophy: An Introductory Bibliography.* Chicago: Swallow, 1972.
Dupré, L. *The Philosophical Foundations of Marxism.* New York: Harcourt, Brace & World, 1966.
Fetscher, I. *Marx and Marxism.* Trans. by N. Lobkowicz and J. Hargreaves. New York: Seabury, 1971.
Fromm, E. *Marx's Concept of Man.* New York: Ungar, 1961.
Garaudy, R. *Marxism in the Twentieth Century.* Trans. by R. Hague. New York: Scribner, 1970.
Hook, S. *From Hegel to Marx.* New York: Reynal & Hitchcock, 1936. Pb. ed., Ann Arbor: University of Michigan Press, 1962.
———. *Toward the Understanding of Karl Marx.* New York: Day, 1933.
Hyppolite, J. *Studies on Marx and Hegel.* Edited and trans. by J. O'Neil. New York: Basic Books, 1969.

Kamenka, E. *The Ethical Foundations of Marxism*. London: Routledge & Kegan Paul, 1962.
_____. *Marxism and Ethics*. London: Macmillan, 1969.
Lichtheim, G. *From Marx to Hegel*. New York: Herder & Herder, 1971.
Livergood, N. D. *Activity in Marx's Philosophy*. New York: Humanities, 1967.
McLellan, D. *Marx Before Marxism*. London: Macmillan, 1970.
_____. *The Thought of Karl Marx: An Introduction*. New York: Harper & Row, 1972.
_____. *The Young Hegelians and Karl Marx*. London: Macmillan, 1969.
Mészáros, I. *Marx's Theory of Alienation*. 2nd ed. London: Merlin, 1970.
Ollman, B. *Alienation: Marx's Conception of Man in Capitalist Society*. London: Cambridge University Press, 1971.
Petrović, G. *Marx in the Mid-Twentieth Century*. Garden City: Doubleday, 1967.
Rotenstreich, N. *Basic Problems of Marx's Philosophy*. New York: Bobbs-Merrill, 1965.
Schacht, R. *Alienation*. Garden City: Doubleday, 1970.
Schaff, A. *Marxism and the Human Individual*. Edited by R. S. Cohen, trans. by O. Wojtasiewicz. New York: McGraw-Hill, 1970.
Schmidt, A. *The Concept of Nature in Marx*. Trans. by B. Fowkes. New York: New Left Books, 1971.
Tucker, R. *Philosophy and Myth in Karl Marx*. 2nd rev. ed. London: Cambridge University Press, 1972.
Turner, D. *On the Philosophy of Karl Marx*. New York: Humanities, 1973.

Chapters 6 and 7: Kierkegaard

WORKS BY KIERKEGAARD

The Concept of Dread. Trans. by W. Lowrie. Princeton: Princeton University Press, 1944; 2nd ed., 1957.
The Concept of Irony. Trans. by L. M. Capel. Bloomington: Indiana University Press, 1965.
Concluding Unscientific Postscript. Trans. by D. F. Swenson and W. Lowrie, Princeton: Princeton University Press, 1941.
Either/Or: A Fragment of Life. 2 vols. Trans. by D. F. Swenson, L. M. Swenson, and W. Lowrie. Princeton: Princeton University Press, 1944. Pb. ed., Garden City: Doubleday, 1959.
Fear and Trembling. Trans. by W. Lowrie. Princeton: Princeton University Press, 1941. Pb. ed. (with *The Sickness Unto Death*), Garden City: Doubleday, 1954.
Philosophical Fragments: Or A Fragment of Philosophy. Trans. by D. F. Swenson, rev. by H. V. Hong. Princeton: Princeton University Press, 1936; 2nd ed., 1962.
The Point of View for My Work as an Author. Trans. by W. Lowrie. London: Oxford University Press, 1939. Rev. and pb. ed., New York: Harper & Row, 1962.
The Present Age and Two Minor Ethico-Religious Treatises. Trans. by A. Dru and W. Lowrie. London: Oxford University Press, 1940. Pb. ed., New York: Harper & Row, 1962.
Purity of Heart Is to Will One Thing. Trans. by D. V. Steere. New York: Harper, 1938. Pb. ed., New York: Harper, 1956.
The Sickness Unto Death. Trans. by W. Lowrie. Princeton: Princeton University Press, 1941. Pb. ed. (with *Fear and Trembling*), Garden City: Doubleday, 1954.

Stages On Life's Way. Trans. by W. Lowrie. Princeton: Princeton University Press, 1940. Pb. ed., New York: Schocken, 1967.

COLLECTIONS AND SELECTIONS FROM KIERKEGAARD'S WRITINGS

The Journals of Kierkegaard. Edited and trans. by A. Dru. London: Oxford University Press, 1938. Rev. and pb. ed., New York: Harper, 1959.
Kierkegaard. Edited by W. H. Auden. New York: McKay, 1952.
A Kierkegaard Anthology. Edited by R. Bretall. New York: Random House, 1959.
Selections from the Writings of Kierkegaard. Edited and trans. by L. M. Hollander. Austin: University of Texas Press, 1923. Rev. and pb. ed., Garden City: Doubleday, 1960.

COMMENTARIES AND STUDIES

Collins, J. *The Mind of Kierkegaard.* Chicago: Regnery, 1953.
Diem, H. *Kierkegaard: An Introduction.* Trans. by D. Green, Richmond: Knox, 1966.
———. *Kierkegaard's Dialectic of Existence.* Trans. by H. Knight. Edinburgh: Oliver & Boyd, 1959.
Garelick, H. M. *The Anti-Christianity of Kierkegaard: A Study of Concluding Unscientific Postscript.* New York: Humanities, 1965.
Gill, J. H., ed. *Essays on Kierkegaard.* Minneapolis: Burgess, 1969.
Haecker, T. *Søren Kierkegaard.* Trans. by A. Dru. London: Oxford University Press, 1936.
Hartnack, J., et. al., eds. *Danish Yearbook of Philosophy.* Vol. 8, *Kierkegaard and Contemporary Philosophy.* New York: Humanities, 1971.
Johnson, R. H. *The Concept of Existence in Concluding Unscientific Postscript.* New York: Humanities, 1973.
Lowrie, W. *Kierkegaard.* London: Oxford University Press, 1938. Rev. and pb. ed. (in 2 vols.), New York: Harper, 1962.
Mackey, L. *Kierkegaard: A Kind of Poet.* Philadelphia: University of Pennsylvania Press, 1971.
Malantschuk, G. *Kierkegaard's Thought.* Edited by H. V. and H. E. Hong. Princeton: Princeton University Press, 1971.
Price, G. *The Narrow Pass: A Study of Kierkegaard's Concept of Man.* New York: McGraw-Hill, 1963.
Shestev, L. *Kierkegaard and Existential Philosophy.* Trans. by E. Hewett. Athens, Ohio: Ohio University Press, 1969.
Shmueli, A. *Kierkegaard and Consciousness.* Trans. by N. Handelmann. Princeton: Princeton University Press, 1971.
Thomas, J. H. *Subjectivity and Paradox.* Oxford: Blackwell, 1957.
Thompson, J. *Kierkegaard.* New York: Knopf, 1973.
———. *The Lonely Labyrinth: Kierkegaard's Pseudonymous Works.* Carbondale: Southern Illinois University Press, 1967.
———, ed. *Kierkegaard: A Collection of Critical Essays.* Garden City: Doubleday, 1972.
Wyschogrod, M. *Kierkegaard and Heidegger: The Ontology of Existence.* New York: Humanities, 1954.

Chapter 8: Nietzsche

WORKS BY NIETZSCHE

The Anti-Christ (with *Twilight of the Idols*). Trans. by R. J. Hollingdale. Baltimore: Penguin, 1968.
Beyond Good and Evil. Trans. by W. Kaufmann. New York: Random House, 1966.
The Birth of Tragedy (with *The Case of Wagner*). Trans. by W. Kaufmann. New York: Random House, 1967.
The Dawn. Vol. IX, *The Complete Works of Friedrich Nietzsche.* Edited by O. Levy, trans. by J. M. Kennedy. Edinburgh, Foulis, 1910. Reissued, New York: Russell & Russell, 1964.
Ecce Homo (with *On the Genealogy of Morals*). Edited and trans. by W. Kaufmann. New York: Random House, 1967.
The Gay Science. Trans. W. Kaufmann. New York: Random House, 1974.
On the Genealogy of Morals (with *Ecce Homo*). Edited and trans. by W. Kaufmann. New York: Random House, 1967.
Thus Spoke Zarathustra. Trans. by W. Kaufmann. New York: Viking, 1966.
Twilight of the Idols (with *The Anti-Christ*). Trans. by R. J. Hollingdale. Baltimore: Penguin, 1968.
The Will to Power. Edited by W. Kaufmann, trans. by W. Kaufmann and R. J. Hollingdale. New York: Random House, 1967.

COLLECTIONS AND SELECTIONS FROM NIETZSCHE'S WRITINGS

The Basic Writings of Nietzsche. Edited and trans. by W. Kaufmann. New York: Random House, 1968.
Nietzsche: A Self-Portrait from His Letters. Edited and trans. by P. Fuss and H. Shapiro. Cambridge, Mass.: Harvard University Press, 1971.
The Portable Nietzsche. Edited and trans. by W. Kaufmann. New York: Viking, 1954.

COMMENTARIES AND STUDIES

Brinton, C. *Nietzsche.* Cambridge, Mass.: Harvard University Press, 1941.
Copleston, F. *Friedrich Nietzsche, Philosopher of Culture.* London: Burns, Oates & Washbourne, 1942.
Danto, A. *Nietzsche as Philosopher.* New York: Macmillan, 1965.
Heidegger, M. *Nietzsche.* 2 vols. Pfullingen: Neske, 1961. (English translation forthcoming.)
Hollingdale, R. J. *Nietzsche: The Man and His Philosophy.* Baton Rouge: Louisiana State University Press, 1965.
Jaspers, K. *Nietzsche: An Introduction to the Understanding of His Philosophical Activity.* Trans. by C. F. Wallraff and J. F. Schmitz. Tucson: University of Arizona Press, 1965. Pb. ed., Chicago: Regnery, 1972.
Kaufmann, W. *Nietzsche: Philosopher, Psychologist, Antichrist.* New York: Random House, 1950; rev. (3rd) ed., 1968.
Löwith, K. *Nietzsches Philosophie der ewigen Wiederkehr des Gleichen.* Stuttgart: Kohlhammer, 1956.

Morgan, G. A. *What Nietzsche Means*. Cambridge, Mass.: Harvard University Press, 1941. Pb. ed., New York: Harper & Row, 1965.

Pfeffer, R. *Nietzsche: Disciple of Dionysus*. Lewisburg: Bucknell University Press, 1972.

Salter, W. M. *Nietzsche the Thinker: A Study*. New York: Ungar, 1968.

Solomon, R. C., ed. *Nietzsche: A Collection of Critical Essays*. Garden City: Doubleday, 1973.

Stambaugh, J. *Nietzsche's Thought of Eternal Return*. Baltimore: Johns Hopkins University Press, 1972.

Wilcox, J. T. *Truth and Value in Nietzsche*. Ann Arbor: University of Michigan Press, 1974.

Chapter 9: Husserl and Heidegger

WORKS BY HEIDEGGER

Being and Time. Trans. by J. Macquarrie and E. Robinson. New York: Harper, 1962.

Discourse on Thinking. Trans. by J. M. Anderson and E. H. Freund. New York: Harper & Row, 1966.

The Essence of Reasons. Trans. by T. Malick. Evanston: Northwestern University Press, 1969.

Existence and Being (four essays, together with a summary of *Being and Time*). Trans. by W. Brock. Chicago: Regnery, 1949; 3rd ed., 1968.

Identity and Difference. Trans. by J. Stambaugh. New York: Harper & Row, 1969.

Kant and the Problem of Metaphysics. Trans. by J. S. Churchill. Bloomington: Indiana University Press, 1962.

"Letter on Humanism." Trans. by E. Lohner. In *Twentieth Century Philosophy*, vol. II, ed. H. Aiken and W. Barrett. New York: Random House, 1962.

On the Way to Language. Trans. by P. D. Hertz. New York: Harper & Row, 1971.

On Time and Being. Trans. by J. Stambaugh. New York: Harper & Row, 1972.

Poetry, Language, Thought. Trans. by A. Hofstadter. New York: Harper & Row, 1971.

The Question of Being. Trans. by J. T. Wilde and W. Kluback. New York: Twayne, 1958.

"The Way Back Into the Ground of Metaphysics." Trans. by W. Kaufmann. In *Existentialism from Dostoevsky to Sartre*, ed. W. Kaufmann. New York: World, 1956.

What Is a Thing? Trans. by W. B. Barton, Jr., and V. Deutsch. Chicago: Regnery, 1967.

What Is Called Thinking? Trans. by F. D. Wieck and J. G. Gray. New York: Harper & Row, 1968.

What Is Philosophy? Trans. by J. T. Wilde and W. Kluback. New York: Twayne, 1958.

COMMENTARIES AND STUDIES

Brock, W. *Existence and Being*. Chicago: Regnery, 1949; 3rd ed., 1968.

Cousineau, R. H. *Heidegger, Humanism and Ethics: An Introduction to the Letter on Humanism*. New York: Humanities, 1972.

Deely, J. N. *The Tradition via Heidegger: An Essay on the Meaning of Being in the Philosophy of Martin Heidegger*. New York: Humanities, 1972.

Gelven, M. *A Commentary on Heidegger's "Being and Time."* New York: Harper & Row, 1970.

Grene, M. *Martin Heidegger*. London: Bowes & Bowes, 1957.

King, M. *Heidegger's Philosophy.* New York: Macmillan, 1964.

Langan, T. *The Meaning of Heidegger.* New York: Columbia University Press, 1959.

Macquarrie, J. *Martin Heidegger.* Richmond: Knox, 1968.

Magnus, B. *Heidegger's Metahistory of Philosophy: Amor Fati, Being and Truth.* New York: Humanities, 1970.

Marx, W. *Heidegger and the Tradition.* Trans. by T. Kisiel and M. Greene. Evanston: Northwestern University Press, 1971.

Mehta, J. L. *The Philosophy of Martin Heidegger.* Rev. ed. New York: Harper & Row, 1972.

Richardson, W. J. *Heidegger: Through Phenomenology to Thought.* 2nd ed. New York: Humanities, 1967.

Schmitt, R. *Martin Heidegger on Being Human.* New York: Random House, 1969.

Spiegelberg, H. *The Phenomenological Movement.* 2nd. ed. Vol. I. New York: Humanities, 1969.

Vicinas, V. *Earth and Gods: An Introduction to the Philosophy of Heidegger.* New York: Humanities, 1961.

WORKS BY HUSSERL

Cartesian Meditations: An Introduction to Phenomenology. Trans. by D. Cairns. New York: Humanities, 1960.

Experience and Judgment: Investigations in a Genealogy of Logic. Edited by L. Landgrebe, trans. by J. S. Churchill and K. Ameriks. Evanston: Northwestern University Press, 1973.

Formal and Transcendental Logic. Trans. by D. Cairns. New York: Humanities, 1969.

The Idea of Phenomenology. Trans. by W. P. Alston and G. Nakhnikian. New York: Humanities, 1964.

Ideas: General Introduction to Pure Phenomenology. Trans. by W. R. Boyce Gibson. New York: Macmillan, 1931. Pb. ed., New York: Collier, 1962.

Logical Investigations. 2 vols. Trans. by J. N. Findlay. New York: Humanities, 1970.

Phenomenology of Internal Time-Consciousness. Edited by M. Heidegger, trans. by J. S. Churchill. Bloomington: Indiana University Press, 1964.

COMMENTARIES AND STUDIES

Bachelard, S. *A Study of Husserl's Formal and Transcendental Logic.* Trans. by L. E. Embree. Evanston: Northwestern University Press, 1968.

Cairns, D. *Guide for Translating Husserl.* New York: Humanities, 1973.

Farber, M. *The Aims of Phenomenology.* New York: Harper & Row, 1964.

———. *The Foundation of Phenomenology.* Cambridge, Mass.: Harvard University Press, 1943. Rev. 3rd ed., Albany: University of New York Press, 1967.

Kockelmanns, J. J. *A First Introduction to Husserl's Phenomenology.* Pittsburgh: Duquesne University Press, 1967.

———, ed. *Phenomenology: The Philosophy of Edmund Husserl and Its Interpretation.* Garden City: Doubleday, 1967.

Lauer, Q. *Phenomenology: Its Genesis and Prospect.* New York: Harper, 1958.

Levin, D. M. *Reason and Evidence in Husserl's Phenomenology.* Evanston: Northwestern University Press, 1970.

Natanson, M. *Edmund Husserl: Philosopher of Infinite Tasks.* Evanston: Northwestern University Press, 1973.

Pivčevič, E. *Husserl and Phenomenology.* London: Hutchinson, 1970.

Ricoeur, P. *Husserl: An Analysis of His Phenomenology.* Trans. by E. G. Ballard and L. E. Embree. Evanston: Northwestern University Press, 1967.

Spiegelberg, H. *The Phenomenological Movement.* 2nd ed. Vol. I. New York: Humanities, 1969.

Tymieniecka, A.-T., ed. *The Later Husserl and the Idea of Phenomenology.* Dordrecht: Nauwelaerts, 1972.

Welch, E. P. *The Philosophy of Edmund Husserl: The Origin and Development of His Phenomenology.* New York: Columbia University Press, 1940.

Chapter 10: Recent European Philosophy

WORKS BY JASPERS

Man in the Modern Age. 2nd ed. Trans. by E. and C. Paul. London: Routledge & Kegan Paul, 1959. Pb. ed., Garden City: Doubleday, 1957.

Philosophical Faith and Revelation. Trans. by E. B. Ashton. New York: Harper & Row, 1967.

Philosophy. 3 vols. Trans. by E. B. Ashton. Chicago: University of Chicago Press, 1969–71.

Philosophy and the World: Selected Essays and Lectures. Trans. by E. B. Ashton. Chicago: Regnery, 1963.

The Philosophy of Existence. Trans. by R. Grabau. Philadelphia: University of Pennsylvania Press, 1971.

The Question of German Guilt. Trans. by E. B. Ashton. New York: Dial, 1947. Pb. ed., New York: Capricorn, 1961.

Reason and Existenz. Trans. by W. Earle. New York: Farrar, Straus and Giroux, 1955.

Truth and Symbol. Trans. by J. T. Wilde, W. Kluback and W. Kimmel. New York: Twayne, 1959.

Von der Wahrheit. Munich: Piper, 1947.

COMMENTARIES AND STUDIES

Allen, E. L. *The Self and Its Hazards: A Guide to the Thought of Karl Jaspers.* New York: Philosophical Library, 1951.

Knudsen, R. *The Idea of Transcendence in the Philosophy of Karl Jaspers.* Kampen, Neth.: Kok, 1958.

Lichtigfeld, A. *Aspects of Jaspers' Philosophy.* 2nd ed. Pretoria: University of South Africa Press, 1971.

Samay, S. *Reason Revisited: The Philosophy of Karl Jaspers.* Notre Dame: University of Notre Dame Press, 1971.

Schilpp, P. A., ed. *The Philosophy of Karl Jaspers.* New York: Tudor, 1957.

Schrag, O. O. *Existence, Existenz, and Transcendence: An Introduction to the Philosophy of Karl Jaspers.* Pittsburgh: Duquesne University Press, 1971.

Wallraff, C. F. *Karl Jaspers: An Introduction to His Philosophy.* Princeton: Princeton University Press, 1970.

WORKS BY SARTRE

Being and Nothingness. Trans. by H. E. Barnes. New York: Philosophical Library, 1956. Pb. ed., New York: Washington Square, 1965.
Critique de la raison dialectique. Part I. Paris: Gallimard, 1960.
Essays in Existentialism. Edited by S. Wahl. New York: Citadel, 1967.
Existentialism and Humanism. Trans. by P. Mairet. London: Methuen, 1948.
Imagination: A Psychological Critique. Trans. by F. Williams. Ann Arbor: University of Michigan Press, 1962.
The Philosophy of Existentialism. Edited by W. Basking. New York: Philosophical Library, 1965.
The Philosophy of Jean-Paul Sartre. Edited by R. D. Cumming. New York: Random House, 1968.
Search for a Method. Trans. by H. E. Barnes. New York: Knopf, 1963. Pb. ed., New York: Random House, 1968.
Sketch for a Theory of the Emotions. Trans. by P. Mairet. London: Methuen, 1962.
The Transcendence of the Ego. Trans. by F. Williams and R. Kirkpatrick. New York: Farrar, Straus and Giroux, 1957.
What Is Literature? Trans. by B. Frechtman. New York: Philosophical Library, 1949. Pb. ed., New York: Washington Square, 1966.

COMMENTARIES AND STUDIES

Barnes, H. E. *Sartre.* Philadelphia: Lippincott, 1973.
Catalano, J. S. *A Commentary on Sartre's "Being and Nothingness."* New York: Harper & Row, 1974.
Desan, W. *The Marxism of Jean-Paul Sartre.* Garden City: Doubleday, 1965.
_____. *The Tragic Finale.* Cambridge, Mass.: Harvard University Press, 1954. Pb. ed., New York: Harper, 1960.
Greene, N. N. *Jean-Paul Sartre: The Existentialist Ethic.* Ann Arbor: University of Michigan Press, 1960.
Grene, M. *Sartre.* New York: Watts, 1973.
Hartmann, K. *Sartre's Ontology.* Evanston: Northwestern University Press, 1966.
Kern, E., ed. *Sartre: A Collection of Critical Essays.* Englewood Cliffs, N. J.: Prentice-Hall, 1962.
Lafarge, R. *Jean-Paul Sartre: His Philosophy.* Trans. by M. S. Kok. Notre Dame: Notre Dame University Press, 1970.
Laing, R. D., and Cooper, D. G. *Reason and Violence: A Decade of Sartre's Philosophy, 1950–1960.* New York: Pantheon, 1971.
MacMahon, J. H. *Humans Being: The World of Jean-Paul Sartre.* Chicago: University of Chicago Press, 1971.
Manser, A. *Sartre: A Philosophic Study.* New York: Oxford University Press, 1967.
Merleau-Ponty, M. *Adventures of the Dialectic.* Trans. by J. Bien. Evanston: Northwestern University Press, 1973.

Warnock, M. *The Philosophy of Sartre.* London: Hutchinson, 1965.
_____, ed. *Sartre: A Collection of Critical Essays.* Garden City: Doubleday, 1971.

OTHER FIGURES

CAMUS

The Myth of Sisyphus. Trans. by J. O'Brien. New York: Knopf, 1955. Pb. ed., New York: Random House, 1958.
The Rebel. Trans. by A. Bower. New York: Knopf, 1954. Pb. ed., New York: Random House, 1960.
Resistance, Rebellion and Death. Trans. by J. O'Brien. New York: Knopf, 1961.

Bree, G. *Albert Camus.* New York: Columbia University Press, 1964.
_____. *Camus and Sartre.* New York: Delacorte, 1972.
O'Brien, C. C. *Albert Camus.* New York: Viking, 1970.
Thody, P. *Camus: A Study of His Work.* New York: Grove, 1957.

HEIDEGGER. See bibliography for chapter 9.

MARCEL

Being and Having. Trans. by K. Farrer. Boston: Beacon, 1951. Pb. ed., Harper & Row, 1965.
Creative Fidelity. Trans. by R. Rosthal. New York: Farrar, Straus & Giroux, 1964.
The Existential Background of Human Dignity. Cambridge, Mass.: Harvard University Press, 1963.
Homo Viator: Introduction to a Metaphysic of Hope. Trans. by E. Craufurd. Chicago: Regnery, 1951. Pb. ed., New York: Harper & Row, 1962.
Man Against Mass Society. Trans. by C. S. Fraser. Chicago: Regnery, 1952. Pb. ed., Regnery, 1967.
Metaphysical Journal. Trans. by B. Woll. Chicago: Regnery, 1952.
The Mystery of Being. 2 vols. Trans. by G. S. Fraser and R. Hague. Chicago: Regnery, 1950–51. Pb. ed., Regnery, 1960.
The Philosophy of Existentialism. Trans. by M. Harari. New York: Philosophical Library, 1949. Pb. ed., New York: Citadel, 1966.
Problematic Man. Trans. by B. Thompson. New York: Herder & Herder, 1967.

Cain, S. *Gabriel Marcel.* New York: Hillary House, 1963.
Gallagher, K. *The Philosophy of Gabriel Marcel.* New York: Fordham University Press, 1962.
Schilpp, P. A., ed. *The Philosophy of Gabriel Marcel.* La Salle, Ill.: Open Court, forthcoming.

MERLEAU-PONTY

Consciousness and the Acquisition of Language. Trans. by H. J. Silverman. Evanston: Northwestern University Press, 1974.
The Phenomenology of Perception. Trans. by C. Smith. London: Routledge & Kegan Paul, 1962.
Sense and Non-Sense. Trans. by H. L. and P. A. Dreyfus. Evanston: Northwestern University Press, 1964.
Signs. Trans. by R. McCreary. Evanston: Northwestern University Press, 1964.

The Structure of Behavior. Trans. by A. Fisher. Boston: Beacon, 1963.

The Visible and the Invisible. Trans. by A. Lingis. Evanston: Northwestern University Press, 1969.

Bannan, J. F. *The Philosophy of Merleau-Ponty.* New York: Harcourt, Brace & World, 1967.

Kwant, R. *From Phenomenology to Metaphysics.* Pittsburgh: Duquesne University Press, 1966.

____. *The Phenomenological Philosophy of Merleau-Ponty.* Pittsburgh: Duquesne University Press, 1963.

Langan, T. *Merleau-Ponty's Critique of Reason.* New Haven: Yale University Press 1966.

Spiegelberg, H. *The Phenomenological Movement.* Vol. II. 2nd ed. New York: Humanities, 1969.

EXISTENTIALISM AND *EXISTENZ*-PHILOSOPHY: GENERAL

Adorno, T. W. *The Jargon of Authenticity.* Trans. by K. Tarnowski. Evanston: Northwestern University Press, 1973.

Barrett, W. *Irrational Man.* Garden City: Doubleday, 1958.

____. *What Is Existentialism?* New York: Grove, 1965.

Blackham, H. J. *Six Existentialist Thinkers.* London: Routledge & Kegan Paul, 1952. Pb. ed., New York: Harper, 1959.

Bochenski, I. M. *Contemporary European Philosophy.* Trans. by D. Nicholl and K. Aschenbrenner. Berkeley: University of California Press, 1960.

Briesach, E. *Introduction to Modern Existentialism.* New York: Grove, 1962.

Brock, W. *Introduction to Contemporary German Philosophy.* London: Cambridge University Press, 1947.

Collins, J. *The Existentialists.* Chicago: Regnery, 1963.

Grene, M. *Introduction to Existentialism.* Chicago: University of Chicago Press, 1959.

Kaufmann, W. *From Shakespeare to Existentialism.* Garden City: Doubleday, 1959.

Macquarrie, J. *Existentialism.* Philadelphia: Westminster, 1972.

Olafson, F. *Principles and Persons: An Ethical Interpretation of Existentialism.* Baltimore: Johns Hopkins University Press, 1967.

Reinhardt, K. F. *The Existentialist Revolt: The Main Themes and Phases of Existentialism.* 2nd ed. New York: Ungar, 1960.

Rintelen, J. v. *Contemporary German Philosophy and Its Background.* Bonn: Bouvier, 1969.

Schrader, G. A., Jr., ed. *Existential Philosophers: Kierkegaard to Merleau-Ponty.* New York: McGraw-Hill, 1967.

Solomon, R. C. *From Rationalism to Existentialism.* New York: Harper & Row, 1972.

Tatarkiewicz, W. *Twentieth Century Philosophy.* Trans. by C. A. Kisiel. Belmont, Calif.: Wadsworth, 1973.

Wahl, J. *Philosophies of Existence.* Trans. by F. M. Lorry. London: Routledge & Kegan Paul, 1969.

Warnock, M. *Existentialism.* London: Oxford University Press, 1970.

____. *Existentialist Ethics.* London: Macmillan, 1967.

Wild, J. *The Challenge of Existentialism.* Bloomington: Indiana University Press, 1959.

WORKS BY PHILOSOPHICAL ANTHROPOLOGISTS

Arendt, H. *The Human Condition.* Chicago: University of Chicago Press, 1958. Pb. ed., Garden City: Doubleday, 1959.

Bolk, L. *Das Problem der Menschwerdung.* Jena: Fischer, 1926.

Bollnow, O. F. *Die Lebensphilosophie.* Berlin: Springer, 1958.

_____. *Mensch und Raum.* Stuttgart: Kohlhammer, 1963.

_____. *Das Neue Bild des Menschen und die pädagogische Aufgabe.* Frankfurt a.M.: Klostermann, 1934.

_____. *Das Wesen der Stimmungen.* Frankfurt a. M.: Klostermann, 1956.

Brüning, W. *Philosophische Anthropologie.* Stuttgart: Klett, 1960.

Bühler, W. *Der Mensch zwischen Übernatur and Unternatur.* Nuremberg: Martin, 1966.

Cassirer, E. *An Essay on Man.* New Haven: Yale University Press, 1944.

_____. *Philosophy of Symbolic Forms.* 3 vols. Trans. by R. Manheim. New Haven: Yale University Press, 1953, 1955, 1957.

Coreth, E. *Was ist der Mensch? Grundzüge einer philosophische Anthropologie.* Innsbruck: Tyrolia, 1973.

Erlich, W. *Philosophische Anthropologie.* Tübingen: Niemeyer, 1957.

Gehlen, A. *Anthropologische Forschung.* Reinbeck bei Hamburg: Rowohlt, 1961.

_____. *Der Mensch: Seine Natur und seine Stellung in der Welt.* 8th ed. Frankfurt a.M.: Athenäum, 1966.

_____. *Studien zur Anthropologie und Soziologie.* Berlin: Luchterhand, 1963.

_____. *Urmensch und Spätkultur.* 2nd ed. Frankfurt a.M.: Athenäum, 1963.

Groethuysen, B. *Anthropologie philosophique.* Paris: Gallimard, 1952.

Häberlin, P. *Der Mensch: Eine philosophische Anthropologie.* Zurich: Schweizer-Spiegel, 1969.

_____. *Leben und Lebensform.* Basel: Schwabe, 1957.

Hengstenberg, H. E. *Mensch und Materie.* Stuttgart: Kohlhammer, 1965.

_____. *Philosophische Anthropologie.* Stuttgart: Kohlhammer, 1957.

_____. *Der Wesensunterschied zwischen Mensch und Tier.* Essen: Fredebeul & Koenen, 1962.

Hofer, H., and Altner, G. *Die Sonderstellung des Menschen.* Stuttgart: Fischer, 1972.

Jonas, H. *The Phenomenon of Life: Toward a Philosophical Biology.* New York: Dell, 1966.

Kamlah, W. *Philosophische Anthropologie.* Mannheim: Bibliographisches Institut, 1972.

Landmann, M. *Das Ende des Individuum.* Stuttgart: Klett, 1971.

_____. *Der Mensch als Schöpfer und Geschöpf der Kultur.* Munich: Reinhardt, 1961.

Litt, T. *Mensch und Welt.* Munich: Reinhardt, 1948. 2nd ed., Heidelberg: Quelle & Meyer, 1961.

_____. *Die Sonderstellung des Menschen im Reiche des Lebendigen.* Wiesbaden: Brockhaus, 1948.

Lorenz, K. *On Aggression.* Trans. by M. K. Wilson. New York: Harcourt, Brace & World, 1966.

Plessner, H. *Conditio Humana.* Pfullingen: Neske, 1964.

_____. *Laughing and Crying.* Trans. by J. S. Churchill and M. Grene. Evanston: Northwestern University Press, 1970.

_____. *Philosophische Anthropologie.* Frankfurt a.M.: Fischer, 1970.

_____. *Die Stufen des Organischen und der Mensch.* 2nd ed. Berlin: de Gruyter, 1965.

_____. *Zwischen Philosophie und Gesellschaft.* Bern: Francke, 1953.

Portmann, A. *Biologie und Geist.* Zurich: Rhein, 1956.

_____. *Biologische Fragmente zu einer Lehre vom Menschen.* 2nd ed. Basel: Schwabe, 1951.

_____. *Zoologie und das neue Bild des Menschen.* 2nd ed. Reinbek bei Hamburg: Rowohlt, 1956.

Ricoeur, P. *Fallible Man.* Trans. by C. Kelbley. Chicago: Gateway, 1965.

_____. *Freedom and Nature.* Trans. by E. V. Kohák. Evanston: Northwestern University Press, 1966.

Rothacker, E. *Mensch und Geschichte.* 2nd ed. Frankfurt a. M.: Athenäum, 1950.

_____. *Philosophische Anthropologie.* 2nd ed. Bonn: Bouvier, 1966.

_____. *Probleme der Kulturanthropologie.* 2nd ed. Bonn: Bouvier, 1965.

_____. *Zur Genealogie des menschlichen Bewusstseins.* Bonn: Bouvier, 1966.

Scheler, M. *Man's Place in Nature.* Trans. by H. Meyerhoff. Boston: Beacon, 1961. Pb. ed., New York: Farrar, Straus & Cudahy, 1962.

_____. *On the Eternal in Man.* Trans. by B. Noble. New York: Harper, 1961.

_____. *Ressentiment.* Edited by L. A. Coser, trans. by W. W. Holdheim. New York: Free Press of Glencoe, 1961. Reissued, New York: Schocken, 1972.

Teilhard de Chardin, P. *The Phenomenon of Man.* Trans. by B. Wall. New York: Harper, 1959. 2nd pb. ed., New York: Harper & Row, 1965.

COMMENTARIES AND STUDIES

Buber, M. *What Is Man?* In *Between Man and Man.* Trans. by R. G. Smith. Boston: Beacon, 1955.

Frings, M. S. *Max Scheler: A Concise Introduction Into the World of a Great Thinker.* Pittsburgh: Duquesne University Press, 1965.

Grene, M. *Approaches to a Philosophical Biology.* New York: Basic Books, 1968.

Hammer, F. *Die exzentrische Position des Menschen: Methode und Grundlinien der philosophische Anthropologie Helmuth Plessners.* Bonn: Bouvier, 1967.

Itzkoff, S. W. *Ernst Cassirer: Scientific Knowledge and the Concept of Man.* Notre Dame: University of Notre Dame Press, 1971.

Jonas, F. *Die Institutionslehre Arnold Gehlens.* Tübingen: Mohr, 1966.

Landmann, M. *Philosophische Anthropologie.* 2nd ed. Berlin: de Gruyter, 1964.

Rasmussen, D. *Mythic-Symbolic Language and Philosophical Anthropology: A Constructive Interpretation of the Thought of Paul Ricoeur.* New York: Humanities, 1971.

Schoeps, H. J. *Was ist der Mensch: Philosophische Anthropologie als Geistesgeschichte der neueren Zeit.* Göttingen: Musterschmidt, 1960.

Weiss, J. *Weltverlust und Subjektivität: Zur Kritik der Institutionslehre Arnold Gehlens.* Freiburg: Romback, 1971.

WORKS OF RELATED INTEREST: STRUCTURALISM

De George, R. T. and F. M., eds. *The Structuralists: From Marx to Levi-Strauss.* Garden City: Doubleday, 1972.

Ehrmann, J., ed. *Structuralism.* Garden City: Doubleday, 1970.

Lane, M., ed. *Introduction to Structuralism*. New York: Basic Books, 1970.

Leach, E. *Levi-Strauss*. New York: Viking, 1970.

Levi-Strauss, C. *Structural Anthropology*. Trans. by C. Jacobson and B. G. Schoepf. New York: Basic Books, 1963. Pb. ed., Garden City: Doubleday, 1967.

Piaget, J. *Structuralism*. Trans. by C. Mashler. New York: Basic Books, 1970.

Index

Kant on, 32–33
Kierkegaard on, 5, 122–23, 126, 139–73
   passim, 245–46
Marx on, 9–10, 113
Nietzsche on, 197, 201–02, 250
Schopenhauer on, 11, 250
See also Existenz; Subjectivity
Institutions, social
   Hegel on, 7, 79, 85, 88–94, 112–13, 145
   Kierkegaard on, 5, 145
   Marx on, 9, 103–04, 110, 112–15
   Nietzsche on, 193
   philosophical anthropology and, 241–42, 251–52
   Schopenhauer on, 12
   See also State
Interpersonal relations. *See* Social life

Jaspers, Karl, 42, 232–39 *passim,* 246, 249
Jesus, 133, 261. *See also* Kierkegaard–on the Incarnation and "the absolute paradox"
Judaism, 114, 162–63, 165–72

Kant, Immanuel, 21–27
   on causality, 23–25, 31, 74–75
   Fichte on, 28, 32
   on freedom, 22, 24–25, 75–76, 77, 78
   on God and the soul, 22, 25, 27
   Hegel on, 44–45, 55, 76–79, 83
   on human nature, 24–25, 32–33, 74–75
   on Hume, 22, 26–27
   and idealism, 22, 30
   on knowledge and experience, 21–27
   passim
   on the mind and the ego, 23–26, 28–29
   on morality, 22, 27, 75, 155
   on objects and things in themselves, 22–27 *passim*
   philosophical method in, 23, 26–27
   philosophical problems in, 21–22, 24–27, 74–75
   on reason and ideas, 24, 25–27, 75–77
   on religion and faith, 22, 27, 45, 259–60
   on the will, 74–75
   on the world, 24
   mentioned, xiv, xvii, 18, 19, 37, 41, 46, 70, 89, 175, 200, 207, 208, 210, 211, 212, 223, 225, 229, 232, 234, 249, 255
Kaufmann, Walter, xvi, 43, 45, 177, 234–35, 264

Kierkegaard Søren, 5–6, 119–74
   on the aesthetic and pleasure, 137–38, 140–45, 151–53, 159–60
   on Christianity, 6, 124, 130, 132–33, 162–68 *passim,* 169–74
   on the ethical, 129, 137–38, 143–48, 151–62, 164, 167
   and *Existenz*-philosophy, 242–43, 245–46
   on faith and "the knight of faith," 5–7, 119–20, 128–33, 145, 166–71, 173
   on God, 5, 7, 11, 120, 126–33 *passim,* 146–47, 150, 160–61, 163–73 *passim,* 245–46
   on happiness, 129–31, 133, 137–73 *passim*
   on Hegel, 120–29 *passim,* 140–49 *passim,* 245
   on human life, 5–6, 11, 122–34 *passim,* 135–74, 243
   on human nature, 5, 119–26, 129–31, 134, 140, 143, 164, 243, 245–46
   on the Incarnation and "the absolute paradox," 127, 129–34 *passim,* 165, 167–73 *passim*
   on knowledge and reason, 121–24, 129, 131, 146–47, 148–51, 251
   on passion, 128–34 *passim,* 168–70
   philosophical method in, 120, 135–36
   philosophical problems in, 120, 135–36, 150–51, 172–73, 243
   on "the public" and publicness, 137–40
   on the religious, 137, 144, 146–47, 154, 157, 160–72
   on subjectivity and individuality, 5–6, 120–34, 139–73 *passim,* 245–46
   mentioned, xiii, 3, 7–15 *passim,* 17, 19, 41, 175, 207, 208, 228, 232, 233, 234, 237, 250, 251, 265
Knowledge
   empiricists on, 20–21
   Hegel on, 6–8, 44, 49–51, 53, 56–60 *passim,* 64–68 *passim,* 82, 102, 125–28, 148, 261
   Heidegger on, 220, 222–25
   Husserl on, 211–13, 216–19
   Kant on, 21–27 *passim*
   Kierkegaard on, 121–24, 148–51
   Marx on, 100–01
   Nietzsche on, 175–76, 181, 190–91
   Schopenhauer on, 12
Knox, T. M., 90, 262–63